North Korea and the Geopolitics of Development

Kevin Gray and Jong-Woon Lee focus on three geopolitical 'moments' that have been crucial to the shaping of the North Korean system: colonialism, the Cold War and the rise of China, to demonstrate how broader processes of geopolitical contestation have fundamentally shaped the emergence and subsequent development of the North Korean political economy. They argue that placing the nexus between geopolitics and development at the centre of the analysis helps explain the country's rapid catch-up industrialisation, its subsequent secular decline followed by collapse in the 1990s and why the reform process has been markedly more conservative compared to other state socialist societies. As such, they draw attention to the specificities of North Korea's experience of late development, but also place it in a broader comparative context by understanding the country not solely through the analytical lens of state socialism but also as an instance of postcolonial national development.

Kevin Gray is a professor in International Relations at the School of Global Studies, University of Sussex.

Jong-Woon Lee is Associate Professor and Director of the Peace Education Center at Hanshin University, South Korea.

T0364206

North Korea and the Geopolitics of Development

Kevin Gray
University of Sussex

Jong-Woon Lee
Hanshin University

Shaftesbury Road, Cambridge CB2 8EA, United Kingdom

One Liberty Plaza, 20th Floor, New York, NY 10006, USA

477 Williamstown Road, Port Melbourne, VIC 3207, Australia

314–321, 3rd Floor, Plot 3, Splendor Forum, Jasola District Centre, New Delhi – 110025, India

103 Penang Road, #05–06/07, Visioncrest Commercial, Singapore 238467

Cambridge University Press is part of Cambridge University Press & Assessment, a department of the University of Cambridge.

We share the University's mission to contribute to society through the pursuit of education, learning and research at the highest international levels of excellence.

www.cambridge.org
Information on this title: www.cambridge.org/9781108826396

DOI: 10.1017/9781108919579

First published 2021
First paperback edition 2022

A catalogue record for this publication is available from the British Library

Library of Congress Cataloging-in-Publication data
Names: Gray, Kevin, 1973- author. | Lee, Jong-Woon, author.
Title: North Korea and the geopolitics of development / Kevin Gray, Jong-Woon Lee.
Description: Cambridge ; New York, NY : Cambridge University Press, 2021. |
    Includes bibliographical references and index.
Identifiers: LCCN 2020042670 (print) | LCCN 2020042671 (ebook) |
    ISBN 9781108843652 (hardback) | ISBN 9781108826396 (paperback) |
    ISBN 9781108919579 (epub)
Subjects: LCSH: Economic development–Korea (North) | Geopolitics–Korea (North) |
    Geopolitics–East Asia. | Korea (North)–Economic conditions. | Korea (North)–
    Foreign economic relations. | Korea (North)–Politics and government.
Classification: LCC HC470.2 .G73 2021 (print) | LCC HC470.2 (ebook) |
    DDC 338.95193–dc23
LC record available at https://lccn.loc.gov/2020042670
LC ebook record available at https://lccn.loc.gov/2020042671

ISBN   978-1-108-84365-2   Hardback
ISBN   978-1-108-82639-6   Paperback

To Yunjeong
Jong-Woon Lee

To my parents
Kevin Gray

Contents

Figures

Tables

Preface

This book seeks to shed light on how geopolitical contestation in the Northeast Asian region served to shape the vicissitudes of North Korea's experience of late development. Though extant analyses of North Korean political economy do make reference to the country's international environment, the emphasis nonetheless tends to be on the domestic level of analysis, with the substantive features of North Korea's developmental model seen as the outcome of the decisions and preferences of the ruling Kim dynasty. Our aim, however, is to put geopolitical dynamics at the very centre of the analysis and to show how the seemingly idiosyncratic North Korean political economy was fundamentally shaped by three key geopolitical moments, namely colonialism and the rise of developmental nationalisms, the structure of Cold War competition that emerged during the post-1945 era, and the more recent momentous shifts associated with the rise of China. In this respect, we analyse North Korea through the lens of catch-up development, understood as the world-historical process whereby newly independent states sought to liberate themselves from the legacies of colonialism and underdevelopment, and to achieve their position amongst the ranks of the modern industrialised nations by means of state-orchestrated projects of national development. At the same time, the capacity of postcolonial states to achieve that goal and the substantive trajectories of their developmental path are profoundly shaped by the aforementioned dynamics of geopolitical contestation. As such, the framework of the development–geopolitics nexus enables us to shed light on the specificity of North Korea's experience, including state-directed industrialisation, its subsequent economic collapse and tentative recovery amidst ongoing marketisation. In contrast to methodologically nationalist approaches, this analytical framework thereby provides a holistic explanation of the particularism of the North Korean trajectory of development, albeit within the universality of the late developmental experience.

Though North Korea is not the information 'black hole' it is sometimes made out to be, researching the country does present its own challenges and requires an eclectic approach towards sources and methods. For example, in terms of historical data, we have endeavoured to draw upon North Korean sources. The reliability of North Korean data might be doubted given the assumed propensity for exaggeration or outright falsification by state socialist countries. All North Korean data are therefore presented with the relevant caveats that they may be subject to some political manipulation. Where possible, North Korean publications are triangulated with other sources. Furthermore, the fact that the authorities ceased to announce detailed economic data as the economy faced increasing difficulties in the 1960s suggests at least some reliability of the data before then. North Korean sources are also utilised to illuminate the regime's policies and thinking on economic issues. Reference is made to historical North Korean newspapers and journals rather than later publications such as Kim Il Sung's Collected Works, which are more subject to retroactive revision.

We have also drawn from reports and secondary literature from South Korean sources. For obvious reasons, South Korea contains the world's largest concentration of research expertise on North Korean political economy outside of the country itself. South Korean academic institutions and research institutes produce vast amounts of information on North Korea, much of which is underutilised in English language publications. In terms of secondary sources, we have endeavoured to show no bias towards the use of English or Korean academic sources. Translations of Korean texts have been carried out by the authors, unless otherwise indicated. In addition, we have also conducted dozens of semi-structured interviews with Chinese government officials and business people in the Sino–North Korean border regions, as well as North Korean defectors residing in South Korea. Needless to say, these have been anonymised to protect the identities of the interviewees. While there are methodological challenges in using defector testimony as a means to gain insight into North Korea, we negotiate such challenges through restricting interviews to relatively matter-of-fact topics such as the role of markets in economic daily life. We also rely on the numerous reports published by international organisations with operations in North Korea. The dearth of contemporary economic data released by Pyongyang is tackled by using the mirror statistics produced by North Korea's key trade partner China, though again this is with the caveat that questions can be raised about the reliability of Chinese data.

There are many people we would like to thank who have in various ways made this book possible. These include Kamran Matin, Adam Cathcart, Louiza Odysseous, Ben Selwyn, Justin Rosenberg, Jamie Doucette, Denny Roy, Lee Jones, Namhee Lee, Jinsoo An, Rorden Wilkinson, Patricia Owens, Shahar Hameiri, Mike Cowin, Jean Lee, James Person, Christine Ahn, Patrick McEachern, Taekyoon Kim, Soojin Park, Sojin Lim, Jeong-Im Hyun, Owen Miller, Soyeun Kim, Stephanie Barrientos, Henry Veltmeyer, Jang-Hwan Joo,

Ihk-Pyo Hong, Sung-Cheol Lee, Moon-Soo Yang, Eul-Chul Lim and Jun-Kee Baek. We would also like to thank the two anonymous reviewers from Cambridge University Press for their highly constructive comments which ultimately assisted in improving the manuscript, as well as Lucy Rhymer and Emily Sharp at Cambridge University Press for their help in ensuring a smooth publication process.

Kevin Gray is grateful to the Woodrow Wilson International Center for Scholars in Washington, DC. A generous nine-month visiting fellowship at the Center in 2017–18 provided the time, resources and mentorship needed to make considerable progress in the writing of the manuscript. Particular thanks are given to two research assistants, Ann Kim and Young Jung, who provided invaluable support. Kevin Gray would also like to express his gratitude to the East-West Center in Honolulu and to POSCO for a generous visiting fellowship there during the summer of 2016, which facilitated part of the research for Chapter 7. Jong-Woon Lee would like to acknowledge research grants from the National Research Foundation of Korea for several fieldwork and data collection trips. Gratitude is also extended to current and former colleagues at Hanshin University, Far East University and the Korea Institute for International Economic Policy, as well as to Hong-Yul Han, Won-Sub Kim, Sang-Nam Park and Sung-Wook Yoon.

Chapter 6 is a significantly revised version of an earlier journal article: Kevin Gray and Jong-Woon Lee, 'Following in China's Footsteps? The Political Economy of North Korean Reform', *The Pacific Review*, 30.1 (2017), pp. 51–73. Chapter 7 draws on two earlier published articles: Jong-Woon Lee and Kevin Gray, 'Neo-Colonialism in South-South Relations?: The Case of China and North Korea', *Development and Change*, 47.2 (2016), pp. 293–316, and Kevin Gray and Jong-Woon Lee, 'The Rescaling of the Chinese State and Sino-North Korean Relations: Beyond State-Centrism', *Journal of Contemporary Asia*, 48.1 (2018), pp. 113–32. Gratitude is expressed towards both Taylor & Francis and John Wiley & Sons for permission to reproduce these articles.

In this book, we have used the McCune–Reischauer system of Korean romanisation, except where alternatives are more commonly used in English, for example, Kim Il Sung rather than Kim Ilsŏng, and Juche rather than Chuch'e. Similarly, place names are given in their typical usage in English rather than the McCune–Reischauer system or indeed official North Korean romanisation, that is, 'Pyongyang' rather than 'Phyongyang'. Romanisation is according to North Korean rather than South Korean usage, for example, Rodong Sinmun rather than Nodong Sinmun. In Korean language references, family names are written first, though in English language references, the family name is written last in the conventional manner.

Introduction: The Development–Geopolitics Nexus in North Korea

To say that North Korea is something of an enigma is to be guilty of considerable understatement. Two seemingly irreconcilable images of the country compete for dominance in the popular imagination. The first and primary reason that North Korea frequently grabs the global headlines is its increasingly sophisticated nuclear weapons and missile programme. The year 2017, for example, saw heightened international concern as Pyongyang not only successfully tested its first hydrogen bomb but also carried out dozens of missile tests, including launches of intercontinental ballistic missiles capable of reaching the US mainland. These rapid advances in nuclear and missile technology despite stringent international sanctions also suggested a growing reliance on indigenous technologies and manufacturing.[1] However, this image of a country with growing technological prowess in weapons of mass destruction competes with that of a poor 'starving' country, whose long-suffering population continues to live under a dictatorship that in every respect appears as an anachronistic throwback to the Soviet Union of the 1930s. Indeed, after decades of extolling the virtues of self-reliant development, North Korea earned the dubious distinction in the 1990s of becoming 'the only literate and urbanized society in human history to suffer mass famine in peacetime'.[2] So-called 'excess deaths' during the famine were estimated to be within a range of around 600,000 to 1 million, or approximately 3–5 per cent of the population.[3] In that decade, the economy also shrank significantly, reportedly averaging 4.2 per cent negative annual growth in consecutive years from 1990 to 1998.[4]

---

[1] *The Atlantic*, 6 September 2017, 'How Did North Korea's Missile and Nuclear Tech Get So Good So Fast?' www.theatlantic.com/international/archive/2017/09/north-korea-tech/538959 [accessed 29 April 2020].

[2] Nicholas Eberstadt, 'What Is Wrong with the North Korean Economy', American Enterprise Institute, 2011, www.aei.org/publication/what-is-wrong-with-the-north-korean-economy [accessed 15 January 2020].

[3] Stephan Haggard and Marcus Noland, *Famine in North Korea: Markets, Aid, and Reform* (New York: Columbia University Press, 2007), p. 76.

[4] Bank of Korea, Economic Statistics System, http://ecos.bok.or.kr [accessed 18 May 2020].

Though the country is, in reality, no longer starving, widespread malnutrition persists as a result of continued challenges faced by the agricultural sector. Indeed, in 2017, the same year that North Korea made rapid advances in its nuclear and missile programme, the World Food Programme reported that 10.3 million North Koreans remained undernourished.[5] For many observers, this juxtaposition of widespread economic hardship amidst technological advancement of the country's nuclear and missile programme forms the basis of a strong normative critique of the misplaced priorities of the North Korean state. Yet, the enigma of North Korea remains. For a country whose Gross Domestic Product (GDP) per capita places it at around 176 out of 193 countries, the requisite capacities in science and technology necessary for an indigenous nuclear programme, such as that of North Korea's, would be beyond the reach of many countries at a similar level of economic development.[6]

If we adopt a diachronic view of the trajectory of the country's development, the North Korean enigma becomes even more pronounced. Following national division and the destruction of the Korean War (1950–53), the country underwent a structural economic transformation that was arguably unparalleled in terms of its breadth and speed. By the end of the 1950s, North Korea had already experienced a significant degree of reconstruction, and in the following decade, North Korea was labelled by the British economist, Joan Robinson, as Asia's first post-war 'miracle economy'.[7] While Robinson's positive portrayal of the North Korean developmental model might be dismissed as that of a sympathetic 'fellow traveller', the country's level of industrialisation and urbanisation did nonetheless place the country ahead of the majority of post-colonial Third World countries, and even compared favourably with the more advanced countries of Eastern Europe.

However, following failed attempts at increasing trade with the non-socialist world in the early 1970s, North Korea experienced a period of sustained economic decline. The diminishing returns of its centrally planned economy along with heightened levels of external indebtedness led to the country's growing reliance on the largesse of its communist neighbours. Furthermore, the collapse of the Soviet Union in the early 1990s alongside China's shift towards a more pragmatic foreign economic policy led to severe shortages in energy, raw materials and foreign currency, and tragically, to a collapse in food production and widespread famine. The fact that this occurred at the epicentre

---

[5] FAO, IFAD, UNICEF, WFP and WHO, *The State of Food Security and Nutrition in the World 2017: Building Resilience for Peace and Food Security* (Rome: FAO, 2017).

[6] 'National Accounts – Analysis of Main Aggregates (AMA)' https://unstats.un.org/unsd/snaama/selbasicFast.asp [accessed 8 March 2018]. Original data is from South Korea's Bank of Korea. It should be noted, however, that the reliability of the Bank of Korea's estimates of North Korean GDP has been widely debated.

[7] Joan Robinson, 'Korean Miracle', *Monthly Review*, 16.9 (1965), pp. 541–49.

of the most dynamic region of the world economy makes North Korea's predicament even more striking. Yet these catastrophic events did not seem to threaten the political stability of the regime. Despite widespread predictions since the 1990s of impending collapse, the distinctive feature of the North Korean regime has not been its fragility but precisely its longevity.

From the early 2000s, the North Korean economy experienced a modest degree of recovery, a process that continued following Kim Jong Un's rise to power in December 2011. There was still widespread poverty in the country, particularly in rural areas, and much of the country's public healthcare system remained dysfunctional. Yet, there was also a process of profound socio-economic change in the country. There were visible signs of economic dynamism in the cities alongside the emergence of a small but influential entrepreneurial class as well as a variety of profit-oriented market activities pursued by individuals and state enterprises. What is even more remarkable is that these domestic transformations took place under an increasingly stringent bilateral and multilateral sanctions regime. However, North Korea's continued policy of nuclearisation alongside the onset of the Trump administration's 'maximum pressure' campaign led to a further tightening of sanctions, raising new questions regarding the sustainability of North Korea's post-crisis economic recovery.

Existing Understandings of North Korean Development

This distinctive trajectory of the rise, collapse and tentative recovery amidst ongoing socio-economic transformation in the context of a politically unreformed socialist state and increasingly adverse external environment provides the main analytical puzzle for this book. As we argue, much of the existing scholarship on North Korean economic development has typically reproduced post-war development theory's internalism and methodological nationalism, whereby the features of a given country's developmental experience are deemed as deriving largely from within that country itself. As a result, we argue that they fail to provide a holistic understanding of the vicissitudes of North Korean development. In existing mainstream approaches, the role of geopolitical contestation is integrated into analyses of North Korean development in a largely *post-hoc* manner. By contrast, we argue not simply that North Korean development should be situated within its broader international context but rather that processes of catch-up industrialisation and geopolitical contestation should be seen as fundamentally co-constitutive.

Much of the literature on North Korean development has either implicitly or explicitly adopted a liberal economic approach. This approach typically regards stalled development in the state socialist and postcolonial worlds as due not to the imperfections of the market but rather due to irrational government interventions that serve to distort the workings of the price mechanism.[8] Autarkic developmental strategies are also criticised for going against Ricardian principles of comparative advantage. By encouraging protectionism and thereby undermining competition, they are seen as merely serving to encourage the rent-seeking activities of domestic entrepreneurs.[9] The economic isolation brought by autarkic policies also leads to scientific and cultural isolation and a suspicious attitude towards exchange with the West, thereby impeding the flow of money, products and capital as well as ideas.[10] Engagement with the world market, on the other hand, is seen as the most effective means of providing aspiring developing countries with the means to achieve greater efficiency through economies of scale.[11] State socialist countries have been subject to particular criticism as a result of low levels of productivity, lack of incentives, as well as an absence of competition between producers. Indeed, it is these chronic inefficiencies that are held responsible for the decline and ultimate collapse of the Soviet and Eastern European economies.[12]

In line with these critiques, liberal economic analyses of the North Korean political economy typically point to the overbearing nature of the state and the resultant distortions of the economy. For example, it has been argued that the North Korean development strategy led to the excessive prioritisation of heavy industry at the expense of consumer goods and services. Furthermore, there was a misallocation of capital investment, with the economy blighted by poor infrastructure, outdated technology, shortages of technology from abroad and a lack of foreign exchange.[13] As in other centrally planned economies, managers of North Korean enterprises spent a great deal of their time dealing with the central authorities to obtain supplies of materials as well as preferential tax or subsidy treatment. However, the soft budget constraint and the lack of bankruptcy laws led to a vicious circle of runaway demand for inputs, hoarding and a deepening shortage of materials.[14] Enterprises typically produced a narrow range of products using techniques that by world standards had become

---

[8] Deepak Lal, *The Poverty of 'Development Economics'* (Cambridge, MA: Harvard University Press, 1983), p. 134.

[9] Anne O. Krueger, 'The Political Economy of the Rent Seeking Society', *The American Economic Review*, 64.3 (1974), pp. 291–303.

[10] János Kornai, *The Socialist System: The Political Economy of Communism* (Princeton, NJ: Princeton University Press, 1992), p. 339.

[11] Bela Balassa, 'Exports and Economic Growth: Further Evidence', *Journal of Development Economics*, 5.2 (1978), pp. 181–89.

[12] Richard E. Ericson, 'The Classical Soviet-Type Economy: Nature of the System and Implications for Reform', *The Journal of Economic Perspectives*, 5.4 (1991), pp. 11–27.

[13] Marcus Noland, 'Prospects for the North Korean Economy', in *North Korea after Kim Il Sung*, ed. by Dae-Sook Suh and Chae-Jin Lee (London: Lynne Rienner, 1998), p. 33.

[14] Myoung-Kyu Kang and Keun Lee, 'Industrial Systems and Reform in North Korea: A Comparison with China', *World Development*, 20.7 (1992), pp. 949–50.

obsolete. Furthermore, the lack of material rewards linked to workers' effort and the neglect of the consumer goods industry served to undermine incentives and productivity.[15]

Similar critiques have also been directed at North Korea's system of collectivised agriculture. It is conceded that prior to the 1980s, despite a shortage of arable land and its short growing season, North Korea achieved impressive increases in agricultural production as a result of land reform, mechanisation, the application of chemical fertilisers and the mass mobilisation of labour power. Nonetheless, the low material incentives inherent in collectivised agriculture subsequently led to declining productivity.[16] As Rüdiger Frank has argued, soft budget constraints, the seller's market and the limited use of money under the planned economy meant that agricultural cooperatives were weakly responsive to price signals. This led to an inefficient allocation of resources and low inputs, as well as the hoarding of resources which further aggravated shortages.[17]

North Korea is also seen as having pursued a policy of economic autarky that served to inhibit 'normal' economic development. Suh Sang-Chul has argued that as with South Korea, the decline of foreign aid in the 1960s meant that North Korea was forced to find new sources of foreign exchange. Yet, as South Korea sought to earn foreign exchange through exports, North Korea strengthened its self-reliant model of development and thereby closed off such a strategy.[18] Furthermore, as domestic industry became more capital and technology-intensive, efficiency in terms of plant size required larger-scale operations that exceeded domestic needs. Thus, North Korea's autarkic approach led to higher production costs. Domestic producers were protected from foreign competition, creating weak incentives for innovation and productivity increases. Autarky also led to a lack of technology transfers from abroad, further contributing to the slowdown in growth.[19] Indeed, in 1984, the dollar value of exports as a ratio of overall Gross National Product (GNP) (based on CIA estimates) stood at just 7 per cent, compared to 21 per cent in Hungary and 32 per cent in South Korea.[20] Furthermore, the fact that for

---

[15] Youn Suk Kim, 'Current North Korean Economy: Overview and Prospects for Change', *North Korean Review*, 4.2 (2008), p. 18.

[16] Phillip Wonhyuk Lim, 'North Korea's Food Crisis', *Korea and World Affairs*, 21.4 (1997), pp. 568–85.

[17] Ruediger Frank, 'Classical Socialism in North Korea and Its Transformation: The Role and the Future of Agriculture', *Harvard Asia Quarterly*, X.2 (2006), pp. 19–20.

[18] Sang-Chul Suh, 'North Korean Industrial Policy and Trade', in *North Korea Today: Strategic and Domestic Issues*, ed. by Robert A. Scalapino and Jun-yop Kim (Berkeley, CA: Institute of East Asian Studies, University of California, 1983), pp. 201–2.

[19] Ibid., p. 204.

[20] Hy-Sang Lee, 'North Korea's Closed Economy: The Hidden Opening', *Asian Survey*, 28.12 (1988), p. 1271.

decades the country traded primarily with non-convertible currency economies exacerbated its shortages of foreign currency. Criticism has also been directed at North Korea's failure to pay its foreign loan commitments since the mid-1970s, which led to a poor credit rating, isolation from the global financial system and difficulty in attracting foreign investment despite facilitative measures the following decade.[21]

As elsewhere in the Socialist Bloc, central planning has been regarded as a significant contributing factor to North Korea's declining economic growth rate. Although it may have played a positive role in the context of post-Korean War reconstruction, the task of central planning became exceedingly complex as the economy expanded. The inefficiency of planning in terms of resource allocation along with the lack of adequate technology resulted in the failure to fulfil planned targets and in continued secular economic decline.[22] As Kim Byung-Yeon has argued, the reduction of aid from the Soviet Union in the late 1950s and the resulting difficulties in securing adequate investment resources led North Korea to combine its central planning system with a mass mobilisation policy that sought to emphasise workers' collective efforts.[23] Nonetheless, the country saw a further centralisation of planning in the 1960s under the slogan of 'unified and detailed planning' at a time when much of the Socialist Bloc was experimenting with 'market socialism'.[24] Indeed, it was not until the 1980s that North Korean made any serious attempt at decentralising economic management.[25]

The liberal economic perspective has also underpinned analyses of the North Korean famine of the 1990s. Stephan Haggard and Marcus Noland have argued, for example, that the famine was a result of several factors including the country's heavy industry-first industrialisation strategy, the policy of self-sufficiency in food despite the shortage of arable land, the collective farm system, industrialised food production, and more broadly, the erosion of traditional farming techniques and the stifling of individual farmers' incentives. Even when North Korea's relations with its allies were drastically transformed at the outset of the 1990s, the regime sought to reduce domestic

---

[21] Hong-Tack Chun, 'Economic Conditions in North Korea and Prospects for Reform', in *North Korea after Kim Il Sung*, ed. by Thomas H. Henriksen and Jongryn Mo (Stanford: Hoover Institution Press, 1997), pp. 32–49; Marcus Noland, 'Why North Korea Will Muddle Through', *Foreign Affairs*, 76.4 (1997), pp. 105–18.

[22] Joseph Sang-Hoon Chung, 'Economic Planning in North Korea', in *North Korea Today: Strategic and Domestic Issues*, ed. by Robert A. Scalapino and Jun-yop Kim (Berkeley, CA: Institute of East Asian Studies, University of California, 1983), pp. 176–82.

[23] Byung-Yeon Kim, *Unveiling the North Korean Economy: Collapse and Transition* (Cambridge: Cambridge University Press, 2017), pp. 57–8.

[24] Phillip H. Park, *Rebuilding North Korea's Economy: Politics and Policy* (Seoul: IFES Kyungnam University, 2016), pp. 53–61.

[25] Ibid., pp. 108–12.

consumption rather than adopt fundamental reforms that would have allowed the country to earn the foreign exchange needed to pay for food imports.[26] North Korea's economic difficulties were not simply deemed to be the result of poor policies, but a result of the very nature of the regime. As Haggard and Noland further argue, '[i]t follows almost as a matter of logic that these problems will not be definitively resolved until the regime is replaced by one that, if not fully democratic, is at least more responsive to the needs of the citizenry'.[27]

Furthermore, attempts to address the shortcomings of this model have been seen as inadequate. In light of China's economic ascent following its market-oriented reforms, critics have emphasised the need for North Korea to introduce similar reforms, including but not limited to the liberalisation of trade, the privatisation of state-owned enterprises (SOEs) and the introduction of private property rights. While North Korea did introduce certain measures in the 1980s such as a joint venture law in 1984 and the establishment of a special economic zone in 1991, the continued poor investment climate is seen as having deterred significant investment by foreign capital.[28] A series of reforms in the early 2000s have similarly been interpreted as limited reforms *within* the system rather than fundamental reform *of* the system. In this view, rather than adopting the Chinese approach, North Korea's reforms shared more in common with the failed attempts at 'market socialism' within the Soviet Bloc during the 1960s.[29] As such, in the post-famine era, North Korean economic policy is understood largely in terms of its continuity with the past. As Yong-Soo Park argues, North Korea's poor economic situation continues to be characterised by shortages in foreign exchange, energy and goods, all of which stem from North Korea's autarkical line.[30]

These liberal economic analyses provide a powerful critique of the distortions caused by North Korea's centrally planned economy and its insular developmental strategy. They correctly draw attention to chronic structural problems as well as to the ideological rigidity that has forestalled serious attempts at addressing those problems. The liberal economic approach is not without its shortcomings, however. First, it focusses primarily on explaining the failures of North Korea's economic and political system. From an analytical perspective, it is by no means self-evident that the relatively successful years of post-war recovery and catch-up industrialisation should be regarded as

---

[26] Haggard and Noland, *Famine in North Korea*, pp. 27.   [27] Ibid., p. 3.
[28] Kongdan Oh and Ralph C. Hassig, 'North Korea between Collapse and Reform', *Asian Survey*, 39.2 (1999), pp. 293–4.
[29] Bernhard Seliger, 'The July 2002 Reforms in North Korea: Liberman-Style Reforms or Road to Transformation?', *North Korean Review*, 1.1 (2005), pp. 22–37.
[30] Yong-Soo Park, 'The Political Economy of Economic Reform in North Korea', *Australian Journal of International Affairs*, 63.4 (2009), p. 531.

little more than a precursor to subsequent stagnation and collapse. Indeed, the focus on market-impeding institutions and autarkic policies runs into difficulties when it is deployed to analyse both the initial successes and subsequent failures of the North Korean economic system. The dominant argument in the literature has been that the 'advantages of backwardness' meant that strategies of extensive growth were relatively easy to achieve, notwithstanding the inherent shortcomings of the centrally planned model.[31] Yet, this tells us little about the specificity of the North Korean experience and exactly how it was that the country was able to undergo what was by most accounts an extraordinarily rapid process of industrialisation and urbanisation in the post-war period.

Second, the distinction between state and market, inherent in liberal economic theory, fails to fully capture the subsequent economic recovery or processes of marketisation in North Korea following the crisis of the 1990s. Indeed, many ordinary North Koreans resorted to market activities as a means of survival, thereby reducing their dependence on the public distribution system. However, while marketisation is understood as a countervailing force outside of and against the state, the evidence suggests the emergence of a more mutually constitutive and co-dependent relationship between state and market that undermines their ontological separation in liberal economic theory. Indeed, the process of marketisation became increasingly inseparable from the economic reform measures, adopted from the early 2000s, which sought to legalise a significant proportion of hitherto illegal and semi-legal market activities.[32]

Third, although the critique of the inefficiencies of central planning and autarky is persuasive, the approach largely limits itself to that critique. In this sense, liberal economics is reflective of a broader predominant approach in the social sciences of methodological nationalism. The latter refers to 'the all-pervasive assumption that the nation-state is the natural and necessary form of society in modernity; the nation-state is taken as the organising principle of modernity'.[33] A key defining feature of methodological nationalism is its 'internalism', which seeks to explain social phenomena by reference to the inner characteristics alone of a given society or type of society.[34] In terms of analysing instances of national development, methodological nationalism explains economic performance with reference to national factors, and in

[31] Ericson, 'Classical Soviet-Type Economy', p. 21.
[32] Yang Moon-Soo, '"Economic Management System in Our Style' Observed through the Revised Laws in the Kim Jong Un Era [Kimjŏngŭn chipkwŏn ihu kaejŏng pŏmnyŏngŭl t'onghae pon 'urisikkyŏngjegwallibangbŏp']', Unification Policy Studies, 26.2 (2017), pp. 101–6.
[33] Daniel Chernilo, 'Social Theory's Methodological Nationalism Myth and Reality', European Journal of Social Theory 9.1 (2006), pp. 5–6.
[34] Justin Rosenberg, 'The "Philosophical Premises" of Uneven and Combined Development', Review of International Studies, 39.3 (2013), pp. 569–97.

particular, to the purposive actions of national governments. In this respect, '[n]ation states are taken to be like rational individuals with preferences, capabilities and responses to the stimuli and opportunities of their strategic environment'.[35] However, because liberal economic theory largely limits itself to internal domestic factors as explanatory variables and neglects the causative role of 'the international', there is little explicit consideration of *why* and in response to *what* historical imperatives specific market-impeding institutions and developmental strategies are adopted. Instead, it places analytical weight on the decisions of policymakers and tends to treat international factors as either epiphenomenal or to be integrated into the analysis in *post-hoc* fashion.

As such, the geopolitical context underpinning North Korea's national project of catch-up industrialisation is at a theoretical level largely elided from the analysis, or at best, there is a failure to integrate 'the international' into the analysis in any systematic way. As a result, such approaches are unable to provide an accurate explanation for the origins of North Korea's political and socio-economic institutions, or to answer the question of *why*, in comparison to the Soviet Union and China, the impetus to reform has been so weak in North Korea. With regards to the latter question, reference is typically made to the cost-benefit calculations of the country's leadership and the latter's aversion to opening the country to forces that may undermine the system of political control over economy and society. Yet in doing so, this underplays both the question of how 'the international' has shaped the dangers and opportunities inherent in such reforms as well as the structural constraints that result from a developmental model that has historically been profoundly shaped by processes of intense geopolitical rivalry.

Dependency theorists, on the other hand, have adopted a quite different approach that does take into account more fully the role of the international system in differentially shaping countries' developmental prospects. Dependency theory has mobilised a strong critique of modernisation and liberal economic theory by arguing that non-Western countries typically found themselves in conditions of underdevelopment not as a result of market-impeding institutions and autarkic developmental policies but rather due to the workings of global capitalism. The advanced economies of the West had, it is argued, achieved their developed status through their exploitation of the non-industrialised peripheral countries, leading to the latter's underdevelopment. Thus, while the now-developed countries may have once been undeveloped, they had never been actively *under*developed, as with many of the

---

[35] Charles Gore, 'Methodological Nationalism and the Misunderstanding of East Asian Industrialisation', *European Journal of Development Research*, 8.1 (1996), pp. 81–82.

non-Western countries in contemporary times.[36] Dependency thus refers to the situation whereby 'the economy of certain countries is conditioned by the development and expansion of another economy to which the former is subjected'.[37] Imperialism, it is argued, imposed a division of labour on the colonial world in which the peripheral countries were reduced to the role of exporters of raw materials to the core and importers of the latter's manufactured goods. Furthermore, this division of labour continued after formal independence, with postcolonial countries suffering from the continued effects of underdevelopment as a result of unequal exchange involving the steady transfer of economic surplus from the periphery to the core.[38] These relations of dependency have also been seen as central to the shaping of class relations within the dependent countries. Situations of dependency typically entail the existence of clientele classes, namely 'those which have a vested interest in the existing international system. These classes carry out certain functions on behalf of foreign interests; in return they enjoy a privileged and increasingly dominant and hegemonic position within their own societies, based largely on economic, political, or military support from abroad'.[39] Given the pervasiveness of these relations of dependency, the main policy prescription that arises from this approach is diametrically opposed to that given by liberal economists. If aspiring developing countries wish to escape conditions of dependency, they must pursue strategies of autarkic development by withdrawing themselves from the global economy and achieving self-sufficiency.[40]

How then has dependency theory been used to explain North Korea's distinctive developmental trajectory? The answer to this question depends on whether the *explanandum* is North Korea's early successes in catch-up industrialisation, the subsequent decline and collapse of its economy, or its subsequent recovery amidst deepening economic relations with China. In the 1970s, for example, several prominent scholars argued that North Korea had been able to achieve autonomous development through radical socialist revolution and delinking from the capitalist world economy.[41] In this view, North Korea was

---

[36] Andre Gunder Frank, 'The Development of Underdevelopment', in *Imperialism and Underdevelopment: A Reader*, ed. by Robert I Rhodes (New York: Monthly Review Press, 1970), pp. 4–5.

[37] Theotonio Dos Santos, 'The Structure of Dependence', *The American Economic Review*, 60.1 (1970), p. 231.

[38] Arghiri Emmanuel, *Unequal Exchange: A Study of the Imperialism of Trade* (New York: Monthly Review Press, 1972).

[39] S. Bodenheimer, 'Dependency and Imperialism: The Roots of Latin American Underdevelopment', *Politics & Society*, 1.November (1971), p. 337.

[40] Vincent Ferraro, 'Dependency Theory: An Introduction', in *The Development Economics Reader*, ed. by Giorgio Secondi (London: Routledge, 2008), pp. 58–64.

[41] Byong Sik Kim, *Modern Korea: The Socialist North, Revolutionary Perspectives in the South, and Unification* (New York: International Publishers, 1970); Ellen Brun and Jacques Hersh,

seen as having outperformed the South Korean 'neo-colony' through reducing its dependence on external supplies of energy, thereby offering a model for Third World countries seeking to pursue economic development while maintaining political independence.[42] There was at the time arguably justification for such views, though it should be noted that the North Korean economy was already facing difficulties by the 1970s. It was North Korea's economic collapse in the 1990s, however, that led to a thoroughgoing reassessment of these earlier arguments. That collapse exposed the fact that despite North Korea's strong rhetoric of self-reliant development, the country had in fact become increasingly dependent on cheap energy imports from its socialist neighbours. The sudden demand by Russia and China that payments for these imports be made in hard currency immediately served to expose the vulnerabilities of the North Korean political economy. As a result, scholars have more recently sought to highlight North Korea's dependency rather than its allegedly successful autarkic post-war development.[43] Indeed, it has been argued, for example, that North Korea's growing trade dependency on China since the mid-2000s can be viewed through the framework of dependency.[44]

Despite placing the workings of the international system at the centre of its analysis, the dependency approach also suffers from several weaknesses. First, the fact that the application of the concept of dependency to different periods of North Korean development leads to diametrically opposed analyses betrays its inability to explain the country's overall developmental trajectory. Second, although North Korea came to be reliant on cheap energy imports from its socialist allies, it is questionable whether this can be regarded as a form of 'dependency' if the latter is taken to point to a fundamentally exploitative relationship between core and the periphery. As we argue below, similar problems can be seen with regards to dependency analyses of relations between the Soviet Union and Eastern Europe, where economic relations were primarily shaped by geopolitical imperatives rather than by any generalised notion of exploitative unequal exchange. Furthermore, attempts to understand Sino–North Korean relations after the 1990s from the perspective of

Socialist Korea: A Case Study in the Strategy of Economic Development (New York: Monthly Review Press, 1976).

[42] See Aidan Foster-Carter, 'North Korea: Development and Self-Reliance. A Critical Appraisal', in *Korea North and South*, ed. by Gavan McCormack and Mark Selden (New York: Monthly Review, 1978), p. 134; Jon Halliday, 'The North Korean Model: Gaps and Questions', *World Development*, 9.9 (1981), p. 895; Gordon White, 'North Korean Chuch'e: The Political Economy of Independence', *Bulletin of Concerned Asian Scholars*, 7.2 (1975), p. 53.

[43] Hyun-Chun Lim and Byung-Kook Kim, 'Rethinking North Korean Self-Reliance: Reality and Facade', in *Dynamic Transformation: Korea, NICs and Beyond*, ed. by Gill-Chin Lim and Wook Chang (Urbana: Consortium on Development Studies, 1990), p. 67.

[44] Nicholas Eberstadt and Alex Coblin, 'Dependencia, North Korea Style', *The Asan Institute for Policy Studies Issue Brief*, 32 (2014).

dependency fail to take into account the prior collapse of the North Korean economy and the role of Chinese trade and investment in facilitating the country's tentative economic recovery. Neither can the notion of economic dependency provide an analytical tool with which to analyse the ultimately (geo)political question of the impact of international sanctions.

As such, both liberal economic and dependency approaches display several shortcomings in providing a comprehensive answer to the puzzle of North Korean development posed above. As we argue, in order to understand the vicissitudes of North Korean development, greater attention needs to be paid towards the nexus between development and geopolitical contestation. Indeed, the oft-repeated and largely inaccurate moniker of 'hermit kingdom' notwithstanding, the history of regional and global geopolitics has fundamentally shaped North Korea's experience of catch-up industrialisation and late development. In order to explore this development–geopolitics nexus further, we examine below three key geopolitical 'moments' that historically have had particular relevance for understanding both global development and the trajectory of late development in North Korea, namely colonialism and the rise of developmental nationalism, the Cold War and the rise of China. We then pose a series of research questions related to each moment that seek to address North Korean development in its international perspective.

Colonialism and the National Developmental Project

The first step in establishing the analytical framework of the development–geopolitics nexus is to examine the origins of 'national development' as a response to the emergence of industrial capitalism and its outward expansion in the nineteenth century through imperialism. A key impact of the rise of industrial capitalism was not the creation of the world 'in its own image', as Karl Marx and Friedrich Engels had argued.[45] Rather, it led to the colonial subjugation of the non-European world and to a sharp and growing economic disparity between the imperialist nations and their colonies. In 1820, for example, Asia, Africa and South America accounted for almost three-fourths of the world population and around two-thirds of world income. By 1950, their share of world income had declined to around one fourth, reflecting the industrialisation of Western Europe and the United States along with the deindustrialisation of Asia.[46] These growing disparities thereby led to the emergence of national communities seeking to pursue projects of 'defensive

---

[45] Karl Marx and Friedrich Engels, *The Communist Manifesto* (Harmondsworth, Middlesex: Penguin Books, 1967), p. 224.

[46] Deepak Nayyar, *Catch Up: Developing Countries in the World Economy* (Oxford: Oxford University Press, 2013), pp. 173–77.

modernisation'.[47] In this respect, the compulsion to develop in response to the military–geopolitical and economic pressures emanating from the more advanced powers can be seen as a general characteristic of late-developing societies.[48] Indeed, political leaders such as Sukarno, Kemal Ataturk, Nkrumah, Nehru, Sun Yat-Sen along with many others all spoke of the need to actively overcome this developmental gap alongside the legacies of colonialism more broadly through projects of catch-up development.

In ideational terms, these defensive modernisations were underpinned by the rise of 'developmental nationalisms' forged through the process of anti-imperialist struggles.[49] The precise forms that these nationalisms took varied widely, however. As Tom Nairn has argued, the Eurocentric worldview had it that the path of modern capitalist development could be followed straightforwardly, and as such, the peripheral countries would be able to catch up with the advanced countries with relative ease.[50] The reality was, however, that they experienced invasion and domination. Elites in the periphery thus felt they had little option but to take matters into their own hands and directly establish the trappings of modernity themselves. However, unable to literally 'copy' the advanced countries, the backward regions were forced to take what they wanted and combine it with their own native social forms. This required the mobilisation of populations through the formation of a militant, inter-class community aware of its own mythical separate identity vis-à-vis the outside forces.[51] As such, nationalism amounted to 'the idealist motor of the forced march out of backwardness or dependency'.[52]

What then can be said about the kinds of institutions that underpinned late development and how their emergence was shaped by geopolitical dynamics? As noted, late development was by definition not simply a process of following the developmental path of 'first mover' England. Alexander Gerschenkron argued, for example, that in Germany late development had occurred in a context whereby an industrial revolution had already taken place in England and the requisite industrial technologies were already existent. This meant that industrial plants were on average larger, ratios of capital to output were higher, and that instead of the more gradual accumulation of capital and its transfer to industry that had taken place in England, Germany also saw the emergence of

---

[47] Philip Curtin, *The World and the West: The European Challenge and the Overseas Response in the Age of Empire* (Cambridge: Cambridge University Press, 2000).

[48] Alexander Anievas, *Capital, the State, and War: Class Conflict and Geopolitics in the Thirty Years' Crisis, 1914–1945* (Ann Arbor: University of Michigan Press, 2014), pp. 45–46.

[49] Radhika Desai, 'Introduction: Nationalisms and Their Understandings in Historical Perspective', *Third World Quarterly*, 29.3 (2008), pp. 399–400.

[50] Tom Nairn, 'The Modern Janus', *New Left Review*, 94 (1975), pp. 8–9.   [51] Ibid., pp. 10–11.

[52] Ibid., p. 14.

large banks designed to finance longer-term industrial investment.[53] However, Russia's greater backwardness and scarcity of capital during its industrialisation drive in the 1890s meant that no banking system could conceivably succeed in attracting sufficient funds to finance large-scale industrialisation. It was therefore the state that stepped in to facilitate the supply of capital for industrialisation through its taxation policies.[54] This emphasis on the role of the state as a facilitator of late development was equally if not more pronounced in postcolonial contexts, reflecting the fact that 'catch up development is inherently political. Since it by definition cannot be organised at the initiative of a single or collective capitalist's short-term interest, catching up *requires* the intervention of the state in order to construct a socialized territorial assemblage able to compete with more advanced productive forces'.[55]

Debates surrounding the causes of successful late development in twentieth-century East Asia further confirm this central role of the state. Against the liberal economic emphasis on the 'invisible hand' of the market, developmental state theorists argue that catch-up industrialisation in Japan, Taiwan and South Korea occurred as a result of a highly effective form of coordination between the state and the capital, though one in which the latter was clearly subjected to the directive capacities of the former through its control over credit.[56] T. J. Pempel's somewhat broader notion of the 'developmental regime' sheds light on the specificity of state–society relations underpinning successful instances of late development as well as on the geopolitical context in which such development occurred. Features of the developmental regime include, amongst others, the existence of a strong state; the state's autonomy from societal interests; land reform and the elimination of the landowner class; hegemonic projects based around the goal of national development; the rejection of reified Western conceptions of the market; independence from foreign capital; and favourable geopolitical relations.[57]

The notion of the developmental regime thus usefully draws attention to the ideational, institutional and geopolitical contexts that have underpinned late

---

[53] Alexander Gerschenkron, *Economic Backwardness in Historical Perspective* (Cambridge, MA: Harvard University Press, 1962), p. 14.

[54] Ibid., pp. 19–20.

[55] Steven Rolf, 'Locating the State: Uneven and Combined Development, the States System and the Political', in *Theoretical Engagements in Geopolitical Economy*, ed. by Radhika Desai (Bingley: Emerald Group, 2015), p. 139.

[56] Chalmers Johnson, *MITI and the Japanese Miracle: The Growth of Industrial Policy, 1925–1975* (Stanford: Stanford University Press, 1982); Robert Wade, *Governing the Market: Economic Theory and the Role of Government in East Asian Industrialization* (Princeton, NJ: Princeton University Press, 1990); Alice H. Amsden, *Asia's Next Giant: South Korea and Late Industrialization* (Oxford: Oxford University Press, 1989).

[57] T. J. Pempel, 'The Developmental Regime in a Changing World Economy', in *The Developmental State*, ed. by Meredith Woo-Cumings (Ithaca, NY: Cornell University Press, 1999), p. 160.

developmental projects more broadly. However, simply recognising the importance of 'favourable geopolitical relations' does not go far enough in recognising how the dynamics of geopolitical contestation are fundamentally constitutive of projects of national development. As we have noted, the emergence of national development as hegemonic ideology occurred in large part due to the violence of imperialism and colonisation, and the resultant developmental gap between the European and non-European worlds. Furthermore, the extent to which aspiring late developers are endowed with the requisite state capacity and autonomy from both domestic and foreign social forces varies greatly in both temporal and spatial terms, and thus needs to be examined with reference to the specificity of geopolitical dynamics in any given situation.

In Asia, for example, the lateness of Japanese development in world-historical time led to a heightened urgency whereby the carving out of a regional sphere of influence was seen as vital to the country's survival as an independent nation. The fact that Japan's colonies of Korea and Taiwan were both contiguous territories facilitated the settling of migrants from the metropole who staffed the large colonial bureaucracies.[58] Indeed, these bureaucracies were significantly larger and more developed than those elsewhere in the colonial world. Though Japan's colonies initially served mainly as agricultural producers and exporters, the late 1930s also saw a degree of colonial industrialisation under Japanese auspices, particularly in Korea.[59] Again, none of this is to deny that Japanese colonialism was a brutal and exploitative experience for the subjugated peoples. Nonetheless, it seems undeniable that the process of state-building as well as the establishment of industry and infrastructure provided a basis for postcolonial industrialisation that was absent in much of the colonial world. Vietnam, for example, has been seen by contrast as a case of 'colonisation without development or modernity'.[60] French colonialism was a more typical example of Western imperialism in that the colonial project was primarily concerned with the extraction of Vietnam's agro-mineral resources with the aim of exploiting differences between the costs of acquisition and the prices that could be obtained on the world market. As such, only a small colonial bureaucracy was required and there was little need for the provision of

---

[58] Bruce Cumings, 'The Origins and Development of the Northeast Asian Political Economy: Industrial Sectors, Product Cycles, and Political Consequences', ed. by Frederic C. Deyo, *International Organization*, 38.01 (1984), pp. 7–11.

[59] Thomas B. Gold, 'Colonial Origins of Taiwanese Capitalism', in *Contending Approaches to the Political Economy of Taiwan*, ed. by Edwin A. Winckler and Susan M. Greenhalgh (Armonk, NY: M. E. Sharpe, 1988), pp. 101–17; Atul Kohli, 'Where Do High Growth Political Economies Come From? The Japanese Lineage of Korea's "Developmental State"', *World Development*, 22.9 (1994), pp. 1269–93.

[60] Bruce Cumings, *Parallax Visions: Making Sense of American-East Asian Relations* (Durham, NC: Duke University Press, 1999), p. 82.

long-term political and social security or intervention in the form of land and labour policies. Conscious developmental efforts were limited to infrastructural projects aimed at facilitating the transport of commodities to the global market.[61] The weak colonial state thus meant that there was nothing like the degree of penetration that the Japanese had achieved in its colonies.

This brief overview of the development–geopolitical nexus during the colonial era thereby raises several questions for the analysis of North Korean development: how exactly did Korea's experience of colonisation shape the emergence of the North Korean developmental regime? Answering this question requires consideration of several subquestions: what were the implications of Japanese colonialism for state–society relations in the post-liberation era? What forms of continuity and discontinuity could be seen between the colonial and postcolonial states? For example, how did colonial land tenure arrangements impact upon state formation in the post-liberation era? To what extent did the legacies of colonial industrialisation shape the North Korea's regime's developmental strategy? The framework of the development–geopolitics nexus also draws attention to the ideological legacies of colonialism and how they shaped the post-liberation developmental strategy. As we will argue, consideration of this question requires paying attention to the Soviet origins of North Korean political institutions as well as their articulation with colonial legacies, alongside their combined impact upon the North Korean developmental regime's emphasis on self-reliant national development.

The Cold War and Late Development

Along with colonialism, the dynamics of the Cold War are central to explaining how geopolitical contestation shaped the possibilities for catch-up industrialisation in the non-Western world. The 1945 juncture led both the United States and the Soviet Union to promote projects of national development in their respective spheres of influence. The United States, for example, established a post-war 'informal empire' made up of formally independent nation states and presided over a dramatic international modernisation project.[62] However, the impact of US nation-building on Third World development was closely intertwined with the legacies of colonialism as well as the uneven geography of the Cold War. For example, the reconstruction of the Northeast Asian regional economy formed a key element in the United States attempts to

---

[61] Martin J. Murray, *The Development of Capitalism in Colonial Indochina (1870–1940)* (Berkeley, CA: University of California Press, 1980), pp. 35–36.

[62] Mark Berger, 'From Nation-Building to State-Building: The Geopolitics of Development, the Nation-State System and the Changing Global Order', *Third World Quarterly*, 27.1 (2006), p. 15.

contain the influence of the Soviet Union in Asia. In postcolonial Taiwan and South Korea, this involved forging an alliance with conservative anti-communist elites and facilitating the repression of the left. These interventions established a degree of continuity between the colonial and postcolonial states, particularly in terms of their relatively developed bureaucracies and institutions of repression, such as the military and the police. The elimination of the landlord class through land reform also served to deradicalise the peasantry and create scope for intersectoral transfers from agriculture to industry, a key mechanism underpinning the catch-up developmental process.[63]

The provision of US aid was also crucial to catch-up industrialisation but varied considerably in line with geopolitical imperatives. Between 1949 and 1961, for example, the United States provided more aid to South Korea and Taiwan (US\$ 4.86 billion and US\$ 3.87 billion, respectively) than it did to the whole of the Latin American and the Caribbean region combined (US\$ 2.22 billion).[64] In addition, the United States provided its Northeast Asian allies with preferential access for their goods to the American market and permitted protectionism against US goods and services in their own markets. This encouraged allies to establish export industries whose primary consumers were in the United States.[65] Military procurement contracts also played an important role, with both South Korea and Taiwan benefitting from contracts provided during the Vietnam War. Yet colonial legacies also affected the degree to which countries in the US orbit were able to productively utilise aid. For example, despite also receiving large amounts of US aid, the South Vietnamese state's lack of absorptive capacity and failure to resolve the land question meant that much aid was wasted on middle-class consumption or on tackling the domestic insurgency. As noted, the French colonial state was primarily extractive, and Vietnam had seen little in the way of industrialisation prior to independence. The postcolonial economy's heavy dependence on the cultivation and export of rice meant that rural elites believed their economic well-being would be threatened if land reform encouraged peasants to consume rice that had formerly been exported.[66]

How then did Soviet hegemony impact on the possibilities for catch-up development in its own sphere? It should be noted first that the notion of

---

[63] Cristóbal Kay, 'Why East Asia Overtook Latin America: Agrarian Reform, Industrialisation and Development', *Third World Quarterly*, 23.6 (2002), pp. 1073–102.

[64] U.S. Overseas Loans and Grants, Obligations and Loan Authorizations https://explorer.usaid .gov/reports [accessed 18 May 2020].

[65] Sheldon W. Simon, 'Regional Security Structures in Asia: The Question of Relevance', in *East Asian Security in the Post-Cold War Era*, ed. by Sheldon W. Simon (Armonk, NY: M. E. Sharpe, 1993), p. 12.

[66] Nancy Wiegersma, *Vietnam: Peasant Land, Peasant Revolution: Patriarchy and Collectivity in the Rural Economy* (Basingstoke: Macmillan, 1988), pp. 175–77.

'superpower conflict' elides the fact that the Soviet Union was itself a key instance of a strong developmental regime seeking to pursue catch-up industrialisation. Soviet industrialisation took the form of a state-guided emulation of a more advanced type of social and productive relations, namely Taylorism and Fordist mass production.[67] Shortly after the revolution, the USSR sought to adopt Frederick Taylor's Principles of Scientific Management, leading to the establishment in 1918 of the League for the Scientific Organisation of Work as well as the Time League. Furthermore, the Central Institute of Labour was established for the purpose of conducting research on scientific management and promoting its adoption throughout Soviet factories. The combination of the import of advanced productive technologies and the mass mobilisation of human labour could be seen in the Stakhanovite movement of the 1930s, which aimed to surpass the labour productivity of the West and prepare the conditions for the transition from socialism to communism.[68] As Russian revolutionary and economist Yevgeni Preobrazhensky argued, the fact that the initial socialist revolution had occurred in a relatively backward and primarily agrarian economy and that revolution elsewhere was no longer expected meant that the Soviet state itself had to take the leading role in facilitating an absolute increase in total output and thus the capital stock.[69]

The manner whereby the Soviet Union sought to develop an economy comparable to that of the advanced industrialised countries bore strong similarities with that of Japan and Germany, both of which relied heavily upon state control to achieve goals of national development, although without the use of socialist ideology to mobilise the working classes.[70] It is for this reason that theorists of state capitalism drew attention to how the hierarchical social relations of production in the Soviet Union were at odds with socialist ideals. According to this view, the Soviet state had become 'capitalistic' in the sense of its functions of administration, supervision and control against the proletariat.[71] As Tony Cliff argued, transformed into a personification of capital, the state had to rid itself of all the remnants of workers' control, substitute conviction in the labour process by coercion and atomise the working class.[72]

---

[67] Kees van der Pijl, 'State Socialism and Passive Revolution', in *Gramsci, Historical Materialism and International Relations*, ed. by Stephen Gill (Cambridge: Cambridge University Press, 1993), p. 246.

[68] Arthur G. Bedeian and Carl R. Phillips, 'Scientific Management and Stakhanovism in the Soviet Union: A Historical Perspective', *International Journal of Social Economics*, 17.10 (1990), pp. 31–34.

[69] James R. Millar, 'A Note on Primitive Accumulation in Marx and Preobrazhensky', *Soviet Studies*, 30.3 (1978), pp. 387–91.

[70] Christopher Chase-Dunn, *Socialist States in the Capitalist World-System* (Beverly Hills: Sage, 1983), p. 37.

[71] C. L. R. James, *State Capitalism and World Revolution* (Oakland, CA: PM Press, 2013), p. 45.

[72] Tony Cliff, *State Capitalism in Russia* (London: Pluto Press, 1974), p. 153.

The same can be said for the postcolonial states that adopted Marxism–Leninism as their official ideology. In reality, there was no inherent contradiction between Marxism–Leninism and strategies of catch-up industrialisation. Much of the colonial world saw the emergence of modern professional and bourgeois classes who often collaborated with colonial rule but also came to resist it through participation in nationalist liberation movements. Where these forces were strong, they often took a communist form, albeit strongly inflected by nationalism.[73] Indeed, as Ronald Suny has argued, 'One of the supreme ironies of the twentieth-century experience must be that nationalism's principal opponent, namely Marxism, has been both empowered by its alliances with nationalism and responsible for creating the conditions for the development of nations in the Second and Third Worlds'.[74] Thus, nationalist movements, often marching under Marxist–Leninist colours, proceeded to construct state-capitalist social orders under which the task of capital accumulation was assumed by a state bureaucracy involved in the exploitation of peasants and workers alike.[75]

As with the United States, the Soviet Union's relations with its own periphery were characterised more by a geopolitical logic rather than simply by exploitative economic relations *per se*. Certainly, moments of exploitation were not absent. Following the Second World War, tensions between the Soviet Union and Yugoslavia, for example, reflected in part attempts by the former to exploit the latter's natural resources and confine Yugoslavia to the role of exporter of raw materials.[76] The Soviet Union also imposed relations of dependency on its own Central Asian republics. The latter thereby saw a significant degree of agricultural specialisation, with a monoculture economy, economic dualism and external control over prices exercised through state monopoly.[77] Furthermore, in the immediate post-war years, the extraction of Eastern European resources played a key role in the reconstruction of the Soviet Union. It has been calculated, for example, that between 1945 and 1953, the Soviet Union extracted from Eastern Europe resources approximately equal to US Marshall Plan aid to Western Europe.[78] This was achieved

---

[73] Desai, 'Nationalisms and Their Understandings', pp. 413–14.

[74] Ronald Grigor Suny, *The Revenge of the Past: Nationalism, Revolution, and the Collapse of the Soviet Union* (Stanford: Stanford University Press, 1993), p. 4.

[75] Alex Callinicos, 'Bourgeois Revolutions and Historical Materialism', *International Socialism*, 43 (1989), 113–71.

[76] David Ray, 'The Dependency Model of Latin American Underdevelopment: Three Basic Fallacies', *Journal of Interamerican Studies and World Affairs*, 15.1 (1973), p. 8.

[77] Gregory Gleason, 'The Political Economy of Dependency under Socialism: The Asian Republics in the USSR', *Studies in Comparative Communism*, 24.4 (1991), p. 352.

[78] Paul Marer, 'Soviet Economic Policy in Eastern Europe', in *Reorientation and Commercial Relations of the Economies of Eastern Europe*, ed. by Joint Economic Committee US Congress (Washington, DC: US Government Printing Office, 1974), p. 144.

through the stripping of factories and infrastructure as well as the relocation of Eastern European labour to the USSR, but also through the arbitrary setting of exchange rates and commodity prices.[79]

Nonetheless, the Stalinist era ultimately saw the creation in the USSR's Eastern European satellites of a model of catch-up industrialisation that adhered closely to the Soviet variant. This consisted of state ownership of the means of production, central planning, the collectivisation of agriculture, rapid industrialisation through repressed consumption and the transfer of forced savings into heavy industry.[80] However, this led to Eastern Europe's increasing reliance upon the Soviet Union for fuels, metals and other raw materials. In exchange for these imports, Eastern Europe exported manufactured goods, though these were typically of poor quality. As such, the emerging structure of trade between the Soviet Union and Eastern Europe actually reversed the 'typical' pattern of dependency whereby the 'dependent' economy exports raw materials and imports finished products.[81] In addition, following de-Stalinisation in the 1950s, popular demands for economic and political reform led Eastern European governments to encourage an increase in public consumption. The willingness of the Soviet Union to shoulder the costs of this increase was underpinned by Eastern Europe's importance to the former's geopolitical security. As a result, the Soviet practice of offering aid in the form of implicit trade subsidies became an established practice. Furthermore, the slowdown of economic growth in the early 1960s across much of Eastern Europe and the correspondingly reduced capacity of elites to respond to domestic demands alongside the related fear of social unrest increased the importance of these subsidies.[82] This led Moscow to complain that as an exporter of primary goods it was being exploited economically in return for political gains, and indeed, trade within the Council for Mutual Economic Assistance (Comecon) actually resulted in a loss for the Soviet Union.[83]

Despite early successes in heavy industrialisation, the inflexible central planning system, outdated management techniques, poor allocation of investment and the preference for capital goods and shortage of consumer products meant that the state socialist economies suffered from increasingly lacklustre

[79] Peter Liberman, *Does Conquest Pay? The Exploitation of Occupied Industrial Societies* (Princeton, NJ: Princeton University Press, 1996), pp. 121–28.
[80] Valerie Bunce, 'The Empire Strikes Back: The Evolution of the Eastern Bloc from a Soviet Asset to a Soviet Liability', *International Organization*, 39.1 (1985), p. 5.
[81] Cal Clark and Donna Bahry, 'Dependent Development: A Socialist Variant', *International Studies Quarterly*, 27.3 (1983), p. 280.
[82] Bunce, 'The Empire Strikes Back', pp. 12–13.
[83] William Zimmerman, 'Dependency Theory and the Soviet-East European Hierarchical Regional System: Initial Tests', *Slavic Review*, 37.4 (1978), p. 617.

economic growth.[84] However, proposals for economic reform and decentralisation throughout the bloc were often met with opposition from party officials and bureaucrats who believed that reform would threaten their power. Eastern European governments instead sought to revitalise their economies through large-scale purchase of sophisticated Western goods and technology. This was facilitated by the détente of the 1970s, which led to a substantial expansion of East-West commerce. Eastern Europe's trade with the West lessened the pressure on the Soviet economy, and through the introduction of Western technology, led to some improvement in terms of the quality and diversity of goods produced in the bloc.[85] However, economic conditions continued to deteriorate as Eastern European governments lacked goods that could be exported to Western markets to pay for their imports. Rapidly rising debt service ratios soon undermined trade with the West, and the rigid internal institutions of these countries prevented them from maximising the benefits from their newly imported technology.[86]

As can be seen, catch-up industrialisation in the post-war era has been highly uneven and profoundly shaped by the dynamics of both colonialism and the Cold War. Many postcolonial countries within the US sphere of influence had some initial developmental successes in the early post-war decades. However, with the exception of a few countries such as South Korea and Taiwan that were on the frontline of the Asian Cold War, these gains were largely stalled by the 1980s as a result of the Third World debt crisis and the rise of global neoliberalism. The Soviet Union also had a profound impact on countries within its sphere of influence, particularly in terms of shaping the institutions and ideology of centrally planned catch-up industrialisation. These interconnections between the Cold War and national development have a number of implications for the analysis of the North Korean experience. North Korea was indeed a country born of the Cold War and one that has continued to be profoundly shaped by it. How then can we understand the Soviet intervention in Korea in 1945 and its articulation with Korea's colonial legacies? What role did the division of the Korean peninsula and its locus on the frontline of the Cold War play in shaping the North's project of national development? How did subsequent geopolitical tensions such as the Sino–Soviet split shape political and economic developments within the country? To what extent did transformations in world capitalism from the 1970s impact upon North Korean development, and how does the country's experience compare and contrast with that of the Soviet Bloc and the postcolonial world? Finally, how did catch-up industrialisation in the context

<hr />

[84] Clark and Bahry, 'Dependent Development', p. 284.
[85] Bunce, 'The Empire Strikes Back', p. 15.
[86] Clark and Bahry, 'Dependent Development', pp. 284–86.

of the Cold War shape the subsequent decline of the North Korean economy and its collapse in the 1990s?

The Rise of China and Global Development

Despite the 'lost decade of development' in the 1980s, the Third World did achieve a respectable level of development during the post-war era, as measured in terms of share in world output. However, this was a highly uneven process and largely attributed to Asia, whereas Latin America barely maintained its share while Africa experienced a continuous decline.[87] By the 1990s, that Asian regional growth had spread to China, which served as a new engine of regional and global growth, thereby radically restructuring the context for global development. Indeed, following the onset of reform in 1978, China's GDP growth averaged nearly 10 per cent a year, the fastest sustained expansion of any major economy in history. It is important to note, however, that by the 1990s, shifts in technology and the organisation of global production would have important implications for the possibilities for continued catch-up industrialisation, both in China and elsewhere. Hitherto, it was possible to analyse the successes of earlier industrialisers in East Asia in terms 'flying geese'.[88] This pointed to a process whereby a regional leader passes its declining industries on to lesser developed countries as it moves up the ladder into more sophisticated industries, thereby driving a regional process of development. As the regional 'miracle' shifted from Northeast Asia towards Southeast Asia and China, however, such conceptualisations failed to capture the increasingly complex organisation of transnational production in the region. As Mitchell Bernard and John Ravenhill have argued, economic integration in East Asia came to be characterised by fragmented product markets, decentralised manufacturing activity and a shift in the organisational setting in which production takes place from the firm to the network.[89]

As such, the path chartered by the late development model based on second industrial revolution technologies has now become all but impassable. Aspiring late developers now confront a world in which production has become dispersed geographically, thereby creating new models of industrial, economic and spatial organisation. Even if developing countries attempt to reproduce particular elements of the late industrialisation experience, they are now more likely to engage with the ubiquitous global value chains that span

---

[87] Nayyar, *Catch Up*, pp. 173–77.

[88] Kaname Akamatsu, 'A Historical Pattern of Economic Growth in Developing Countries', *The Developing Economies*, 1.S1 (1962), pp. 3–25.

[89] Mitchell Bernard and John Ravenhill, 'Beyond Product Cycles and Flying Geese: Regionalization, Hierarchy, and the Industrialization of East Asia', *World Politics*, 47.2 (1995), p. 172.

both developed and developing countries across a variety of core industries.[90] This is a challenge that has also confronted China. Despite these shifts in global production, the Chinese government sought to build an SOE sector comprised of Japanese and South Korean-style national champions in vertically integrated pillar industries. However, the Chinese economy today is much larger and more diversified than the Japanese and South Korean economies were at the height of their state-led growth. Due to the decentralisation of political authority since 1978, the state is much less unified than its East Asian neighbours were. Furthermore, as signified by the terms of China's World Trade Organization (WTO) accession, the world's wealthiest countries no longer tolerate the sorts of protectionism they once did with regard to earlier East Asian industrialisers.[91] The challenges of new technologies and organisation of production, questions about state capacity and the more restrictive international environment all suggest that China has not replicated the earlier East Asian developmental states but has instead come to serve as a final production platform for the region's exports market. At the same time, earlier Asian industrialisers have narrowed their industrial bases to the production and trade of parts and components within this broader regional production network.[92]

Despite these developmental challenges, the sheer scope of China's rise and its newfound status as the world's second-largest economy means that it does nonetheless have important implications for development elsewhere. Much of the debate surrounds the question of the extent to which China may be serving to challenge contemporary global neoliberalism. For example, it has been argued that China has challenged neoliberalism by projecting its growing power through constitutionalised global governance, thereby consolidating its long-term strategy of 'consensual development'.[93] China is also seen as having played a leading role in providing both neighbouring and distant countries in the global south with alternatives to the trade, investment and assistance of the West and of western-dominated international financial

[90] D. Hugh Whittaker, Tianbiao Zhu, Timothy Sturgeon, Mon Han Tsai and Toshie Okita, 'Compressed Development', *Studies in Comparative International Development*, 45.4 (2010), p. 441.

[91] Edward S. Steinfeld, 'China's Shallow Integration: Networked Production and the New Challenges for Late Industrialization', *World Development*, 32.11 (2004), p. 1979.

[92] Martin Hart-Landsberg and Paul Burkett, 'China and the Dynamics of Transnational Capital Accumulation', in *Marxist Perspectives on South Korea in the Global Economy*, ed. by Martin Hart-Landsberg, Seongjin Jeong and Richard Westra (Aldershot: Ashgate, 2007), p. 13.

[93] Gerard Strange, 'China's Post-Listian Rise: Beyond Radical Globalisation Theory and the Political Economy of Neoliberal Hegemony', *New Political Economy*, 15.5 (2011), pp. 539–59.

institutions.[94] This suggests that the unipolar world dominated by the United States is beginning to recede, with the rise of China and other emerging powers leading to a more multipolar international order.

Others, however, have viewed China's emerging relations with the global South as representing a resurgent form of neocolonialism in South–South relations. China is, in this view, regarded as primarily concerned with securing resources for its rapidly growing economy. From this more critical perspective, observers have characterised China, along with other rising powers, as having promoted neoliberal practices that facilitate capital accumulation, resource extraction and the expansion of their markets.[95] As David Harvey has argued, China effectively dominates Asia as a regional hegemon and is in the process of reasserting its imperial traditions in the region and beyond.[96] Outside of Asia, this debate has perhaps been most prominent with regard to China's impact on African development. Attention has been paid, for example, to the way that China's bilateral aid has been used to obtain broader rights in African oil and mineral extraction.[97] Furthermore, it has been noted that the influx of cheap Chinese goods into African countries has decimated indigenous textile industries.[98]

The challenge posed by the rise of China is deemed as having both material and ideational dimensions. It has raised questions about the representativeness of international organisations such as the International Monetary Fund (IMF), The World Bank and the Asian Development Bank. Due to resistance to China's efforts to reform the governance of these financial institutions, particularly from the United States, Beijing has also moved to establish alternative institutions that reflect more fully its own ideas concerning development, such as the New Development Bank and the Asian Infrastructure Investment Bank. Perhaps most ambitiously, in 2013, China unveiled the One Belt One Road project, more recently known as the Belt and Road Initiative (BRI). The BRI's broad aims are to deepen connectivity and cooperation amongst Eurasian countries. On the one hand, the BRI reflects the fact that since the global financial crisis, China's foreign policy has become more assertive and willing to use the country's financial influence to pursue its economic interests

---

[94] Deborah Bräutigam, *The Dragon's Gift: The Real Story of China in Africa* (Oxford: Oxford University Press, 2009); May Tan-Mullins, Giles Mohan and Marcus Power, 'Redefining "Aid" in the China–Africa Context', *Development and Change*, 41.5 (2010), pp. 857–81.

[95] Patrick Bond, 'BRICS and the Tendency to Sub-Imperialism', Pambazuka News [Online], 2014, www.pambazuka.net/en/category/features/91303 [accessed 29 April 2020].

[96] David Harvey, *A Brief History of Neoliberalism* (Oxford: Oxford University Press, 2005), p. 140.

[97] Pádraig R. Carmody and Francis Y. Owusu, 'Competing Hegemons? Chinese versus American Geo-Economic Strategies in Africa', *Political Geography*, 26.5 (2007), pp. 505–8.

[98] Lawrence Edwards and Rhys Jenkins, 'The Impact of Chinese Import Penetration on the South African Manufacturing Sector', *The Journal of Development Studies,* 51.4 (2013), pp. 447–63.

abroad.[99] Yet, the BRI can also be seen to reflect domestic imperatives including the need to tackle security challenges in both China's immediate neighbours to the West and in its own Western regions. It also reflects ongoing problems of overcapacity within the Chinese economy and the shift to a model of political economy more heavily weighted towards domestic consumption. As such, the BRI seeks to create alternative investment opportunities, particularly for the SOEs that have been engaged in extensive infrastructural projects within the country for a decade or more.[100] The BRI's strong emphasis on infrastructure thereby serves to fulfil acute needs in Asia though at the same time has the potential to create new relations of dependency. Furthermore, as the case of US opposition to the Asian Infrastructure Investment Bank suggests, China's BRI project and its associated institutions are closely implicated in the intensifying geopolitical rivalries in the region since the early 2010s.

The rise of China thus has enormous implications for global development. How then has the rise of China impacted upon the recovery of the North Korean economy? To what extent can China's deepening economic relations with North Korea be seen as a form of neocolonialism or an emergent form of South–South cooperation? What is the relationship between deepening economic relations with China and ongoing processes of marketisation in North Korea? Furthermore, how should that process of marketisation be conceptualised? Questions also exist surrounding the ideational influence of the Chinese model. To what extent has North Korea sought to emulate features of China's reform and opening? Why have North Korean experiments with market reform been relatively limited compared to that of China? What is China's role in the international sanctions regime that has been established in recent years? Finally, China's own rise has been situated within broader shifts in global production that to a certain extent challenges the very notion of 'national development'. What implications does this have for how North Korea formulates its own developmental strategy and the degree to which such a strategy might be successful?

This historical overview of how the nexus between geopolitics and development has operated through the colonial era, the Cold War and the rise of China thus provides a framework for analysing the processes whereby aspiring developing countries seek to attain their place within the industrialised world through state-led modernisation. The rise of industrial capitalism and its outward expansion through imperialism has been crucial to the shaping of

---

[99] Hong Yu, 'Motivation behind China's "One Belt, One Road" Initiatives and Establishment of the Asian Infrastructure Investment Bank', *Journal of Contemporary China*, 26.105 (2017), p. 356.

[100] Peter Ferdinand, 'Westward Ho – the China Dream and "One Belt, One Road": Chinese Foreign Policy under Xi Jinping', *International Affairs*, 92.4 (2016), pp. 951–52.

the prospects for late development in the postcolonial world, both in terms of giving rise to the very notion of catch-up industrialisation itself but also in terms of producing developmental regimes that are either more or less conducive to the mobilisation of society towards late developmental goals. Its manifestly repressive and exploitative nature notwithstanding, imperialism had profound albeit spatially differentiated implications for the extent to which postcolonial societies were able to successfully pursue such goals. It strongly shaped the key institutions, patterns of state–society relations and ideological imperatives that would underpin developmental efforts. During the postcolonial era, the specificities of developing nations' positions vis-à-vis the strategic competition between the United States and the Soviet Union also profoundly shaped the vicissitudes of catch-up industrialisation. Developmental assistance was one key mechanism through which this occurred, though the absorptive capacity of the state, its capacity for mobilising human and material resources, along with prevailing ideas regarding the optimum degree of enmeshment with the international economy were also shaped by the legacies of colonialism and the (geo)politics of decolonisation. Following the end of the Cold War, the relative shift in the locus of the world economy towards China along with changes in the nature of global production also created a new set of constraints and opportunities for states seeking to realise late developmental goals.

It should be noted, however, that we do not argue that geopolitical contestation simply determines developmental outcomes at the national level. External pressures, whether military or economic, are ultimately mediated through domestic social and political struggles. Indeed, a shortcoming of both liberal economic and dependency approaches is their failure to take into the role of domestic politics in shaping how countries respond to the changing international environment. As Peter Gourevitch has argued, 'the international system, be it in an economic or politico-military form, is undetermining. The environment may exert strong pulls but short of actual occupation, some leeway in the response to that environment remains'.[101] Gourevitch suggests coalitional analysis as a means of examining how the need to gain support for a policy shapes outcomes and thus how domestic politics matters.[102] Although North Korea's authoritarian political culture and opaque policymaking would seemingly preclude such analysis, it is the case that the political contestation that existed until the mid-1950s was a formative moment in shaping North Korean economic policy. The transition towards the monolithic ideological system in the 1960s also had important path-dependent implications for how the regime would respond to geopolitical challenges going forward.

---

[101] Peter Gourevitch, 'The Second Image Reversed: The International Sources of Domestic Politics', *International Organization*, 32.4 (1978), p. 900.
[102] Ibid., pp. 904–5.

The analytical attention to domestic politics and agency thus also helps to dispel potential criticism that the development–geopolitics nexus somehow absolves the North Korean leadership for its manifest economic mismanagement. The mediation of 'the international' through domestic politics suggests instead that the relationship between geopolitics and development should be seen as situated in a dialectical relationship and as mutually constitutive, rather than unidirectional.

Outline of the Argument

In Chapter 1, we argue that the establishment of the North Korean developmental regime can be understood as an outcome of multiple historical lineages, including Korea's experience of colonial rule and national division alongside the adoption of the Soviet model of the party-state in the post-liberation era. The ascendancy of Kim Il Sung coincided with the emergence of a virulent form of postcolonial nationalism that strongly shaped the country's subsequent developmental trajectory. State-building involved a series of so-called 'bourgeois democratic reforms' including a rapid land-to-the-tiller reform that addressed longstanding peasant grievances and ensured a degree of initial popular support for the new regime. These reforms also served to integrate popular demands into a state-led project of modernisation and late development. Understood as a process of what Antonio Gramsci referred to as 'passive revolution', these top-down measures would have important implications as to the degree to which the state would be able to mobilise society around catch-up industrialisation goals.

In Chapter 2, we examine the recovery of the North Korean economy following the Korean War and the country's extraordinarily rapid process of industrialisation and social transformation in the 1950s. The nationalist impulse that underpinned the country's heavy industrialisation programme stemmed from the geopolitical insecurity faced by the North Korean state but was enabled by the massive external aid that the country received from elsewhere in the Socialist Bloc. As noted above, these pressures and opportunities were mediated through domestic political struggles. The factional disputes of the 1950s were in part related to competing views regarding the country's optimum position within the socialist international division of labour, and the contentious nature of these debates was a reflection of the factions' divergent origins. This chapter also draws attention to the decline of international aid to North Korea towards the latter part of the decade and the role that decline played in the increasing reliance on mass mobilisation campaigns.

In Chapter 3, we examine the shifting geopolitical environment of the 1960s and its immediate impact on the performance of the First Seven-Year Plan as well as the long-term developmental implications of the regime's militarised response. The emerging Sino–Soviet split raised important questions regarding the reliability of North Korea's socialist allies and further strengthened the impetus towards heavy industrialisation and the building of an independent defence industrial sector. Furthermore, geopolitical challenges were intensified by the establishment of a military regime in South Korea and the increased economic and security cooperation within the South Korea–Japan–United States triangle. These external pressures served to heighten the militaristic dimension to North Korea's development goals and its emphasis on the self-reliant model of catch-up industrialisation. However, the negative consequences of this deepening militarisation of the country became increasingly visible in the 1960s. This chapter also examines the ideological underpinnings of the North Korean developmental project in terms of the ascendance of *Juche* thought, and how the latter subsequently evolved as the ruling state ideology.

In Chapter 4, we examine North Korea's secular economic decline between the 1970s and the 1990s. As elsewhere in the Socialist Bloc, the early 1970s saw declining growth rates and superpower détente, leading to growing economic engagement with Western Europe and Japan. However, North Korea faced burgeoning foreign debts and defaulted on repayment. Locked out of world capital markets, North Korea made some attempts to attract foreign direct investment in the 1980s, though these attempts were limited and largely unsuccessful. North Korea instead became increasingly reliant on support from the Soviet Union and China. However, the collapse of the Soviet Union along with the pragmatic turn in China's foreign economic policy in the early 1990s immediately exposed this excessive reliance. North Korea's 'advantages of backwardness' had thus become a curse, leading to collapse and mass famine. The almost complete elimination of civil society under the monolithic ideological system along with the rise of Military First Politics meant, however, that the country's socio-political system was relatively impervious to the transformations taking place elsewhere in the socialist world.

In Chapter 5, we examine how North Korea's geopolitical environment charted in the earlier chapters shaped the emergence of a distinctive relationship between state and market in the post-crisis era. The crisis of the 1990s led the North Korean population to rely on markets for food and everyday goods, though marketisation thereafter expanded to the services, transport, construction, light industry and agricultural sectors. Though marketisation had its genesis in the paralysis of the public distribution system, we argue that it was greatly facilitated by supportive state policies. For example, the state took a leading role in furthering the process of marketisation through the establishment of permanent 'general markets' as well as the establishment of a mobile communications sector, both prerequisites for a marketised economy. Furthermore, while much of the existing literature has presented state and market as situated in a zero-sum relationship, we argue that the rise of the market at the same time profoundly transformed the state sector. The SOEs became increasingly involved in market activities, and the growing entrepreneurial class entered into partnerships with government organs and officials as a means of negotiating the continued lack of private property rights.

In Chapter 6, we examine the degree to which the Kim Jong Un government sought to reform its economy in line with China's economic reforms. We pay attention to the reform measures carried out under the slogan of 'Our-Style Economic Management Method', particularly in the realm of agricultural and industrial management and the development of special economic zones. As we argue, these economic reforms sought to establish a favourable environment for continued marketisation. While the political considerations of North Korean policymakers led to an explicit rejection of Chinese-style reform, there were nonetheless clear parallels between North Korean reforms and those of post-1978 China. Structural differences between their political economies and in their international environment meant, however, that the reforms had divergent impacts. North Korea had experienced a much greater degree of industrial decline than China by the outset of its reform process, a fact that also hindered the recovery of the agricultural sector, while its adverse environment provided a particularly inauspicious context for bold economic reforms, and in particular, for the attraction of foreign investment.

In Chapter 7, we examine the more direct material impact of the rise of China on the North Korean economy through the lens of the broader debate regarding China and global development. We argue that while in the early post-crisis period, North Korea's trade relations with China resembled the resource dependency found in many Global South countries, North Korea subsequently became increasingly integrated into cross-border regional production networks, with textile manufacturing being outsourced to North Korean producers as a result of ongoing economic shifts within China itself. Although this relationship can superficially be conceptualised as a form of dependency, North Korea's crisis preceded rather than followed its growing economic relations with China. In this sense, China can be said to have played a facilitative role in North Korea's economic recovery. However, along with the imposition of stringent international sanctions against North Korea, increased import dependency on China led to a policy emphasis on domestic import substitution, a strategy that saw some successes in the light industrial sector.

The final substantive chapter examines the impact of international sanctions on the North Korean political economy. On the one hand, sanctions served to exacerbate the tendency whereby North Korea became dependent on the booming Chinese economy. Until 2016, sanctions largely failed to exert any broad macroeconomic shock on North Korea, and indeed, they coincided with the country's post-crisis recovery. In addition, we examine the political impacts of sanctions against North Korea. While the regime resisted the demands made by the 'senders' of the sanctions, they did serve to strengthen the leadership's commitment to a self-reliant economy that was becoming increasingly anachronistic in an era of globalised capitalism. We also argue that since 2017, the impact of sanctions under the slogan of 'maximum pressure' was more visible, though was differentiated according to the economic sector, region and social strata. The conclusion of the book recaps the main arguments, but also examines the recent shift towards an emphasis on economic construction under Kim Jong Un. The conclusion also makes some projections concerning North Korea's future developmental trajectory.

1 State-Building and Late Development in North Korea

The state emblem of North Korea adopted in 1948 in most respects looks remarkably similar to those of other state socialist countries (see Figure 1.1). Bordered by rice plants on each side to signify the country's modernised agricultural sector, the top of the emblem depicts a shining red star above a snow-capped mountain range.[1] The centre of the emblem features a symbol of industrial modernity, the Supung Dam, a hydroelectric power station situated on the Yalu River on the border with China. The Supung Dam is a curious choice for the centrepiece of the emblem as its history seemingly runs counter to the ethos of self-reliance that came to dominate the country's developmental discourse. The dam was built by Japan during the colonial era for the purposes of supplying energy to the Manchukuo puppet state and to Japanese-owned industrial facilities in northern Korea. Construction began in October 1937 following the outbreak of the Sino–Japanese War, and the dam was completed in 1943, just two years prior to Japan's surrender. Capable of producing 700,000 kW, the dam was at the time the world's second largest after the Grand Coulee Dam in the US state of Washington.[2] Following Korea's liberation in 1945 and the establishment of a nascent state structure north of the 38th parallel, the dam was nationalised, and in May 1948, as two separate governments were established on the peninsula, the North Korean authorities halted the transmission of power to the South. However, in June 1952 at the height of the Korean War, the dam was heavily damaged as a result of a two-day bombing campaign by the US Air Force. With Soviet aid and technical assistance, the repair of the dam began in 1954 and it resumed operations in the autumn of 1958.

The story of the Supung Dam thus mirrors North Korea's early developmental history more broadly, including its colonial origins, the destruction of the Korean War, and the role of external aid in national reconstruction after the

---

[1] In 1993, the emblem was modified to make the mountain range visibly identifiable as Mt Paektu.

[2] Aaron Stephen Moore, 'The Yalu River Era of Developing Asia: Japanese Expertise, Colonial Power, and the Construction of Sup'ung Dam', *The Journal of Asian Studies*, 72.1 (2013), p. 116.

Figure 1.1: The state emblem of North Korea.
Source: Getty Images.

war's end. In this chapter, we focus on this early history by examining how the geopolitics of colonialism, decolonisation, and the emergent global Cold War acted to shape North Korean state-building and early efforts at catch-up industrialisation. Existing scholarship on the issue tends to be characterised by an unhelpful dichotomy between those that see the country as having undergone a process of 'Sovietisation' and those that emphasise the revolutionary nature of the post-1945 conjuncture. In contrast, we argue that early state-building in North Korea might more accurately be described as a process of passive revolution, understood as state-led modernisation from above alongside the forestalling of an independent popular will at odds with the overriding ethos of industrialism. As we argue, the specificities of Korea's colonial history meant that at the time of liberation in 1945, the Soviet occupying forces in concert with the emergent North Korean leadership were compelled to address pent-up social tensions in order to establish the basis for a hegemonic socialist state. Towards this aim, a series of so-called democratic reforms were enacted, including land reform, labour and gender equality laws, and the establishment of mass organisations. These reforms played a central role in the mobilisation of society towards developmental goals. We also examine how the colonial origins of North Korea's developmental regime shaped the leadership's heavy emphasis on autonomous national development. As we argue, the material and ideational legacies of colonial rule alongside the emergent geopolitical dynamics of the Cold War would have a profound impact on the country's post-liberation developmental policy.

1.1   Colonial Legacies and National Division

Korea's fate in the late nineteenth and early twentieth centuries was intimately related to the broader geopolitical shifts associated with the increased presence of the Western imperialist powers in East Asia, the decline of the Sinocentric world order, and the rise of modern Japan. Korea's strategic location meant that China, Japan, and increasingly Russia were engaged in an intense struggle for dominance over the peninsula in the late nineteenth century. Hitherto, Choson dynasty Korea had earned the title of the 'Hermit Kingdom' as a result of its policy of seclusion. Given its tributary status within the Sinocentric world order, the country had largely limited its diplomatic relations to China. As China's power in the region declined, however, Japan emerged as the region's dominant military and economic power. Attempts by China to maintain its traditional influence in Korea alongside the growing imperial ambitions of Japan as well as Russia culminated in the First Sino–Japanese War (1894–95) and the Russo–Japanese War (1904–5). Japan's decisive victory in these two wars effectively served to eliminate China and Russia as rivals for the domination of Korea. Japan was also successful in 1905 in obtaining consent from the Western powers for its suzerainty over the peninsula through the second Anglo–Japanese alliance and the secret Taft–Katsura Agreement, the latter of which amounted to US approval of Japan's colonisation of Korea in return for Japan's recognition of American control over the Philippines.[3] Japan subsequently proceeded to annex Korea by force, and in August 1910, the country was made a formal Japanese colony.

---

[3] Carter J. Eckert, Ki-baik Lee, Young Ick Lew, Michael Robinson and Edward W. Wagner, *Korea Old and New: A History* (Cambridge, MA: Harvard University Press, 1990), pp. 238–39.

Korea was thoroughly transformed by the colonial experience, and in ways that diverged from the typical pattern of European colonial rule. Japanese colonial rule was shaped by the country's own developmental experience and the fact that it too had taken place within a context of intense imperialist rivalry in Asia. Following the Meiji Restoration, Japan could not simply follow a gradual industrialisation process such as that which had occurred in England but had to proactively overcome its economic backwardness through a project of defensive modernisation from above. In doing so, the Japanese state was compelled to take the lead in the mobilisation of domestic resources and the search for natural resources and labour abroad. The fact that Korea, in contrast to the colonial territories of the European imperial powers, was geographically much closer to its imperial metropole provided the latter with the opportunity to exert greater authority and influence over its colony. As Bruce Cumings has argued, the lateness of the Japanese imperialism led to greater emphasis on the state as transformative agent. As such, the strong Meiji state was 'projected onto Korea in the form of a colonial apparatus with enormous strength, autonomy, and resulting extractive and manipulative powers'.[4]

Colonial administration in Korea was, therefore, highly developed. The number of Japanese administrators in proportion to colonial subjects was, for example, much higher in Korea than in Europe's colonies. Whereas the similarly sized French colony of Vietnam was ruled with around 3,000 French officials, Korea was ruled by 87,552 officials, of whom 52,270 were Japanese.[5] This political and administrative control was backed by garrison forces and a police force that in 1943 numbered at around 22,000. The colonial government was, as a result, highly authoritarian and wielded extensive executive, legislative and judicial powers.[6] All Korea's colonial governors were either generals or admirals who dealt with any resistance from the Korean population through overtly repressive methods.

What then was the impact of Japanese colonialism on Korea's economic development? In the literature on South Korean political economy, there has been a long-standing debate over the question of whether Japanese colonialism promoted or retarded Korea's modernisation and development. M. Shahid Alam has argued, for example, that 'When examined from the perspective of economic development, [South] Korea's servitude under Japanese colonialism proved fortunate for her in more ways than one ... The benefits that the

---

[4] Bruce Cumings, *The Origins of the Korean War, Vol. I: Liberation and the Emergence of Separate Regimes 1945–1947* (Princeton, NJ: Princeton University Press, 1981), p. 5.

[5] Eckert et al., *Korea Old and New*, p. 257.

[6] Han-Kyo Kim, 'The Japanese Colonial Administration in Korea: An Overview', in *Korea Under Japanese Colonial Rule: Studies of the Policy and Techniques of Japanese Colonialism*, ed. by Andrew C. Nahm (Kalamazoo, MI: The Center for Korean Studies, Western Michigan University, 1973), p. 43.

Koreans derived from it in the long run were quite considerable'.[7] On the other hand, in official North Korean historiography as well as in mainstream South Korean historiography, notions of colonial modernisation have largely been rejected due to their implicit or at times explicit celebration of Japanese colonial rule. However, such debates have tended to dwell on modernisation at the expense of its coloniality.[8] While there is little doubt that Korea experienced a degree of economic growth during the colonial era, this occurred within the context of an economically dependent relationship with Japan aimed at satisfying the latter's material demands rather than benefiting the Korean population in any substantive sense. In the early colonial era, Korea largely served as a supplier of staple food to the industrialising Japanese economy and as a market for the latter's manufactured goods.[9]

Indeed, the colonial authorities initially concentrated on increasing grain production through facilitating growth in agricultural inputs and intensification of cultivation. This led to a 2 per cent annual increase in rice production per unit of land in the years between 1910 and 1940.[10] However, the coloniality of this modernisation effort was apparent in the simultaneous dramatic increase in rice exports. According to one estimate, rice exports rose from 16 per cent of production in 1910–15 to 44 per cent in 1930–36, with rice imports from Korea making up over half of all Japanese rice imports between 1925 and 1938.[11] As a result, per capita consumption of rice in Korea declined by 36.8 per cent between 1915 and 1933. Although there was a slight increase in the consumption of millet, Koreans' overall consumption of cereals and beans declined by 17.9 per cent during that era.[12]

Moreover, the colonial authorities along with Japan's Oriental Development Company took over large tracts of Korean farmland and sold it under terms that were favourable to land-hungry Japanese settlers and private land companies. As a result, the number of Japanese landowners in Korea saw a sharp increase. This colonial land grab led many small-scale Korean farmers to lose their land and become either full or semi-tenants, with the number of full tenants rising from 29 per cent of total farm households in 1913–17 to 56 per

---

[7] M. Shahid Alam, *Governments and Markets in Economic Development Strategies: Lessons from Korea, Taiwan, and Japan* (New York: Praeger Publishers, 1989), p. 248.

[8] Suzy Kim, *Everyday Life in the North Korean Revolution, 1945–1950* (Ithaca, NY: Cornell University Press, 2013), pp. 8–9.

[9] Carter J. Eckert, 'The South Korean Bourgeoisie: A Class in Search of Hegemony', *Journal of Korean Studies*, 7 (1990), p. 118.

[10] Atul Kohli, 'Where Do High Growth Political Economies Come From? The Japanese Lineage of Korea's 'Developmental State'', *World Development*, 22.9 (1994), p. 1278.

[11] Paul W. Kuznets, *Economic Growth and Structure in the Republic of Korea* (New Haven, CT: Yale University Press, 1977), p. 14.

[12] Andrew J. Grajdanzev, *Modern Korea* (New York: The John Day Company, 1944), pp. 118–19.

cent in 1938.[13] There was, however, a great deal of continuity in the substance of traditional land ownership patterns. While the traditional landholding system was put on a rational–legal basis with new contract laws, many Korean landlords retained their landholdings and became key agents in the disciplining of peasants and in extracting their rice for export. New contractual property rights served to strengthen the hold of these landlords and heighten the exploitation of the peasantry.[14] Land rent was usually collected in kind as a proportion of annual output, with rent averaging around half the crop, although in some cases collections reached 90 per cent.[15] Many peasants were consequently impoverished and either became agricultural labourers or migrated to Manchuria, the Russian Far East or to Japan to escape starvation at home. According to the available data, between 1936 and 1940, around 565,229 Koreans emigrated to Manchuria and 456,483 to Japan.[16]

During the early colonial era, the authorities also sought to discourage industrial development through the passing of the Company Law, which stipulated that any newly established corporation in Korea was required to obtain a charter from the colonial authorities. This thereby discouraged the establishment of any large corporations in Korea that might compete with Japan's own export industries.[17] However, the Great Depression brought fundamental changes to colonial rule as Japan experienced a severe recession and launched its war of aggression in northern China. Japan reoriented its economic priorities in colonial Korea from agricultural to industrial development. Indeed, Japan was one of the few imperial powers to establish heavy industries in its colonies.[18] As we shall see, this had important implications for post-colonial industrialisation in both North and South Korea. Nearly all the important industrial enterprises in colonial Korea were established during this period. Investment in industry grew from 2.8 billion yen in 1940 to 3.4 billion yen in 1944.[19] In order to fulfil the Japanese empire's military needs, there was

---

[13] Alam, *Governments and Markets*, p. 249.

[14] Bruce Cumings, *Korea's Place in the Sun: A Modern History* (New York: W. W. Norton and Company, 1997), p. 151.

[15] Kuznets, *Economic Growth and Structure*, p. 17.

[16] Tai-Hwan Kwon, 'International Migration of Koreans and the Korean Community in China', *Korea Journal of Population and Development*, 26.1 (1997), pp. 5–6.

[17] Chul Won Kang, 'An Analysis of Japanese Policy and Economic Change in Korea', in *Korea Under Japanese Colonial Rule: Studies of the Policy and Techniques of Japanese Colonialism*, ed. by Andrew C. Nahm (Kalamazoo, MI: The Center for Korean Studies, Western Michigan University, 1973), p. 79.

[18] Bruce Cumings, 'The Legacy of Japanese Colonialism in Korea', in *The Japanese Colonial Empire, 1895–1945*, ed. by Ramon H. Myers and Mark R. Peattie (Princeton, NJ: Princeton University Press, 1984), p. 482.

[19] Jeon Hyun Soo, 'The Nationalisation of Major Industry and the Planning of the People's Economy [Sanŏbŭi kugyuhwawa inmin'gyŏngjeŭi kyehoekhwa: Kongŏbŭl chungsimŭro]', *Review of North Korean Studies*, 2.1 (1999), p. 67.

a rapid increase in the production of strategic materials such as steel, metals and chemicals, as well as in mining. It was at this juncture that large-scale hydroelectric power plants such as the Supung Dam were built to supply these energy-intensive industries. This encouraged further Japanese investments in heavy industry, particularly in the north of the country, such as the mass chemicals complex established in Hungnam on the north-eastern coast of Korea.[20] This spatially uneven pattern of industrialisation would have an important impact on the subsequent trajectories of the two Koreas following liberation.

Colonial Korea thus saw rapid economic growth, with the annual average rate of growth in the gross output of goods at 5.4 per cent.[21] This was accompanied by significant structural shifts: the share of agriculture in net commodity product dropped from 84.6 per cent in 1910–12 to 49.6 per cent in 1939–41, while the share of the manufacturing sector increased from 6.7 per cent to 29 per cent during the same period.[22] Within the manufacturing sector, the heavy and chemical industries saw particularly rapid growth, from 16.5 per cent of total manufacturing value in 1930 to 49.5 per cent in 1943.[23] The colonial authorities also invested in physical infrastructure, including an extensive rail network. As Jun Uchida has argued, just as railways were a central element of Japan's national development, the colonisation of Korea brought similar developments to the extent that by 1945 Korea possessed the most developed railway system in Asia outside of Japan.[24]

While the colonial era arguably did leave behind a basic foundation for future economic development in North Korea, the qualitative pattern of growth nonetheless displayed many of the features of colonial exploitation found elsewhere. The benefits of increased production in Korea went mainly to Japan to support the latter's imperial expansion into Asia. The output of relatively developed industrial sectors such as mining, iron and chemicals was limited to crude materials and semi-finished industrial goods that were shipped to Japan for final processing. Furthermore, the machine-tools industry, essential for balanced industrial growth, was left underdeveloped in Korea. In Japan, machine tools accounted for 22.5 per cent of all industrial production in

---

[20] Yang Moon-Soo, *The Structure of the North Korean Economy: The Mechanism of North Korean Development and Slowdown [Pukhan'gyŏngjeŭi kujo: Kyŏngjegaebalgwa ch'imch'aeŭi mek'anijŭm]* (Seoul: Seoul National University Press, 2001), pp. 54–55.

[21] Betty L. King, 'Japanese Colonialism and Korean Economic Development, 1910–1945', *Asian Studies – Journal of Critical Perspectives on Asia*, 13.3 (1975), p. 10.

[22] Kuznets, *Economic Growth and Structure*, p. 19.

[23] Yang Moon-Soo, *Structure of the North Korean Economy*, p. 57.

[24] Jun Uchida, '"A Scramble for Freight": The Politics of Collaboration along and across the Railway Tracks of Korea under Japanese Rule', *Comparative Studies in Society and History*, 51.1 (2009), p. 119.

1940, whereas in colonial Korea, it accounted for just 3.6 per cent.[25] Despite growth in the light industrial sector, Korea continued to import finished consumer goods from Japan and experienced relative stagnation in terms of technology and product quality. Furthermore, as with European imperialism, Korea saw little in the way of the formation of an indigenous professional class. Nearly all managers, engineers and technicians were Japanese, whereas Koreans were at best employed as support staff. A degree of industrial growth notwithstanding, Korea effectively remained an economic satellite within a Japan-centred regional imperial economy. One consequence of this was that the sudden economic break with Japan in August 1945 immediately had a damaging impact. In the northern half of the country, around 1,000 enterprises were forced to halt operations following the Japanese surrender. In addition, 53 factories and 242 mines were either partially or completely destroyed as a result of deliberate sabotage by the retreating Japanese, with the rail network also paralysed.[26]

This disruption was exacerbated by the territorial division of the peninsula by the United States and the Soviet Union, which split an integrated albeit uneven national economy in half. As noted, the heavy industries and large-scale mining operations were concentrated in northern Korea. According to the available data, about 80 per cent of heavy industries and 90 per cent of electric power generation facilities were concentrated in the north of the country. At the time of national division, southern Korea accounted for about 45 per cent of Korean land and 65 per cent of the population. It also possessed 69 per cent of light industry, 82 per cent of commerce and 63 per cent of agricultural production.[27] By contrast, southern Korea's larger labour force, its tradition-ally more developed commerce, and its better quality agricultural land and climatic conditions led the Japanese to concentrate on the development of agriculture, light industry and the service sector there. Prior to liberation, northern Korea had therefore relied on the south for staple food and consumer goods, while the south had depended on the north for chemical fertiliser, mineral resources and electric power. Division meant therefore that post-liberation North Korea faced an immediate food crisis as well as shortage of basic consumer goods, while the South suffered from an acute shortage of raw materials and electric power, leading to a sharp slowdown in manufacturing.

When discussing the legacies of colonialism, however, just as important in terms of Korea's post-1945 experience was how the bitter experience of thirty-five years of colonial rule shaped the emergence of modern Korean nationalism. As Carter Eckert argues, Koreans had long been aware of their

[25] Yang Moon-Soo, *Structure of the North Korean Economy*, p. 56.
[26] Jeon Hyun Soo, 'Nationalisation of Major Industry', pp. 69–70.
[27] Jon Halliday, 'The North Korean Enigma', *New Left Review*, 127 (1981), p. 24.

cultural and linguistic differences from people around them. Yet, while there may have been a degree of loyalty towards the Korean monarch in the premodern era, there would have been little in the way of loyalty towards the abstract concept of 'Korea' as a nation state.[28] The nineteenth century, however, saw the rise of modern nationalism amidst growing confrontation with foreign powers. During the colonial era, Korean nationalism saw further development as a result of the spread of literacy through education and the fact that Koreans were brought together as never before through the building of railways, the intensification of economic contacts and internal migration to the new administrative centres. These trends were intensified by the harsh and arbitrary rule of the military and police, racial discrimination and the disruption of traditional modes of life in villages and urban neighbourhoods.[29]

Korean nationalism therefore also took the form of an anti-imperialist ideology that emphasised confronting the foreign challenge through the modernisation of state and society. Following the March 1st uprising in 1919 against colonial rule, the colonial authorities made certain concessions through the adoption of a conciliatory policy aimed at cultural assimilation, the goal of bolstering pro-Japanese collaborators and the weakening of Korean national consciousness. By the 1930s, however, the Sino–Japanese and Pacific Wars had led to increased repression in Korea. Nationalist sentiments were intensified as a result of Japan's strengthened assimilation policies such as *naisen ittai* (Japanese and Koreans as one body) and through forcing Koreans to take Japanese names, engage in Shinto worship and speak the Japanese language. The war also led the colonial government to introduce a series of coercive labour mobilisation programmes. As such, the harsh nature of colonial rule combined with Korea's pre-existing sense of nationhood led many Koreans to take part in anti-Japanese activities both at home and abroad.

As can be seen, the legacies of colonialism in Korea are complex and multifaceted. In material terms, colonialism bequeathed an industrial structure that was unbalanced and dependent but nonetheless was arguably developed to a degree unparalleled within the colonial world. However, colonialism also led to pent-up social tensions to the extent that Korea found itself in 1945 at a revolutionary juncture. In order to establish viable developmental regimes, post-colonial leaderships in both the North and South were compelled to address these tensions through a combination of coercive and consensual measures. Furthermore, as elsewhere in the post-colonial world, political leaders in both Koreas took it for granted that true

---

[28] Carter J. Eckert, *Offspring of Empire: The Koch'ang Kims and the Colonial Origins of Korean Capitalism, 1876–1945* (Seattle: University of Washington Press, 1991), p. 226.
[29] Michael Robinson, *Korea's Twentieth-Century Odyssey: A Short History* (Honolulu: Hawaii University Press, 2007), p. 46.

independence vis-à-vis foreign powers could only be achieved through emulating the advanced industrialised countries through a process of state-led catch-up industrialisation.

1.2   Post-1945 Geopolitics and State-Building in the North

The partition of Korea in 1945 was a direct outcome of the emergent geopolitical conflict between the superpowers, with very little input from Koreans themselves. Internationally, as a colonial appendage of Japan, Korea was largely a forgotten country prior to the outbreak of the Pacific War in 1941. At the Cairo Conference in November 1943, the legality of Korea's colonial status was discussed by the leaders of the United States, Britain and China for the first time since the country's annexation by Japan in 1910. The resulting Cairo Declaration stated that 'The aforesaid three great powers, mindful of the enslavement of the people of Korea, are determined that in due course Korea shall become free and independent'.[30] The Soviet Union declared war on Japan on 9 August 1945 and the Soviet 25th Army crossed the Tumen River into northern Korea. However, concrete plans for the occupation of the Korean peninsula were not finalised until after Japan's unconditional surrender on 15 August. The Supreme Commander of the Allied Powers in the Pacific, General Douglas MacArthur, issued General Order No. 1.[31] Aimed at managing the Japanese surrender, the General Order dictated that the surrender of Japanese forces north of the 38th parallel would be overseen by the Soviet Union while the surrender of those south of the parallel would be overseen by the United States.[32] The Soviet military adhered to the General Order and did not advance south of the 38th parallel. These actions were matched by those of the US military following their arrival at Incheon on 8 September.

As is well known, this arrangement meant that the Japanese surrender led not to Korea's 'liberation' in any substantive sense but ultimately to the peninsula's permanent division into two mutually antagonistic states. Both the United States and the Soviet Union were confronted with nascent political structures that had been set up by Koreans in the immediate aftermath of the surrender. The self-governing Korean authority, the Committee for the Preparation of Korean Independence (*Chosŏn kŏn'gukchunbiwiwŏnhoe*,

---

[30] 'The Cairo Declaration', 26 November 1943, History and Public Policy Program Digital Archive, Foreign Relations of the United States, Diplomatic Papers, The Conferences at Cairo and Tehran, 1943 (Washington, DC: United States Government Printing Office, 1961), 448–49, https://digitalarchive.wilsoncenter.org/document/122101 [accessed 19 May 2020].

[31] 'General Order No. 1 – Office of the Supreme Commander for the Allied Powers', 2 September 1945, www.mofa.go.jp/mofaj/files/000097066.pdf [accessed 19 May 2020].

[32] Myung-Ki Kim, *The Korean War and International Law* (Claremont, CA: Paragon House, 1991), pp. 16–19.

CPKI) had been established in Seoul on 16 August, and was initially a coalition of leftist, rightist and centrist figures who had been active in the independence movement. Despite growing internal tensions and the questioning of its legitimacy by other political groups, the CPKI's goal of preparing for a 'fully independent state' through the formation of a democratic government received broad popular support, and by the end of August, 145 branches had been established across the peninsula.[33] While many organisations were established at the national and grassroots levels, there was no political force organised solely on either a northern or southern basis in the immediate post-liberation era. The majority of Koreans were not cognisant of the division and regarded the occupation by US and Soviet troops as a temporary measure. It was broadly assumed that an independent Korea would be ruled by a central government from the traditional political capital of Seoul.[34]

However, the United States and the Soviet Union worked upon the assumption that Koreans did not have the capacity to establish their own independent government, and perhaps more importantly, that self-government would not be conducive to Washington and Moscow's respective geopolitical interests. As a result, United States and Soviet troops landed in Korea not only as liberators but as occupying forces. In the south, the United States established a military government in September 1945 known as the United States Army Military Government in Korea. This military government viewed the CPKI as a leftist organisation and immediately moved to suppress it.[35] However, while it is true that many within the CPKI and local People's Committees adhered to socialism, this did not necessarily signify a deeply held worldview, support for the Soviet Union or a commitment to Marxist internationalism. Rather it represented commitment to the elimination of Japanese influence in Korea, to mass politics, and more broadly, to the elimination of feudal legacies and to levelling social reforms.[36] However, deeply concerned about the spread of communist influence in the region, the presence of self-avowed communists was enough to alarm the American authorities. As such, the latter instead sponsored the rightist political forces led by wealthy landlords and businessmen, many of whom had collaborated with the Japanese. Conservative political leader Rhee Syngman, a returnee from the United States, obtained significant support from the Americans and played a key role in the repression of leftist organisations

---

[33] Kim Hak-joon, *Korean Partition and the Soviet Military Rule of North Korea under International Politics among Major Powers (1863–January 1946)* [*Kangdaeguk kwŏllyŏgjŏngch'i araesŏŭi hanbando punhalgwa Soryŏnŭi Pukhan'gunjŏnggaesi (1863 nyŏn 1946 nyŏn 1 wŏl)*] (Seoul: Seoul National University Press, 2008), p. 684.
[34] Ibid., p. 689.
[35] Leon Gordenker, *The United Nations and the Peaceful Unification of Korea: The Politics of Field Operations, 1947–1950* (The Hague: Martinus Nijhoff, 1959), p. 5.
[36] Cumings, *Origins of the Korean War: Volume I*, p. 86.

and in establishing an alternative strongly anti-communist government south of the 38th parallel.[37]

As with the United States in the south, the Soviet Union sought to establish a regime in the north that was favourable to its own interests. The Soviet 25th Army established its headquarters in Pyongyang on 26 August 1945, while stationing its regional command offices in major cities and counties across the north. In contrast to the south, however, the Soviet Union did not directly establish a military government but instead allowed for local administration by the grassroots People's Committee organisations at the city, county and provincial levels. However, the Soviet forces did intervene to enable leftist groups and communists to take the lead in these organisations.[38] Furthermore, on 8 February 1946, the Soviet military set up a bureau in charge of civil affairs, known as the North Korean Provisional People's Committee (*Pukchosŏn limshiinminwiwŏnhoe*, NKPPC). The NKPPC formed the central governing organ of the emergent North Korean state, with guerrilla fighter Kim Il Sung appointed as chairman. While the NKPPC was led by Koreans, however, it had to go through a process of consultation with the Soviet-occupying authorities, which in turn received its directives from Moscow.[39] As such, the Soviet Union maintained its influence in North Korea after the formation of the NKPPC. Indeed, Soviet troops stayed in the country until 1948 and several hundred Soviet advisors stayed for longer to train North Korean cadres. The Soviet Union also exerted a strong cultural influence during this time and held a monopoly on the country's external trade. In this sense, it could be said that during the late 1940s at least, the Soviet Union's influence in the country paralleled the influence it had in its Eastern European satellites during the same period.[40] The authority of rising Korean political figures such as Kim Il Sung was therefore limited at this time and depended on the extent to which they aligned themselves with Soviet interests.

It should be noted, however, that while Kim Il Sung was selected by the Soviet Union to lead the embryonic North Korean state, his dominance was by no means absolute from the outset. The communist camp was made up of several communist factions that both competed and cooperated with each other. Kim Il Sung himself had emerged in the 1930s as the leader of a band

[37] Ralph N. Clough, *Embattled Korea: The Rivalry for International Support* (Boulder, CO: Westview Press, 1987), pp. 9–10.

[38] Kim Gwang-Oon, *The History of North Korean Politics I: The Establishment of Party, State and Military [Pukhan chŏngch'isa yŏn'gu 1: Kŏndang, kŏn'guk, kŏn'gunŭi yŏgsa]* (Seoul: Sunin, 2003), pp. 69–80.

[39] Paik Haksoon, *The History of Power in North Korea: Ideas, Identities, and Structures [Pukhan kwŏllyŏgŭi yŏgsa: Sasang, chŏngch'esŏng, kujo]* (Seoul: Hanul Books, 2010), pp. 91–92.

[40] Erik van Ree, *Socialism in One Zone: Stalin's Policy in Korea, 1945–1947* (Oxford: Berg, 1989), p. 174.

of guerrillas in southern Manchuria engaged in armed struggle against the Japanese. In 1940, he was forced to retreat to a Soviet military camp near Khabarovsk, where he became a Captain in the Soviet Red Army.[41] Kim's guerrilla experience underpinned the legitimacy of his rule in post-liberation North Korea, yet at the same time, he was also regarded by the Soviet Union as a loyal ally who would faithfully follow Moscow's policy towards the Korean peninsula and accept the model and experience of the Soviet party state.[42] At the age of just thirty-three, Kim was introduced to the citizens of Pyongyang at a rally on 14 October 1945, although it was not until 17 December that Kim became the head of the communist party. Kim's power was initially shared with three other major communist factions: 1) the domestic faction, consisting of communists who had operated inside Korea during the colonial era, such as Pak Hon Yong; 2) the China-aligned Yan'an faction consisting of Koreans who had served in the Chinese Red Army, such as Mu Chong, Kim Tu Bong and Choi Chang Ik; 3) the Soviet–Korean faction consisting of ethnic Koreans from the Soviet Union, such as Ho Ka-i and Pak Chang Ok. Although competition between Kim's Manchurian guerrillas and the other communist factions continued well into the 1950s, they mostly cooperated in the establishment of the party-state during the late 1940s.

In the immediate post-liberation era, there also existed a non-communist nationalist camp. This included figures such as Christian nationalist Cho Man Sik, who headed the South Pyongan Province Committee for the Preparation for Korean Independence, and on 3 November 1945, established the Democratic Party based on landed, industrial and commercial interests. In the early stages of the occupation, the Soviet authorities sought to cooperate with the non-communist camp centred around Cho to facilitate what it termed a 'bourgeois democratic revolution.' This approach was based upon the Menshevik two-stage theory of revolution, whereby feudal and colonial legacies would be eliminated, and a subsequent socialist revolution would be established through a strategy of class collaboration.[43] As a contemporary report to Moscow, from Soviet officers on the ground, detailed: the aim was to establish 'a united bloc of democracy based on the Communist Party, the Democratic Party, the Democratic Union of Youth, the women's democratic organization, trade unions, and other anti-Japanese democratic organizations and place headed by Kim Il Sung, a national hero of Korea best-known and

---

[41] For details on Kim Il Sung's anti-Japanese strike force activities in the Manchurian region and his activities in the Far East Army 88th Brigade, see the pioneering work of Dae-Sook Suh *Kim Il Sung: The North Korean Leader* (New York: Columbia University Press, 1988).

[42] Paik Haksoon, *History of Power in North Korea*, pp. 40–41.

[43] Alzo David-West, 'Stalinism, Post-Stalinism, and Neo-Capitalism: To Be or Not to Be?', *North Korean Review*, 4.2 (2008), p. 63.

loved by all the people'.[44] However, the proposal of a four-power trusteeship at the Moscow Conference of December 1945 led to the elimination of non-communist nationalists such as Cho from the political scene. Cho strongly opposed the trusteeship plan, and as a result, refused to work with the Soviet authorities. This refusal ultimately led to Cho's house arrest in 1946 and the replacement of the Democratic Party leadership with communists.[45]

In addition to eliminating the non-communist camp from the political scene, the Soviet Union placed a key emphasis on the development of the North Korean communist party. The historically fractious nature of the Korean communist movement and the role of Japanese repression meant that by the time of liberation in 1945, there had been no functioning communist party on the peninsula. On 11 September, the Korean Communist Party was established by communist activist Pak Hon Yong of the domestic faction. However, the fact that the party was established not in the Soviet-occupied north but in Seoul meant that it was largely outside of the control of the Soviet authorities. As such, the latter sought to establish a separate communist party organisation in the North friendly to its interests. On 12 October 1945, Soviet forces granted permission for the formation of political parties and social organisations, and the following day, a group of around seventy communists established the Northern Branch of the Korean Communist Party (*Chosŏn'gongsandang Pukchosŏnbunguk*).[46] This party was still weak, however, as its membership numbered only around 4,500 in December 1945.[47] Following the formation of the NKPPC as the governing institution, there were further moves to build an independent party structure in the North. In April 1946, the name of the party was changed to the North Korean Communist Party (NKCP, *Pukchosŏn Gongsandang*), and in late August 1946, there was a further transformation as the NKCP merged with the Yan'an faction's Choson New People's Party to form a united front party, the North Korean Workers' Party (*Pukchosŏn Rodongdang*). This paralleled the unification in November that year of three leftist parties in the South to create the South Korean Workers' Party, although the latter had already been in decline as Pak Hon Yong and other key activists fled to the North as a result of the repression of the US military government. Following the formal establishment of two separate states on the Korean peninsula, the North Korean Workers' Party absorbed its

[44] 'Soviet Report on Communists in Korea, 1945', 1945, History and Public Policy Program Digital Archive, AGShVS RF. F. 172. OP 614631. D. 23 pp. 21–26. Translated by Gary Goldberg. http://digitalarchive.wilsoncenter.org/document/114890 [accessed 19 May 2020].
[45] Robert A. Scalapino and Chong-Sik Lee, *Communism in Korea: Part 1. The Movement* (Berkeley, CA: University of California Press, 1972), pp. 337–40.
[46] Kim Gwang-Oon, *History of North Korean Politics*, pp. 143–56.
[47] Son Jon Hu, *The History of Land Reform in North Korea [Urinara t'ojigaehyŏksa]* (Pyongyang: Science and Encyclopedia Publishing Company, 1983), p. 257.

southern counterpart in June 1949 to create the Korean Workers' Party (KWP, *Chosŏn Rodongdang*).

As with the United States in the South, therefore, the Soviet Union was similarly involved in strengthening political groups favourable to its own interests, thereby playing a key role in making permanent what was initially supposed to be a temporary division line along the 38th parallel. It is not surprising then that efforts by Washington and Moscow to find a resolution to the so-called Korean problem were unsuccessful. As noted, at the Moscow Conference of December 1945, the Foreign Ministers of the United States, Britain and the Soviet Union agreed to establish a Joint Soviet–American Commission to assist in the creation of a provisional Korean democratic government and a four-power trusteeship over the country within five years. However, subsequent negotiations ended in an impasse due to widely divergent views as to how to resolve the Korean issue. On 14 November 1947, the General Assembly adopted a resolution proposed by the United States to hold national elections throughout the peninsula to establish a Korean government. These elections would be held under the auspices of the United Nations Temporary Commission on Korea (UNTCOK), which consisted of representatives from nine UN-member nations.[48]

Upon its arrival in Seoul on 8 January 1948, UNTCOK was blocked from entering the North by the Soviet and North Korean authorities. After failing to gain access to the North, UNTCOK consulted with the Interim Committee of the General Assembly over whether to implement the General Assembly resolution in South Korea alone. The United States was supportive of this proposal while other members of UNTCOK expressed concerns that an election limited to the South would create two rival governments on the peninsula, thus making the division permanent.[49] The US position was finally adopted by the Interim Committee in February 1948, with general elections held in the South on 10 May 1948. The National Assembly in Seoul adopted a constitution and elected Rhee Syngman as President of the Republic of Korea, with the South Korean government itself inaugurated on 15 August 1948. Three weeks later on the 9th of September, the government of the Democratic People's Republic of Korea (DPRK) was formally established. Korea had thus been formally divided into two states, with both claiming to be the only legitimate state on the peninsula.

National division not only led to the short-term economic disruption outlined above but it also fundamentally shaped the future developmental

---

[48] Rosalyn Higgins, *United Nations Peacekeeping 1946–1967: Documents and Commentary. Vol. 2. Asia* (Oxford: Oxford University Press, 1970), p. 155.

[49] Leland M. Goodrich, *Korea: A Study of US Policy in the United Nations* (New York: Council on Foreign Relations, 1956), pp. 45–46.

trajectories of both Koreas. It created two separate entities that had no prece-
dent in Korean history since the establishment of the Koryo dynasty in the
tenth century. As Cumings has argued, 'There was no internal pretext for
dividing Korea ... the thirty-eighth parallel was a line never noticed by the
people of, say, Kaesŏng, the Koryŏ capital, which the parallel cut in half. And
then it became the only line that mattered to Koreans, a boundary to be
removed by any means necessary'.[50] In the North, the fact of national division
profoundly shaped the leadership's strategy of heavy industrialisation and
decisions regarding the spatial location of industry and infrastructure. As we
shall see in later chapters, inter-Korean rivalry and the broader geopolitical
competition in Northeast Asia also meant that military spending came to
account for an increasing share of North Korea's budget, which in turn
contributed towards the slowdown of the economy from the 1960s. These
legacies also influenced the caution with which the country's leadership
approached liberalising economic reforms and external opening, thereby constituting a key point of contrast with more successful cases of reformed
socialism such as China and Vietnam.

1.3   North Korea's Passive Revolution

Given the dominant role of the Soviet Union in the establishment of the North
Korean state and in shaping its political landscape, it is not surprising that a
key argument put forward in some of the early Western as well as South
Korean literature was that the country underwent a process of 'Sovietisation' in
the immediate post-liberation era.[51] This view reflects early Cold War tendencies amongst US policymakers to see all instances of national communism as
being directed from Moscow.[52] It also reflects a tendency in mainstream South
Korean scholarship to emphasise the foreign and allegedly 'non-Korean'
character of the North Korean regime. Similar arguments can be found in the
broader literature on state socialism and post-communist transitions, whereby a
sharp distinction is typically drawn between countries that underwent socialist
transitions as a result of domestic revolutions and those that had socialism
imposed externally.[53] Early analyses placed North Korea within the latter

---

[50] Cumings, *Korea's Place in the Sun*, p. 186.

[51] Department of State, *North Korea: A Case Study of a Soviet Satellite* (Washington, DC: US
Government Printing Office, 1961); Oh Youngjin, *The Soviet Army's North Korea: One
Testament [Sogunŭi Pukhan: Hanaŭi chŭngŏn]* (Seoul: Central Culture Publishing, 1983).

[52] Marc J. Selverstone, *Constructing the Monolith: The United States, Great Britain, and
International Communism, 1945–1950* (Cambridge, MA: Harvard University Press, 2009).

[53] see Kornai, *The Socialist System*, p. 22; Steven Saxonberg, *Transitions and Non-Transitions
from Communism: Regime Survival in China, Cuba, North Korea, and Vietnam* (Cambridge:
Cambridge University Press, 2013), pp. 20–21.

camp, as representing a case of 'transplantation' rather than revolution.[54] Yoon T. Kuark argued in the 1960s, for example, that '[s]ince the end of the Second World War ... North Korea has become a thoroughly orthodox Communist state with but few deviations from the Russian type'.[55] Suh Dae-Sook similarly argued that the fact the northern half of the Korean peninsula lacked the social conditions conducive towards a communist takeover was ultimately irrelevant. Sovietisation did not depend on the popularity of the reforms but was a process carried out from above by the cadres that the Soviet forces had either brought with them or trained in the country itself.[56]

It is certainly difficult to deny the profound impact that the Soviet Union had on the shape and character of the North Korean state. Indeed, the 1948 constitution was closely modelled after the USSR's 1936 constitution,[57] although the North Korean constitution made no reference to the vanguard role of the communist party. This reflected both the facts that North Korea was initially regarded by the Soviet Union as at the 'bourgeois democratic stage' of development and that its process of party building was still embryonic. Notwithstanding this key difference, the institutional structure of the North Korean state bore strong similarities to that of the Soviet Union. In ideological terms, North Korea professed a strong adherence to Marxist–Leninist ideology that had few deviations from its Soviet variant. The strong imprint of the Soviet model would also be seen in the realm of economic management in terms of the mobilisation and allocation of surplus through central planning, the country's relatively autarkic relationship with the world economy and the priority given to industry over agriculture and to heavy over light industry. As noted in the previous chapter, North Korean central planning existed alongside strong emphasis on the mass mobilisation of society towards developmental goals.

However, understanding state-building simply as a process of 'Sovietisation' risks missing the specificity of the North Korean experience in terms of the influence of domestic socio-economic conditions inherited from the colonial era. More recent scholarship has therefore sought to emphasise the postcolonial revolutionary impetus underpinning North Korean state-building in the late 1940s. Charles Armstrong has argued, for example, that notwithstanding a high degree of Soviet influence, Korea's status as a largely agrarian country emerging from colonial rule problematises any simple analogy with

---

[54] Lim and Kim, 'Rethinking North Korean Self-Reliance', p. 59.

[55] Yoon T. Kuark, 'North Korea's Industrial Development during the Post-War Period', *The China Quarterly*, 14 June (1963), p. 51.

[56] Dae Sook Suh, 'A Preconceived Formula for Sovietization: The Communist Takeover of North Korea', *Journal of East and West Studies*, 1.1 (1973), p. 113.

[57] Dae-Kyu Yoon, 'The Constitution of North Korea: Its Changes and Implications', *Fordham International Law Journal*, 27.4 (2003), p. 1292.

the Soviet Union's Eastern European satellites and explains the rapid indigenisation of communism in North Korea. As such, the analytical distinction between externally imposed communist regimes and those that came about through domestic revolution does little to shed light on the substantive character of the North Korean state.[58] As Barry Gills has argued, a revolution did indeed take place in North Korea between 1945 and 1946. Successful in the North and aborted in the South, this revolution was ultimately based upon the socio-economic conditions generated by colonialism. Following the Japanese surrender, popular demands were made for land reform, the cancellation of debts, the right to employment, democracy and full independence. Furthermore, the success of this revolution owed much to the fact that colonialism had left behind a weak Korean bourgeoisie and landowning class as well as a power vacuum following the departure of the Japanese in 1945.[59] Furthermore, Suzy Kim has drawn attention to how it was primarily the realm of 'everyday life' that became the most important arena for North Koreans to experience the revolution. The land reform, the People's Committee elections, a literacy campaign and the experience of collective life through participation in the new mass organisations constituted the mechanisms whereby the revolution and the pursuit of socialist modernity were institutionalised into everyday life.[60]

However, this 'revolutionary' rupture of the late 1940s was quickly subsumed into a state-led project of development. This reflected the more general pattern whereby the globally uneven spread of capitalist industrialisation created a strong impetus for postcolonial states to take a leading role in mobilising society towards developmental goals. In this respect, the North Korean experience can more accurately be understood as one of what Antonio Gramsci understood as 'passive revolution'.[61] This refers to a state-led initiative aimed at facilitating modernisation and late development from above in response to geopolitical pressures. At the same time, passive revolution involves a pre-emptive and selective adoption of certain subaltern demands as part of a broader attempt at forestalling the development of a collective will.[62] As noted in the previous chapter, the dominant role of the state in facilitating catch-up industrialisation has been a recurrent feature of late

---

[58] Charles K. Armstrong, *The North Korean Revolution, 1945–1950* (Ithaca: Cornell University Press, 2003), pp. 3–4.

[59] Barry Gills, 'North Korea and the Crisis of Socialism: The Historical Ironies of National Division', *Third World Quarterly*, 13.1 (1992), pp. 108–9.

[60] Kim, *Everyday Life in the North Korean Revolution*.

[61] Antonio Gramsci, *Selections from the Prison Notebooks of Antonio Gramsci* (London: Lawrence and Wishart, 1971), pp. 104–6.

[62] Kevin Gray, *Labour and Development in East Asia: Social Forces and Passive Revolution* (London: Routledge, 2015), pp. 22–28.

development, and in North Korea, the state has arguably pursued this goal to a level of intensity unparalleled elsewhere in the postcolonial world. What emerged in 1945, therefore, cannot be adequately understood in terms of either the external imposition of state socialism or an indigenous revolution, but rather was a process of nationalist state-led modernisation and industrialisation that partially absorbed popular demands but ultimately facilitated passive revolution.

Indeed, following its establishment, the NKPPC proceeded under Soviet auspices to carry out such radical reforms as land reform, the nationalisation of Japanese-owned industry and the enactment of labour and gender equality laws, all of which had far-reaching consequences.[63] These reforms played a key role in liquidating the remnants of the colonial economic structure and in laying the foundations for national development. They also served to assuage the considerable social tensions created by the colonial experience thereby serving to establish a degree of support for the new regime. The most significant of these was the land reform. On 5 March 1946, the NKPPC officially proclaimed the Agrarian Reform Law, according to which all land owned by the Japanese, land belonging to Korean 'traitors' as a result of collaboration with the colonial authorities, land owned by Koreans in excess of five *chŏngbo* and land cultivated by tenants was confiscated and redistributed to land-poor farmers, landless tenants and agricultural labourers.[64] As a result, 1,000,325 *chŏngbo*, amounting to approximately 53 per cent of the total land under cultivation in North Korea, was confiscated by the state. Of this, 981,390 *chŏngbo* of land was subsequently redistributed to 724,522 households.[65] This amounted to more than 70 per cent of the total number of farm households in the country. In addition, orchards, livestock farms, forests and irrigation facilities were confiscated and transferred to regional People's Committees or to other state organs.

In contrast to the South Korean land reform carried out in 1948 and 1950, the North Korean reform took the form of confiscation without compensation. With the aim of abolishing the feudal tenancy system, confiscations were to be carried out mainly against around 44,000 large landowners. Five *chŏngbo* of land was deemed by the NKPPC as the maximum that any farm household could cultivate with its own manpower. Large landowners were therefore defined as those whose landholdings were above this threshold. Indeed, under

---

[63] Eui-Gak Hwang, *The Korean Economies: A Comparison of North and South* (Oxford: Clarendon Press, 1993), p. 33.

[64] One *chŏngbo* is almost equivalent to one hectare (0.992 ha).

[65] DPRK Academy of Sciences, *The Development of the People's Economy in Korea after Liberation [Haebanghu urinaraŭi inmin'gyŏngjebaljŏn]* (Pyongyang: Academy of Sciences Publishing House, 1960), pp. 7–10; Son Jon Hu, *The Experience of Land Reform [T'ojigaehyŏk kyŏnghŏm]* (Pyongyang: Social Science Publishing Company, 1983), p. 72.

the principle that land ownership was only to be granted to direct cultivators, all land leased under tenancy conditions was subject to confiscation regardless of the background of the owners or the scale of their holdings. As a result, smaller landowners with landholdings of under five *chŏngbo* would still have their land confiscated if they did not farm it themselves and it was instead cultivated by tenants or farmhands. On the other hand, even if large landowners had holdings of over five *chŏngbo,* their land would not be confiscated if they and their families farmed it all themselves, though such cases were rare. If part of the land was farmed themselves and part leased to others, then only the leased land would be confiscated.[66] Although the landlord class was eliminated, the reform did not dispossess relatively wealthy self-cultivating landowners, and as a result, a considerable income gap among farm households continued to exist in the North.

In addition to breaking the power of the landowner class, the redistribution of confiscated land laid the basis for increased food production. Indeed, the fragmented nature of land ownership at the end of the colonial era was seen as a fetter on agricultural production. In 1940, 72 per cent of all farms were less than one *chŏngbo* in size.[67] Reflecting the state's efforts to increase production, the land to be redistributed was calculated according to the number of family members in the receiving household and the number of labourers within that family. The most land was given to working-age males aged between 18 and 60 and females aged between 18 and 50. The precise amount was also dependent on qualitative factors such as the fertility of the land, the ratio between rice paddies and fields and conditions for cultivation. This minimised the unfair distribution of land and was a key factor in the reform's success.[68] According to Article 10 of the Agrarian Reform Law, farmers were also prohibited from buying, selling, renting or mortgaging the redistributed land. This meant that there was limited opportunity for speculation and that farmers' surplus capital was more likely to be reinvested into agricultural production.[69] After the land reform, on 27 June 1946, the NKPPC instituted the agricultural commodity tax, under which farmers had to give 25 per cent of their produce to the state.[70]

[66] Son Jon Hu, *History of Land Reform in North Korea,* pp. 111–70.
[67] Joseph Sang-Hoon Chung, *The North Korean Economy: Structure and Development* (Stanford: Hoover Institution Press, 1974), pp. 4–5.
[68] Son Jon Hu, *History of Land Reform in North Korea,* pp. 178–85.
[69] Chung, *North Korean Economy,* pp. 7–9.
[70] Kim Sung Jun, 'The Development of Agricultural Management in Korea [Urinara non-gch'on'gyŏngniŭi palchŏn]', in *The Development of the People's Economy in Korea 1948–1958 [Urinaraŭi inmin'gyŏngje palchŏn 1948–1958],* ed. by Kim Il Sung University Department of Economics (Pyongyang: State Publishing Company, 1958), p. 152.

As such, the land reform was a key step towards generating the surpluses required for broader industrialisation. North Korea was of course by no means unique in viewing land reform as the basis of subsequent national development. Following the end of the Second World War, governments of newly independent nations typically viewed the generation of agricultural surpluses as essential for industrialisation and emphasised agricultural modernisation as a means of increasing both land and labour productivity.[71] In East Asia too, the demand for land redistribution existed in socialist countries such as North Korea, China and North Vietnam as well as in US-aligned South Korea and Taiwan. Except for a few cases, however, the majority of land reforms elsewhere in the postcolonial world faced strong opposition from powerful landlord classes and/or the intervention of former colonial powers. By contrast, the North Korean land reform of 1946 was largely successful and completed in just 23 days with minimal bloodshed. Jon Halliday has even gone as far as to argue that the North Korean land reform '... was the most peaceful and the fastest land reform in Asia (or, to my knowledge, anywhere in the world)'.[72]

This success of the land reform can be attributed to several enabling factors closely related to the specificities of Korea's liberation. Following August 1945, Japanese landowners fled the country. The partition of the peninsula also served to separate Korean absentee landlords residing in the south from their lands in the north and encouraged northern landlords fearful of the emerging political climate there to flee south. Along with the presence of Soviet troops, the national division served to prevent the landlord class from organising any resistance to the reform.[73] Arguably, the most important factor, however, was that of popular support. The fact that the 1946 reform took the form of a 'land to the tiller' redistribution rather than a more radical collectivisation (though that did come later) also helped to generate support from the peasantry. As noted in Table 1.1, the land that was distributed to the People's Committees rather than to individual farmers amounted to no more than 2 per cent.

Popular support reflected the highly uneven pattern of landholdings at the time of liberation. As we have seen, Japanese colonialism had by 1945 left behind a relatively strong industrial and commercial base, but as in many other newly independent countries of the Third World, agriculture remained the dominant economic activity. In 1946, the year of the land reform, private

[71] Charles Peter Timmer, 'Agriculture and Economic Development Revisited', *Agricultural Systems*, 40.1–3 (1992), p. 27.
[72] Halliday, 'The North Korean Enigma', p. 25.
[73] The early North Korean literature highlighted the occupying Soviet forces as creating favourable conditions for the success of the reform, but from the late 1950s, emphasis was placed on Kim Il Sung's guidance along with the party's 'correct measures'.

Table 1.1 *Confiscation and Redistribution through Land Reform*

	Total Land		Total Arable Land	Agricultural Households	
	Area (*chŏngbo*)	Percentage		Households	Percentage
Confiscation of land belonging to:					
Japanese/Japanese government	112,623	11.3	111,561	12,919	3.1
National traitors and fugitives	13,272	1.3	12,518	1,366	0.3
Landlords with more than 5 *chŏngbo*	237,746	23.8	231,716	29,683	7.0
Landlords with entire land farmed by tenants	263,436	26.3	259,150	145,688	34.5
Landlords with partial land farmed by tenants	358,053	35.8	354,093	228,866	54.1
Religious organisations	15,195	1.5	14,916	4,124	1.0
Total	1,000,325	100.0	983,954	422,646	100.0
Land Redistributed to:					
Agricultural labourers	22,387	2.3	21,960	17,137	2.4
Landless farmers	603,407	61.5	589,377	442,973	61.1
Land-poor farmers	345,974	35.3	344,134	260,501	36.0
Landlords migrated from other areas	9,622	0.9	9,598	3,911	0.5
People's Committees	18,935	-	18,885	-	-
Total	981,390	100.0	965,069	724,522	100.0

Note: 'Landlords with entire land farmed by tenants' refers to those with less than five *chŏngbo* of land who lease all of it to tenants. 'Landlords with partial land farmed by tenants' refers to those with less than five *chŏngbo* and who lease part of their land to be continually farmed by tenants. Source: modified from DPRK Central Bureau of Statistics, *Statistics on the Development of the DPRK's People's Economy 1946-1960 [1946-1960 Chosŏnminjujuŭiinmin'gonghwaguk inmin'gyŏngjebaljŏn t'onggyejib]* (Pyongyang: State Publishing House, 1961), pp. 59–60.

farmers accounted for 74.1 per cent of the employed population, and agriculture accounted for 59.1 per cent of North Korea's total economic production.[74] However, patterns of land ownership in colonial Korea had seen a gradual shift from owner farmers to tenants and farm labourers. By 1945, nearly 56.7 per cent of all farming households in northern Korea were poor peasants who owned only 5.4 per cent of arable land in the country. By contrast, a small group of large landlords who made up 4 per cent of farming households

---

[74] DPRK Central Bureau of Statistics, *Statistics on the Development of the DPRK's People's Economy 1946–1960*, pp. 19–24.

occupied 58.2 per cent of arable land.[75] There was, therefore, a clear popular impetus for land reform following liberation.

The 1946 land reform also enabled the swift consolidation of popular support for the new regime. Indeed, the goal of the reform was precisely to swiftly break the power of the landowning classes, eliminate Japanese collaborators and incorporate peasants into the emergent political system and win their support.[76] As in China, poor peasants and agricultural labourers played a key role in the 11,500 rural committees that were organised to carry out the land reform. So-called anti-traitor meetings were held in which all peasants were obliged to participate in order to expose the 'pro-Japanese' landlords. Through establishing a loyal village leadership, the North Korean state had, by the end of the reform, succeeded in penetrating the countryside to the lowest level.[77] The reform also marked the communist party's transformation into a mass party. In December 1945, the Northern Branch of the Korean Communist Party reportedly had only 4,530 members, with farmers accounting for 34 per cent of its membership. This grew from 26,000 in April 1946 to 366,000 in August of the same year when the North Korean Workers' Party was formed. Thus, within just four months of the land reform, party membership had increased roughly 14-fold. In early 1948, membership recorded 708,000 members, of whom 374,000 had been poor peasants prior to the land reform.[78] As such, the communist party's membership had by 1948 reached 7.5 per cent of an overall population of around 9.3 million. The popularity of the reform also translated into increased support for Kim Il Sung, who was widely seen as its key instigator.

To what extent did the land reform improve productivity in the agricultural sector? The rationale of the reform was that the direct ownership of land by cultivators would increase farmers' incentives. This logic was reflected in the headline of a *Rodong Sinmun* editorial on 5 April 1947: 'Farmers! If you wish your land to be yours forever, struggle to increase the harvest through diligent farming!'[79] It is difficult, however, to calculate the precise impact of the land reform as it coincided with other profound socio-economic and political changes in North Korea. Liberation from colonial rule and national division, for example, had led to a sharp dip in food production, to which the authorities responded by launching a campaign to increase grain production through the

---

[75] Son Jon Hu, *Experience of Land Reform*, p. 3.
[76] Armstrong, *North Korean Revolution*, p. 75.
[77] Cumings, *Origins of the Korean War: Volume I*, pp. 414–15.
[78] Son Jon Hu, *History of Land Reform in North Korea*, p. 257.
[79] *Rodong Sinmun*, 5 April 1947, 'Farmers! If you wish your land to be yours forever, struggle to increase the harvest through diligent farming! [Nongmindŭriyŏ! Punyŏbadŭn t'ojirŭl yŏngguhi tangsindŭrŭi soyuga toege haryŏmyŏn nongsarŭl pujirŏnhi hamŭrossŏ suhwakkorŭl nop'igi wihayŏ ssauja]'.

expansion of irrigation, increased supply of fertiliser and agricultural equipment, restoration of agricultural land and establishment of agricultural banks.[80] Despite these efforts, North Korean sources suggest that grain production only recovered gradually. It was not until 1948 that grain production recovered to pre-liberation levels, increasing from 1.9 million tonnes in 1946 to 2.1 million tonnes in 1947, and to 2.67 million tonnes in 1948, thereby comparing favourably to the 2.42 million tonnes of 1944.[81]

In addition to the land reform, the NKPPC also introduced new labour and gender equality laws. In June 1946, the Labour Law of North Korean Workers and Office Employees was passed, which made provisions for an equal wage system, an eight-hour day and six-day week, regulations concerning child and female labour and rules concerning labour organisations. All workers were to be enrolled into the North Korean General Federation of Trade Unions. Similarly, the Law on North Korean Equal Rights between Men and Women was passed the following month, which guaranteed equal rights for men and women in national, economic, cultural, social and political life, and in elections, work and education. The law abolished certain traditional customs and guaranteed free marriage, the divorce of women and women's right of succession to property. It also outlawed prostitution and the existence of concubines.[82]

Furthermore, between August and October 1946, the NKPPC carried out the nationalisation of Japanese-owned industry. In late 1945, almost all major Japanese-owned businesses, including factories, power plants, mines and transport infrastructure, were confiscated by the Soviet authorities. As in Eastern Europe, there had been an initial attempt by the occupying Soviet forces to transfer industrial equipment and mineral resources back to the Soviet Union as war booty, but in July 1946, Moscow made the decision to hand over the former Japanese-owned industries to the North Korean authorities.[83] As such, on 10 August 1946, the NKPPC formally nationalised all enterprises and industrial assets previously owned by the Japanese and their collaborators by enacting the Law on the Nationalisation of Industries, Railway, Transport, Communication and Banks, etc. As a result, a total of 1,034 Japanese-owned enterprises amounting to 72.4 per cent of North Korean industrial output in 1946 were nationalised.[84]

---

[80] Kim Sung Jun, 'The Development of Agricultural Management in Korea', pp. 154–55.
[81] KCNA, *Korean Central Almanac 1959 [Chosŏnjungangyŏn'gam 1959]* (Pyongyang: KCNA, 1959), p. 196.
[82] Youn-Soo Kim, 'The Economy of the KDPR – Its Development, Organization and Functioning', in *The Economy of the Korean Democratic People's Republic 1945–1977*, ed. by Youn-Soo Kim (Kiel: German Korea-Studies Group, 1979), p. 23.
[83] Jeon Hyun Soo, 'Nationalisation of Major Industry', pp. 82–90.
[84] DPRK Academy of Sciences, *Development of the People's Economy*, pp. 7–10.

In contrast to the rapid nationalisation of Japanese-owned enterprises, the socialisation of small-scale private manufacturing and commerce took place in a more gradual manner. Small-scale handicraft production, retail, services and petty market trading, for the most part, remained in private hands during the early post-liberation period. In line with the principles of the bourgeois democratic revolution, the NKPPC announced in October 1946 a policy of guaranteeing private property rights and encouraging investment by national capitalists and individual traders. Indeed, chronic shortages of basic consumer necessities and resultant high levels of inflation were causing considerable public hardship. As such, the North Korean authorities' cooperative stance towards small-scale capital was seen as essential in terms of maintaining the production of basic necessities.[85] Nonetheless, the state's direct involvement in the commercial sector saw a gradual increase in the late 1940s. For example, the state established a food distribution system for urban workers in 1946 and introduced state-designated prices for some basic goods in 1947, leading to an expansion of state-owned and cooperative shops. Whereas in 1946 there was just one state-owned store and 950 cooperative stores in North Korea, by 1949 this had grown to 1,371 and 1,994, respectively.[86] This thereby increased the role of the state in the commercial sector and laid the foundation for greater central planning and state intervention in the economy.

The democratic reforms were accompanied by the establishment of mass organisations including the North Korean Farmers' League, the North Korean Democratic Youth League, the North Korean General Federation of Trade Unions, the North Korean Women's Federation and the General Federation of North Korean Writers and Artists. As Suzy Kim has argued, these organisations were expected to act as 'transmission belts' connecting the party with the masses from the provinces down to the counties, townships and villages. Through conducting meetings, study sessions, and holding internal elections to nominate their own leaders by majority vote, they provided a form of collective life for the vast majority of North Koreans.[87] Regardless of whether the early period of state-building represented a revolutionary or democratic moment in North Korea, however, it is difficult to deny that over time these corporatist mass organisations were crucial in the party-state's efforts to forestall the emergence of an independent civil society. Although it has been argued that these organisations were central to eliciting a degree of consent on the part of the North Korean public,[88] they were all created, operated and

---

[85] Jeon Hyun Soo, 'Nationalisation of Major Industry', pp. 98–99.

[86] DPRK Central Bureau of Statistics, *Statistics on the Development*, p. 135.

[87] Kim, *Everyday Life in the North Korean Revolution*, pp. 112–13.

[88] Yong Sub Choi, 'North Korea's Hegemonic Rule and Its Collapse', *The Pacific Review*, 30.5 (2017), p. 787.

closely monitored by the Korean Workers' Party. By inserting the party into every organised social interaction, the regime thereby sought to obstruct the development of oppositional thought or activity.[89] As with the democratic reforms, the establishment of these organisations can be seen as part of the passive revolutionary dynamic of the selective adoption by the developmental regime of popular demands combined with measures designed to prevent the emergence of a collective will.

1.4   Conclusion

As we have argued, while the Soviet Union exerted a strong influence on North Korean state-building after 1945, the country should also be understood in terms of its postcolonial lineage. Three and a half decades of colonial rule had a profound impact on North Korea's experience of late development. It contributed to the emergence of modern Korean nationalism, an essential ideational underpinning of catch-up industrialisation. Pent-up social grievances surrounding land ownership patterns also meant that the post-liberation regime was able to achieve a degree of popular support and legitimacy by means of a thoroughgoing land-to-the-tiller reform. The uneven geography of colonial industrialisation meant that North Korea was upon liberation relatively well endowed with heavy industries compared to the South. The country was thereby arguably unique amongst postcolonial societies in that a national development strategy based on heavy industries was within the realm of possibility. As we shall see, however, this colonial legacy ultimately proved to be a double-edged sword in that this developmental bias subsequently served to constrain the country's capacity to adapt to future changes in its external environment, including the extent to which the authorities were prepared to pursue Chinese-style 'reform and opening'.

Following liberation, the unfolding logic of the Cold War meant that North Korea was and would continue to be at the epicentre of a global rivalry that would continue to be interpreted by the country's leadership as an existential threat. Furthermore, the extreme destruction of the fratricidal Korean War would only serve to deepen this sense of threat. In this respect, the legacies of colonialism, the role of the Soviet Union in facilitating the country's post-war recovery and industrialisation, national division and the emergent global Cold War, all shed light on how the development–geopolitics nexus has operated in the North Korean context. As we have also seen, these external threats and opportunities were mediated through a domestic process of passive revolution, whereby the project of catch-up industrialisation took the form of

---

[89] Daniel Byman and Jennifer Lind, 'Pyongyang's Survival Strategy: Tools of Authoritarian Control in North Korea', *International Security*, 35.1 (2010), p. 49.

the emergence of a regime aimed at mobilising the population towards developmental goals while forestalling genuine popular sovereignty. External geopolitical dynamics did not, therefore, translate automatically into specific developmental policies at the domestic level. Rather, they were mediated through and contested by specific political forces within the country. In the next chapter, we will examine in more detail how disputes over developmental strategy in the 1950s reflected the divergent origins of particular groupings within the Korean communist movement.

2   Post-War Reconstruction and Catch-Up Industrialisation

By the late 1940s, North Korea had seen the establishment of a developmental regime that was strongly shaped by both its colonial history as well as the Soviet occupation in the immediate post-liberation period. Along with the division of the Korean peninsula, these multiple lineages imparted a strong emphasis on autonomous national development on the part of the North Korean leadership. In this chapter, we examine how the development–geopolitics nexus operated in terms of North Korea's subsequent experience of catch-up industrialisation. Following the widespread destruction of the Korean War, Kim Il Sung and his regime pursued a Soviet-style strategy of building a national economy based upon a strong heavy-industrial sector. Yet this was not an expression of subservience or dependency vis-à-vis the USSR but an effort at countering potential economic and political dependency. Paradoxically, however, the strategy was only possible through massive external assistance from the socialist bloc. The result was that following the war North Korea saw an extraordinarily rapid process of industrialisation and urbanisation to the extent that within a decade the country could be compared to the more advanced countries of Eastern Europe.

In addition to its role in establishing an autonomous defence sector, a key logic of Kim Il Sung's heavy industry–first strategy was that it would supply the inputs necessary for a strong and self-reliant light industrial and agricultural sector. Despite claims of 'simultaneous development' across economic sectors, however, heavy industry was in reality prioritised. Indeed, heavy industry's monopolisation of resources required significant sacrifices on the part of the population, particularly as declining levels of foreign aid led to increased emphasis on the mass mobilisation of labour. This developmental strategy did not go unchallenged, however. As we have already noted, North Korean politics were characterised by a relative degree of pluralism during the first decade after liberation. In particular, the factional disputes of the mid-1950s were in part a reflection of divergent ideas surrounding strategies of late development and North Korea's position within the 'socialist division of labour'.[1] Indeed, new ideas emerging within the Soviet Union following Joseph Stalin's death encouraged domestic dissent vis-à-vis Kim Il Sung's heavy industry–first strategy. By the late 1950s, however, Kim had largely defeated his factional opponents and was able to pursue his developmental strategy unhindered. At the same time, the political turmoil of the late 1950s left the regime increasingly distrustful of its socialist allies and served to exaggerate the regime's isolationist tendencies, a trend that would become even more pronounced in the following decades.

2.1 Post-War Reconstruction and Development Policy

Following the state-building of the immediate post-liberation era, the North Korean authorities embarked upon a process officially referred to as that of 'peaceful reconstruction'. In concrete terms, this took the form of two one-year plans (1947 and 1948) followed by a two-year plan (1949–50). These plans were aimed at further eliminating the vestiges of Japanese colonial rule and the disruption caused by national division, and at establishing the basis of a viable North Korean economy. In line with these aims, the Central Bank of Korea (Chosŏnjungangŭnhaeng) implemented a currency reform in December 1947 which brought an end to the use of the Japanese colonial currency and the military notes issued by the occupying Soviet forces. This period also saw a marked improvement in the fiscal basis of the new state. As key industrial plants were rehabilitated, the state's budgetary income in 1949 had increased by 233 per cent compared to that of 1947. Furthermore, the proportion of income derived from the state-owned sector grew from 44.5 per cent in 1946 to 73 per cent in 1949.[2] Despite these early achievements, the Two-Year Plan of 1949–50 experienced difficulties due to ongoing shortages of capital. Following Kim Il Sung's March 1949 visit to the Soviet Union, Moscow agreed to provide a concessional loan for the next three years together with a treaty on economic and cultural cooperation. The loan was insufficient to fulfil the plan's targets, however. In 1950, the North Korean government budget was overspent by 1.5 billion won, leading the authorities to issue public bonds in May that year in an attempt to fill the revenue gap.[3]

[1] Paik Haksoon, *History of Power in North Korea*, p. 231.
[2] An Kwang Jup, 'The Development of Finance in Korea [Urinara chaejŏngŭi palchŏn]', in *The Development of the People's Economy in Korea, 1948–1958 [Urinaraŭi inmin'gyŏngje palchŏn 1948–1958]*, ed. by Kim Il Sung University, Department of Economics (Pyongyang: State Publishing Company, 1958), p. 277.
[3] *Rodong Sinmun*, 16 May 1950, 'People's economic development bonds have been issued with the enthusiastic demand of the people [Inmindŭrŭi yŏllyŏrhan yomang soge inmin'gyŏngjebalchŏn ch'aegwŏnŭn parhaengdoeŏtta]'.

Whatever progress had been made in terms of economic recovery was largely reversed by the outbreak of the Korean War in June 1950. Three years of heavy fighting led to massive physical destruction and loss of life.[4] The war is estimated to have led to over four million casualties, including two million North Korean civilians and 500,000 North Korean soldiers, which together amounted to around 20 per cent of North Korea's entire population.[5] The country's industrial base was also severely damaged, with the resulting dislocations reportedly reducing gross industrial production in 1953 to 64 per cent of its 1949 level.[6] Except for sectors essential for the maintenance of war supplies, all industries saw a significant decline in production. In 1953, electricity generation had fallen by 73.5 per cent compared to 1949 levels, and the output of the fuel, metallurgical, chemical and construction material sectors recorded a drop of 88.7 per cent, 89.5 per cent, 78.3 per cent and 63.7 per cent, respectively, during the same period.[7] In addition, the majority of urban public buildings were destroyed, including around 5,000 schools and 1,000 medical facility buildings. A further 600,000 civilian houses were destroyed. In the agricultural sector, the damage of paddy and non-paddy fields led to a reduction in the area of cultivated land by around 90,000 *chŏngbo* and a decline in grain production to 88 per cent of pre-war levels.[8]

Through leaving behind an even more entrenched system of national division, the war had a profound impact on North Korean developmental strategy. On 8 August 1953, twelve days after the armistice was signed, the Sixth Joint Plenum of the KWP Central Committee adopted a policy of economic recovery that prioritised heavy industry.[9] In his opening report entitled 'The Struggle for Restoration and Development of the Post-War People's Economy and the Subsequent Duties of the Party in Relation to the Signing

---

[4] As General MacArthur himself testified to Congress in May 1951, two years prior to the end of the war, 'The War in Korea has almost destroyed that nation of 20,000,000 people. I have never seen such devastation . . . . If you go on indefinitely, you are perpetuating a slaughter such as I have never heard of in the history of mankind' (Reported in 'The Military Situation in the Far East', United States Government Printing Office, Washington, DC, 1951, p. 82).

[5] Martin Hart-Landsberg, *Korea: Division, Reunification, and U.S. Foreign Policy* (New York: Monthly Review Press, 1998), p. 133.

[6] DPRK Academy of Sciences, *Development of the People's Economy*, p. 99.

[7] Kim Jong Il, 'The Development of Industry in Korea [Urinara kongŏbŭi palchŏn]', in *The Development of the People's Economy in Korea, 1948–1958 [Urinaraŭi inmin'gyŏngje palchŏn 1948–1958]*, ed. by Kim Il Sung University, Department of Economics (Pyongyang: State Publishing Company, 1958), p. 123.

[8] DPRK Academy of Sciences, *Development of the People's Economy*, pp. 98–99.

[9] Suh Dong-Man, *The History of Socialist System Formation in North Chosun 1945–1961 [Pukchosŏn sahoejuŭi ch'eje sŏngnipsa 1945–1961]* (Seoul: Sunin, 2005), p. 604; Kim Sung-bo, *North Korean History 1: The Experience of State Building and People's Democracy 1945–1960 [Pukhanŭi yŏksa 1: Kŏn'guggwa inminminjujuŭi kyŏnghŏm 1945–1960]* (Seoul: Critical Review of History, 2011), p. 175.

of the Armistice Agreement', Kim Il Sung outlined the reasoning behind this strategy:

'The scope of the destruction of the people's economy as a result of the war has been massive and severe. It is impossible for us to completely reconstruct every sector of the people's economy at the same time .... In relation to post-war reconstruction, we urgently need to prioritise the reconstruction of key factories and enterprises. Without distinguishing between the early and later stages of industrial reconstruction, the overall recovery and development of the people's economy could be retarded, leading to the massive wastage of funds, resources, materials and labour power'.[10]

As such, the steel, machine tools, shipbuilding, mining, electricity generation, chemicals and construction materials sectors were all to be prioritised in terms of investment. Heavy industry was seen as essential in the building of an autonomous defence sector, with security considerations also influencing the geographical location of industrial facilities. As Kim Il Sung further argued, the fact that colonial-era factories had been concentrated in the coastal regions to facilitate the shipping of their output to Japan meant that they were located far away from sources of energy and were exposed to heavy naval shelling during the war. Given the urgency and expense of post-war reconstruction, Kim recognised that while some damaged factories would have to be rebuilt in their original location, new factories in strategic sectors would be located in the country's interior.[11] As such, North Korea saw the emergence of a distinctive economic geography in which key machine tools and other defence-related factories were, for the most part, located in the mountainous border region of Jagang Province.[12]

These were, therefore, the basic principles that underpinned the Three-Year Plan (1954–56) adopted at the Seventh Session of the Supreme People's Assembly on 23 April 1954 (see Table 2.1). The plan's official goal was 'the priority development of heavy industry with simultaneous development in agriculture and light industry'.[13] The notion of 'simultaneous development' was based on the notion that the recovery and development of heavy industry would supply the necessary inputs for light industry and agriculture. As such, there would be no trade-off between prioritising heavy industrialisation and

---

[10] Kim Il Sung, *On the Recovery and Development of the Post-War People's Economy [Chŏnhu inmin'gyŏngje pokkubalchŏnŭl wihayŏ]* (Pyongyang: Korean Workers' Party Publishing House, 1956), pp. 3–5.

[11] Ibid., pp. 4–7.

[12] This spatial location of industry had far-reaching consequences. Following the famine of the mid-1990s, UN organisations and NGOs began to supply humanitarian aid to North Korea. However, due to security-related concerns resulting from the concentration of machinery and defence-related factories, humanitarian organisations were blocked from entering Jagang Province.

[13] Youn-Soo Kim, 'Economy of the KDPR, p. 35.

Table 2.1 *Economic plans during the post-war reconstruction period*

	Basic goals	Announced results
Three-Year Plan (1954–56)	• Recovery to pre-war levels. • A total of 75 per cent increase in national income over 1953 levels. • A 2.6-fold increase in total industrial production. • A total of 119 per cent increase in the grain harvest over 1949 levels.	• A total of 160 per cent increase in national income over 1953 levels. • A 2.8-fold increase in industrial production. • A total of 196 per cent increase in labour productivity. • A total of 126 per cent increase in grain production over 1946 levels.
Five-Year Plan (1957–60)	• Establishment of the basis for industrialisation. • A 2.6-fold increase in industrial production. • Priority to heavy industrialisation and simultaneous development of light industry and agriculture. • Production of 3,760,000 tonnes of grain. • Basic resolution of the food, clothes and shelter problem for citizens.	• A 2.2-fold increase in national income. • A 3.5-fold increase in industrial production. • Average annual industrial growth: 36.6 per cent. • Annual growth rate of machinery and metal industry: 49.6 per cent. • A total of 140 per cent increase in labour productivity. • Production of 3,803,000 tonnes of grain. • Achievement of the plan's targets one year early.

Source: Modified from KDI, *The Economic Indicators of North Korea [Pukhan'gyŏngjejip'yojip]* (Seoul: Korea Development Institute, 1996), p. 37.

improving the people's livelihood.[14] For Kim Il Sung, North Korea would be able to pursue such a strategy due to its advantages of backwardness and the specificity of the country's external alliances. Along with North Korea's experience of reconstruction in the late 1940s and its rich mineral resources, Kim argued that economic and technical aid from the socialist countries would form an important basis for the country's recovery and development.[15]

---

[14] KCNA, *Korean Central Almanac 1959*, pp. 2–3.
[15] Kim Il Sung, *On the Recovery and Development*, pp. 76–77.

In contrast to Stalin's Soviet Union, a heavy industry–first strategy in North Korea would therefore not necessarily imply the sacrifice of living standards.[16] While the Soviet Union's geopolitical pressures compelled it to build a heavy-industrial sector by drawing finite resources away from consumption, external aid would enable North Korea to avoid this path.

There is little doubt that socialist bloc assistance played a key role in North Korea's post-war reconstruction and development. It served to relieve domestic constraints and enhance the state's capacity to invest in various industrial projects. The reason for this generosity was the country's position on the frontline of the emerging Asian Cold War. North Korea's geopolitical importance to the Soviet Union and China paralleled that of South Korea to the United States, with Moscow and Beijing seeking to preserve their ideological ally of North Korea as a geopolitical buffer state. Furthermore, as Moscow became increasingly sceptical regarding its relations with Mao Zedong's China, it viewed its alliance with Pyongyang as critical not just in terms of countering US predominance in the region but also in terms of maintaining its national interests vis-à-vis China.[17] Beijing had a similar rationale for seeking to maintain North Korea as an ally. In the early twentieth century, the Korean peninsula had formed the corridor through which imperial Japan facilitated its military expansion into China. Following the Korean War, therefore, Beijing's support of North Korea as a bulwark against US encroachment became a consistent strategic objective.[18]

Under these circumstances, the socialist bloc was willing to commit substantial resources to enable North Korea's post-war reconstruction. This assistance was offered largely in the form of pledges by individual donor countries of material and technical support for specific industrial sectors and regions in North Korea. On 20 December 1953, following trips to both the Soviet Union and China, Kim Il Sung reported to the Sixth Session of the Supreme People's Assembly that North Korea was '... not an isolated island but part of the socialist bloc, which included the USSR, the most industrialised country in the world, as well as China and several other people's democracies .... It is not the case that everything that is required by our people's economy must be made by

---

[16] KCNA, *Korean Central Almanac 1959*, p. 3.

[17] Bruce Cumings, *The Origins of the Korean War, Vol. II. The Roaring of the Cataract, 1947–1950* (Princeton, NJ: Princeton University Press, 1990), pp. 327–31.

[18] Benjamin Habib, 'The Enforcement Problem in Resolution 2094 and the United Nations Security Council Sanctions Regime: Sanctioning North Korea', *Australian Journal of International Affairs*, 70.1 (2016), p. 60.

our own hands. If that view exists, then it is fundamentally wrong in today's situation'.[19]

According to North Korean sources, Moscow provided one billion roubles of grants to North Korea, with two-thirds of that figure to be disbursed by 1954 and the remainder by 1955. Despite post-Stalinist ideas emerging in the Soviet Union regarding the integration of its allies into the 'socialist division of labour', this aid was focused on the reconstruction of North Korea's existing industrial base. It was mostly tied to specific projects, including assistance in the form of machinery and equipment, building materials and technical assistance for the reconstruction of Kim Chaek Iron and Steel Complex, Seongjin Steelworks, Hungnam Fertiliser Factory, Seunghori Cement Factory, Nampo smelting factory, Supung Dam and Pyongyang Textile Factory. However, the aid also included the building of new factories, such as those related to meat processing, textiles, fish canning, hydrochloric acid, paint and varnish, tractor repair and the building of a central radio station. Aid also took the form of the supply of agricultural machinery and tools, synthetic fertilisers, breeding cattle, horses, fishing boats, buses, textiles and other necessities, as well as equipment for hospitals and schools, along with materials for a central scientific–technical library. The Soviet Union also halved the debt which North Korea had incurred prior to the war as part of the 1949 treaty on economic and cultural assistance.[20] As a result, projects built with Soviet aid provided for percentages ranging from 30 to 100 per cent of national output in numerous sectors such as energy, metallurgy, chemicals, building materials and light industry.[21]

In addition, Beijing forgave all North Korean debts to China, including those incurred as a result of military aid during the Korean War, and provided a grant of 800 million yuan for the period between 1954 and 1957.[22] Reflecting China's lower level of industrial development compared to the Soviet Union, Beijing's aid was centred more on raw materials, food, building materials and light industrial goods, thereby helping to ease North Korea's shortages of basic

---

[19] Kim Il Sung, 'The Report of the Work of the DPRK Government Delegations Visiting the Soviet Union, the People's Republic of China and People's Democratic Countries [Ssoryŏn chunghwainmin'gonghwaguk mit inminminjujuŭi chegukkadŭrŭl pangmunhan Chosŏnminjujuŭiinmin'gonghwaguk chŏngbudaep'yodanŭi saŏp kyŏnggwa pogo]'. Reprinted by the Korean Central News Agency, *Korean Central Almanac, 1954–1955 [1954–1955 nyŏnp'an Chosŏnjungangnyŏn'gam]* (Pyongyang: KCNA, 1955), p. 28.

[20] Ibid., pp. 21–22.

[21] Erik van Ree, 'The Limits of Juche: North Korea's Dependence on Soviet Industrial Aid, 1953–1976', *Journal of Communist Studies*, 5.1 (1989), p. 59.

[22] 'Li Fuchun's Report on Sino–Korean Trade Negotiations', 30 September 1957, History and Public Policy Program Digital Archive, State Planning Commission Archives. Obtained for NKIDP by Shen Zhihua and translated for NKIDP by Jeffrey Wang, http://digitalarchive.wilsoncenter.org/document/114171 [accessed 19 May 2020].

necessities.[23] Furthermore, Chinese troops stationed in North Korea after the war provided manpower for the building or repair of railways, bridges, public buildings and farming-related facilities.[24] Czechoslovakia provided aid in the form of car and car-parts factories, a tool factory, the rebuilding of a cement plant and three hydroelectric power plants. Poland assisted with the repair and renovation of steam locomotives and railway cars, as well as repairs to three coal mines. Hungary provided aid for the building of chemical, weights and measures, and machine-tools factories. Romania built cement, pharmaceutical and brick factories, and sent ten passenger railcars, ten fishing boats, thirty trucks and a variety of other materials and necessities. Bulgaria provided silk textiles, window glass and equipment for brick and wood product factories.[25] Assistance was also provided by Mongolia and Albania. Out of all the Eastern European countries, East Germany provided the greatest amount of assistance to North Korea, which included taking responsibility for the reconstruction of the city of Hamhung between 1954 and 1962.[26] This included rebuilding the city's infrastructure through the provision of equipment, machinery and advanced technology.

The significance of this aid can therefore hardly be overestimated. As can be seen in Table 2.2, aid amounted to 34 per cent of North Korea's state budget in 1954, 21.7 per cent in 1955 and 16.5 per cent in 1956. North Korean sources report that gross industrial output grew at an average annual rate of 42 per cent, meaning that 1956 levels were 2.8 times that of 1953 and 1.8 times that of 1949. Furthermore, it was reported that around 240 large-scale industrial enterprises had been completely or partially reconstructed, and around 80 new enterprises were built.[27] External assistance was not the only factor at play in the successful completion of the plan, however. The plan was also accompanied by the massive mobilisation of labour. As could be seen in the slogan of 'all out for the reconstruction and development of the people's economy for the strengthening of the

---

[23] KCNA, *Korean Central Almanac, 1954–1955*, p. 22.

[24] *Rodong Sinmun*, 16 December 1954, 'Through cooperation with our Chinese brothers, reconstruction of the locomotive repair and management office in West Pyongyang is advancing [Chungguk hyŏngjedŭrŭi hyŏpchoro sŏp'yŏngyang kigwan'gu pokku kongsa chinch'ŏk]'.

[25] 'Political Report No. 8 of the Embassy of the People's Republic of Poland in the Democratic People's Republic of Korea for the Period of 1 December to 31 December 1953', 31 December 1953, History and Public Policy Program Digital Archive, Polish Foreign Ministry Archive. Obtained for NKIDP by Jakub Poprocki and translated for NKIDP by Maya Latynski, http://digitalarchive.wilsoncenter.org/document/114962 [accessed 19 May 2020].

[26] Rüdiger Frank, 'Lessons from the Past: The First Wave of Developmental Assistance to North Korea and the German Reconstruction of Hamhùng', *Pacific Focus*, 23.1 (2008), pp. 46–74.

[27] DPRK Academy of Sciences, *Development of the People's Economy*, pp. 125–26.

Table 2.2 *The state budget during the Three-Year Plan*

		1954	1955	1956
Total budget revenue		90,183	108,157	99,254
Proportion of total income	Income from state-owned sector (%)	52.6	69.1	74.6
	Foreign aid (%)	34.0	21.7	16.5
	Tax income from citizens (%)	13.4	9.2	8.9
Total (%)		100	100	100

Note: Budget revenue unit is million won.
Source: DPRK Academy of Sciences, *The Development of the People's Economy in Korea after Liberation*, p. 123.

democratic base', post-war reconstruction drew heavily on the experience of wartime mobilisation. Furthermore, this reliance on mass mobilisation was to become more or less a permanent feature of the North Korean economic model.[28]

However, while the quantitative goals of the Three-Year Plan were, for the most part, achieved and surpassed, questions can be raised with regards to the extent to which the goal of 'simultaneous development' was successful. Indeed, the available data suggest that in reality Kim Il Sung's heavy industry–first strategy took place at the *expense* of light industry and agriculture. During the Three-Year Plan, 39.9 billion won was invested in the industrial sector, of which 80 per cent was devoted to heavy industry.[29] With the partial exception of the textile industry, the light industrial sector saw much slower recovery as a result. Concrete figures relating to the goal of increasing the production of basic necessities to twice the level of 1949 were not released upon the completion of the plan, suggesting a failure to meet that target. Indeed, a delegation from the Communist Party of the Soviet Union at the KWP Third Party Congress in April 1956 reported that although there had been significant progress in industrial reconstruction, '. . . the 1949 level of production has still not been achieved in the main consumer goods and the population's supply

---

[28] Hazel Smith, *North Korea: Markets and Military Rule* (Cambridge: Cambridge University Press, 2015), p. 106.
[29] Rhee Myong Seo, 'Our Party's Economic Policy on Heavy Industry-First Growth and the Simultaneous Development of Light Industry and Agriculture [Chunggongŏbŭi usŏnjŏk changsŏnggwa kyŏnggongŏp mit nongŏbŭi tongsijŏk palchŏne taehan uri tangŭi kyŏngjejŏngch'aek]', in *The Constructions of Socialist Economy in Our Country [Urinaraesŏŭi sahoejuŭi kyŏngje kŏnsŏl]*, ed. by DPRK Academy of Sciences, Economics and Legal Research Institute (Pyongyang: Academy of Sciences Publishing House, 1958), p. 101.

Table 2.3 *Announced results of the Three-Year Plan*

Item	Unit	1956 production level	1956 levels as a proportion of 1949 (%)	1956 levels as a proportion of 1953 (%)
Electricity	Billion kWh	5.1	86	500
Coal	Million tonnes	3.9	98	550
Pig iron	1,000 tonnes	187.2	113	–
Electric motors	1,000	8.8	1,320	–
Lathes	1	507	–	–
Farming machinery and implements	Million won	378	1,640	1,110
Pumps	1,000	5.8	1,370	1,600
Chemical fertilizer	1,000 tonnes	195	49	–
Ammonium sulfate	1,000 tonnes	139	43	–
Caustic soda	1,000 tonnes	6.1	66	2,010
Carbide	1,000 tonnes	99	72	1,610
Cement	1,000 tonnes	597	111	2,250
Bricks	Millions	694.2	1,570	4,020
Roofing tiles	Millions	58.9	710	–
Plate glass	Thousand square metres	1,960	–	–
Hardwood	Million square metres	2.6	160	250
Timber	Million square metres	1.1	199	370
Cotton fabric	Million metres	73.6	780	350
Silk fabrics	Million metres	3.4	106	400
Socks	Million pairs	10.1	152	210
Shoes	Million pairs	17.5	–	250
Fish products	1,000 tonnes	365	133	300

Source: Rodong Sinmun, 24 February 1957, 'DPRK State Planning Commission Report on the Results of the 1954–1956 DPRK People's Economic Reconstruction and Development Three-Year Plan [1954–1956 nyŏn Chosŏnminjujuŭiinmin'gonghwaguk inmin'gyŏngjebokkubalchŏn 3 kaenyŏn kyehoek shirhaengch'onghwae kwanhan Chosŏnminjujuŭiinmin'gonghwaguk kukkagyehoegwiwŏnhoe chungangt'onggyegugŭi podo]'.

with consumer goods is extremely insufficient, which delays the development of trade turnover and measures to improve the population's standard of living'.[30]

---

[30] 'Memo from K. Koval to the CPSU CC, "Concerning the main issues of the economic situation of the DPRK"' April, 1956, History and Public Policy Program Digital Archive, RGANI Fond 5, Opis 28, Delo 412. Translated by Gary Goldberg. http://digitalarchive.wilsoncenter.org/document/120799 [accessed 19 May 2020].

The unbalanced pattern of North Korea's post-war reconstruction was even more visible in the agricultural sector.[31] As a result of the war, grain production fell from 2.65 million tonnes in 1949 to 2.23 million tonnes in 1954.[32] This had a negative impact upon the food distribution system, and in the mid-1950s, there were reports of starvation amongst poorer farmers. During the Three-Year Plan, agricultural investment was increased from the originally planned 5.6 billion won to 7.4 billion won.[33] The authorities reported that as a result of wage increases and a reduction in the state-designated prices of consumer goods, workers' purchasing power had increased and livelihoods had improved.[34] However, overall investment in agriculture remained inadequate and amounted to only a small fraction of that invested in heavy industry. In 1955, ongoing shortages in food and basic necessities led to inflation and a decline in real purchasing power, which in turn led to increased discontent amongst urban workers.[35] The government thereby increased its compulsory purchases of grain, which further antagonised farmers and worsened food shortages in the countryside. Errors in the execution of its planning in the agricultural sector were even admitted by the authorities.[36] As we shall see, these difficulties contributed to opposition to Kim Il Sung's post-war reconstruction policies.[37]

Between 1 June and 19 July 1956, just as the Three-Year Plan was coming to an end, Kim Il Sung embarked upon a long trip to the USSR, Mongolia and to seven countries in Eastern Europe to secure further aid for the subsequent Five-Year Plan. With its main task as the 'further strengthening of the economic foundation of socialism and the fundamental resolution of the people's problems of food, clothing and shelter', the Five-Year Plan's aims included a continued focus on the development of heavy industry, with the goal of a 2.6-fold increase in industrial output and an increase in grain production to the level of 3.76 million tonnes by 1961.[38] The amount of aid promised by North Korea's socialist allies was lower than before, however, as Kim Il Sung stated

---

[31] Baek Jun-Kee, 'North Korea's Political Changes and Power Realignment in the 1950s Following the Korean War Armistice [Chŏngjŏn hu 1950 nyŏndae Pukhanŭi chŏngch'i pyŏn-donggwa kwŏllyŏk chaep'yŏn]', *Review of North Korean Studies*, 2.2 (1999), pp. 22–23.

[32] KCNA, *Korean Central Almanac 1958 [Chosŏnjungangyŏn'gam 1958]* (Pyongyang: KCNA, 1958), p. 196.

[33] An Kwang Jup, 'Development of Finance in Korea', p. 297.

[34] For example, *Rodong Sinmun*, 17 December 1954, 'People's purchasing power grows day by day [Inmindŭrŭi kumaeryŏkŭn nallo sŏngjang]'; *Rodong Sinmun*, 28 December 1954, 'Constant promotion of people's welfare [Inmin pongniŭi pudanhan chŭngjin]'.

[35] Baek Jun-Kee, 'North Korea's Political Changes', pp. 22–24.

[36] *Rodong Sinmun*, 10 December 1955, 'The accurate formulation of the 1956 agricultural plan [1956 nyŏndo nongsan'gyehoegŭi chŏnghwakhan surip]'.

[37] Baek Jun-Kee, 'North Korea's Political Changes', p. 18.

[38] KWP, *Reports and Decisions on the DPRK People's Economy First Five Year Plan (1957–1961) [Chosŏn Minjujuŭi Inmin'gonghwaguk inmin'gyŏngjebalchŏn che 1 ch'a 5*

in his speech to the August plenary of the KWP Central Committee following his return, '... the new aid will rapidly help the recovery of our people's economy, and will play an important role in improving the people's livelihood .... Once again, we deeply thank fraternal governments and peoples for the love and support that they have expressed, via our delegation, to our people, and for their new and enormous material assistance'.[39]

However, the majority of heavy industrial-aid projects discussed in Kim's 1953 report to the Sixth Session of the Supreme People's Assembly was not explicitly mentioned in this speech. Reference was made more generally to Soviet aid in terms of steel, textiles, cotton, rice, oil, cables, cars, tractors and wood, as well as technical assistance in the fields of agriculture, fisheries and science and technology. The only reference to a specific industrial project was that of the restoration of Hungnam Fertiliser Factory. As we will see, the emergence of the new policy line in the Soviet Union following Nikita Khrushchev's rise to power had led to opposition in Moscow to Kim Il Sung's heavy industry–first strategy and thereby contributed to tensions with Pyongyang. There was, as a result, a decline in the overall amount of aid, particularly with regards to heavy-industrial projects. The East European countries also shifted their support from heavy industry towards basic necessities, though there was continued support for reconstruction projects that had been part of the Three-Year Plan.

Nonetheless, it can be seen that aid from North Korea's socialist allies played a central role in facilitating reconstruction and development in the 1950s. According to Avram Agov's calculations, total economic aid, loans and military aid from North Korea's socialist allies amounted to over five billion roubles (see Table 2.4). On a per capita basis, socialist aid to North Korea actually exceeded that of US aid to South Korea. Furthermore, while much US aid consisted of consumer products, fraternal aid to North Korea was focused on reconstructed and newly built factories, thereby having a more direct economic impact on North Korean industrialisation. The lower cost of imports from the Socialist Bloc also meant that aid could deliver more goods and equipment.[40] Thus, despite the cost of withdrawing from the capitalist world economy, North Korea in this crucial period of recovery benefitted from the struggle between the two antagonistic blocs. In contrast to theories of 'socialist dependency', economic relations between North Korea and its allies

kaenyŏn (1957–1961) kyehoege kwanhan pogo mit kyŏlchŏngsŏ] (Pyongyang: Korean Workers' Party Publishing House, 1958), pp. 68–78.

[39] Kim Il Sung, On the Summary of the Work of the Government Delegation Visiting Fraternal States and Some of the Challenges Facing Our Party [Hyŏngjejŏk che kukkarŭl pangmunhan chŏngbu taep'yodanŭi saŏp ch'onghwawa uri tangŭi tangmyŏnhan myŏtkaji kwaŏptŭre kwanhayŏ] (Pyongyang: Korean Workers Party, 1956), p. 7.

[40] Ibid., p. 221.

Table 2.4 *Socialist aid to North Korea, 1954–1961*

(Unit: million roubles)

Country, region	Economic aid	Loans	Military aid	Total
USSR	1,160	140	500	1,800
China	1,808	N/A	N/A	1,808
Eastern Europe	1,042	351.5	16	1,410
East Germany	372	N/A	N/A	372
Poland	335	N/A	16	351
Czechoslovakia	113	344	N/A	457
Romania	90	N/A	N/A	90
Bulgaria	76.4	N/A	N/A	76.4
Hungary	52.5	7.5	N/A	60
Albania	2.46	N/A	N/A	2.46
Mongolia	1.76	N/A	N/A	1.76
Vietnam	0.44	N/A	N/A	0.44
Total	4,012.2	491.5	516	5,091.7

Source: Avram Asenov Agov, 'North Korea in the Socialist World: Integration and Divergence, 1945–1970. The Crossroads of Politics and Economics'. (PhD Thesis: University of British Columbia, 2010), p. 219.

at this time diverged from the typical model of capitalist dependent development. Relations were (geo)politically constituted rather than characterised by relations of economic exploitation. However, declining levels of aid in the late 1950s and 1960s would force the North Korean leadership to rely increasingly on domestic resources to achieve its developmental goals.

2.2   Collectivisation and Nationalisation

Following the Korean War, the North Korean political economy increasingly came to resemble the Soviet model, with the socialisation of the means of production becoming a key policy objective. The 'democratic reforms' of the late 1940s had led to an economy characterised by a mix of private and public ownership. Although state intervention in the economy increased markedly as a result of the nationalisation of Japanese-owned property, the private sector continued to play a dominant role in the early post-liberation era. During the Korean War, however, private economic activities began to see a decline, although, in 1953, state-ownership still accounted for only 45.1 per cent of total economic output and cooperative ownership for just 5.4 per cent.[41] In line with the aims of the land-to-the-tiller reform, the private ownership of land

[41] DPRK Central Bureau of Statistics, *Statistics on the Development*, p. 23.

remained widespread, accounting for 91.5 per cent of gross agricultural output.[42] However, the North Korean authorities believed that this dual economic structure served to hinder economic planning. As such, the year 1954 saw the launch of a policy of agricultural collectivisation, or 'cooperativisation' (*hyŏptonghwa*) in North Korean terminology. This policy was seen as instrumental to efforts to increase agricultural production through the strengthening of direct administrative control. As Kim Sung Jun of the Faculty of Economics at Kim Il Sung University argued:

Cooperativisation will make it possible for agriculture to develop rapidly in line with industry and enable it to develop in a planned way. While large-scale industry on a national scale has been developing on the basis of the state plan, the management of petty agriculture remains isolated and decentralised, and influenced by autonomous market forces ... Under these conditions, agriculture cannot develop rapidly and serves as a barrier to industrial development. Therefore, from the perspective of the unified planned development of industry and agriculture, it is necessary to shift from small-scale agricultural management to large scale cooperative management based on social ownership of the means of production ... and to eradicate capitalist exploitative elements in the villages.[43]

However, the collectivisation of agriculture was also an attempt at quickening the pace of agricultural development without increasing investment or redirecting resources away from heavy industry.[44] Furthermore, it was a response to North Korea's acute labour shortages resulting from massive wartime casualties and exodus to the South. According to official statistics, the population had fallen from 9.6 million at the end of 1949 to 8.5 million in December 1953.[45] The population deficit was particularly acute amongst young males, thereby contributing to labour shortages in both agriculture and industry. Collectivisation was thus considered by the authorities as a means of freeing up labour reserves and utilising land more efficiently. However, this policy of collectivisation ran counter to the state's post-liberation policy of granting ownership rights of land to individual farmers and allowing farmers to sell their surplus in local markets.

Agricultural collectivisation progressed rapidly and extensively in the mid-1950s. Three types of cooperatives were established: namely labour, land and socialist cooperatives, thereby roughly mirroring the mutual aid, producer and collective cooperatives found in China. However, rather than the staged approach pursued in the latter, North Korean collectivisation was distinctive

[42] DPRK Academy of Sciences, *Development of the People's Economy*, p. 108.
[43] Kim Sung Jun, 'Development of Agricultural Management in Korea', pp. 169–70.
[44] Masao Okonogi, 'North Korean Communism: In Search of Its Prototype', in *Korean Studies: New Pacific Currents*, ed. by Dae-Sook Suh (Honolulu: University of Hawai'i, 1994), p. 185.
[45] DPRK Central Bureau of Statistics, *Statistics on the Development*, p. 18.

Table 2.5 *Agricultural collectivisation in North Korea*

Year	Number of agricultural cooperatives	Households included in agricultural cooperatives		Arable land included in agricultural cooperatives	
		Number of households	% Share in total households	Land area (*Chŏngbo*)	Percentage of total land
1953	806	11,879	1.2	11,000	0.6
1954	10,098	332,662	31.8	576,000	30.9
1955	12,132	511,323	49.0	885,000	48.6
1956	15,825	864,837	80.9	1,397,000	77.9
1957	16,032	1,025,106	95.6	1,684,000	93.7
1958	3,843	1,055,015	100.0	1,791,000	100.0

Note: 1953–57 figures based on December; 1958 figures based on November.
Source: DPRK Central Bureau of Statistics, *Statistics on the Development of the DPRK's People's Economy 1946–1960*, p. 61.

in that a majority of the cooperatives (74 per cent) were socialist from the outset.[46] The proportion of arable land under the control of cooperatives grew rapidly from 0.6 per cent in 1953 to 48.6 per cent in 1955, and then to 93.7 per cent in 1957 (see Table 2.5). By August 1958, all farms had been collectivised. At the same time, the share of private farms in gross agricultural output decreased dramatically from around 92 per cent in 1953 to 11.8 per cent in 1957, with private farming completely eliminated the following year.[47]

The collectivisation of agriculture also led to a sharp decline in the role of market traders and handicraft manufacturers of daily necessities. Such activities had taken place mostly based on the family unit, with the number of workers in each unit generally not exceeding three or four. From 1954, however, the authorities began to regulate against such activities and adopted measures to absorb handicraft workers into production cooperatives. The buying and selling of surplus grain in marketplaces were also prohibited, with trade in food products and the operation of restaurants only allowed to take place via the state's official mechanisms.[48] Thus, along with private farming, petty commerce and handicraft production had also entirely disappeared from the North Korean economy by 1958.

---

[46] Glenn D. Paige, 'North Korea and the Emulation of Russian and Chinese Behavior', in *Communist Strategies in Asia: A Comparative Analysis of Governments and Parties*, ed. by Arthur Doak Barnett (New York: Praeger, 1963), p. 240.
[47] KCNA, *Korean Central Almanac 1958*, p. 177.
[48] DPRK Academy of Sciences, *Development of the People's Economy*, p. 151.

2.3   Development Strategy and North Korean Politics

North Korean development policy was by no means determined in any mechanistic sense by the legacies of colonialism or by the country's external geopolitical environment. These influences were rather mediated through domestic political struggles. As noted in the previous chapter, North Korean politics, in the late 1940s, was characterised by a relative degree of plurality, involving both competition and cooperation between several political factions. While Kim Il Sung's position was paramount, there was effectively a collective leadership system based upon Kim Il Sung's Manchurian guerrillas, the Soviet Koreans, the Yan'an Koreans and the domestic Koreans.[49] By the end of the Korean War, however, Kim Il Sung had successfully removed several of his key competitors.

After the purge of General Mu Chong, a leader of the Yan'an faction, during the early stages of the war, Kim Il Sung in late 1951 moved against Ho Ka-i, the leader of the Soviet faction. Ho Ka-i had come to Korea in 1945 and, on the basis of his past experience in the communist party apparatus in Tashkent, played an important role in the establishment of the North Korean Workers' Party.[50] In September 1948, he became the Party's First Secretary, which led to an emerging division of power. Ho Ka-i and other Soviet faction figures dominated the central positions in the KWP and controlled its internal affairs. Kim Il Sung, on the other hand, held the party's highest formal position as General Secretary of the Central Committee, though his real power lay in his position as State Premier, which gave him control over the government and military affairs.[51] Following the start of the armistice negotiations in the summer of 1951, Kim Il Sung turned his attention to improving the organisational strength of the party, which led to growing tensions with Ho Ka-i on issues of party organisation.[52] As a result, the following November Ho Ka-i was demoted, and at the Sixth Joint Plenum of the KWP Central Committee on 4 August 1953, it was reported that he had committed suicide.[53] The Soviet faction was thus weakened, though it survived until the mid-1950s.

A more decisive move was made against the domestic faction centred around the South Korean Workers' Party, and its leader, Pak Hon Yong. As noted in the previous chapter, although there were tensions between Kim Il Sung and Pak over the structure of the communist party and its leadership

[49] Paik Haksoon, *History of Power in North Korea,* pp. 36–39.
[50] Kim Kook-Hoo, *Pyongyang's Soviet Korean Elites [P'yŏngyangŭi k'areisŭk'i ellit'ŭrŭl]* (Seoul: Hanul Books, 2013), p. 162.
[51] Paik Haksoon, *History of Power in North Korea,* pp. 73–76.
[52] Kim Sung-bo, *North Korean History 1,* p. 15.   [53] Dae-Sook Suh, *Kim Il Sung,* p.126.

during the immediate post-liberation period, Pak moved to the North in late 1946 and took the position of Vice Premier and Minister of Foreign Affairs from September 1948. However, North Korea's failed war of reunification was used by Kim to dispose of Pak. In the late 1950s, as the North Korean army retreated in the face of the US/UN intervention, Kim Il Sung was left vulnerable to accusations that he was responsible for this failure and thus sought to redirect blame towards Pak for his erroneous prediction that large-scale mass uprisings led by his southern supporters would take place. Towards the end of the war, Pak and twelve key figures of the domestic faction were accused by Kim of plotting a coup d'état and spying for the United States.[54] He was imprisoned in late 1953 and reportedly executed in 1956. As a result, the domestic faction was completely eliminated, and thousands of its members who had fled from the South were expelled from the party.

The Korean War, therefore, left Kim Il Sung and his Manchurian guerrilla faction in a strengthened position. However, most figures associated with the Soviet and Yan'an factions remained in their positions for the time being. As Paik Haksoon has argued, given the fact that the USSR and China still had considerable influence in the country and were a key source of military and economic aid, it was difficult for Kim at this time to eliminate the Soviet and Yan'an factions entirely. Kim Il Sung continued to cooperate with them and distributed key positions in the party, cabinet and the regional organisations to Soviet and Yan'an figures. Soviet Korean Pak Chang Ok was, for example, appointed in March 1954 as Vice Premier and President of the State Planning Commission.[55] At the same time, however, Kim also appointed his own allies to key positions, thereby strengthening his own political power. The Korean War also strengthened Kim Il Sung's growing personality cult. In 1952, on his 40th birthday, Kim's official biography was published along with the first volume of his collected works. Furthermore, in February 1953, on the fifth anniversary of the founding of the Korean People's Army, Kim was awarded the title of 'Marshal'. As such, North Korean political culture increasingly came to resemble that of Stalinist Russia.[56] Indeed, it was at this time that the phrase 'respected great leader' (kyŏngaehanŭn suryŏng) made its formal appearance in government documents and state laws.[57]

---

[54] Lee Jong-Seok, *A New Approach to Understanding Contemporary North Korea [Saero ssŭn hyŏndae Pukhanŭi ihae]* (Seoul: Critical Review of History, 2000), pp. 417–18.

[55] Paik Haksoon, *History of Power in North Korea*, pp. 312–15.

[56] Suh Dong-Man, 'North Korea's Political Struggles and Ideology Situation in the 1950s [1950 nyŏndae Pukhanŭi chŏngch'igaldŭnggwa idaeollogi sanghwan]', in *North and South Korea's Choice and Refraction [1950 nyŏndae nambukhanŭi sŏnt'aeggwa kuljŏl]*, ed. by The Institute of Korean Historical Studies (Seoul: Critical Review of History, 1998), pp. 324–26.

[57] For example, in April 1954, the Three Year Plan for the Recovery of the DPRK People's Economy, 1954–1956 passed in the Supreme People's Assembly included the term 'Under the leadership of our respected leader Marshall Kim Il Sung'.

Although the war had seen the elimination of the domestic faction alongside the weakening of the Soviet and Yan'an factions, factional political infighting intensified in the mid-1950s. As James Person has argued, this was not solely a result of personalistic animosities or the unprincipled pursuit of political power but increasingly related to substantive issues such as nationalism versus internationalism, the industrial economy versus the consumer economy and individual versus collective leadership.[58] As noted, these debates came to the fore as a result of the profound political changes taking place in the Soviet Union following Stalin's death in March 1953. Indeed, in the socialist camp, there was a move away from autarkic national planning towards an increased emphasis on the idea of international economic integration and national specialisation within a 'rational' socialist international division of labour.[59] Furthermore, in his famous 'secret speech' in February 1956 at the 20th Congress of the Communist Party of the Soviet Union (CPSU), Nikita Khrushchev denounced Stalin's excesses, including the widespread use of terror during the Great Purges of the 1930s; the failure to adequately prepare for the Nazi invasion of 1941; the mismanagement of the war effort; the deportation of entire nationality groups during the war (including ethnic Koreans who were forcibly removed from the Russian Far East to the Central Asian republics); the purging of political leaders in Leningrad and Georgia; Stalin's policy towards Yugoslavia which had led to the latter's severance of its relations with the Soviet Union; and, with particular implications for Kim Il Sung, the excessive cult of personality surrounding Stalin. The Khrushchev era thus led to a considerable degree of liberalisation in the Soviet Bloc, which included the dismantling of the cult of personality and the reform of the Stalinist political system.

These trends served to bolster opposition to Kim Il Sung's politics within North Korea. The Soviet and Yan'an factions supported the principle of collective leadership while openly attacking Kim Il Sung's cult of personality.[60] They engaged Kim Il Sung and his allies in a debate on economic policy, arguing for a shift away from heavy industrialisation towards an emphasis on the production of consumer goods.[61] Kim's critics also argued that the rapid collectivisation of agriculture was premature given the country's still relatively low level of industrialisation and shortage of modern agricultural machinery.[62] They pushed for North Korea's greater integration into the socialist division of

---

[58] James F. Person, 'North Korea in 1956: Reconsidering the August Plenum and the Sino–Soviet Joint Intervention', *Cold War History*, 19.2 (2019), p. 255.

[59] Gordon White, 'North Korean Chuch'e', p. 47.

[60] Lee Jong-Seok, *New Approach*, pp. 74–77.

[61] Young Chul Chung, 'The Suryŏng System as the Institution of Collectivist Development', *Journal of Korean Studies*, 12.1 (2007), p. 52.

[62] Paik Haksoon, *History of Power in North Korea*, pp. 255–58.

labour through immediate membership of Comecon, which would ostensibly involve the export of natural resources and import of consumer goods. The rationale was that this would bring about more immediate improvements in living standards as well as stability and security for the war-torn economy within the larger socialist community.

As Kim Il Sung later reflected in his speech in January 1958 at the Ministry of Light Industry Diligent Workers Meeting, at the root of such debates was the question of whether to prioritise the immediate improvement of people's livelihood over the longer-term building of an autonomous industrial base:

> 'There were some people who had doubts about the correctness of the Party's economic policies ... If we had brought in consumer goods such as daily necessities or cloth and rice as aid from our allies, as these anti-Party factions had argued, then at that time we could have lived well. But if we had done that, the days ahead would have been dark, and every year we would have to obtain cloth and rice from a different country... Therefore, the Party defeated the defamation and plotting of these anti-Party elements and put heavy industry at the centre while pursuing the simultaneous development of light industry and agriculture'.[63]

Kim is referring here to the so-called 'August Incident,' whereby at the Joint Plenum of the KWP's Central Committee on 30 August 1956, Kim was attacked by key figures of the Soviet and Yan'an factions. After reporting on his long overseas trip earlier that summer, Kim claimed that the only personality cult in North Korea was the one that his factional opponents were building around themselves.[64] According to Kim, the KWP had been trying to correct the practice of the personality cult for several years and had learned from the CPSU's experience of dealing with Stalin's personality cult through educating party members and the masses. However, a group of Soviet Koreans such as Pak Chang Ok and members associated with the Yan'an group such as Choi Chang Ik criticised Kim for his own personality cult as well as for concentrating on heavy industry while neglecting light industry and the provision of food, clothing and shelter.[65] Kim Il Sung had, however, received prior notification of the Soviet and Yan'an factions' impending attack and had carefully planned his response. Kim and his supporters thus proceeded to label the Soviet and Yan'an figures as part of an 'anti-Party factional conspiracy' and were successful in expelling them from the party.[66]

---

[63] KCNA, *Korean Central Almanac 1959*, p. 3.

[64] Kim Il Sung, *On the Summary of the Work of the Government Delegation Visiting Fraternal States and Some of the Challenges Facing Our Party*, pp. 42–44.

[65] Adrian Buzo, *The Guerilla Dynasty: Politics and Leadership in North Korea* (London: I B Tauris, 1999), p. 25.

[66] Baek Jun-Kee, 'North Korea's Political Changes', pp. 41–46.

While Kim Il Sung succeeded in purging the leaders of the Yan'an and Soviet factions, their international connections meant that their purge could not fail to attract the attention of Moscow and Beijing. In September 1956, the two countries sent a joint delegation to Pyongyang consisting of Soviet First Deputy Anastas Mikoyan and Chinese Minister of Defence Marshal Peng Dehuai to request that Kim reinstate those who had been purged and release other individuals from prison. Demonstrating the continued influence of the country's foreign allies, the leaders of the two factions were thereby officially pardoned and rehabilitated at the second plenum of the KWP Central Committee on 23 September. However, not long after the joint delegation's departure, Kim Il Sung again took measures to eliminate his factional adversaries. The leader of the Soviet faction, Pak Chang Ok, was eventually executed and the majority of Soviet Koreans were removed from their party and governmental posts, leading many of them to return to the Soviet Union. The campaign also removed the Yan'an faction's Kim Tu Bong from his position of Chairman of the Presidium of the Supreme People's Assembly. The purge was not limited to factional leaders but quickly expanded to the whole of North Korean society. Along with enhanced ideological education and surveillance, more than 30,000 were arrested and imprisoned between 1957 and 1959, including low-ranking cadres in regional organs and social organisations. So-called 'reactionary elements' deemed lacking in loyalty to Kim Il Sung's leadership were targeted, many of whom had no prior involvement in the factional disputes.[67]

Despite the resumption of the purges, Moscow and Beijing failed to make the kind of decisive intervention they had made in September 1956. This failure was in part a result of the shifting international climate resulting from the popular protest in Poland and in Hungary and the fear in Moscow that these democratic experiments were getting out of control.[68] The Soviet Union also experienced a domestic political crisis in 1957. While Khrushchev's anti-Stalinist line was challenged, he successfully consolidated his power by defeating Georgy Malenkov and other key rivals within the collective leadership.[69] In China too, tentative liberalisation in the form of the Hundred Flowers movement was quickly followed by the repressive Anti-Rightist Campaign, which involved the persecution of those who had too enthusiastically supported reformist ideals.[70] In any case, it can be argued that despite their misgivings, Kim Il Sung's critics ultimately supported him at the helm of North Korea. Both Moscow and Beijing were aware that no one in the North

---

[67] Baek Jun-Kee, 'North Korea's Political Changes', pp. 52–60.
[68] Andrei N. Lankov, 'Kim Takes Control: The "Great Purge" in North Korea, 1956-1960', *Korean Studies*, 26.1 (2002), pp. 101–2.
[69] Ibid., p. 102.　　[70] Ibid., pp. 102–3.

Korean leadership elicited the widespread popular support enjoyed by Kim, and thus disposing of him was not an option.[71] Furthermore, Khrushchev may have considered figures such as Pak Chang Ok as simply too moderate. As Erik van Ree has argued, 'At a time when the communist bloc was in danger of falling apart owing to weakened discipline it would have been wise to support an orthodox leader such as Kim Il Sung'.[72]

The ultimate outcome of the August Incident was, therefore, the firm establishment of Kim Il Sung's unchallenged autocratic rule in North Korea. This signified a clear shift from the immediate post-liberation era when identification with either the Soviet Union or China constituted the key to holding political influence in North Korea to a situation in which those same connections became a political liability.[73] Needless to say, the interventions of the Soviet Union and China in 1956 were not appreciated by Kim Il Sung. As we shall see in the next chapter, in the midst of worsening relations with these socialist allies in the 1960s respectively, Pyongyang labelled the USSR and China as 'great power chauvinists' for having interfered in North Korean internal politics in 1956. Furthermore, this outside interference provided further justification for Kim to strengthen his grip on power and gave him greater leeway to pursue national autonomy through the building of a self-sufficient economy based on heavy industry. These events also shaped the emergence of *Juche* ideology, which would henceforth be established as the guiding ethos of North Korea's catch-up development project.

2.4   Mass Mobilisation and Catch-Up Industrialisation

Increasingly tense relations between North Korea and its socialist allies contributed towards declining levels of external aid available to support its Five-Year Plan (1957-61). The proportion of aid in the state budget fell from 21.7 per cent in 1955 to 12.2 per cent in 1957, and to 4.5 per cent in 1958.[74] Indeed, North Korean documents make frequent mention of the economic difficulties caused by this decline. As a result, the authorities placed greater emphasis on the mobilisation of labour as a means of stimulating production. Following liberation, mass mobilisation had already become a feature of economic life in North Korea, and took such forms as the Production Increase Shock Movement and the Production Increase and Competition Movement, and the Collective Innovation Movement.[75] In 1958, a new

[71] Person, 'North Korea in 1956', p. 273.   [72] van Ree, 'Limits of Juche', p. 54.

[73] Glenn D. Paige and Dong Jun Lee, 'The Post-War Politics of Communist Korea', *The China Quarterly*, 14, June (1963), p. 23.

[74] DPRK Academy of Sciences, *Development of the People's Economy*, p. 182.

[75] Suh Dong-Man, *History of Socialist System Formation*, p. 604.

campaign known as the *Chŏllima* movement was launched, named after a mythical horse that could run 1,000 *li* in a day.[76] As Kim Il Sung asserted at the 3rd Session of the Second Supreme People's Assembly in June 1958, 'At the call of the party, all workers are riding the *Chŏllima* towards socialism. In the cities and villages, in the factories and mines, and in the fisheries and forests, the workers' revolutionary momentum and enthusiasm are reaching extraordinary heights. This is a revolutionary tide that has not been seen in our country's history before'.[77]

Work teams began to be formed in Kangson Steel Mill in March 1959, and the movement developed rapidly thereafter.[78] In 1960 alone, 19,721 work teams were established, with 356,627 workers taking part in the movement. Workers were encouraged to surpass their assigned quotas and devise more efficient working methods. Teams of workers who succeeded in doing so were labelled as '*Chŏllima* work teams'.[79] The movement was not confined to industry, but permeated every facet of life, including agriculture, transportation, commerce, education and culture. For example, in the field of education, it was reported that by March 1961, a total of 3,200 classes consisting of 147,000 students had taken part, with a total of 163 classes awarded the title of '*Chŏllima* class'.[80] As can be seen from slogans such as 'let's live and work in accordance with communism', the *Chŏllima* work team movement was based on the goal of transforming all workers into 'new communists' through the practice of collectivism in the workplace and daily life. In doing so, the aim was to enhance workers' consciousness of the need for self-sacrifice for the sake of collective interests.[81] At the KWP's Fourth Party Congress in September 1961, the *Chŏllima* movement was defined as the overall party line. As the Albanian delegation to the Congress reported, 'The enthusiasm and the optimism were very visible, especially amongst the people, in all the meetings and conversations we had with them. They were embodied in the

---

[76] While North Korean sources date the origins of the *Chŏllima* movement to a speech made by Kim Il Sung to the leaders of Kangson Steel Mill on 28 December 1956, the majority of Western scholars have dated the movement from 1958. See Peter Graham Moody, 'Chollima, the Thousand Li Flying Horse: Neo-Traditionalism at Work in North Korea', *Sungkyun Journal of East Asian Studies*, 13.2 (2013), p. 215.

[77] *Rodong Sinmun*, 13 June 1958, 'A great doctrine – ride the Chollima for the successful carrying out of the First Five Year Plan! – a great milestone for the building of socialism [Widaehan kangnyŏng – che 1 ch'a 5 kaenyŏn kyehoegŭi sŏnggwajŏk suhaengŭl wihayŏ ch'ŏllimaro tallija! sahoejuŭi kŏnsŏrŭi widaehan rijŏngp'yo]'.

[78] *Rodong Sinmun*, 10 March 1959, 'Resolution on the launch of the Chŏllima Work Team Movement, a new form of socialist competition [Saeroun sahoejuŭijŏk kyŏngjaeng hyŏngt'aein ch'ŏllima chagŏppan undongŭl palgi kyŏruimun]'.

[79] Dae-Sook Suh, *Kim Il Sung*, p. 164.

[80] KCNA, *Korean Central Almanac 1961 [Chosŏnjungangnyŏn'gam 1961]* (Pyongyang: KCNA, 1961), pp. 197–99.

[81] Youn-Soo Kim, 'Economy of the KDPR', p. 51.

great and massive movement, the [*Chŏllima*] ... which had developed into a great popular push for bigger steps ahead'.[82]

With parallels to the language used in China, the North Korean government referred to this period as the 'great tide of socialism' (*sahoejuŭi kŏnsorŭi taegojo*). Indeed, the *Chŏllima* movement bore more than a passing resemblance to China's Great Leap Forward campaign in its aim of accelerating economic growth through the intensive mobilisation of labour.[83] Parallels between the two countries could also be seen in the reorganisation in the late 1950s of North Korea's agricultural cooperative farms and China's merger of cooperatives into communes at the *xiang* level.[84] As indicated in Table 2.5, October 1958 saw the combination of approximately 13,000 North Korean collective farms into 3,843 larger farms. This meant that their boundaries were made coterminous with the lowest rural administrative unit, the *ri* (village). Given that there were 3,745 *ri* in 1957, nearly all cooperative farms were involved in this restructuring process. By 1958, about 60 per cent of collective farms consisted of between 201 and 1,000 households.[85] The chairman of the People's Committee at the *ri* level thus became the chairman of the *ri* agricultural cooperative, and as in China, agricultural cooperatives came to play a role not only in food production but also in the provision of healthcare, education and cultural life in rural areas. These developments thereby represented a shift from the faithful implementation of the Soviet model towards a degree of borrowing from the Chinese experience. There is little evidence to suggest, however, that this was due to any direct political pressure from Beijing. The Yan'an faction had already been eliminated from North Korean politics and Chinese troops had left the country by 1958. Rather, this borrowing reflected the leadership's pragmatic view that Chinese innovations provided solutions to contemporary North Korean developmental challenges.[86]

As with China, North Korea saw the mass mobilisation of labour as a means of skipping developmental stages and facilitating a process of state-led catch-up industrialisation. Kim Il Sung visited China in late November and early December 1958, where he observed first-hand the Great Leap Forward and the agricultural communes. When he returned, he spoke of the 'great successes' that the Chinese were achieving in socialist construction and repeated Mao's

[82] 'Report on the Work of the Delegation of the ALP to the 4th Congress of the Korean Workers' Party', September 07, 1961, History and Public Policy Program Digital Archive, AQPPSH, MPP Korese, V. 1961, D4. Obtained by Ana Lalaj and translated by Enkel Daljani. http://digitalarchive.wilsoncenter.org/document/114424 [accessed 19 May 2020].

[83] Chin O. Chung, *Pyongyang between Peking and Moscow: North Korea's Involvement in the Sino-Soviet Dispute, 1958–1975* (University, Alabama: University of Alabama Press, 1978), pp. 32–33.

[84] Paige, 'North Korea and the Emulation', pp. 244–45.

[85] DPRK Central Bureau of Statistics, *Statistics on the Development*, p. 65.

[86] Paige, 'North Korea and the Emulation', pp. 243–44.

claim that China would overtake and outstrip Britain in the production of steel and other major goods within the next few years.[87] In this respect, Kim Il Sung's endorsement of the Chinese model of development implicitly refuted the universal validity of the Soviet model. In response, Khrushchev announced in his report to the 21st Congress of the CPSU in early 1959 that the transition to communism was a natural historic process that could not be bypassed. Development was thus a linear process that would be long and gradual. Only the increased production of material goods could accelerate the transition towards communism. As such, the USSR claimed that both Europe and Asia should follow the 'correct' Soviet road to development.[88]

There were, however, instructive differences between China and North Korea that had important consequences. The disastrous outcome of China's Great Leap Forward was in the first instance the result of a poor harvest caused by droughts and floods. The impact of these natural disasters was exacerbated, however, by the poorly and hastily built irrigation system and the fact that a great deal of rural labour had been diverted into the building of 'backyard furnaces', which proved to be a resounding failure.[89] North Korea, on the other hand, had opted for a more centralised steel industry that was more appropriate to the size of the country. Furthermore, by the late 1950s, industry already played a more important role in the North Korean economy and was therefore to some extent able to export industrial products to pay for the import of food and thereby ward off potential famine.[90] In any case, in 1960, following a further attack by Khrushchev on the concept of agricultural communes, the North Korean government slowed down its collectivisation programme. On the one hand, Pyongyang did not wish to overtly offend the USSR but also recognised the problems of the Chinese-style approach and the ensuing economic chaos there. North Korea thus had not abandoned the idea of the USSR as leader of the world socialist camp, and its emulation of Chinese policies during this period can be viewed simply as a pragmatic consideration of whether they would be effective or not.[91]

To what extent then did North Korea's post-war development policies 'work'? Overall, despite significant challenges, the performance of the North Korean economy between 1953 and 1960 by most measures was impressive. The country recovered to pre-war economic levels through the Three-Year Plan and continued its rapid industrialisation during the subsequent Five-Year Plan. The latter's targets were reportedly achieved two and half years early, in

[87] Chin O. Chung, *Pyongyang between Peking and Moscow*, p. 33.   [88] Ibid., p. 34.
[89] Zhihong Zhang, 'Rural Industrialization in China: From Backyard Furnaces to Township and Village Enterprise', *East Asia: An International Quarterly*, 17.3 (1999), p. 64.
[90] Joungwon Alexander Kim, 'The "Peak of Socialism" in North Korea: The Five and Seven Year Plans', *Asian Survey*, 5.5 (1965), pp. 260–61.
[91] Chin O. Chung, *Pyongyang between Peking and Moscow*, pp. 35–37.

Table 2.6 *Industrial production as a percentage of national income*

	1950 (%)	1966 (%)
Bulgaria	37	45
Czechoslovakia	63	66
East Germany	56	64
Hungary	48	57
Poland	47	52
Romania	43	49
USSR	58	51
Yugoslavia	52	46
North Korea[a]	36	62

Note: [a]Figure for 1949 and 1964. Percentage of 'total social output' (*sahoe ch'ongsaengsan*).
Source: Jozef Wilczynski, *The economics of socialism: principles governing the operation of the centrally planned economies in the USSR and Eastern Europe under the New System*. (London: Allen and Unwin, 1972), p. 70; KCNA, *Korean Central Almanac 1965 [Chosŏnjungangnyŏn'gam 1965]* (Pyongyang: KCNA, 1965), p. 477.

June 1959. Thus, after one 'buffer year', the Five-Year Plan was officially brought to a close in late 1960. According to North Korean sources, by the end of the Five-Year Plan in 1960, gross industrial output was 9.9 times that of 1953, thereby seeing an average annual growth rate of 39 per cent.[92] Whereas in 1953, the industrial sector accounted for 30.7 per cent of North Korean total production, this had grown to 40.1 per cent by 1956 and again to 57.1 per cent by 1960. Agriculture declined from 41.6 per cent in 1953 to 23.6 per cent by 1960. Although agricultural growth was slower than that of industry, the period of 1953–60 also saw a 195 per cent increase in agricultural output with an average annual growth rate of around 10 per cent. Grain production reached over 3 million tonnes for the first time in 1957 and saw a further increase to 3.8 million tonnes in 1960. Though its growth was slower compared to other crops, rice yields reached 1.54 million tonnes in 1960, a 25 per cent rise over that of 1953. The country also saw a significant growth in population during this period, with the population in 1960 recorded at 10,789,000, a growth of 2.3 million since the end of the war. As a consequence of post-war industrialisation and migration from rural areas, the urban population reportedly increased from 17.7 per cent of the whole population in December 1953 to

---

[92] The data is drawn from several North Korean sources such as the 1961 report of Central Bureau of Statistics and the yearbooks of the Korean Central News Agency.

Table 2.7 *Urban population in state socialist societies*

	1950 (%)	1960 (%)
Bulgaria	27.5	38.0
Hungary	37.8	41.7
East Germany	70.9	72.0
Poland	36.9	48.3
Romania	25.2	32.4
USSR	40.2	49.9
Czechoslovakia	51.5	57.4
China	-	13.6
North Korea[a]	17.7	40.6

Note: [a]Figure for 1953.
Source: David Lane, *The Rise and Fall of State Socialism*
(London: Polity Press, 1996), p. 157; DPRK Central Bureau of
Statistics, *Statistics on the Development of the DPRK's People's
Economy*, p. 20.

40.6 per cent at the end of 1960 (see Table 2.7). North Korea also made significant gains in education during this period, with the total number of enrolled students in North Korea increasing from 1,176,000 to 2,530,000. Compulsory education was extended to include primary school children in 1956 and to middle school children in 1958.

Though questions might be raised about the reliability of North Korea's official data for the 1950s, it is indisputable that the country saw a high rate of industrialisation and urbanisation. What is particularly striking is how by the mid-1960s, North Korea's industrial production as a share of national income was comparable with the more industrialised countries of Eastern Europe (see Table 2.6). North Korea's industrial growth can also be compared favourably to the majority of Third World countries over the same period and resembles the growth rates seen in Japan in the 1950s and South Korea and Taiwan in the 1970s. However, it should be noted that these gains were influenced by the relative ease of post-war reconstruction compared to 'normal' growth, as well as to the availability of foreign aid and technology during the 1950s.[93] Furthermore, the state's focus on heavy industrialisation at the expense of light industry and agriculture had negative implications for living standards. Indeed, as a proportion of total investment in the industrial sector, investment

[93] Joseph Sang-Hoon Chung, 'Economic Planning', p. 182.

in heavy industry increased from 81 per cent during the period of the Three-Year Plan to 83 per cent during the Five-Year Plan.[94] Furthermore, the collectivisation of agriculture and the elimination of private commerce meant that North Korea's economic model increasingly took the form of a forced accumulation system based upon the repression of public consumption through low incomes and low prices for agricultural products.[95]

2.5   Conclusion

As we have seen, the post-war developmental trajectory of North Korea was strongly shaped by intense geopolitical rivalry, including the experience of the adoption of the Soviet model of centrally planned industrialisation, the provision of generous aid for the reconstruction of the North Korean economy and the ongoing tensions surrounding the divided Korean peninsula. These external influences did not determine North Korean development policy in any mechanistic sense but were mediated through domestic political struggles and the resulting establishment of Kim Il Sung's autocratic rule. As a result, North Korea placed an extraordinarily high premium on rapid catch-up industrialisation centred on the heavy and defence industries. Yet in the late 1950s, when 'fraternal aid' began to decline, North Korea also engaged in the pragmatic emulation of elements of the Chinese model, and in particular, the latter's reliance on mass mobilisation. This would have a long-term impact on North Korean developmental ideology. In the 1972 'Socialist Constitution', explicit mention was made of the *Chŏllima* movement as part of the 'general line in the building of socialism'.[96] Furthermore, at the time of the crisis of the 1990s, the movement was again stressed as a mode of mass mobilisation and collective thought consciousness. As a *Rodong Sinmun* editorial argued in December 1993, 'When we energetically struggle, armed with the spirit and the vigour of the height of the *Chŏllima* era, we can overcome any difficulty. In the forward march of socialism, it becomes possible to achieve miracles and innovation within ceasing'.[97] This strong path dependency is also indicative of the manner in which the purge of forces critical of Kim Il Sung in the latter half of the 1950s meant that debate in the realm of the economic policy largely

---

[94] An Kwang Jup, Development of Finance, p. 297; DPRK Academy of Sciences, *Development of the People's Economy*, p. 164.

[95] Suh Dong-Man, *History of Socialist System Formation*, p. 764; Lee Tae-Sup, *North Korea's Economic Crisis and System Change [Pukhanŭi kyŏngje wigiwa ch'eje pyŏnhwa]* (Seoul: Sunin, 2009), pp. 20–23.

[96] Article 13, 1972 constitution.

[97] *Rodong Sinmun*, 28 December 1993, 'Advance energetically, armed with the spirit and the vigour of the height of the Chollima era [Ch'ŏllima taegojo sidaeŭi kŭ chŏngsin, kŭ kibaekŭro himch'age chŏnjinhaja]'.

disappeared and that North Korea's society and culture became increasingly ossified. While this approach had enabled the country to quickly recover from the destruction of the Korean War and establish a foundation for a modern industrial development, it had negative implications for North Korea's ability to adapt to future geopolitical and economic shifts.

Geopolitics, therefore, played a critical role in shaping the emergence of the North Korean developmental regime. The notion of an existential threat to national survival was without a doubt promoted by the government for the purposes of achieving national unity and maintaining the legitimacy of authoritarian rule. In this respect, North Korea was little different from its southern neighbour. North Korea was also by no means a passive actor within this geopolitical contestation, not least through the decision to launch its failed war of reunification on 25 June 1950. Nonetheless, it is difficult to deny the objective reality of the North's precarious existence. Both the experience of colonial subjugation and the destruction and trauma of the Korean War underpinned a strong drive for self-reliant national development. Central to this was the presence of already-industrialised socialist allies which were able to provide significant levels of developmental assistance. For North Korea, the ability to rely on such external support was, as we have seen, explicitly cited by Kim Il Sung as a key factor enabling the country to pursue a more independent economic policy than would otherwise have been the case. This fact also led Kim Il Sung to believe that North Korea could pursue a heavy industry–first strategy without sacrificing living standards, though, in reality, this strategy would prove to be a failure. As we shall see, these tendencies were further intensified in the 1960s as a result of growing tensions not only between the capitalist and socialist worlds but also within the latter.

3 Geopolitical Contestation and the Challenge to North Korean Development

Following the Korean War, North Korea actively sought to challenge the conditions of economic dependency faced by many postcolonial Third World countries. Kim Il Sung's defeat of his factional adversaries in the mid-1950s meant that he had relatively free rein to pursue a strategy of heavy industrialisation as the basis of autonomous national development. This process was, however, highly dependent on generous assistance from North Korea's socialist allies, and as that assistance began to decline in the late 1950s, there was increased emphasis on the mobilisation of domestic resources such as labour. As we argue in this chapter, the following decade saw further development of the distinctive North Korean political economy. New management methods were introduced for enterprises, factories and cooperative farms, and the country's centralised system of economic planning was expanded. The *Ch'ŏngsan-ri* Method and the *Taean* Work System, for example, were applied to agriculture and industry respectively and served to enhance the KWP's role in economic management. At the same time, the introduction of 'unified and detailed planning' served to centralise economic planning to an unprecedented degree, at a time when much of the socialist world was experimenting with 'market socialism'.

In this chapter, we also examine the ideological underpinnings of North Korean developmentalism in the form of the emergence of *Juche* thought (*chuch'e sasang*). The ascendance of *Juche* thought can be understood as a means of legitimising the mobilisation of society towards the single-minded pursuit of catch-up developmental goals. Although *Juche* thought does have some distinctive features reflecting the specific context from which it arose, we argue that *Juche* thought should be seen as a variant of the strong development nationalisms that typically underpinned late developmental projects in both the state socialist and postcolonial worlds. However, from the late 1960s, *Juche* thought increasingly took the form of ideological justification of the Kim Il Sung regime's monolithic political system and hereditary succession, and as such, its previous emphasis on postcolonial catch-up development was somewhat diluted.

As we shall also see, the North Korean political economy suffered from several difficulties from the 1960s. As many of the state socialist countries discovered, while the Soviet model of central planning was effective during the early stages of extensive catch-up development, it was much less able to facilitate the transition towards qualitative intensive economic growth. In addition, North Korea faced a series of geopolitical challenges that were arguably unparalleled amongst the state socialist countries. The deepening Sino–Soviet conflict raised serious questions regarding the reliability of North Korea's external alliances and served to exaggerate the autarkic tendencies in the country's approach to industrialisation. At the same time, as a divided country, competition with the South lent a particularly militaristic dimension to North Korea's late developmental goals. These pressures drove the authorities to direct even more resources towards the heavy industry with the goal of building a strong domestic defence sector. However, the burden of increased militarisation served to exacerbate economic imbalances and led to the stalling of the catch-up industrialisation project.

3.1   Modifications to Economic Management

With parallels to China, from the late 1950s North Korean discourse surrounding economic management made increasing reference to the notion of the 'mass line'. As Mao Zedong had argued from the wartime base of Yan'an in 1943, '... all correct leadership is necessarily "from the masses, to the masses". This means: take the ideas of the masses (scattered and unsystematic ideas) and concentrate them (through study turn them into concentrated and systematic ideas), then go to the masses and propagate and explain these ideas until the masses embrace them as their own, hold fast to them and translate them into action, and test the correctness of these ideas in such action'.[1] In North Korea, however, the 'mass line' took a more hierarchical form. While the cadre was constantly called upon to go to the masses, it was not so much to learn from the masses but to teach and instruct the masses, the model of which was Kim Il Sung's 'on-the-spot' guidance visits.[2] The mass line was centred around physical labour under the leadership of the party cadres, with a strong emphasis on non-material rewards. The workplace formed the primary locus in which workers participated in this mass line dynamic, but they were also expected to participate as unpaid labour through their mass organisations.[3]

---

[1] Tse-Tung Mao, *Selected Works of Mao Tse-Tung: Volume III* (Peking: Foreign Languages Press, 1965), p. 119.
[2] D. Gordon White, 'The Democratic People's Republic of Korea through the Eyes of a Visiting Sinologist', *The China Quarterly*, 63. September (1975), pp. 520–21.
[3] Smith, *North Korea*, p. 144.

This mass line approach could be seen clearly in the mass mobilisation campaigns discussed in the previous chapter, such as the *Chŏllima* movement. The early 1960s also saw the introduction of two new systems of agricultural and industrial management, known as the *Ch'ŏngsan-ri* Method and the *Taean Work System*. These new systems were a response to the increasing difficulties emerging in the realm of central planning during the previous Five-Year Plan.[4] Both placed rhetorical emphasis on the role of the revolutionary enthusiasm of the masses in the building of an independent socialist economy and on tackling bureaucratisation and over-centralisation, yet they also served to strengthen direct administrative control over lower-level organisations.[5] The *Ch'ŏngsan-ri* Method, for example, emerged following Kim Il Sung's February 1960 on-the-spot guidance visit to *Ch'ŏngsan-ri* cooperative farm in Kangso County, South Pyongan Province. Rather than a strictly hierarchical system, the *Ch'ŏngsan-ri* Method required county party officials to mingle with agricultural workers to learn about their work and help resolve problems collectively. As such, the system was based upon the principle that party and administrative officials at higher levels needed to help and listen to those at the lower level.[6] On the 30th anniversary of the establishment of the *Ch'ŏngsan-ri* Method, Vice President Pak Sung Chul described the essence of the system as follows:

'The basic principle of the *Ch'ŏngsan-ri* Method is that the higher-level organisations help those at a lower level, and the superiors help those below them by always going down to the local level to gain a deep understanding of the situation, to establish the correct way to solve problems, and in all areas, to prioritise political work and mobilise the fervour of mass consciousness in order to carry out revolutionary tasks'.[7]

At the same time, however, the *Ch'ŏngsan-ri* Method put the farms under the control of the KWP, thereby giving central and regional party organisations superiority over the Cabinet's ministries and regional administrative organs.[8]

---

[4] Joungwon Alexander Kim, 'The "Peak of Socialism" in North Korea', pp. 257–59.

[5] Byong Sik Kim, *Modern Korea: The Socialist North, Revolution Perspectives in the South, and Unification* (New York: International Publishers, 1970), pp. 111–35.

[6] *Kŭlloja*, February 1963, 'The *Ch'ŏngsan-ri* Method is a powerful weapon for the promotion of socialist construction – On the third anniversary of Comrade Kim Il Sung's on-the-spot guidance at Ch'ŏngsan-ri [Ch'ŏngsanni pangbŏbŭn sahoejuŭi kŏnsŏrŭl ch'okchinhanŭn wiryŏkhan mugiida - Kimilsŏng tongjiŭi ch'ŏngsanli hyŏnjijido 3 chunyŏne chehayŏ]', pp. 8–14.

[7] *Rodong Sinmun*, 9 February 1990, 'Firmly grasp *Ch'ŏngsan-ri* spirit and the *Ch'ŏngsan-ri* method, and strongly achieve the construction of socialism – The report of, member of the KWP Central Committee Politburo and Vice President Comrade Pak Sung Chul at the Central Report Meeting [Ch'ŏngsanni chŏngsin, ch'ŏngsanni pangbŏbŭl t'ŭnt'ŭnhi t'ŭrŏchwigo sahoejuŭi kŏnsŏrŭl himitke tagŭch'ija - chungangbogodaehoeesŏ han chosŏnnodongdang chungangwiwŏnhoe chŏngch'iguk wiwŏnimyŏ bujusŏgin paksŏngch'ŏl tongjiŭi pogo]'.

[8] Park Hyeong Jung, 'Introduction of Party-Centered Industrial Management System in the First Half of the 1960's in North Korea [1960 nyŏndae chŏnban'gi Pukhanesŏ chibangdang chungsimŭi kongŏpkwallich'egye surip kwajŏnggwa naeyong]', *Review of North Korean Studies*, 6.2 (2003), pp. 94–95.

A similar combination of mass line dynamics and strengthened party control could be seen in the *Taean* Work System. Announced in December 1961 following a visit by Kim Il Sung to the *Taean* Electrical Machine Factory in Nampo, the *Taean* Work System served to strengthen the KWP's leadership in the realm of factory management.[9] From the immediate post-liberation era to the end of the 1950s, North Korea's enterprise management had hitherto resembled the single manager system established in the Soviet Union during the 1930s. Under that system, an enterprise director appointed by the relevant industrial ministry held responsibility for all management activities. The *Taean* Work System replaced this with a system of collective leadership in the form of the factory party committee, which held authority over both the enterprise director and chief technician.[10] In this respect, the adoption of the *Taean* Work System thereby bore strong parallels with the 1956 enterprise management reforms in China.[11]

These centralising tendencies under party leadership could also be seen in the central planning system, precisely at the time when countries elsewhere in the Socialist Bloc were experimenting with decentralising reforms. 'Unified planning' (*kyehoegŭi irwŏnhwa*) and 'detailed planning' (*kyehoegŭi sebuhwa*) were introduced in 1965 as a means of strengthening the KWP's control over economic management and coordinating economic activities at all levels to reduce wastage and increase output as well as avoid disequilibrium between sectors. This thereby amounted to a comprehensive planning system, with up to 100,000 products included under the plans.[12] In terms of its operation, unified and detailed planning saw the establishment of regional administrative planning commissions in the provinces under the direct supervision of the State Planning Commission, thereby making it possible for state commissioners to go into factories and supervise the execution of the plan. There were also changes in the plan formulation procedures designed to resolve the situation common to centrally planned systems whereby planners asked for maximum output from production units and sought to minimise the supply of inputs, and

---

[9] According to the Korean Academy of Social Sciences Dictionary of the Economy, the *Taean* Work System represents a 'unified and centralised production guidance system.' Its introduction was specifically a response to the problem of shortages of raw materials in factories, which arose as a result of higher-level organs failing to take responsibility for the supply of materials by passing this responsibility down to lower production units. The authorities saw this not as a problem inherent to central planning *per se,* but rather as a more specific one of 'bureaucratism'. Under the *Taean* Work System, the upper-level organs would take responsibility for the supply of materials, thereby enabling factories to concentrate on production. Research Institute of Juche Economics - Academy of Social Sciences, *Dictionary of the Economy [Kyŏngjesajŏn]*, (Pyongyang: Social Science Publishing House, 1985), pp. 461–62.

[10] KIEP, *2002 North Korean Economy Report [2002 Pukhan'gyŏngjebaeksŏ]* (Seoul: Korea Institute for International Economic Policy, 2003), p. 79.

[11] Park Hyeong Jung, 'Introduction of Party-Centered Industrial Management System', p. 93.

[12] Kang and Lee, 'Industrial Systems', p. 953.

producers requested maximum inputs while seeking to minimise effort and output. The solution was therefore to encourage more worker participation in the planning process.[13]

For the next three decades, the North Korean regime maintained this system of economic management based on the *Ch'ŏngsan-ri* Method, the *Taean* Work System and unified and detailed planning, despite the fact that they contributed to the country's chronic inefficiency.[14] Material incentives were weak as economic management largely utilised political, ideological, and in general, non-material methods of motivating workers and managers.[15] As the party became more deeply involved in economic management, cadres and bureaucrats became resistant to any notion of economic reform and instead focused on political goals rather than economic logic.[16]

In terms of the sectoral emphasis of North Korean developmental strategy, the early 1960s saw a continued emphasis on the building of an autonomous heavy-industrial sector. This emphasis underpinned the goals of the First Seven-Year Plan (1961–67) announced in August 1960 (see Table 3.1), once again defying Soviet efforts to induce 'cooperative planning' amongst the socialist countries. At the Fourth Party Congress in September 1961, the authorities argued that whereas the previous Five-Year Plan had laid the basis for an industrial economy, the Seven-Year Plan would consolidate the basis of an independent national economy, with quantitative goals of an annual industrial growth rate of 18 per cent.[17]

However, the decision to extend the First Seven-Year Plan by three years was indicative of the serious problems within the North Korean economy. At the Fifth Party Congress in November 1970, Kim Il Sung argued that North Korea's greatest achievement had been its 'transformation into a socialist

---

[13] Phillip H. Park, *The Development Strategy of Self-Reliance (Juche) and Rural Development in the Democratic People's Republic of Korea* (London: Routledge, 2002), p. 36.

[14] The economic management system established in the 1960s largely survived intact until the 1980s, despite its manifest inefficiency. However, the economic crisis of the 1990s and the advance of marketisation served to undermine the existing system of economic management and led to the collapse of central planning in much of the country. While North Korea's legal system and its official documents continued to adhere to the system, the expansion of management autonomy, growing market trade and the differentiation of workers' incomes all meant that the *Taean* Work System and the *Ch'ŏngsan-ri* Method were no longer effective. In April 2019, the *Taean* Work System was finally removed from the Constitution and replaced with the Socialist Enterprise Responsibility Management System.

[15] Joseph Sang-Hoon Chung, 'North Korea's "Seven Year Plan" (1961–70): Economic Performance and Reforms', *Asian Survey*, 12.6 (1972), p. 544.

[16] Park Hyeong Jung, 'Introduction of Party-Centered Industrial Management System', pp. 94–95.

[17] *Rodong Sinmun*, 17 September 1961, 'On the DPRK's Seven Year Plan for the Development of the People's Economy (1961–1967) – the First Vice Premier of the DPRK Cabinet Kim Il [Chosŏn Minjujuŭi Inmin'gonghwaguk inmin'gyŏngjebalchŏn 7 kaenyŏn (1961–1967) kyehoege taehayŏ – Chosŏn Minjujuŭi Inmin'gonghwaguk naegak che1 pususang Kimil]'.

Table 3.1 *First Seven-Year Plan (1961–67)*

Basic tasks and targets of the plans	Economic results as announced by the North Korean government
• Establishment of an autonomous industrial system. • Technological development and the improvement of people's livelihood. • Dual '*Pyŏngjin*' line of economic and defence construction. • A 2.7-fold increase in national income. • A 3.2-fold increase in overall industrial production. • Grain harvest of 6–7 million tonnes.	• National income: no announcement. • A 3.3-fold increase in industrial production. • A total of 12.8 per cent average annual growth in the industrial sector. • Annual growth rate of machinery and metal industries: 18.4 per cent. • A total of 147.5 per cent increase in labour productivity. • No announcement on the grain harvest. • Extension of the plan by three years to 1970.

Source: Modified from KDI, *Economic Indicators of North Korea*, pp. 37–8.
Note: The goal of the dual *Pyŏngjin* line of economic and defence construction was not announced until late 1962.

industrialised nation'.[18] The industrial growth rate between 1961 and 1970 was reported as having seen a 12.8 per cent annual increase, with the volume of industrial production increasing 3.3 times over a decade.[19] Yet the government's silence on other key targets of the Seven-Year Plan suggested the extent of the difficulties it was facing. In the literature, several causes have been cited: diminishing returns on investment, the rigidity of central planning, unrealistic economic plans, the shortage of advanced technology, economic bottlenecks and inefficient resource allocation resulting from the emphasis on self-reliance and heavy industrialisation. Indeed, the fact that the slowdown of the Eastern European countries occurred during the same period suggests that these problems were common to all the centrally planned economies.[20] Nonetheless, a further cause specific to North Korea was the excessive military

[18] *Rodong Sinmum,* 3 November 1970, 'Report presented by KWP Central Committee General Secretary Kim Il Sung at the 5th Congress of the KWP [Chosŏnnodongdang che 5 ch'adaehoeesŏ han chungangwiwŏnhoe saŏpch'onghwa pogo – Chosŏnnodongdang chungangwiwŏnhoe ch'ongbisŏ Kimilsŏng]'.
[19] *Rodong Sinmun,* 10 November 1970, 'On the DPRK's Six Year Plan for the Development of the Peoples' Economy (1971–1976) – DPRK Cabinet First Vice Premier Kim Il [Chosŏn Minjujuŭi Inmin'gonghwaguk inmin'gyŏngjebalchŏn 6 kaenyŏn (1971–1976) kyehoege taehayŏ – Chosŏn Minjujuŭi Inmin'gonghwaguk naegak che 1 pususang Kimil]'.
[20] Jan Vanous, 'East European Economic Slowdown', *Problems of Communism*, 31.July–August (1982), pp. 1–19.

spending alongside declining economic assistance from the Socialist Bloc in the context of an increasingly adverse geopolitical environment.

3.2   Geopolitical Shifts and the Militarisation of North Korean Development

As we have seen, North Korea relied heavily on Soviet and Chinese assistance for its security following the Korean War. Due to North Korea's strategic role as 'forward defence state' vis-à-vis US-aligned East Asia, the Soviet Union provided a substantial amount of military aid along with strong security guarantees. China also deployed over 400,000 soldiers in North Korea until their gradual withdrawal by October 1958.[21] With these external guarantees, North Korea was able to focus on rehabilitating its war-devastated economy rather than strengthening its military capacity.[22] However, the dramatic deterioration in North Korea's external security environment in the early 1960s had a significant impact on the country's development strategy. The most important geopolitical challenge facing North Korea was the fallout of its two key socialist allies. Sino–Soviet tensions arose as a result of Beijing's opposition to Khrushchev's de-Stalinisation campaign and, in late 1959, its disappointment over Moscow's position with regards to growing Sino–Indian border tensions. After the bitter debate at the Bucharest Conference of the World Communist and Workers' Parties in June 1960 along with the Soviet Union's termination of technical aid to China and withdrawal of Russian experts, the Sino–Soviet split developed into open confrontation. Both countries viewed the other as having deviated from the 'correct' Marxist–Leninist line, with Beijing criticising Khrushchev's Soviet Union as 'revisionist' and the latter criticising China as 'dogmatist'.[23] These tensions deteriorated even to the point of military clashes in Zhenbao (Damansky) Island on the Ussuri River in March 1969.

These tensions could not but have an adverse impact on North Korea. Initially, Pyongyang sought to adopt a neutral position in order to protect its own political independence and ensure continued provision of assistance by both countries.[24] However, Moscow and Beijing both sought to draw North

---

[21] Kim Yong Hyun, 'A Study on the Militarizing State of North Korea: The 1950s–1960s [Pukhanŭi kunsagukkahwae kwanhan yŏn'gu: 1950–1960 nyŏndaerŭl chungsimŭro]' (PhD thesis: Dongguk University, 2001), pp. 78–81.

[22] Sung-Joo Han, 'North Korea's Security Policy and Military Strategy', in *North Korea Today: Strategic and Domestic Issues*, ed. by Robert A. Scalapino and Jun-yop Kim (Berkeley, CA: Institute of East Asian Studies, University of California Press, 1983), p. 146.

[23] Lee Jong-Seok, *Research on the Korean Workers' Party: Focus on Changes in Leadership Thought and Structural Change [Chosŏnnodongdang yŏn'gu: chidosasanggwa kujo pyŏnhwarŭl chungsimŭro]* (Seoul: Critical Review of History, 1995), p. 75.

[24] Robert A. Scalapino, 'Korea: The Politics of Change', *Asian Survey*, 3.1 (1963), p. 38.

Korea into their respective orbits through the signing of mutual defence treaties with Pyongyang. During Kim Il Sung's visit to Moscow on 6 July 1961, the two countries signed the Treaty of Friendship, Cooperation and Mutual Assistance. Five days later, Kim signed a Sino–DPRK mutual aid treaty with Chinese Premier Zhou Enlai in Beijing. At the heart of both treaties was a clause mandating the automatic military involvement of the ally in the case of either party's security emergency.[25] As the Sino–Soviet dispute intensified, the Soviet Union placed increased pressure on North Korea, along with other Asian socialist states such as North Vietnam and Mongolia as part of its broader effort, to isolate China. Moscow also continued to pressure Pyongyang to drop its policy of economic self-reliance and integrate itself within the broader socialist division of labour. This pressure involved a sharp decline in the Soviet Union's provision of aid to North Korea.[26] Pyongyang, however, continued to insist on self-reliance as a 'correct international revolutionary principle' and sent a clear message to Moscow that it would chart an independent course with or without Soviet assistance.[27]

These developments led North Korea to adopt an increasingly pro-Beijing stance. In 1962, Pyongyang provided clear rhetorical support to Beijing during the Sino–Indian border conflict and began to make veiled criticisms of Soviet foreign policy.[28] These improved Sino–North Korean relations were confirmed by an agreement concluded in October that year to resolve outstanding border demarcation issues between the two countries. Though the Soviet Union was not explicitly mentioned by name, North Korean state media criticised Moscow's attacks on China. For example, the February 1963 edition of *Kŭlloja*, the KWP Central Committee's political theory magazine, argued that '. . . the unilateral attack and isolation of the Chinese Communist Party, which occupies an important position within our socialist camp, threatens the unity of the camp and seriously harms peace and the common socialist

[25] For the text of the treaties and content of the joint communiqués, see: KCNA, *Korean Central Almanac 1962 [Chosŏnjungangnyŏn'gam 1962]* (Pyongyang: KCNA, 1962), pp. 157–63. The treaty with the Soviet Union was in the first instance valid for ten years, and if prior to its expiry the two parties so desired, it could be extended for a five-year term. On September 1996, five years after the collapse of the Soviet Union, Russia made the decision not to extend the treaty. In the term of the Sino–North Korean treaty, there was no time limit. Instead, it was based upon the principle that unless there was an agreement between the parties to revise or cancel the treaty, it would continue to be effective. As such, despite the establishment of diplomatic relations between South Korea and China in 1992, the 1961 Sino–North Korean security treaty officially remains in force.

[26] Jane P. Shapiro, 'Soviet Policy towards North Korea and Korean Unification', *Pacific Affairs*, 48.3 (1975), p. 339.

[27] Chin O. Chung, *Pyongyang between Peking and Moscow*, pp. 77–78.

[28] Lee Jong-Seok, *Research on the Korean Workers' Party*, p. 76.

achievement'.[29] The Soviet Union's withdrawal of missiles from Cuba in October 1962, in particular, served to heighten North Korean doubts regarding Khrushchev's commitment to the security of its socialist allies, and in particular, to that of North Korea in the event of any potential renewed conflict on the peninsula.[30] As such, Pyongyang increasingly came to share Beijing's view of the Soviet Union as a 'great power chauvinist' that was subordinating the interests of its communist allies to the goal of peaceful coexistence with the United States.[31]

This termination of Soviet assistance contributed to the aforementioned failure to reach the targets of the Seven-Year Plan. A full three-page editorial in *Rodong Sinmun* on 28 October 1963 entitled 'Let's Advocate the Socialist Camp' put forward a strong critique of Soviet policy, and in particular, of Moscow's attempts at intervention in North Korea's domestic affairs:

'Today the international communist movement is being severely tested, and the differences of opinion within the international communist movement are becoming increasingly serious. Some people have moved far from Marxism–Leninism and the principles of proletariat internationalism, and have fallen into the muddy waters of revisionism . . . Some people are using foreign aid as an excuse to interfere in the internal politics of fraternal parties and countries and are unilaterally imposing their wishes . . . Seeking to enforce their subjective opinions without knowing the situations of other parties creates great harm to the socialist revolution and to socialist construction'.[32]

The apparent convergence between North Korean and Chinese worldviews reflected in part the fact that both were divided countries and involved in a direct military stand-off with the United States, thereby placing them at odds with Moscow's line of peaceful coexistence. The fact that both were at similar stages in their respective revolutions and national developmental projects also underpinned their uncompromising stance towards US hegemony, though that stance was also useful in terms of mobilising their respective populations.[33] Yet, after the fall of Khrushchev in October 1964, relations between Pyongyang and Moscow quickly began to improve again. Following a meeting in Moscow between North Korea's First Vice-Premier Kim Il and the new Soviet leader Leonid Brezhnev in November 1964, Soviet Premier Alexei

[29] *Kŭlloja*, February 1963, 'Let's defend the unification of the socialist camp and strengthen the unity of the international communist movement [Sahoejuŭi chinyŏngŭi t'ongirŭl suhohamyŏ kukchegongsanjuŭi undongŭi tan'gyŏrŭl kanghwahaja', p. 3.

[30] Donald S. Zagoria, 'North Korea: Between Moscow and Beijing', in *North Korea Today: Strategic and Domestic Issues*, ed. by Robert A. Scalapino and Jun-yop Kim (Berkeley, CA: Institute of East Asian Studies, University of California Press, 1983), pp. 354–65.

[31] Scalapino, 'Korea', pp. 38–39.

[32] *Rodong Sinmun*, 28 October 1963, 'Let's advocate the socialist camp [Sahoejuŭi chinyŏngŭl onghohaja]'.

[33] Chin O. Chung, *Pyongyang between Peking and Moscow*, pp. 104–7.

Kosygin visited Pyongyang in February 1965.[34] In welcoming Kosygin, Kim Il Sung recalled the 'unbreakable bond of friendship' between the two countries and voiced the conviction that the visit would not merely strengthen that bond but would contribute to the unity of the socialist camp. There was also renewed vigour in Soviet–North Korean cultural relations, with Pyongyang toning down its attacks on Soviet revisionism and its policy of peaceful coexistence. This led in turn to an increase in Moscow's provision of economic and military assistance to North Korea. A *Rodong Sinmun* editorial on the occasion of the 20th anniversary of the liberation of Korea from Japanese colonial rule made glowing reference to the role of the Soviet Union in Korea's liberation, with no reference to China's assistance during the Korean War.[35] This reflected the fact that while North Korea's earlier shift towards China had largely been a pragmatic response to immediate challenges, this could not form the basis of a long-term strategy for North Korea. The relatively developed nature of North Korean industry and the intensifying geopolitical competition with US-aligned South Korea meant that there was a heightened need for imports of advanced industrial and military technology from the USSR.[36]

This Soviet–North Korean rapprochement occurred in the context of souring relations with Beijing. Pyongyang became increasingly distrustful of what it regarded as China's 'dogmatist' attitude, as manifested in Beijing's rejection of a Soviet proposal in 1965 for international negotiations amongst the socialist countries to establish a joint response to the Vietnam War.[37] However, the deterioration of relations with China was not solely a result of Pyongyang's own manoeuvring. The political and social chaos of the Cultural Revolution was a contributing factor. In 1967, Red Guards made strong verbal attacks against Kim Il Sung as Khrushchev-like revisionist and reportedly even spread unfounded rumours regarding an alleged coup d'état in Pyongyang, to which the Korean Central News Agency was forced to make an urgent statement of clarification.[38] However, in 1969, as the Cultural Revolution began to subside, relations between Beijing and Pyongyang once again began to improve. A North Korean delegation headed by Chairman of the Presidium of the Supreme People's Assembly Choi Yong Gon, a veteran of the armed anti-Japanese movement with close relations to the Chinese leadership, accepted a formal invitation from Beijing to attend an event on 1 October 1969 to

---

[34] *New York Times*, 11 February 1965, 'Moscow Announces New Trip', p. 13.

[35] B. C. Koh, 'North Korea and Its Quest for Autonomy', *Pacific Affairs*, 87.4 (2014), p. 777.

[36] Balázs Szalontai, *Kim Il Sung in the Khrushchev Era: Soviet–DPRK Relations and the Roots of North Korean Despotism, 1953–1964* (Washington, DC: Woodrow Wilson Center Press, 2005), p. 207.

[37] Lee Jong-Seok, *Research on the Korean Workers' Party*, p. 80.

[38] See *Rodong Sinmun*, 27 January 1967, 'Statement of the DPR Korean Central News Agency [Chosŏn Minjujuŭi Inmin'gonghwaguk chungangt'ongsinsaŭi sŏngmyŏng]'.

commemorate the 20th anniversary of the founding of the Chinese state. Furthermore, in April 1970, Chinese Premier Zhou Enlai visited Pyongyang, with Kim Il Sung returning the visit to Beijing the following October.[39]

Throughout these shifting alliances, North Korea nonetheless stressed the importance of independence from both China and the USSR, and continued to emphasise self-reliant economic development. As a *Rodong Sinmun* editorial in August 1966 argued 'our Party creatively applied Marxism–Leninism to the reality of the Korean revolution and established its own independent guidance theory. This is reflected in our Party's lines and policies'.[40] Pyongyang's primary aim in this period was to fulfil the goals of the Seven-Year Plan by the end of the decade and strengthen its own military capabilities, while avoiding subordination to either the Soviet Union or China.[41] Nonetheless, the widening rift between Moscow and Beijing posed a significant security dilemma for the North Korean regime through weakening unity within the Socialist Bloc at a time when the country was engaged in a sharp confrontation with US-aligned East Asia.

Indeed, in the 1960s, North Korea was also faced with the emergence of a military regime in the South. In the previous decade, South Korea had experienced relatively limited post-war reconstruction alongside ongoing political instability. Student demonstrations in April 1960 toppled the Rhee Syngman regime and led to the onset of the coalition government headed by Chang Myon. However, political unrest and economic stagnation continued, and in May 1961, a military coup d'état led by Major General Park Chung-Hee overthrew the civilian government. Park's military regime mobilised a strong ideology of anti-communism in order to legitimise its anti-democratic tendencies. Far more than simply a government policy, anti-communism came to establish a hegemonic position within South Korea's national consciousness.[42] The challenge was not just ideational, however. The Park government also embarked upon a strategy of rapid catch-up development through widespread state intervention and export-oriented industrialisation.

In the 1950s, Pyongyang had believed that the US preference for the status quo on the peninsula meant that possibility of offensive military action by the South was unlikely.[43] In the early 1960s, however, the United States became increasingly embroiled in the Vietnam War. Seoul also sent its first combat

---

[39] Lee Jong-Seok, *Research on North Korean–Chinese Relations at the Time of the Cultural Revolution [Munhwadaehyŏngmyŏng sigi Pukhan-Chungguk gwan'gye yŏn'gu]* (Seongnam: Sejong Institute, 2015), pp. 23–27.

[40] *Rodong Sinmun*, 12 August 1966, 'Let's advocate autonomy [Chajusŏngŭl onghohaja]'.

[41] Chin O. Chung, *Pyongyang between Peking and Moscow*, p. 133.

[42] Roland Bleiker, *Divided Korea: Toward a Culture of Reconciliation* (Minneapolis: University of Minnesota Press, 2005), pp. 12–13.

[43] Sung-Joo Han, 'North Korea's Security Policy', p. 148.

troops to South Vietnam in 1965, and moved to normalise diplomatic relations with Tokyo that same year, thereby marking increased economic and military cooperation within the South Korea–Japan–United States triangle.[44] For Pyongyang, these developments suggested a shift in American policy from defensive to offensive posture in Asia, thereby serving to heighten the country's siege mentality. Evidence of this could be seen in Kim Il Sung's report to the KWP's Second Party Delegates Conference on 5 October 1966:

'Through bilateral military agreements between the American imperialists, the Sato government of Japan and the South Korean puppet government, a triangular military alliance is in reality forming ... Comrades, in recent years, the socialist camp and the international communist movement have been undergoing a great test. Contemporary revisionism and dogmatism have created a severe setback in the development of the international revolutionary movement ... Today, the aggression of the American imperialists is getting stronger and their conspiracy to expand the war is becoming more and more visible. Park Chung-Hee of South Korea is actively preparing for a new war under the direction of the US imperialists and is already directly involved in the US imperialists' aggressive war in Vietnam. The situation is becoming more tense and there is an increased risk of war in our country and throughout Asia'.[45]

The North Korean leadership responded to these challenges by giving greater emphasis to self-reliance in defence alongside the broader militarisation of North Korean society. In December 1962, at the Fifth Plenum of the Fourth Central Committee of the KWP, the so-called 'Four Military Lines' (*4 tae kunsarosŏn*) were announced. These included: 1) the militarisation of the people, including the arming of the working class, both ideologically and politically; 2) the fortification of the entire country through the construction of defensive facilities; 3) the training of all soldiers ideologically, politically and technically; and 4) the modernisation of the military.[46] At the same KWP plenary, the '*Pyŏngjin*' Dual Line of Economic and Defence Construction was adopted. This *Pyŏngjin* line represented the ascendance of military-related goals relative to those of economic development that had dominated since the 1953 armistice.[47] Indeed, it was explicitly recognised that the policy of

[44] Se Jin Kim, 'South Korea's Involvement in Vietnam and Its Economic and Political Impact', *Asian Survey*, 10.6 (1970), pp. 519–32.

[45] Kim Il Sung, *The Present Situation and the Tasks of Our Party [Hyŏnjŏngsewa uri tangŭi kwaŏp]* (Pyongyang: Korean Workers' Party Publishing House, 1966), pp. 9, 21, 50–51.

[46] Seong-yong Park, 'North Korea's Military Policy under the Kim Jong-Un Regime', *Journal of Asian Public Policy*, 9.1 (2016), p. 61.

[47] The militaristic turn had long-term implications, shaping both the rise of Military First Politics (*sŏn'gun chŏngch'i*) during the Kim Jong Il era as well as the *Pyŏngjin* Dual Line of the construction of the economy and nuclear weapons capability. As the shared terminology suggests, the latter in particular had clear parallels here with the *Pyŏngjin* line of the 1960s, and indeed, Kim Jong Un explicitly mentioned this in a speech given at the plenary meeting of the KWP Central Committee on 31 March 2013. The difference was, however, that in the 1960s the dual line represented a shift from the primary focus on economic reconstruction and

militarisation might have negative implications for economic growth. As the authorities argued, 'Even if the development of the people's economy is in part restricted, we first need to strengthen national defence'.[48] In concrete terms, the plenary designated 1963 as a further 'buffer year' and adjusted the Seven-Year Plan's goal of increasing annual industrial production by 18 per cent downwards to 11 per cent.[49]

The policy of militarisation also underpinned North Korea's increasingly belligerent foreign policy and its provocative actions against the South. Following the KWP Party Delegates Conference in October 1966, there were increased incidents of violence along the demilitarised zone (DMZ) and at sea, culminating in an attack on the South Korean presidential Blue House by North Korean commandos in January 1968. North Korea's seizure of the US spy ship, the USS *Pueblo* two days later further heightened military tensions on the peninsula. Various explanations have been given for this belligerent turn, including that Pyongyang was seeking to hinder the US-led war effort in Vietnam by drawing the United States and South Korean attention and resources to the Korean DMZ,[50] that Kim Il Sung remained resolutely opposed to any notion of peaceful coexistence and favoured aiding wars of national liberation as part of an 'all out fight' against US imperialism,[51] or that Pyongyang was seeking to generate a security crisis as a means of distracting public attention from its domestic economic difficulties and instability in the country's foreign relations.[52] However, the heightened tensions of the late 1960s were not generated by Pyongyang alone but were part of a cycle of provocation and counter-provocation. On the South Korean side, this reflected an aggressive strategy on the part of the Park Chung-Hee government to utilise the security crisis as a means of extracting military aid from the United States amidst ongoing negotiations with Washington over South Korean troop dispatches to Vietnam.[53]

In any case, these tensions can be seen as both cause and consequence of North Korea's continued militarisation and led to the share of defence

development towards greater emphasis on militarisation, whereas Kim Jong Un's *Pyŏngjin* line took the opposite direction, from the rhetorical focus on 'military first' objectives to include greater emphasis on economic recovery.

[48] *Rodong Sinmun*, 16 December 1962, 'Report related to the fifth Plenary of the fourth KWP Central Committee [Tang chungangwiwŏnhoe che 4 ki che 5 ch'a chŏnwŏn hoeŭie kwanhan podo]'.

[49] Szalontai, *Kim Il Sung in the Khrushchev Era*, p. 195.

[50] Glenn D. Paige, '1966: Korea Creates the Future', *Asian Survey*, 7.1 (1967), p. 27.

[51] Soon Sung Cho, 'Korea: Election Year', *Asian Survey*, 8.1 (1968), pp. 40–41.

[52] Mitchell Lerner, '"Mostly Propaganda in Nature": Kim Il Sung, the Juche Ideology, and the Second Korean War', *Wilson Center Working Paper*, 2010, pp. 25–26.

[53] Tae-Gyun Park, 'Beyond the Myth: Reassessing the Security Crisis on the Korean Peninsula during the Mid-1960s', *Pacific Affairs*, 82.1 (2009), pp. 93–110.

Table 3.2 *Estimates on North Korea's budget spending and defence expenditure*

(Units: thousands North Korean won, %)

Year	Total annual budgets	Expenditure for people's economy		Expenditure for social and cultural sectors		Defence expenditure	
		Amounts	Share	Amounts	Share	Amounts	Share
1958	1,321,414					63,563	4.8
1959	1,649,212	1,135,300	68.9	382,341	23.2	63,483	3.7
1960	1,967,870		69.2		24.5	61,000	3.1
1961	2,338,000	1,707,904	73.0	500,332	21.4	58,450	2.5
1962	2,728,760	1,979,576	72.5	616,700	22.6	70,950	2.6
1963	3,028,210	2,240,880	74.0	653,700	21.5	57,540	1.9
1964	3,418,240	2,377,210	69.5	704,160	20.6	198,260	5.8
1965	3,476,130	2,363,760	68.0	684,220	19.7	278,090	8.0
1966	3,571,400	2,443,780	68.4	616,910	17.3	357,140	10.0
1967	3,948,230	1,970,170	49.9	690,940	17.5	1,200,260	30.4
1968	4,812,890	2,353,500	48.9	829,130	17.0	1,559,380	32.4
1969	5,048,570	2,397,890	47.5	994,950	19.7	1,565,000	31.0
1970	6,002,690	2,821,260	47.0	1,193,940	19.9	1,878,840	31.3
1971	6,301,680	2,783,790	44.2	1,444,670	22.9	1,959,820	31.1
1972	7,388,610	4,099,320	55.5	1,878,070	25.4	1,256,060	17.0
1973	8,313,910	4,755,540	57.2	2,103,440	25.3	1,280,340	15.4
1974	9,672,190	5,513,930	57.0	2,397,920	24.8	1,557,220	16.1
1975	11,367,480	6,506,880	57.2	2,757,620	24.3	1,864,270	16.4
1976	12,325,500	6,918,280	56.2	3,083,010	25.0	2,065,370	16.7
1977	13,349,200	7,681,740	56.8	3,391,310	25.4	2,095,820	15.7
1978	14,743,600	8,450,870	57.3	3,638,880	24.7	2,344,230	15.9
1979	16,972,600	10,073,440	59.4	4,010,050	23.6	2,562,860	15.1

Source: modified from ROK Ministry of Unification, *North Korean Economic Statistics [Pukhan Kyŏngje t'onggyejip]* (Seoul: Ministry of Unification, 1996), pp. 139–42. The MOU's estimated figures are based upon the annual budget expenditures reported in North Korean publications such as the Korean Central Almanac and Rodong Sinmun.

expenditures in the national budget rising sharply to over 30 per cent in the late 1960s (see Table 3.2). While many observers are sceptical of official North Korean military expenditure figures, the fact of a sharp increase in defence spending during that decade seems undeniable. This increase occurred along-side the continued militarisation of society in accordance with the 'Four Military Lines'. For example, in 1963, a paramilitary organisation consisting of discharged soldiers known as the North Korean Reserve Forces (*kyododae*) was established. In 1970, the Red Youth Guard, an organisation made up of high school students, was also formed. As a result, the young and old alike were all integrated into the country's military structure.[54] An official statement regarding the rapid increase in military expenditures at the time by the North Korean leadership can be found in the report of the First Vice-Premier Kim Il in November 1970:

'Following the *Pyŏngjin* Line of Economic and Defence Construction laid down by Comrade Kim Il Sung, the Party has actively endeavoured to build national defence by adjusting the development speed of the people's economy. In 1960, the portion of the state budget spending devoted to the defence sector was 19 per cent, but between 1967 and 1969, after the Party Delegates Conference, this was increased to 31.3 per cent of the state's budget for strengthening the nation's defence power. In the last nine years, enormous funds worth approximately 8 billion won have been spent on the construction of defence'.[55]

The militarisation of society can also be seen in the growing ideological significance assigned to Kim Il Sung's anti-Japanese guerrilla struggle. Kim's leadership and the military brotherhood and solidarity of his guerrilla comrades were emphasised as the highest example of communists and their collectivist sacrifice. From the early 1960s, the 'following and learning' of the spirit and method of the anti-Japanese guerrilla struggle was propagated throughout North Korean society. The *Ch'ŏngsan-ri* Method and *Taean* Work System were key mechanisms through which this occurred, with mass education on the work method of the anti-Japanese guerrillas and military-style collectivist's methods.[56] Given Kim Il Sung's tightened grip on power, it is hardly surprising that the anti-Japanese guerrilla, who was resilient in the face of hardship and eternally loyal to the Supreme Commander, would become the role model for society.[57] The external geopolitical environment did not, therefore, lead to the militarisation of society in any mechanistic sense. The external threat was mediated through the worldview of those political forces that had become dominant in North Korea and thereby came to constitute the ideological underpinning of the country's developmental project.

As indicated, this policy of militarisation placed an extraordinary burden on the North Korean economy. In 1966, for the first time since the Korean War, the economy reportedly experienced negative

[54] Kim Yong Hyun, 'Study on the Militarizing State', p. 124.
[55] *Rodong Sinmun,* 10 November 1970, 'On the DPRK's Six Year Plan for the Development of the Peoples' Economy (1971–1976) – DPRK Cabinet First Vice Premier Kim Il [Chosŏn Minjujuŭi Inmin'gonghwaguk inmin'gyŏngjebalchŏn 6 kaenyŏn (1971–1976) kyehoege tae-hayŏ – Chosŏn Minjujuŭi Inmin'gonghwaguk naegak che 1 pususang Kimil]'.
[56] Lee Tae-Sup, *North Korea's Economic Crisis,* pp. 120–23.
[57] Buzo, *Guerilla Dynasty,* pp. 70–71.

growth.[58] The authorities thus decided in October that year to extend the First Seven-Year Plan by three years. Despite deepening economic imbalances, however, the regime continued to channel investment into those heavy industries with close linkages to the defence sector, such as machine tools, chemicals and steel. As First Vice-Premier Kim Il further revealed, the proportion of heavy industries in the state's overall industrial investment between 1961 to 1969 amounted to over 80 per cent. Investment in light industry and agriculture thus saw a continued decline, with a negative impact on public livelihood.[59]

In the 1970s, stalled economic growth forced the government to reduce military spending from 31.1 per cent of the annual expenditures in 1971 to 17 per cent in 1972. North Korean military spending has since failed to keep up with that of the South.[60] Nonetheless, it has continued to exert a considerable burden on North Korean economic development. According to US Department of State's figures, North Korea's average annual military expenditure between the years of 2005 and 2015 was US$ 3.06 billion (or US$ 126 per capita), placing the country 49th in the world. However, South Korea's military expenditures amounted to US$ 32.3 billion (or US$ 656 per capita), placing the country 10th. As such, North Korea's military spending has fallen to just a fraction of that of South Korea, a situation which is exacerbated by the North's lack of any external military alliance resembling that of the United States–South Korea alliance. In terms of the economic burden, however, North Korea's military spending accounts for 23.3 per cent of its estimated GDP, the highest rate in the world. South Korea's military spending, on the other hand, accounts for just 2.6 per cent of its GDP, placing it 45th in world rankings.[61] While not all of North Korea's economic problems can be reduced to the burden of military spending alone, it is no coincidence that the declining growth rate in the mid-1960s was contemporaneous with the expansion of its defence expenditures.

3.3   *Juche* Thought and the Development–Geopolitics Nexus

The shifting geopolitical environment of the 1960s coincided with the ascendance of *Juche* thought as North Korea's official state ideology. *Juche* can be understood as the most succinct expression of the country's developmental nationalism, and it bore a strong correlation to the autarkist ethos that

[58] Lee Tae-Sup, *North Korea's Economic Crisis*, pp. 161–62.
[59] *Rodong Sinmun,* 10 November 1970, 'On the DPRK's Six Year Plan'.
[60] Chung-in Moon and Sangkeun Lee, 'Military Spending and the Arms Race on the Korean Peninsula', *Asian Perspective*, 33.4 (2009), pp. 78–80.
[61] US Department of State: 'World Military Expenditures and Arms Transfers 2017'. www.state .gov/t/avc/rls/rpt/wmeat/ [accessed 22 December 2018].

underpinned the country's catch-up industrialisation project. As noted in the Introduction, nationalist projects of catch-up industrialisation in the postcolonial world have typically been underpinned by strong developmental nationalisms. These nationalisms served to establish the goal of emulating the more advanced and developed countries as well as facilitate the mobilisation of society around those goals. Indeed, the historical record suggests that catch-up industrialisation has demanded extraordinary sacrifices on the part of populations, including the repression of consumption and livings standards as well as of democratic freedoms. The task of eliciting active consent to the goal of development has therefore been dependent on the formulation of a legitimising hegemonic national-popular ideology that serves to justify such sacrifices. As Gerschenkron has argued, the precise form of this ideology may take different forms, but they share in common the fact that '... [i]n a backward country the great and sudden industrialization effort calls for a New Deal in emotions'.[62] Postcolonial developmental nationalisms thus tend to share in common the fact that they present the project of late development as a prerequisite for national survival and autonomy in the face of geopolitical challenges.

In the early stages of North Korean state formation, official ideology drew heavily on the orthodox Marxism–Leninism of the Soviet Union. This external ideological influence was by no means in contradiction with the strong nationalism of the Korean communist movement. Radical Korean nationalists regarded Soviet-style state socialism as an effective means to achieve liberation from the legacies of colonial rule and to pursue the goal of national development. The fact that the Soviet Union was the only major country to give material assistance to anti-colonial struggles meant that, after coming to power, Korean nationalists did not see close ties to the USSR as contradictory to the aims of national independence but rather as a necessary condition for that independence.[63] However, the consolidation of Kim Il Sung's independence vis-à-vis his erstwhile Soviet backers alongside the growing geopolitical pressures outlined above led to the indigenisation of Marxism–Leninism in the form of the ascendance of *Juche* thought as the official state ideology.

The precise meaning of *Juche* has been subject to numerous and shifting interpretations. The literal translation of the term is 'subject', though the term is more typically interpreted in the English language literature as denoting 'self-reliance' or 'national autonomy'. Usage of the term predates the establishment of the North Korean state.[64] As James Person notes, *Juche* as an

---

[62] Gerschenkron, *Economic Backwardness*, pp. 24–25.
[63] Armstrong, *North Korean Revolution*, pp. 4–5.
[64] For a useful overview of the origins of the term, see B. R. Myers, *North Korea's Juche Myth* (Busan: Sthele Press, 2015), pp. 10–14.

expression of national subjectivity had been part of nationalist discourse in East Asia since the late nineteenth century. In Korea, the term initially emerged as part of an effort to produce an autonomous Korean subjectivity led by activists and thinkers from across the political spectrum.[65] The history of colonial subjugation can be seen as having played a key role in nurturing a normative commitment to autonomy amongst Korean intellectuals.[66]

It has been argued that the rise of *Juche* to the position of North Korea's official state ideology was closely shaped by the experience of Kim Il Sung and his guerrilla comrades during the anti-Japanese struggle of the 1930s, and that this contributed to the post-liberation regime's ideas of national independence and self-reliance. The first recorded use by Kim Il Sung of the term, however, took place in the context of the factional politics of the mid-1950s, and specifically, in his December 1955 speech to KWP propagandists and agitators, titled 'On Eliminating Dogmatism and Formalism and Establishing Juche in Ideological Work'.[67] Kim's call for the establishment of *Juche* in ideological work reflected the fact that in the early years of state-building, Soviet influence was prevalent not just in terms of the country's emulation of political institutions and economic policy but also in the educational and cultural sphere.[68] From the late 1940s, large numbers of Russian books and journals were translated into Korean, students were being sent to study in the Soviet Union and elsewhere in the socialist camp and many North Koreans watched Soviet films as a part of their ideological indoctrination.[69] This emulation of Soviet cultural, political and economic practices was seen by Kim as part of a broader practice of what is known in Korean as '*sadaejuŭi*' or 'flunkeyism', a remnant of Korea's long history of glorifying the cultures, traditions and political practices of more advanced countries. Kim's 1955 speech might therefore be interpreted as an attempt to 'decolonise' the Korean mind. Indeed, the establishment of an autonomous Korean subjectivity meant, in turn, abandoning *sadaejuŭi* for the purposes of national subject formation and instilling a sense of national pride.[70]

Kim's 1955 speech also took place in the context of the de-Stalinisation taking place within the Soviet Union following Stalin's death. As we saw in the previous chapter, one of the key factors underpinning the factional disputes

[65] James F. Person, 'North Korea's Chuch'e Philosophy', in *Routledge Handbook of Modern Korean History*, ed. by Michael J. Seth (London: Routledge, 2016), p. 211.

[66] Keith Howard, 'Juche and Culture: What's New?', in *North Korea in the New World Order*, ed. by Hazel Smith, Chris Rhodes, Diana Pritchard and Kevin Magill (Basingstoke: Macmillan, 1996), pp. 170–71.

[67] Lee Jong-Seok, *New Approach*, p. 146.

[68] Kim Il Sung, *On Juche Ideology [Chuch'esasange taehayŏ]* (Pyongyang: Korean Workers' Party Publishing House, 1977), pp. 145–72.

[69] Jae-Cheon Lim, *Kim Jong Il's Leadership of North Korea* (London: Routledge, 2009), p. 19.

[70] Person, 'North Korea's Chuch'e Philosophy', p. 214.

of the mid-1950s was the sharp contention between Kim Il Sung's heavy industry–first strategy and the new modes of thinking prevailing in the Soviet Union. The call to establish *Juche* can therefore be understood as an expedient means by which Kim could attack his foreign-aligned opponents and portray them as alien to Korea and as subordinate to the interests of Moscow and Beijing.[71] As Kim remarked in his December 1955 speech, 'It is important to acquire the revolutionary truth and the Marxist–Leninist truth in carrying out work, and it is important to apply that truth to the actual conditions in our country. There can be no principle that you have to follow the Soviet style. Some people say that the Soviet style is good, or the Chinese style is good, but now it's time to make our style'.[72] These comments cannot, however, be regarded in any sense as 'anti-Soviet' *per se* since Kim's speeches in the late 1950s were also peppered with statements of praise for the Soviet Union and for Marxism–Leninism. Rather, *Juche* was a call for putting the interests of the Korean revolution first and applying Marxism–Leninism to local conditions. Indeed, at the Fourth Congress of the KWP in September 1961, the North Korean leadership evaluated the success of the Five-Year Plan as the period when 'the Marxist–Leninist principle was applied to the actual conditions of our country in a *Juche*-like manner'.[73]

In this sense, Franz Schurmann's distinction between pure and practical ideology in Maoist China is also apt in the case of North Korea. As Schurmann argues, pure ideology refers to values, that is, moral and ethical conceptions about right and wrong. Practical ideology, on the other hand, refers to norms, that is, rules which prescribe behaviour and are thus expected to have direct action consequences. In China, pure ideology took the form of Marxist–Leninist theory and its stress on the importance of the materialist forces of world history centred around class conflict. Indeed, the Sino–Soviet split notwithstanding, this view of history assigned a particular role to the Soviet Union, the first socialist state and object of emulation and vision of the golden age. Practical ideology, on the other hand, could be seen as the ideology for action that emerges in the concrete conditions of the country concerned. Mao Zedong's thought, therefore, emerged out of the unification of universal truth and concrete practice, thus fulfilling the role of practical ideology in the Chinese case.[74] As such, it was entirely possible to be critical of the wholesale importation of foreign ideologies that had not been adapted to local conditions while remaining faithful to Marxism–Leninism. In this respect, Kim's

---

[71] Lee Jong-Seok, *New Approach*, pp. 147–48.   [72] Kim Il Sung, *On Juche Ideology*, p. 155.

[73] *Rodong Sinmun*, 11 September 1961, 'Congratulations to the Fourth Party Congress – the Congress of the Glorious Victors [Che 4 ch'a tang taehoerŭl yŏllyŏrhi ch'ukhahanda – yŏnggwangsŭrŏun sŭngnijadŭrŭi taehoe]'.

[74] Franz Schurmann, *Ideology and Organization in Communist China* (Berkeley, CA: University of California Press, 1966), pp. 38–46.

1955 speech had close parallels with Mao's 1940 speech 'On New Democracy', which argued that China had suffered from the mechanical absorption of foreign material and that it was necessary to integrate Marxism's universal truths with the concrete practice of the Chinese revolution. In this vein, Mao argued that 'Chinese culture should have its own form, its own national form. National in form and new-democratic in content – such is our new culture today'.[75]

Although Kim Il Sung raised the concept of *Juche* in 1955, there were no attempts to establish it as a system of thought until the late 1950s. Kim was at that time still reticent about the possibility of any ideology that might be seen as a competitor to Marxism–Leninism due to continued reliance on Soviet aid. It was not until the deepening of the Sino–Soviet dispute that Kim further elaborated on the substantive content of *Juche* thought.[76] Following the suspension of Soviet economic and military assistance in 1962, Kim increasingly emphasised the need for an autonomous developmental path through stressing the spirit of 'self-regeneration' (*charyŏk kaengsaeng*) by means of reliance on one's own strength rather than that of others.[77] As a *Rodong Sinmun* editorial on 19 December 1962 put it, '*Juche* thought is a fundamental principle that our Party firmly holds in its actions'.[78]

Juche thought henceforth came to be associated more fully with the ethos of self-reliance rather than simply the application of Marxism–Leninism to local conditions. This emphasis can be seen in Kim Il Sung's April 1965 speech at a meeting at the Ali Archam Academy of Social Sciences held to mark the tenth anniversary of the Bandung Conference. According to Kim, 'Establishing *Juche* means maintaining the principle of solving all the problems of revolution and construction independently, in accordance with the reality of one's own country and mainly by its one's own power'.[79] The establishment of *Juche* was thereby argued by Kim to encapsulate a strategy of 'independence in thought, independence in politics, self-reliance in the economy, and self-defence in the military'.[80]

This strong normative emphasis on autonomous national development was by no means unique to North Korea. As the history of Third Worldism shows, strong norms of autonomy and self-reliance were typical for countries

---

[75] Tse-Tung Mao, *Selected Works of Mao Tse-Tung: Volume II* (Peking: Foreign Languages Press, 1965), p. 381.
[76] Dae-Sook Suh, *Kim Il Sung*, pp. 307–8.
[77] *Külloja*, 15 March 1962, 'Self-regeneration is the revolution ethos of communists [Charyŏkkaengsaengŭn kongsanjuŭijadŭrŭi hyŏngmyŏngjŏk kip'ungida]', pp. 2–7.
[78] Lee Jong-Seok, *New Approach*, p. 159.
[79] *Rodong Sinmun*, 17 April 1965, 'On socialist construction in the DPRK and the revolution in South Korea – Kim Il Sung [Chosŏnminjujuŭiinmin'gonghwagugesŏŭi sahoejuŭi kŏnsŏlgwa namjosŏn hyŏngmyŏnge taehayŏ - Kimilsŏng]'.
[80] Ibid.

emerging from long periods of colonial rule.[81] In the case of India, for example, the experience of nearly two centuries of British colonial rule shaped the emergence of a political ideology that above all stressed social, political and economic dependence. Jawaharlal Nehru's experience of dealing with the British convinced him of the risks of allying himself with any great power, and as such, India's post-independence foreign policy was centred around non-alignment and economic self-reliance.[82] As Nehru argued, 'While benefiting from foreign experiences – more especially, in the constitutional sense, from England and the United States – we did not wish to copy any foreign models. We believed that India had, by virtue of her long history and traditions, an individuality of her own and we should retain this without adhering to outworn ideas or traditions'.[83] *Juche's* strong emphasis on national autonomy can thus be seen as a variant, if a particularly virulent one, of a more general post-colonial ideology of developmental nationalism.

Furthermore, as the occasion of Kim's participation in the 1965 anniversary meeting of the Bandung Conference suggests, the 1960s saw North Korea's heightened engagement in South–South diplomacy vis-à-vis decolonising nations. This strategy represents, in part, North Korea's increased room for diplomatic manoeuvre following the Sino–Soviet split. It was also, however, an element of the ongoing competition with South Korea for international recognition and legitimacy, and in particular, for concrete diplomatic support in forums such as the United Nations General Assembly. Indeed, until the early 1980s, North Korea largely outperformed the South in this respect as a result of the close correspondence between North Korean and Third Worldist values of anti-colonialism, anti-imperialism, national liberation and non-alignment.[84] On the one hand, Pyongyang sought to raise its status within the Non-Aligned Movement by means of providing economic as well as military assistance to revolutionary movements in Africa, Asia and Latin America. On the other hand, a degree of self-interest was certainly at the forefront of this engagement with the Third World. North Korea sought economic benefits, diplomatic support and validation of Kim Il Sung's personality cult through the promotion of *Juche* abroad.[85] Nonetheless, there was no necessary contradiction between the nationalism of *Juche* and the internationalism of the Third

[81] Vijay Prashad, *The Darker Nations: A People's History of the Third World* (New York: New Press, 2007).

[82] Nitya Singh and Wootae Lee, 'Survival from Economic Sanctions: A Comparative Case Study of India and North Korea', *Journal of Asian Public Policy*, 4.2 (2011), p. 175.

[83] Jawaharlal Nehru, 'Changing India', *Foreign Affairs*, 41.3 (1963), p. 455.

[84] Barry K. Gills, *Korea versus Korea: A Case of Contested Legitimacy* (London: Routledge, 1996), pp. 99–100.

[85] Benjamin Young, 'The Struggle for Legitimacy – North Korea's Relations With Africa, 1965–1992', *BAKS Papers*, 16 (2015), pp. 100–101.

World solidarity movement. As Vijay Prashad has argued, anti-colonial nationalisms tended to adopt an internationalist ethos that looked outward to other anti-colonial nations as their fellows. Third World nationalisms were thus better understood as a form of 'internationalist nationalism'.[86]

3.4   The Establishment of the Monolithic Ideological and Political System

Juche thought was not a static system of ideology but continued to develop in response to international and domestic stimuli. In the late 1960s, *Juche* thought underwent further significant changes that coincided with the intensified monopolisation of power by Kim Il Sung. Following the factional struggles of the previous decade, Kim Il Sung's position within the North Korean polity had already become largely unassailable. However, in 1967, a further purge took place of high-ranking officials associated with the so-called 'Kapsan faction', which had previously been aligned with Kim Il Sung's Manchurian guerrillas. At the 15th Plenum of the 4th KWP Central Committee in May 1967, Kim accused Pak Kum Chol of the KWP Politburo Standing Committee and Central Committee Secretariat along with other high-ranking Kapsan members of engaging in 'anti-party and anti-revolutionary scheming'. Their subsequent purge appears to have been a result of their opposition to the emerging cult of the anti-Japanese Manchurian guerrilla and the intensification of Kim Il Sung's absolute political authority.[87] In any case, the purge paved the way for even greater centralisation of power around Kim Il Sung.

As a result, *Juche* was further developed to justify Kim's increased hold on power. In a speech delivered to the Supreme People's Assembly on 16 December 1967, Kim Il Sung outlined the 'Monolithic Ideological System' (*yuilsasangch'egye*), which served to formally establish *Juche* thought as the state ideology. In his speech, Kim outlined a ten-point platform for establishing the principles of *Juche* in the fields of politics, economics and national defence, as well as in national reunification, international trade, science and technology, and international affairs. Arguably, the most important principle of the Monolithic Ideological System was absolute loyalty to Kim himself.[88] As a 1968 *Rodong Sinmun* New Year's editorial argued, 'We do not know any ideology other than that of Comrade Kim Il Sung's revolutionary thought and the *Juche* thought of our party. At any time and everywhere, we

---

[86] Prashad, *Darker Nations*, p. 12.
[87] Paik Haksoon, *History of Power in North Korea*, p. 601.
[88] James Person, 'The 1967 Purge of the Gapsan Faction and Establishment of the Monolithic Ideological System', 14th December 2013, NKIDP e-Dossier no. 15, Available: www.wilsoncenter.org/publication/the-1967-purge-the-gapsan-faction-and-establishment-the-monolithic-ideological-system [accessed 14 May 2020].

will defend the party and the *Suryŏng* [Great Leader] with our life and think and act according to his intentions'.[89] This elevation of *Juche* thought led to the suppression of any remnant of ideological pluralism in North Korea. *Juche* was thereby transformed into a justification for Kim Il Sung's monolithic system.[90] As Mitchell Lerner argues, it came to emphasise '. . . the role of the single leader, the [*Suryŏng*], as an almost God-like figure without whose guidance the masses would be unable to act collectively, develop revolutionary consciousness, or discern the correct path towards their socialist identity'.[91]

Juche thought's role as official state ideology was enshrined in the new 'Socialist Constitution of the Democratic People's Republic of Korea' adopted in December 1972. As the constitution stated, 'The Democratic People's Republic of Korea is guided in its activity by the *Juche* thought of the Korean Workers' Party, which is a creative application of Marxism–Leninism to our country's reality'.[92] Despite this wording, *Juche* thought came to occupy a status that suggests at least a partial displacement of Marxism–Leninism as the official state ideology, thus making the transition from practical to pure ideology.[93] As the status of *Juche* thought became more prominent, there were conscious attempts to provide it with a more philosophical basis. Though the principles of self-reliance and independence continued to form the core of *Juche*, from the late 1960s it evolved from a political slogan into a legitimate worldview (*weltanshchauung*) with a philosophical structure. In response to questions from journalists of the Japanese Mainichi Newspapers, Kim Il Sung remarked in September 1972 that, 'Put simply, the *Juche* thought holds that the master of the revolution and construction is the people, and that the people have the power to drive revolution and construction. In other words, it is the thought that only man holds control over his own destiny, and only he has the power to shape his destiny'.[94] *Juche* thought thus took the form of a philosophical statement regarding man's relationship with nature and society. Earlier manifestations of *Juche* thought were of course highly voluntaristic, but this later philosophical turn made this voluntaristic

---

[89] *Rodong Sinmun*, 1 January 1968, 'Let's take the great ten platforms of the Great Leader and move forward strongly towards the New Year's victory [Suryŏngŭi widaehan 10 tae chŏnggangŭl nop'i pattŭlgo saehae saesŭngnirŭl hyanghayŏ himch'age chŏnjinhaja]'.

[90] Lee Jong-Seok, *New Approach*, pp. 128–29.

[91] Lerner, 'Mostly Propaganda in Nature', p. 17.

[92] The term 'Marxism–Leninism' was even dropped from the constitution in 1992. However, the displacement of Marxism–Leninism by *Juche* thought has not been complete in North Korea. The 2010 KWP Bylaws, for example, maintain a commitment to Marxism–Leninism: 'The KWP seeks to strengthen education in *Juche* thought and opposes all kinds of reactionary opportunistic thought such as capitalist ideology, feudal Confucian ideology, revisionism, dogmatism and flunkeyism, and upholds the revolutionary principles of Marxism–Leninism'.

[93] Young Chul Chung, 'The Suryŏng System as the Institution of Collectivist Development', p. 62.

[94] Kim Il Sung, *On Juche Ideology*, p. 517.

strain even more pronounced to the extent that some observers have argued that whereas Marx had served to put Hegel's philosophy back on its feet, Kim Il Sung had put it back on its head.[95]

As noted in our discussion of the 'mass line', the emphasis on the role of human will in North Korea's late developmental project was in reality weighted towards the will of the *Suryŏng*, the Great Leader. In his 1982 elaboration of *Juche* thought, Kim Jong Il made this explicit in his examination of the relations between the leader, the party and the masses. For Kim Jong Il, the leader is the errorless brain, the masses are the body that can live only through loyalty to the leader, and the party is the nervous system that provides the organisational linkage between the masses and the leader.[96] Certainly, in contrast to the experience of England as the first mover in industrialisation, successful late development has often recognised the role of powerful modernising leaders such as Park Chung-Hee, Chiang Ching-Kuo, Lee Kuan Yew and others. In North Korea, however, the emphasis on the role of the modernising great leader has arguably been taken to extremes not seen elsewhere. In this sense, the voluntaristic slogan of 'man is the master of everything' has been in contradiction with the elimination of individualism and ideological pluralism in the North Korean society and with the strong cult of personality surrounding Kim Il Sung and his family.

Juche thought was also modified to justify hereditary succession from Kim Il Sung to Kim Jong Il. In February 1974, Kim Jong Il became a member of the politburo at the Plenum of the Party Central Committee, where he was designated as his father's official successor. In April of the same year, Kim Jong Il proclaimed the 'Ten Principles of Establishing a Monolithic Ideology System of the Party', which emphasised that Kim Il Sung's thought should be followed unconditionally. Indeed, Kim Jong Il's 1982 treatise on *Juche* in itself served to establish his authority in terms of doctrinal matters, thereby further securing his succession to the leadership of the monolithic ideological system.[97]

3.5 Conclusion

In this chapter, we have seen how the relatively benign geopolitical environment that underpinned the rapid post-Korean War reconstruction and structural

[95] Rudiger Frank, 'North Korea's Autonomy 1965–2015', *Pacific Affairs*, 87.3 (2015), p. 797; Charles K. Armstrong, 'The Role and Influence of Ideology', in *North Korea in Transition: Politics, Economy, and Society*, ed. by Kyung-Ae Park and Scott Snyder (Plymouth: Rowman and Littlefield, 2013), p. 8.
[96] Sung Chull Kim, *North Korea under Kim Jong Il: From Consolidation to Systemic Dissonance* (New York: SUNY Press, 2012), p. 125.
[97] Chung Young Chul, *Research on Kim Jong Il's Leadership [Kimjŏngil ridŏsip yŏn'gu]* (Seoul: Sunin, 2005), pp. 338–53.

transformations of the 1950s gave way to the more uncertain geopolitical environment of the 1960s. The deepening Sino–Soviet conflict and the emergence of the military regime in South Korea were interpreted by the North Korean leadership as a grave threat to the country's security. The response was to embark upon a costly process of militarisation. The policy of prioritisation of heavy industry gave way to the *Pyŏngin* dual line of economic and defence construction. However, the burden that this placed on North Korea's overall economic development was significant. To be sure, the phenomena of the increasing strain of military spending was common to many postcolonial Third World nations. As precious capital was increasingly directed towards the military, these countries saw at this time a drastic reduction in social spending.[98] In North Korea, Kim Il Sung's heavy industry–first strategy did lead to a respectable level of industrial growth during the 1960s, but the extension of the First Seven-Year Plan gives some indication as to the pressures that the economy was facing as a result of its increasing militarisation.

This militarised response to external geopolitical challenges was by no means predetermined. As we have seen, the guerrilla heritage of the North Korean leadership was apparent in terms of the sectoral allocation of resources as well as the elevation of the military as a model for the organisation of society, a response that would have a long-lasting impact on North Korea's political culture. For example, the era of Military First Politics that was to emerge under Kim Jong Il in the 1990s and the *Pyŏngin* line of economic and nuclear development under Kim Jong Un in the 2010s clearly had their roots in the militarisation of the 1960s. The tension between, on the one hand, defence and heavy industry, and on the other, light industry and agriculture, also continued to have deleterious consequences for living standards. North Korea's status as a divided country and the unresolved status of the Korean War thus played a significant role in producing and perpetuating this unbalanced developmental pattern. The 1960s also saw the emergence of institutions of economic management that came to define the distinctiveness of the North Korean political economy, such as the *Ch'ŏngsan-ri* Method, the *Taean* Work System and the unified and detailed planning system. However, all of these innovations have been held responsible for the economic stagnation of subsequent decades.

This chapter has also examined the ideological underpinnings of the North Korean developmental project in terms of the emergence of *Juche* thought, and how it subsequently evolved in response to North Korea's domestic and geopolitical challenges. Key formative movements in this regard include the factional politics of the 1950s and the political expediency of emphasising the

---

[98] Prashad, *Darker Nations*, p. 173.

indigenous nature of the Korean revolution over its external Soviet and Chinese influences; the Sino–Soviet split and the nationalist imperative for North Korea to avoid leaning to one side and to maintain the country's own distinctive trajectory; and the need to legitimise the North Korean monolithic leadership system centred around Kim Il Sung as well as Kim Jong Il's hereditary succession. Though the concept of *Juche* has its roots in Korea's early modern history and colonial experience, the geopolitical dynamics of the 1960s provided the immediate context for its emergence as the official state ideology. By the end of the 1960s, however, North Korea's industrialisation project was clearly in difficulty. As we examine in the next chapter, the country sought to break out of this situation through a process of unprecedented economic opening with the West and Japan, though this did not prevent the country from entering a period of terminal decline that culminated in the catastrophic collapse of the 1990s.

4   Economic Decline and the Crisis of the 1990s

The proximate cause of North Korea's economic collapse of the 1990s was the geopolitical and geo-economic shifts associated with the end of the Cold War. However, the crisis followed two decades of secular decline following the failed attempt in the 1970s at increasing trade with Western Europe and Japan. The shift in trade towards the non-socialist world was enabled by the favourable climate of détente and the successful post-war recovery of the Western European and Japanese economies. On the one hand, this strategy reflected a broader trend amongst the centrally planned economies whereby the exhaustion of the extensive growth model led to the import of foreign technologies and capital as a means of improving efficiency and sustaining continued growth.[1] It also had parallels with the catch-up industrialisation strategies adopted by a number of Third World postcolonial countries seeking to overcome the legacies of imperialism. However, as elsewhere, North Korea became increasingly vulnerable to the vicissitudes of the capitalist world economy and found itself unable to service its burgeoning foreign debts and saw a decline in its credit rating as a result. This failed opening thus left the country even more isolated by the end of the 1970s. In an attempt to reverse the country's ongoing economic decline, the authorities adopted several reform measures in the 1980s, though the results of these efforts were largely disappointing. As a result, North Korea became increasingly reliant on imports from its socialist allies at concessional 'friendship prices'.

The end of the Cold War led to a sudden halt in this assistance from the Socialist Bloc and exposed the fundamental contradictions of North Korea's catch-up developmental model. While the goal of self-sufficiency in agriculture and industry was one that was historically born of geopolitical expediency, the profound transformations in North Korea's external environment during the early 1990s made that goal impossible to achieve. For example, North Korea's goal of self-sufficiency in food production had been achieved through the establishment of an agricultural sector that was highly

---

[1] Franklyn D. Holzman and Robert Legvold, 'The Economics and Politics of East–West Relations', *International Organization*, 29.1 (1975), pp. 275–320.

112

industrialised and energy-dependent. As a result, the termination of Soviet and Chinese friendship prices had an immediate and devastating impact on food production. The energy crisis combined with the extreme climatic events of the mid-1990s led to a famine of unprecedented scale. The sudden decline in energy imports also let to a dramatic curtailment of industrial production. This was exacerbated as workers engaged in the widespread pilfering of factory materials and equipment as a survival mechanism, with many leaving their workplaces in search of food. As we shall see, the collapse shook the North Korean system to its core. While the apparent resilience of the political system defied widespread predictions of North Korea's impending collapse, there was a shift towards what came to be known as 'military-first politics', though as we argue, this elevation of the role of the military was more rhetorical and for the immediate purposes of crisis management than a reflection of a genuine shift in the locus of power away from the party state. The impact on the economic system was profound, however, and had implications that would leave no part of North Korean society unaffected.

4.1   North Korea's Failed Opening of the 1970s

During the 1970s, Pyongyang continued its *Pyŏngjin* line of economic and defence-related construction. Politically, this involved the purge of any remaining resistance to Kim Il Sung's rule amidst the emergence of an increasingly monolithic totalitarian state. The ongoing centralisation of power around Kim Il Sung was enshrined in the 1972 Socialist Constitution, under which Kim was appointed to the newly created position of President. The Preamble of the KWP Bylaws also formally stated that 'the Korean Workers' Party is the party of the *Suryŏng* [great leader] Kim Il Sung'. The North Korean polity thereby saw the entrenchment of a vertical power structure under which the *Suryŏng* headed the party, government and military, with the KWP seeing a relative decline in its stature.[2] As noted in the previous chapter, *Juche* thought continued to be promoted as the state's ruling ideology.

This deepening of authoritarianism coincided with a shift in North Korea's foreign trade relations. Between 1962 and 1970, the total value of North Korea's imports rose from US\$ 190.4 million to US\$ 394.9 million, while exports increased from US\$ 169 million to US\$ 307.9 million. At the same time, however, North Korea's trade with its socialist allies (mainly the Soviet Union and China) fell from 96 per cent of North Korea's total foreign trade to 83 per cent. By 1974, this had fallen again to 51 per cent (see Table 4.1). This decline was largely a result of the increasing share of Western Europe and

---

[2]   Paik Haksoon, *The History of Power in North Korea*, p. 609.

Table 4.1 *Estimates on North Korea's trade in the 1960s and 1970s*
(Unit: US$ 1,000)

Year	Total	Exports	Socialist countries	Capitalist countries	Imports	Socialist countries	Capitalist countries
1962	359,434	169,041	162,893	6,148	190,393	183,725	6,668
1964	408,840	192,435	171,841	20,594	216,405	195,989	20,416
1966	525,077	238,994	208,617	30,377	286,083	254,970	31,112
1968	586,504	255,364	206,876	48,488	331,140	280,700	50,439
1969	662,269	274,151	220,192	53,959	388,118	295,059	93,059
1970	702,810	307,909	249,014	58,896	394,901	335,523	59,378
1971	953,062	333,072	269,748	63,325	619,989	554,655	65,335
1972	1,111,281	413,899	336,521	77,377	697,382	542,393	154,989
1973	1,425,504	498,533	371,695	126,837	926,972	594,316	332,655
1974	2,078,417	713,115	467,750	245,366	1,365,302	599,005	766,297
1975	2,018,803	820,304	503,088	317,216	1,198,499	675,478	523,021
1976	1,516,230	578,784	373,942	204,842	937,446	607,671	329,776
1977	1,606,738	775,482	447,864	327,617	831,257	545,854	285,403
1978	2,233,260	1,200,450	658,476	541,974	1,032,810	602,613	430,197
1979	2,860,606	1,476,131	858,234	617,896	1,384,475	807,038	577,436

Source: Kang-Taeg Lim, 'North Korea's Foreign Trade, 1962–1992', p. 23, 27, 33.

Note: The growth in trade with capitalist countries refers to Japan, developing countries and those countries that were members of the Organisation for Economic Co-operation and Development (OECD). The latter group largely refers to Western Europe. North Korean trade with the United States was mostly non-existent due to strict sanctions in place from the time of the Korean War. Trade with Western Europe and Japan accounted for between 78 and 95 per cent of all trade with capitalist countries during the 1970s.

Japan in North Korea's external trade. Until the mid-1950s, North Korea's trade relations with the non-socialist world had been almost non-existent. In 1954, however, the United States abandoned its policy of pressuring members of the North American Treaty Organization to refrain from trade with the country. Thus, in 1956, Japan began to conduct trade with North Korea, and this was soon followed by the United Kingdom, France, West Germany and other countries.[3] Western Europe and Japan's share of North Korea's trade grew accordingly from 3 per cent in 1962 to 14 per cent in 1970, and reached a peak of 41 per cent in 1974.[4]

As a result, there emerged in the 1970s a trading relationship whereby North Korean imports from the non-socialist countries consisted of large machinery and transport goods (38 per cent) and manufactured goods (21.7 per cent). These imports were mainly from Western Europe and Japan and reflected North Korea's acute need for new technology and equipment. North Korea also imported foodstuffs (14.5 per cent), chemicals (10.3 per cent) and raw materials (7.4 per cent), the bulk of which came from non-socialist developing countries.[5] North Korean exports to the non-socialist countries, on the other hand, consisted largely of basic industrial goods (56.4 per cent), such as non-ferrous metals, iron and steel, textile yarn and fabrics and non-metallic mineral manufactures. These exports were roughly equally divided between Western Europe/Japan and the non-socialist developing countries. After industrial goods, North Korean exports to non-socialist countries, and in particular to Japan, included foodstuffs (16.7 per cent) and raw materials (15.4 per cent).[6]

The fact that technologies and equipment could increasingly only be obtained from outside of the Socialist Bloc reflected ongoing structural changes in the North Korean economy. Rapid industrial growth during the 1950s and 1960s had occurred alongside substantial changes in the structure of national output and employment. The share of industry in North Korea's national output increased from 23.2 per cent in 1946 to 40.1 per cent in 1956, and again to 62.3 per cent in 1963. At the same time, agriculture declined from 59.1 per cent to 26.6 per cent and then again to 19.3 per cent.[7] A corresponding shift took place in the structure of employment. The proportion of North Korean workers employed in secondary industries rose from

[3] Horst Brezinski, 'International Economic Relations between the KDPR and Western Europe', in *The Economy of the Korean Democratic People's Republic 1945–1977*, ed. by Youn-Soo Kim (Kiel: German Korea-Studies Group, 1979), pp. 202.

[4] Kang-Taeg Lim, 'North Korea's Foreign Trade, 1962–1992' (PhD thesis: University at Albany, State University of New York, 1995), pp. 131–32.

[5] Joseph Sang-Hoon Chung, 'Foreign Trade of North Korea: Performance, Policy and Prospects', in *North Korea in a Regional and Global Context*, ed. by Robert A. Scalapino and Hongkoo Lee (Berkeley, CA: Institute of East Asian Studies, University of California Press, 1986), p. 100.

[6] Ibid., p. 96.   [7] Eui-Gak Hwang, *Korean Economies*, p. 43.

12 per cent in 1945 to 42 per cent in 1965, while the agricultural sector having accounted for three-quarters of the total labour force in 1945 only represented about 40 per cent in 1965.

However, as liberal economic analyses have pointed out, the underlying strategy of extensive growth had by the 1960s largely exhausted itself. There developed an acute need for more advanced technologies and capital investments in order to maintain growth, particularly in the heavy industry, transportation and energy infrastructure sectors. But North Korea faced considerable obstacles in achieving further industrialisation by relying on domestic resources alone. The large military build-up including the establishment of an extensive armaments industry also hindered the reallocation of domestic resources towards technological development. With the North Korean authorities unable to finance industrial upgrading, labour productivity saw a continuous decline. Though reliable data on North Korea's technological development and industrial productivity are unavailable, the declining annual growth rate during the 1960s suggests that technology was unable to keep pace with changes in the country's industrial structure.

The government's stress from the 1960s on technological innovation provides an indication of the extent to which the upgrading of existing industrial facilities was considered a pressing challenge. The Six-Year Plan launched at the 5th KWP Congress in November 1970 explicitly sought to '... promote and develop the achievements of industrialisation, to advance the technological revolution to new heights, to strengthen the material technical basis of socialism, and to liberate workers from hard labour in all sectors of the people's economy' (see Table 4.2).[8] In his speech at the Congress, Kim Il Sung emphasised the need to reduce the gap between heavy and light labour and between industrial and agricultural labour, along with other goals such as freeing women from the heavy burden of family work. The goals of the Six-Year Plan also included an increase in the number of university and technical graduates working in factories and cooperative farms to over 10 per cent, and to increase the number of technicians and experts across the country to over one million.[9] One approach towards achieving these goals was to rely on tried and tested methods of mass mobilisation. With parallels to China's Cultural Revolution, the year 1972 saw the launch of the 'Three Revolution Teams

[8] *Rodong Sinmun,* 10 November 1970, 'On the DPRK's Six-Year Plan for the Development of the Peoples' Economy (1971–1976) – DPRK Cabinet First Vice-Premier Kim Il [Chosŏn Minjujuŭi Inmin'gonghwaguk inmin'gyŏngjebalchŏn 6 kaenyŏn (1971–1976) kyehoege taehayŏ – Chosŏn Minjujuŭi Inmin'gonghwaguk naegak che 1 pususang Kimil]'.

[9] *Rodong Sinmum,* 3 November 1970, 'Report presented by KWP Central Committee General Secretary Kim Il Sung at the 5th Congress of the KWP [Chosŏn rodongdang che 5 ch'adaehoeesŏ han chungangwiwŏnhoe saŏpch'onghwa pogo – Chosŏn rodongdang chungangwiwŏnhoe ch'ongbisŏ Kimilsŏng]'.

Table 4.2 *North Korea's economic plans between the 1970s and 1980s*

	Basic tasks and targets of the plans	Economic results as announced by the North Korean government
Six-Year Plan (1971–76)	• Strengthen the material and technological basis of socialism. • The modernisation of industrial facilities and the promotion of the technological revolution. • A 1.8-fold increase in national income. • A 2.2-fold increase in industrial production. • Grain harvest of 7–7.5 million tonnes.	• A 1.8-fold increase in national income. • A 2.5-fold increase in industrial production. • Average annual industrial growth rate or 16.3 %. • Annual growth rate of machinery and metal industry: 19.1 % • A total of 155 % increase in labour productivity. • Grain harvest of 8 million tonnes in 1976. • Year 1977 designated as 'buffer year'.
Second Seven-Year Plan (1978–84)	• The *Juche*-isation, modernisation and scientifisation of the people's economy. • The strengthening of the movement for reducing production costs and making savings. • Modernisation of the transportation sector. • Strengthening of the independent accounting system. • Increase in foreign trade. • A 1.9-fold increase in national income. • A 2.2-fold increase in industrial production. • Grain harvest of ten million tonnes.	• No announcement on national income. • A 2.2-fold increase in industrial production. • A total of 178 % increase in electricity generation. • A total of 185 % increase in steel production. • Grain harvest of ten million ton. • Designation of 1985–6 as a readjustment period. • No announcement on results of industrial and agriculture sector after the readjustment period.
Third Seven-Year Plan (1987–93)	• The *Juche*-isation, modernisation and scientifisation of the people's economy. • Promotion of the development of science and technology. • Expansion of trade and foreign economic cooperation. • A 1.7-fold increase in national income. • A 1.9-fold increase in industrial production. • A 1.4-fold increase in agricultural production.	• A 1.5-fold increase in industrial production. • A 1.3-fold increase in electricity generation. • A 1.4-fold increase in coal production. • A 1.6-fold increase in non-ferrous metals. • A 1.3-fold increase in steel production. • A 1.5-fold increase in chemical fertilizers. • Designation of 1994–6 as a buffer period.

Source: Modified from KDI, *Economic Indicators of North Korea*, p. 38.

Movement' (*3 tae hyŏngmyŏngsojoundong*). This movement sought to dispatch teams of young party officials and university students with specialist technical skills to individual factories, enterprises and cooperative farms in order to tackle problems at the production site and educate workers in technology.[10] As in China, however, the students typically lacked relevant experience in either agriculture or industry, and thus failed to bring about productivity gains.[11]

North Korea's technological impasse could not therefore be addressed through the mobilisation of domestic resources but required the import of foreign technologies. Yet, the Soviet Union was increasingly unable to fulfil North Korea's needs in this respect. The country had made significant technological progress until the 1960s, particularly in the aerospace, nuclear and machine industries. However, technological progress in heavy industry was not accompanied by development in other manufacturing sectors such as telecommunications, electronics, transportation and light industrial machinery. Furthermore, a large proportion of Soviet industrial manufactures, based on advanced technology, were produced not for export but domestic use.[12] North Korea's rapid industrialisation in the post-war period also meant that the technological gap with the Soviet Union had in any case narrowed. The industrialising North Korean economy indeed compared favourably with China, and thus, the latter was seen by Pyongyang as even less of a potential source of new technologies.

Trade between North Korea and its socialist allies was in any case complicated by the fact that as centrally planned economies, such trade did not follow market dynamics. As János Kornai has argued, trade between centrally planned economies took place on the basis of national-level agreements, whereby a given country sought to maximise purchases of 'hard goods' for which it had an acute need, while seeking to sell 'soft goods' of which it had a surplus and was unable to sell to capitalist countries.[13] The prices paid for goods often varied widely from international market prices. This meant that

---

[10] Jang In Sook, 'North Korea's Development of the Crisis and Reorganization of Mass Movement Line in the 1970s [1970 nyŏndae Pukhanŭi palchŏnwigiwa taejungundongnosŏn chaejŏngnip]', *Journal of North Korean Studies*, 15.1 (2011), pp. 258–67.

[11] *Smith*, North Korea, p. 148.

[12] András Köves, 'Socialist Economy and the World-Economy', *Review (Fernand Braudel Center)*, 5.1 (1981), p. 116.

[13] Kornai, *The Socialist System*, pp. 351–55. An example of such an agreement in the North Korean case was the multi-year trade agreement titled the 'Agreement on Mutual Supply and Payment of Goods between 1966–1970', signed with the Soviet Union in June 1966. See Cho Myung-chul, *Economic Relations between North Korea and Russia and Their Implications for Economic Cooperation between Two Koreas [Pukhan'gwa Rŏsia saiŭi kyŏngjehyŏmnyŏk hyŏnhwanggwa nambukkyŏnghyŏbe chunŭn sisajŏm]* (Seoul: Korean Institute for International Economic Policy, 2003), pp. 29–34.

one country might benefit from the arrangement more than the other, leading to charges of 'economic exploitation'. For instance, the prices of Soviet crude oil and petroleum exports to Socialist Bloc countries were until the 1960s higher than that sold to the capitalist countries. Soviet exports of crude oil to the non-socialist world were priced at US$ 2.55/barrel in 1957, falling to US$ 1.50 in 1967, whereas crude oil exports to the socialist world were priced at US$ 3.28/barrel in 1957, falling to US$ 2.10 in 1967.[14] The North Korean leadership was certainly well aware of this problem. In 1964, when relations between North Korea and the Khrushchev regime reached their lowest level, *Rodong Sinmun* published the following critique:

'In the process of providing assistance to the rebuilding our factories, you have sold us facilities … and materials at prices far above those prevailing in the international market, while taking away in return many tons of gold, huge quantities of precious metals, and other raw materials at prices substantially higher than those prevailing in the international market. When you talk about the aid you have given us, is it not reasonable that you also mention the above fact: that you took away from us the product of our painstaking labor at a time when our life was most difficult to bear?'[15]

These exploitative trade relations occurred alongside a continued decline in economic assistance from the Soviet Union and China. Despite the restoration of Soviet–North Korean relations following Khrushchev's replacement by the Brezhnev–Kosygin leadership in the mid-1960s, economic and technical assistance from the Soviet Union continued to fall short of North Korean expectations. Indeed, economic aid from the Soviet Union increasingly took the form of loans rather than grants.

How then did North Korea's partial reintegration into the capitalist world market in the early 1970s affect the country's developmental trajectory? In the short term at least, the effects were positive. As noted, the Six-Year Plan (1971–76) sought to strengthen the technological basis of the economy and achieve a growth in national income by 180 per cent and an increase in industrial production by 220 per cent (see Table 4.2). In August 1975, the authorities announced that the plan's goals had been achieved 16 months early, with industrial output achieving a 2.5-fold increase. While the targets relating to the steel, cement and transport sectors were not met, North Korea's overall economic performance for the first half of the 1970s was markedly better than in the previous decade. The 1970s also saw an increase in agricultural output. Though North Korean data on grain production in the 1970s is incomplete, the announced figures suggest that grain production increased from 7.7 million

---

[14] Robert E. Ebel, *Communist Trade in Oil and Gas: An Evaluation of the Future Export Capability of the Soviet Bloc* (New York: Praeger, 1970), pp. 58–59.
[15] Quoted in Byung Chul Koh, *The Foreign Policy of North Korea* (New York: Praeger, 1969), p. 79.

tonnes in 1975 to 8 million tonnes in 1976, and again to 9 million tonnes in 1979.[16] Though there are some questions as to whether these figures are exaggerated and/or whether the official figures refer to husked or hulled rice, they suggest on their own terms continued improvement during the late 1970s.[17]

This improved economic performance was underpinned by several other developments. For example, though still high by international standards, military spending as a proportion of the annual government budget saw a relative decline in the 1970s. Defence expenditures accounted for 31.1 per cent of the budget in 1971 but for the rest of the decade, they fell to around 15–17 per cent. At the same time, expenditures for 'the people's economy' (*inmin gyŏngjebi*), increased from 44.2 per cent in 1971 to around 56–57 per cent for the rest of the decade.[18] Furthermore, this shift coincided with an increase in the absolute size of the national budget.

Despite the positive role played by the import of foreign technologies during this period, North Korea subsequently faced problems common to other Second and Third World countries pursuing similar strategies, namely that of increasing balance of payments difficulties. According to a survey by Nicholas Eberstadt, North Korea enjoyed a trade surplus of US$ 20.6 million with the non-socialist countries in 1971. However, this turned into a trade deficit of US$ 73.1 million in 1972, and by 1975, this had reached US$ 229.6 million. North Korea's trade deficit with Japan, its largest trade partner amongst the non-socialist countries, rose from US$ 4.2 million in 1971 to US$ 118 million in 1974, and then US$ 139 million in 1975.[19] This deficit was to a large extent financed by the commercial loans from Western Europe and Japan. Indeed, in 1972, Japan had become the first non-socialist country to provide long-term trade credits to North Korea for the purchasing of its own products, and this was followed by several Western European countries.[20]

However, as the trade deficit grew, North Korea faced serious difficulties in repaying its loans. In 1975, North Korea failed to pay its foreign loan commitments at the scheduled time, leading Western European and Japanese commercial bank creditors to halt lending. North Korea's international credit rating deteriorated as a result, thereby preventing access to further commercial loans. Thus, despite the initial positive results, the rapid expansion of North Korea's

---

[16] KDI, *Economic Indicators of North Korea*, p. 91.

[17] Hy-Sang Lee, 'Supply and Demand for Grains in North Korea: A Historical Movement Model for 1966–1993', *Korea and World Affairs*, 18.3 (1994), p. 530.

[18] MOU, *North Korean Economic Statistics*, p. 139.

[19] Nicholas Eberstadt, 'Financial Transfers from Japan to North Korea: Estimating the Unreported Flows', *Asian Survey*, 36.5 (1996), p. 530.

[20] Brezinski, 'International Economic Relations between the KDPR and Western Europe', p. 203.

foreign trade during the first half of the 1970s ultimately had a highly adverse impact on the country's economy. While the government has not released data on its external indebtedness, it has been estimated that North Korea's commercial loans from Western counties amounted to approximately US\$ 1.3 billion by 1975.[21] By 1976, North Korea's total outstanding debt to socialist and non-socialist countries is estimated to have reached US\$ 2.4 billion.[22]

This debt crisis reflected the fact that North Korea had failed to treat international trade as an engine of economic growth, as had the East Asian newly industrialising countries. As such, the authorities overlooked the importance of balancing foreign trade and developing export industries based on comparative advantage. North Korea was hardly unique in this regard, however. The country's foreign debt crisis was analogous to the debt-fuelled industrialisation seen elsewhere in the Third World.[23] Indeed, the global wave of decolonisation in the 1950s and 1960s had led many newly independent states to seek to overcome the legacies of the colonial international division of labour through launching catch-up industrialisation programmes. In addition to foreign borrowing, these countries typically sought to fund their industrialisation programmes through the export of raw materials and simple manufactures. However, they too were subsequently faced with declining terms of trade due to the slowdown of the global economy in the 1970s. Stagflation in the advanced industrial economies caused by the oil crisis further undermined the export earnings of Third World countries and caused serious balance of payments problems, which they sought to overcome through further borrowing. In this respect, North Korea's foreign debt and balance of payment difficulties in the 1970s can be seen as part of a more generalised crisis of Third World development.

North Korea's trade pattern of exporting relatively simple commodities and importing manufactured goods similarly left it vulnerable to the world economic crisis and raised the costs of machinery and transport equipment imports while driving down export earnings. For example, following an increase in 1973–74, the prices of North Korea's key mineral exports to Japan of talc, natural steatite, iron and zinc ores and metalliferous non-ferrous wastes, all saw a decline, which meant that the country's mineral export earnings could not offset the jump in the price of imported petroleum.[24] North Korea thereby

---

[21] KDI, *Economic Indicators of North Korea*, p. 161.

[22] Yang Moon-Soo, 'North Korea's External Loans: Trends and Characteristics [Pukhanŭi taeoech'aemu munje: ch'usewa t'ŭkching]', *KDI Review of the North Korean Economy*, 14.3 (2012), p. 24.

[23] Jeff Frieden, 'Third World Indebted Industrialization: International Finance and State Capitalism in Mexico, Brazil, Algeria, and South Korea', *International Organization*, 35.3 (1981), p. 407.

[24] Kang-Taeg Lim, 'North Korea's Foreign Trade, 1962–1992', pp. 27–28.

lost substantial amounts of foreign exchange due to the worsening terms of trade, and had, therefore, integrated itself into the world market at the worst possible time. Once engaged in the world economy, even an ostensibly self-reliant economy such as North Korea's was vulnerable to the imported effects of the world economic crisis.[25]

The broader crisis of Third World development was not limited to the economic sphere but also had political implications in terms of fatally weakening the Non-Aligned Movement (NAM).[26] In the context of the ongoing Sino–Soviet split, North Korea concentrated much of its diplomatic activity on the NAM during the 1970s and had greatly expanded its foreign relations with several Asian and African postcolonial nations. Between 1973 and 1974, Pyongyang had, for example, established diplomatic relations with twenty-eight Third World countries. Furthermore, in May 1975, Kim Il Sung visited Algeria and Mauritania to improve relations with Africa, and on his return visited Yugoslavia, a leading member of the NAM. North Korea joined the NAM Foreign Ministers' Meeting in Peru on 25 August 1975, and in May 1976, was approved as a member of the Group of 77.[27] By the 1980s, however, the Third World debt crisis and the rise of global neoliberalism served to eclipse the NAM and its calls for a more just international economic order. As such, the crisis of the 1970s was both a crisis of development as well as a narrowing of the political space that developing countries had sought to carve out in the context of ongoing Cold War rivalry.

4.2   Experimentation with Economic Reform

Following the failed opening of the 1970s, North Korea experienced deepening economic stagnation. Western Europe and Japan's share in North Korea's total trade declined as the country reoriented its trade back towards the Socialist Bloc, albeit at the same time seeking to expand its economic relations with the Third World countries. In response to these ongoing challenges, the North Korean authorities re-emphasised the principle of self-reliance while stressing full utilisation of domestic resources and technology. However, excessive investment in heavy industry and over-reliance on the mass mobilisation of labour continued to produce meagre results, and the inefficiency of central planning exacerbated the country's economic problems. For example, unstable and insufficient energy supplies along with insufficiently

---

[25] Gills, 'North Korea and the Crisis of Socialism', p. 116.

[26] Prashad, *The Darker Nations*, pp. 207–23.

[27] Social Science Publishing Company, *DPRK History of Foreign Relations 2 [Chosŏnminjujuŭi Inmin'gonghwaguk taeoegwan'gyesa 2]* (Pyongyang: Social Science Publishing Company, 1987), pp. 141–43.

developed transport infrastructure continued to hamper industrial production, and the availability of consumer goods saw a continued decline. These ongoing structural problems were evident in the fact that although the North Korean authorities had declared the early completion of the Six-Year Plan (1971–76) in August 1975, there followed a further 'buffer period' for readjustment.

Similar problems beset the subsequent Second Seven-Year Plan (1978–84), which was also based on the goals of self-reliance and technical modernisation (see Table 4.2). In early 1984, without releasing any concrete data, it was claimed that the plan had successfully achieved an average annual industrial growth rate of 12.2 per cent.[28] However, this claim was dubious, as it was clear that the economy continued to be blighted by worn-out production facilities and a shortage of capital and advanced technology. In 1981, 1983 and 1984, the annual increase in industrial output under the plan was not announced, and the fact that the declaration of the plan's completion in February 1985 was made by the Central Bureau of Statistics rather than the North Korean leadership itself suggested ongoing poor economic performance.[29] Two years later, the North Korean government launched the Third Seven-Year Plan in 1987. The substantive goals of the plan differed little from the goals of the previous plan, further suggesting lack of progress.

In response to these ongoing economic challenges, the North Korean government adopted in the 1980s several new policies aimed at the selective introduction of market dynamics. Experimentation with 'market socialism' was, of course, by no means limited to North Korea. The Soviet Union, for example, launched several marketising reforms in the 1960s, though these ultimately failed as a result of bureaucratic resistance.[30] In that same decade, however, North Korea's economic management system had actually seen further centralisation. As noted in the previous chapter, the system of unified and detailed planning introduced in 1965 represented an attempt to expand the KWP's oversight over economic planning and coordination of economic activities at all levels. As the economy grew more complex, unified and detailed planning became increasingly ineffective.[31] The reforms of the 1980s thus took the form of the partial decentralisation of decision-making rights and the relaxation of central planning.

One of the most important of these reforms related to the so-called 'independent accounting system' (tongnip ch'aesanje, IAS), which aimed to

---

[28] Eui-Gak Hwang, *Korean Economies*, p. 45.

[29] KIEP, *2002 North Korean Economy Report*, p. 98.

[30] Vladimir Kontorovich, 'Lessons of the 1965 Soviet Economic Reform', *Soviet Studies*, 40.2 (1988), p. 311.

[31] Phillip H. Park, *Rebuilding North Korea's Economy*, pp. 59–68.

increase the role of cost accounting and profit creation in SOE management. The origins of the IAS date back to the early post-war era. According to North Korean sources, some newly nationalised enterprises adopted the IAS as early as November 1946, although it was applied more widely in the mid-1950s. Simply put, the aim of the IAS was to allow a portion of operating funds to be retained by the enterprise.[32] These funds could then be distributed in accordance with each worker's contribution, although funds were typically granted to work teams rather than individuals so as to increase incentives without encouraging individualism.[33] However, the rise of unified and detailed planning in the 1960s served to undermine management autonomy and the role of the IAS. By the 1980s, the IAS was again seen as a solution to ongoing economic decline and as a means of restoring economic growth.[34]

Thus, at the 10th Session of the Sixth Central Committee of the KWP in December 1984, the IAS was revised to provide more autonomy to SOEs and to increase their financial accountability. Enterprises were required to cover expenses from their own revenues after the requisite contributions were made to state finances. Remaining funds could then be used for the expansion of production and for workers' welfare and cultural projects.[35] However, there was something of a gap between the stated intentions of the IAS and how it was implemented in practice. In the mid- to late-1980s, the proportion of profits that enterprises were allowed to retain remained relatively small, with the state continuing to absorb the bulk of SOE profits.[36] As such, the reforms did little to overcome soft budget constraints and the runaway demand for inputs. The problem of hoarding, endemic to SOEs in centrally planned systems, persisted, and with the absence of bankruptcy laws, it was difficult for the North Korean authorities to enforce discipline on SOEs.[37]

The revival of the IAS was accompanied by the formation of what were known as 'unified enterprises' (ryŏnhapkiŏpso). The unified enterprise was a system in which a group of factories and enterprises work together as part of a

[32] An Kwang Jup, 'Development of Finance in Korea', pp. 275–95.

[33] Phillip H. Park, 'Introduction: Economic Reform and Institutional Change in the DPRK', in The Dynamics of Change in North Korea: An Institutionalist Perspective, ed. by Phillip H. Park (Seoul: IFES Kyungnam University, 2009), p. 16.

[34] Myung-Kyu Kang, 'Industrial Management and Reforms in North Korea', in Economic Reforms in the Socialist World, ed. by Stanislaw Gomulka, Yong-Chool Ha and Cae-One Kim (Armont, NY: M. E. Sharpe, 1989), pp. 203–4.

[35] Kang and Lee, 'Industrial Systems and Reform in North Korea', pp. 948–49.

[36] Moon Soo Yang and Kevin Shepard, 'Changes in North Korea's Corporate Governance', in The Dynamics of Change in North Korea: An Institutionalist Perspective, ed. by Phillip H. Park (Seoul: IFES Kyungnam University, 2009), p. 171.

[37] Lim Soo-Ho, The Co-Existence of Plan and Market: The Outlook for North Korea's Economic Reform and Systemic Change [Kyehoeggwa sijangŭi kongjon: Pukhanŭi kyŏngjegaehyŏggwa ch'ejebyŏnhwa chŏnmang] (Seoul: Samsung Economic Research Institute, 2008), pp. 52–55.

single complex.[38] Each enterprise was allowed to manage its own business activities, including the establishment of its own plan, albeit under the guidance of the State Planning Commission. The significance of this organisational form was that the unified enterprise served to increase the role of the internal market within the enterprise.[39] Though originally established on an experimental basis in 1974, the mid-1980s saw the formation of unified enterprises throughout North Korean industry. By September 1986, there were around 120 unified enterprises.[40] These included major enterprises such as Kim Chaek Iron and Steel Complex, Hwanghae Steel, 2.8 Vinylon Complex, Hungnam Fertiliser Complex, Taean Heavy Industry Complex, Pyongyang Thermal Power Plant, Sungri Motor Plant and Sangwon Cement. Again, the emergence of unified enterprises, in theory, represented the decentralisation of decision-making rights. However, the fact that key decisions on investment and production were still made and supervised by higher-level agencies meant that management autonomy was in reality only allowed in very limited areas. In particular, the system of the centralised supply of materials and assignment of labour force remained in place, while unified enterprises were still required to fulfil production goals set by the planning authorities.[41]

In the mid-1980s, the North Korean authorities unveiled a further initiative, known as the 'August 3rd People's Consumer Goods Production Movement'. This was aimed at addressing the failure of the central planning system to produce light industrial consumer goods of sufficient quantity and quality.[42] The term 'August 3rd' referred to the fact that the programme was announced on the occasion of Kim Jong Il's visit to the National Light Industry Exhibition in Pyongyang on 3 August 1984. The movement involved the establishment of 'daily necessities production units' in factories and enterprises to produce everyday goods such as clothes, footwear, school supplies, kitchen utensils and other household items through the utilisation of waste and idle material. As such, the movement was based on longstanding principles of self-reliance and the frugal use of resources. A further feature of the movement was the introduction of a new material incentive system through the establishment of direct-sales outlets (8.3 *chingmaejŏm*) in each county and township. As the production and sales of the goods took place outside of

---

[38] Park, *Rebuilding North Korea's Economy*, p. 71.   [39] Ibid., pp. 89–94.

[40] Lim Soo-Ho, *Co-Existence of Plan and Market*, p. 58.

[41] KIEP, *2002 North Korean Economy Report*, pp. 120–21.

[42] Choi Bong-Dae and Koo Kab-Woo, 'Implications of the Implementation of the Formation Process of North Korean Cities' "Farmers' Markets": Centred on the cases of Sinuiju, Chongjin and Hyesan in North Korea during the 1950s–1980s [Pukhan tosi 'nongminsijang' hyŏngsŏng kwajŏngŭi yihaengnonjŏk hamŭi: 1950–1980 nyŏndae Sinŭiju, Ch'ŏngjin, Hyesanŭi saryerŭl chungsimŭro]', *Review of North Korean Studies*, 6.2 (2003), p. 171.

the central planning index, factories were provided with a means to engage in profit-oriented production.[43]

However, this attempt to resolve the chronic shortage of consumer goods was again met with mixed results. The movement sought to squeeze more consumer goods out of an industrial structure geared towards heavy industry, and was, in reality, a reflection of a continued unwillingness to reallocate state investment resources away from heavy towards light industry.[44] The fact that the goods were produced through the utilisation of by-product and waste materials rather than the supply of new investment funds or materials meant that the goods were of limited quantity and quality. Indeed, August 3rd goods were largely unable to compete with the Chinese products that flooded into North Korea's burgeoning informal markets following the economic crisis of the 1990s. As will be discussed in the next chapter, however, the movement did establish a space for market-oriented production outside the state's central planning mechanism that would subsequently become more significant.

Finally, efforts were made to attract foreign investment. In September 1984, influenced in part by the successes of China's economic opening, the North Korean authorities promulgated the Law of Equity and Contractual Joint Ventures. Furthermore, in December 1991, the government announced the establishment of the Rajin-Sonbong Free Economic and Trade Zone in the north-eastern part of the country, close to the Chinese and Russian borders. However, these efforts were again met with disappointing results. Between the promulgation of the joint venture law and the end of 1993, North Korea received just 140 foreign investment projects to the combined value of US$ 150 million. Investments by pro-Pyongyang ethnic Koreans in Japan amounted to nearly 90 per cent of the 116 projects of which details are known, while the Soviet Union, China and Poland invested in two to four projects each. Investments by Western countries included one each from the United States (by Korean Americans), Denmark, and Italy, France, Hong Kong and Australia. Furthermore, rather than high technology sectors, the investments tended to be focused on food, textiles and other light industrial products, as well as department stores, coffee shops, restaurants and other services.[45] In terms of relieving North Korea's shortage of capital and technology, they thereby appeared to have a minimal effect. The Rason-Sonbong Zone similarly lay undeveloped for two decades.

Reasons for these failures include political rigidity, the regime's unwillingness to make fundamental reforms, inadequate infrastructure, lack of an appropriate institutional framework, a relatively small domestic market and a

[43] Ibid., p. 172.   [44] Hy-Sang Lee, 'North Korea's Closed Economy', p. 1269.
[45] Young Namkoong, 'An Analysis of North Korea's Policy to Attract Foreign Capital: Management and Achievement', *Korea and World Affairs*, 19.3 (1995), pp. 468–69.

poor reputation for the repayment of foreign debt.[46] North Korea was thereby unable to take advantage of the highly favourable external climate of the 1980s, namely low-interest rates in international capital markets, the mobility of transnational corporations and growing foreign direct investment in the Northeast Asian region. Indeed, the Japanese *yen* appreciated by 46 per cent in the three years following the September 1985 Plaza Accord, leading to a sharp decline in Japan's export competitiveness and to a massive relocation of industry offshore, particularly to Southeast Asia and China.[47] North Korea was almost completely bypassed by this mass wave of outward foreign investment, and as a result, the country's economic decline continued.

4.3   The End of the Cold War and North Korea's Economic Collapse

North Korea was unable to prevent the unprecedented collapse and widespread famine of the 1990s. The proximate cause of the crisis was the profound geopolitical shock of the end of the Cold War. This shock followed a period of increasing economic reliance on the Soviet Union. Relations between Moscow and Pyongyang had seen a marked improvement in the mid-1980s, a development that coincided with the worsening of US–USSR relations in the form of the so-called 'Second Cold War'.[48] A Soviet–North Korean 'Agreement on Trade and Economic Cooperation between 1986 and 1990' was reached in February 1986, which sought to increase the size of bilateral trade by 2.7 times compared with the past five years.[49] As such, the Soviet share of North Korea's total trade volume increased from about 27 per cent in 1980 to 57 per cent in 1988.[50] This growth in trade was accompanied by a sharp rise in North Korea's trade deficit with the USSR, although trade was conducted on a concessional basis.[51] North Korea was particularly dependent upon the Soviet Union for refined oil, lubricants and equipment in order to support the industrial and energy sectors of its economy.

By the late 1980s, however, North Korea's existing alliances were threatened by the Soviet Union's increasingly pragmatic foreign policy, and in particular, by Seoul's own policy of engagement with the Socialist Bloc.

---

[46] Ibid., p. 475.
[47] Walter Hatch and Kozo Yamamura, *Asia in Japan's Embrace: Building a Regional Production Alliance* (Cambridge: Cambridge University Press, 1996).
[48] Alexander Zhebin, 'Russia and North Korea: An Emerging, Uneasy Partnership', *Asian Survey*, 35.8 (1995), pp. 727–31.
[49] Cho Myung-chul, *Economic Relations between North Korea and Russia*, p. 34.
[50] Nicholas Eberstadt, Marc Rubin and Albina Tretyakova, 'The Collapse of Soviet and Russian Trade with the DPRK, 1989–1993: Impact and Implications', *The Korean Journal of National Unification*, 4 (1995), p. 92.
[51] Vladimir B. Yakubovsky, 'Economic Relations between Russia and the DPRK: Problems and Perspectives', *Korea and World Affairs*, 20.3 (1996), p. 452.

The Roh Tae-Woo administration's (1988–93) *Nordpolitik* sought to normalise diplomatic relations with the socialist countries and, in doing so, provide South Korean enterprises with access to new markets. The establishment of closer relations with Moscow was also seen as instrumental in tackling Pyongyang's policy of arms build-up towards the South and in encouraging inter-Korean dialogue.[52] However, it was Moscow's need for new sources of investment in the context of South Korea's status as the world's fastest-growing economy that underpinned the success of Seoul's new foreign policy approach.[53]

Moscow's policy towards the Korean peninsula thus shifted from preoccupation with ideological and security considerations to the pursuit of economic benefits. Faced with its own economic difficulties, the Gorbachev regime came to view South Korea as a source of potential demand for Soviet raw materials and as a source of consumer goods. Moscow also hoped that South Korean firms would invest in the Siberian and Russian Far East regions.[54] Trade between South Korea and the Soviet Union thereby saw a rapid expansion within the short period of 1988–90, with Seoul also committing credits of US\$ 3 billion to Moscow as economic assistance.[55] The two countries also normalised diplomatic relations on 30 September 1990. Needless to say, the warming of relations between the two countries was a worrying development for North Korea.

Due to the Soviet Union's worsening economic situation, Moscow began to demand that North Korea conduct its bilateral trade based on cash payments at world market prices, thereby abandoning the existing system of soft trading arrangements. As a result, North Korea–Soviet trade started to see a sharp decline in 1989 after having reached a peak the year before. North Korea's imports from the Soviet Union plummeted in 1991 to one-third of the average level in 1987–90, and by 1993, imports from Russia had fallen to less than a tenth.[56] Between 1990 and 1991, North Korean exports to the USSR/Russia fell by over 60 per cent, and in 1993, they were less than 6 per cent of what they had been in the 1987–90 period.[57] As Michael Mazarr has argued, the sudden end of the Soviet Union's long tradition of economic and

---

[52] Kook-Chin Kim, 'South Korea's Policy toward Russia: A Korean View', *Journal of Northeast Asian Studies*, 13.3 (1994), pp. 9–10.

[53] John Curtis Perry, 'Dateline North Korea: A Communist Holdout', *Foreign Policy*, 80.Autumn (1990), p. 173.

[54] Seung-Ho Joo, 'Soviet Policy toward the Two Koreas, 1985–1991: The New Political Thinking and Power', *Journal of Northeast Asian Studies*, 14.2 (1995), pp. 31–32.

[55] Kook-Chin Kim, 'South Korea's Policy toward Russia', p. 4.

[56] Eberstadt et al., 'The Collapse of Soviet and Russian Trade with the DPRK', p. 98

[57] Ibid., p. 101.

political support for North Korea meant that the latter became one of the 'orphans of *glasnost*'.[58]

To make the matters worse, on 24 August 1992, China also established full diplomatic ties with South Korea. Though Sino–US relations had warmed in the 1970s, Beijing and Pyongyang sought to maintain their alliance, and on the surface at least, North Korea did not oppose China's subsequent reform and opening. However, China's continued economic growth led to a deepening of its trade relations with South Korea. As the existing multi-year Sino–North Korean trade agreement came to an end in January 1992, China halted its soft trading arrangements with North Korea and demanded the use of international exchange rates and hard currency payments. As a result, Sino–North Korean trade saw a decline of 39 per cent between 1993 and 1995, and a further decline of 33 per cent by 1999.[59] This sudden realignment of trading relations with North Korea's socialist allies had a particular impact on the country's energy imports. Overall imports of crude oil and petroleum products declined from 2.2 million tonnes per year in 1986–87 to 1 million in 1994–95. Imports of coking coal saw an even sharper decline, from 330,000 tonnes in 1986 to less than 100,000 tonnes in 1995.[60]

The immediate effect of these realignments was to send the North Korean economy into a vicious cycle of decline. The sharp decline in imports of petroleum and industrial equipment, for example, exerted a significant shock on the energy, transport and manufacturing sectors. Transportation bottlenecks hampered the domestic production and delivery of coal, which led to reduced operation of thermal power plants and industrial facilities that used coal as the primary energy source. As coal accounted for about 70 per cent of North Korea's energy needs in 1990, this, in turn, had a devastating impact upon railways and on manufacturing, which was already suffering from the collapse in imports of machinery and equipment.[61] Along with the reduced output of iron ore mines, shortages of energy and imported coking coal curtailed production at the Kim Chaek Iron and Steel Complex and at other steel mills, which served to further constrict the operation of machine-tools factories and the supply of domestic machinery.[62] Thus, in the early 1990s, North Korean

[58] Michael J. Mazarr, 'Orphans of Glasnost: Cuba, North Korea and US Policy', *Korea and World Affairs*, 15.1 (1991), pp. 58–84.

[59] Scott Snyder, *China's Rise and the Two Koreas: Politics, Economics, Security* (Boulder, CO: Lynne Rienner, 2009), pp. 111–2.

[60] Nicholas Eberstadt, *The North Korean Economy: Between Crisis and Catastrophe* (New Brunswick, New Jersey: Transaction Publishers, 2007), p. 116.

[61] Lee Seog-Ki, Kim Suk-Jin, Kim Kye Hwan and Yang Moon-Soo, *North Korean Industries and Firms in the 2000s: Recovery and Operation Mechanism [2000 nyŏndae Pukhanŭi sanŏpgwa kiŏp: hoebok silt'aewa chakdong pangsik]* (Seoul: Korea Institute for Industrial Economics and Trade, 2010). pp. 73–74.

[62] Ibid., p. 75.

industry operated at a rate well below its capacity. Between 1989 and 1994, cement production fell by 51 per cent and chemical fertiliser by 23 per cent. Steel production saw a decline of 46 per cent between 1991 and 1994.[63] This decline thereby further undermined the country's ability to earn foreign exchange and purchase inputs from abroad.

These dynamics also had a devastating impact on North Korean agriculture. Despite the country's scarcity of arable land and its short growing season, North Korea had, until the 1970s, achieved an impressive level of agricultural development. As we have seen, the continued increase in agricultural output during the post-liberation era was largely achieved on the basis of land reform, collectivisation, extensive development of drainage and irrigation facilities, high levels of mechanisation and electrification, as well as mass mobilisation of labour. However, the growth in North Korea's grain production was also coupled with the broader worldwide trend whereby Green Revolution technologies brought about the remarkable expansion of grain production in developing countries from the late 1960s. North Korea made efforts to increase productivity in the agricultural sector through the diffusion of high-yield varieties and the widespread application of chemical fertilisers. The Six-Year Plan (1971–76) placed particular emphasis on the building of new fertiliser plants, such as the Namhung Youth Chemical Complex, which was built with equipment imported from Western Europe as part of the country's short-lived era of trading relations with the non-socialist world.[64] North Korean official figures suggest that, as a result, the country improved its annual grain production from 4.5 million tonnes in 1965 to 8 million tonnes in 1976, and then to 10 million tonnes in 1984.[65]

Nonetheless, North Korean grain production began to stagnate in the 1980s, before collapsing in the 1990s. Critics of North Korean agriculture have often pointed to the collectivised agricultural management system as having played a key role in the failure of the sector in the 1990s. Kongdan Oh and Ralph Hassig argue, for example, that the collective farms do not impart sufficient motivation to workers, who are often paid according to how many days they work, rather than how much work they do. Furthermore, edicts from above about what crops to plant deprive farmers of the decision-making autonomy that would otherwise enable the land to be used more effectively.[66] Stephan Haggard and Marcus Noland also view North Korea's policy of self-sufficiency in food production as a fundamentally misguided policy given

---

[63] Park, *Rebuilding North Korea's Economy*, p. 114.

[64] Hy-Sang Lee, 'Supply and Demand for Grains in North Korea', pp. 517–19.

[65] KDI, *Economic Indicators of North Korea*, p. 91.

[66] Kongdan Oh and Ralph C. Hassig, *North Korea through the Looking Glass* (Washington, DC: Brookings Institution, 2000), p. 61.

the country's high ratio of population to arable land. A more rational policy would have been to reduce dependence on domestic sources of supply rather than increase it.[67] As these authors suggest, the inefficiencies of collective farming and the appropriateness of self-sufficiency in food production no doubt constitute a key weakness in North Korea's agricultural sector.

Though there is truth to these critiques, they do not by themselves explain the timing of the crisis in the 1990s or why the agricultural sector was so vulnerable to the geopolitical shifts associated with the end of the Cold War. In this respect, North Korea's agricultural system can be seen as an extension of the country's broader catch-up industrialisation model. As Chong-Ae Yu has argued, the North Korean agricultural crisis stems more generally from the unsustainable practices of modern industrial agriculture and its dependence on industrial inputs. As such, the country's postcolonial development along with the global drive for industrial agriculture as the dominant mode of food production formed the fundamental underpinnings of the crisis of the 1990s.[68]

The vulnerability of North Korean agriculture to any potential reduction in the material inputs was precisely what happened when the country's relations with its socialist allies deteriorated. As noted, declining imports of energy and industrial equipment limited the operations of North Korea's petrochemical factories, the main source of fertilisers and pesticides. They also lowered the operational use of existing agricultural machinery, such as tractors and rice transplanters. Chemical fertiliser production in 1996 only reached a level of about two-sevenths of the country's overall capacity, and imported pesticides saw a rapid decline from 1,099 tonnes in 1991 to 146 tonnes in 1993. As a result, the per hectare consumption of chemical fertilisers declined from 1,000 kg in 1989 to 500 kg in 1995.[69] Indeed, signs of growing food shortages were apparent as early as 1991, as evidenced by the government's launch of the 'let's eat two meals a day' campaign. Food rations for urban residents (on average 700 grams per day for a worker and 300 grams for each family dependent) had been reduced. However, natural disasters such as floods in 1995 and 1996 and a drought in 1997 further aggravated North Korea's food situation and led to the collapse of the Public Distribution System (PDS). As a result, from the mid-1990s, North Korea descended into a state of famine.

In the past, the PDS had functioned as the core of the socialist system and served to guarantee the people's basic livelihood and was a means of social control. The collapse of the PDS meant that a large percentage of the

[67] Stephan Haggard and Marcus Noland, *Hard Target: Sanctions, Inducements, and the Case of North Korea* (Stanford: Stanford University Press, 2017), p. 107.
[68] Chong-Ae Yu, 'The Rise and Demise of Industrial Agriculture in North Korea', *Journal of Korean Studies*, 12.1 (2007), p. 81.
[69] Lim, 'North Korea's Food Crisis', p. 579.

population was left extremely vulnerable with no access to food or basic necessities. The fact that people left their workplaces to find food further contributed to the ongoing collapse of industrial production. The crisis led to severe and widespread malnutrition, with the worst cases affecting children's centres and baby homes. There was also severe damage to water and sanitation facilities, and the country's health system was unable to cope due to a lack of basic medical inputs.[70] Precise estimates of the numbers that perished due to starvation in the 1990s are unavailable, though the most sophisticated attempts to measure excess deaths put them in the range of roughly 600,000 to one million, or approximately 3–5 per cent of the population.[71] In any case, the famine was clearly a human catastrophe and gave North Korea the dubious distinction of becoming one of few countries in the post-war era to experience a widespread famine in peacetime.

4.4   Crisis Management and Military-First Politics

The economic collapse and resulting famine led to large-scale humanitarian assistance from abroad. In August 1995, North Korea formally requested international emergency relief through the United Nations Office. Humanitarian assistance to North Korea was centred on the UN Consolidated Inter-Agency Appeal for the DPRK and lasted for ten years until 2004. Aid was also given on a bilateral basis. From 1995, the United States provided humanitarian aid to North Korea, and by 2001, had provided 1.8 million tonnes of food aid to the value of US$ 591 million.[72] This international effort coincided with a relative improvement in North Korea's foreign relations. The first North Korean nuclear crisis led to the Geneva Agreement of October 1994, under which the United States agreed to provide two light-water reactors and supply heavy fuel oil as *quid pro quo* for North Korea's return to the Non-Proliferation Treaty and commitment to nuclear safety safeguards under the supervision of the International Atomic Energy Agency. North Korea's foreign relations saw further improvement in the wake of the Inter-Korean Summit on 15 June 2000. Bilateral aid from individual countries, UN agencies, international NGOs and religious organisations saw an increase, with humanitarian aid worth US$ 378 million in 2001 and US$ 360 million in 2002 provided to North Korea.[73]

---

[70] Hazel Smith, *Hungry for Peace: International Security, Humanitarian Assistance, and Social Change in North Korea* (Washington, DC: United States Institute of Peace, pp. 68–72.

[71] Stephan Haggard and Marcus Noland, *Famine in North Korea: Markets, Aid, and Reform* (New York: Columbia University Press, 2009), p. 76.

[72] Hazel Smith, 'Overcoming Humanitarian Dilemmas in the DPRK (North Korea)', *United States Institute of Peace Special Report* (2002), p. 4.

[73] UNOCHA, Financial Tracking Service (http://fts.unocha.org).

While the crisis of the 1990s was first and foremost economic in nature, North Korea's political system was by no means left unaffected. Kim Il Sung died at the age of 82 years old in July 1994, while his son and successor Kim Jong Il announced a mourning period of three years. Faced with the worst crisis in its history, the 1996 New Year editorial in *Rodong Sinmun* stressed the spirit of the 'arduous march'. This was a reference to the escape of the anti-Japanese partisans led by Kim Il Sung from the onslaught of the Japanese troops in Southern Manchuria, and as such, came to serve as an ideological slogan exhorting citizens to overcome difficulties in order to protect the North Korean system. The North Korean authorities also declared the post-Kim Il Sung era as one of 'Yuhun Politics', a somewhat difficult to translate term with strong Confucian undertones that point to the unwavering adherence to the policy line established by the departed Supreme Leader. Yet, Kim Il Sung's death did lead to a key shift in North Korean politics towards an emphasis on the role of the military in state and society. Indeed, it has been widely argued that Military-First Politics (*sŏn'gun chŏngch'i*) represented a shift away from the subordination of the military to the civilian leadership that had existed under Kim Il Sung.[74]

In organisational terms, Military-First Politics was manifested in the rising stature of the National Defence Commission (NDC). The NDC was elevated to a branch of government as a result of the constitutional revision of 1992, with Kim Jong Il elected as chairman. The argument that Military-First Politics displaced the party state also rests on the fact that Kim Jong Il staffed the NDC with military elites who were in charge of the key institutions responsible for the security of the regime.[75] Kim Jong Il's on-the-spot guidance tours included military-related sites to a much greater extent than those of Kim Il Sung, while Kim Jong Il's entourage on these visits, frequently taken as an indicator of the real holders of influence within the North Korean political system, were increasingly made up of military figures.[76] Under Kim Jong Il's rule, military elites enjoyed higher positions in the hierarchy, and had seemingly become the backbone of state governance.[77] Indeed, Military-First Politics in the 1990s was also accompanied by the promotion of the military as an object of emulation. A 'civil-military unity campaign' was launched under which factories, enterprises, cooperative farms as well as educational institutions were instructed to host seminars to express thanks and provide material support to

---

[74] See Smith, *Hungry for Peace*, p. 79.
[75] Jongseok Woo, 'Kim Jong-Il's Military-First Politics and beyond: Military Control Mechanisms and the Problem of Power Succession', *Communist and Post-Communist Studies*, 47.2 (2014), p. 123.
[76] KINU, *Trends in Kim Jong Il's On-the-Spot-Guidance [Kim Chŏngil Hyŏnjijido Tonghyang 1994-2011]* (Seoul: Korea Institute for National Unification, 2011).
[77] Seong-yong Park, 'North Korea's Military Policy under the Kim Jong-Un Regime', p. 63.

the Korean People's Army. This campaign was also aimed at minimising discontent within the military amidst the rapidly deteriorating economic situation.[78]

Given the Marxist–Leninist origins of North Korean state ideology, this elevation of the stature of the military certainly does appear to be an anomaly and in marked contrast to other state socialist countries that typically viewed the working class as the main driving force of the revolution. Even under Kim Il Sung, North Korea had designated the workers, peasants and intellectuals as the key revolutionary forces rather than the military.[79] In explaining why North Korea took this path under Kim Jong Il, it is difficult to overestimate the sense of existential crisis that the onset of the post-Cold War system and economic collapse posed to the regime. The emphasis on the military as a bedrock of political stability was a means of countering these rising internal and external threats and keeping the military loyal. The military was not only to provide security but play a key role in maintaining system stability and ideological strengthening, as well as to mobilise soldiers as labour-power for mass construction sites, such as hydropower station construction, road building, etc., thereby giving the military a key role in the economic sector.[80] Yet, underpinning this strategy was the North Korean leadership's broader interpretation of the causes of the collapse of socialism in the Soviet bloc. It was believed that the latter had occurred because the Soviet leadership had failed to understand the leading role of the military and had allowed it to become politically and ideologically disarmed. As such, the North Korean leadership concluded that the party, the people and the socialist system could only be preserved through the barrel of a gun.[81]

However, although the military increased in importance and prestige, this did not mean that the military had literally taken control of the party and government. As Tae-Sup Lee has argued, the army was neither superior to the party nor the dominant political power within the North Korean system. In the Kim Jong Il era, Military-First Politics was led by the party with the goal of strengthening the military's support for the party.[82] Certainly, there did appear to be a decline in the party's activities. For example, there were no party congresses after 1980 or plenums of the Central Committee after 1993. It is also suspected that there were no Secretariat or Politburo meetings after Kim Il Sung's death. However, these were institutions of the party's collective leadership. Following the factional disputes of 1956, the Kapsan purge in 1967 and

---

[78] Young-Tai Jeung, *North Korea's Civil-Military-Party Relations and Regime Stability* (Seoul: Korea Institute for National Unification, 2007), pp. 23–26.

[79] Ibid., p. 16.

[80] Tae-Sup Lee, *North Korea's Economic Crisis and System Change*, pp. 331–2.

[81] Young-Tai Jeung, *North Korea's Civil-Military-Party Relations and Regime Stability*, p. 22.

[82] Tae-Sup Lee, *North Korea's Economic Crisis and System Change*, pp. 327–32.

the emergence of the *Suryŏng* system, the KWP effectively became the personal party of Kim Il Sung and Kim Jong Il. As such, the party's collective leadership organs largely became meaningless and ceased to operate.[83] In that sense, it was not a decline of the party *per se* but rather that the emphasis in the party appeared to have shifted towards the Secretariat, the key KWP institution that discusses and makes decisions on internal and other working-level issues and supervises the implementation of such matters, through, for example, the Organisation and Guidance Department.[84] Under Military-First Politics, there was no fundamental change to the 'Party-commands-the-military' structure in which the party guides and controls the military politically and ideologically. With the exception of Kim Jong Il, military leaders sitting on the NDC did not appear to actively participate in national-level decision-making processes. Even after the onset of Military-First Politics, party-dominant political characteristics were still maintained.[85] As such, Military-First Politics should be seen as a form of crisis management that did not displace the traditional party state, and indeed, the rising stature of the party during the Kim Jong Un era would appear to confirm this view.

4.5   Conclusion

Both liberal economic and dependency analyses have identified North Korea's autarkic economic strategy as one of the most salient characteristics of the country's developmental model. As we have seen, however, North Korea did embark upon an unprecedented pursuit of trade relations with the non-socialist countries in the 1970s, though this was largely for the purpose of maintaining its self-reliant developmental path. The failure of this strategy should, however, also be understood as part of a more generalised crisis of Third World development, whereby the oil crisis and stagflation in the West problematised the continued funding of Import substitution industrialisation (ISI) programmes underpinned by the export of natural resources. The fact that North Korea did not, in contrast to elsewhere in the Third World, subsequently undergo International Monetary Fund-mandated structural adjustment and instead pursued a series of rather cautious economic reforms meant that the country was ill-placed to take advantage of the boom in foreign investment in the East Asian region in the subsequent decade. In particular, the promulgation of the country's first joint venture law in 1984 and establishment of the

[83] Cheong Seong-Chang, *Contemporary North Korean Politics: History, Ideology and Power System [Hyŏndae Pukhanŭi chŏngch'i: Yŏksa – inyŏm – kwŏllyŏgch'aegye]* (Seoul: Hanul Academy, 2011), p. 288.
[84] MOU, *Understanding North Korea* (Seoul: Ministry of Unification, 2014), p. 66.
[85] Young-Tai Jeung, *North Korea's Civil-Military-Party Relations and Regime Stability,* p. 20.

Rajin-Sonbong Special Economic Zone in 1991 were largely failures. Furthermore, the contradictions of the country's heavy industry–first catch-up developmental model led the country to a full-blown crisis in the 1990s as a result of the rapid transformation of North Korea's external alliances. As we have argued, North Korea's dependence on the largesse of its socialist allies constituted a fundamental weakness of that model, and with the geopolitical transitions of that decade, the country's model of development quickly became unsustainable.

The crisis of the 1990s has continued to cast a dark shadow on the country's subsequent economic development. Although the country began to see a limited degree of recovery from the mid-2000s, poor agricultural productivity and continued food shortages remained key challenges that required addressing the inefficiency of the collective farming system and the shortages of key inputs such as fuel, fertiliser, pesticides and farm machinery. Industry also suffered from a lack of key inputs such as energy, machinery and materials, and factories were blighted by continued inefficiency. As will be argued in the next chapter, the crisis also meant that many ordinary North Koreans had little choice but to resort to private economic activities in order to survive. However, marketisation subsequently extended beyond simply the proliferation of physical marketplaces and came to influence all areas of social and economic life in North Korea. In doing so, it fundamentally transformed the nature of the North Korean state itself along with its relation to society.

5   Marketisation and the Transformation of the North Korean State

As we have seen, North Korea's economic collapse in the 1990s was profoundly shaped by the country's position within the broader dynamics of geopolitical contestation and by how those dynamics historically shaped the country's experience of catch-up industrialisation. The prioritisation of heavy industry, the single-minded pursuit of militarisation, the instability of North Korea's external alliances, failed economic reform and opening in the context of a crisis of global development, growing external dependence on energy imports and the abrupt end of the Cold War, all contributed towards the crisis. In turn, geopolitical dynamics can thus also be said to have shaped the resulting socio-economic and political transformations in North Korea in the form of marketisation.

Faced with the collapse of the Public Distribution System (PDS), ordinary North Koreans became increasingly dependent on the market for their survival. In the first instance, this was evident in the emergence of informal marketplaces trading in food and basic necessities. Thereafter, market dynamics spread to a variety of sectors including services, manufacturing, mining, seafood and fisheries, transport and real estate. This process has often been referred to as one of marketisation or capitalism from below.[1] In such views, the state is typically seen as situated in an uneasy relationship with these spontaneous grassroots processes. The currency reform of 2009, for example, whereby the authorities sought to dispossess the emergent entrepreneurial class of their new-found wealth, is held up as evidence of the socialist state's hostility towards the market.[2] The rise of the market and of an entrepreneurial class has also been seen as constituting an ongoing potential challenge to the

---

[1] Peter Ward, Andrei Lankov and Jiyoung Kim, 'Capitalism from Below with North Korean Characteristics: The State, Capitalist Class Formation, and Foreign Investment in Comparative Perspective', *Asian Perspective*, 43.3 (2019), pp. 533–55; Stephan Haggard and Marcus Noland, 'Reform from Below: Behavioral and Institutional Change in North Korea', *Journal of Economic Behavior and Organization*, 73.2 (2010), p.134; Smith, *North Korea*, pp. 211–34.

[2] Rüdiger Frank, 'Socialist Neoconservatism and North Korean Foreign Policy', in *New Challenges of North Korean Foreign Policy*, ed. by Kyung-Ae Park (Basingstoke: Palgrave MacMillan, 2010), pp. 3–42.

state's authority.[3] In this view, there are parallels with mainstream understandings of the collapse of state socialism in Eastern Europe, whereby an autonomous realm of civil society is seen as having emerged to challenge the authoritarian state and facilitate a transition towards democracy.[4]

On the one hand, such views reflect the liberal ontological distinction between the state and market/civil society and between the public and private. Here the private realm of the market or civil society is defined as an arena of activity, association, interests and identities operating separately from the state. They also frequently take the form of a normative conception that regards the preservation of the distinction between public and private as a necessary condition of a liberal democratic polity and successful market economy, and the absence of this boundary as a key characteristic of totalitarianism.[5] However, as Karl Polanyi argued with reference to the case of England, the rise of the market economy was actively facilitated by the modern state. The latter played a key role in bringing about the changes needed in the social structure and in human society that would form the basis of a competitive capitalist economy. Specifically, this involved the creation of markets in land and labour, which would then be sold in accordance with supply and demand.[6] Given that the market has historically been created and regulated by the state, the distinction between the two should be viewed as methodological rather than ontological, and not one that is 'real' *per se*.[7]

The literature on North Korean marketisation has not entirely neglected certain forms of interdependence between state and market actors, arguing that there is, in fact, widespread collusion between officials and market actors at various levels of the economy.[8] Hazel Smith argues, for example, that '... [m]arketisation generated incentives for poorly paid officials to waive and reduce penalties such that the legal system became much more porous and less of an absolute bulwark of state repression'.[9] Furthermore, state enterprises became key players in market activities while the KWP and the military

[3] Alexander Dukalskis, 'North Korea's Shadow Economy: A Force for Authoritarian Resilience or Corrosion?', *Europe - Asia Studies*, 68.3 (2016), pp. 487–507.

[4] Marcia A. Weigle and Jim Butterfield, 'Civil Society in Reforming Communist Regimes: The Logic of Emergence', *Comparative Politics*, 25.1 (1992), pp. 1–23; Zbigniew Rau, *The Reemergence of Civil Society in Eastern Europe and the Soviet Union* (Boulder, CO: Westview Press, 1991).

[5] Corinna-Barbara Francis, 'Quasi-Public, Quasi-Private Trends in Emerging Market Economies: The Case of China', *Comparative Politics*, 33.3 (2001), p. 277.

[6] Karl Polanyi, *The Great Transformation* (Boston, MA: Beacon Press, 1944), pp. 71–80.

[7] Ian Bruff, 'Overcoming the State/Market Dichotomy', in *Critical International Political Economy: Dialogue, Debate and Dissensus*, ed. by Stuart Shields, Ian Bruff and Huw Macartney (Basingstoke: Palgrave Macmillan, 2011), pp. 86–87.

[8] Hyung-min Joo, 'Visualizing the Invisible Hands: The Shadow Economy in North Korea', *Economy and Society*, 39.1 (2010), p. 133.

[9] Smith, *North Korea*, p. 212.

contributed towards marketisation through the establishment of trading companies. Despite the ostensible 'marketisation of the Party', however, Smith still notes an unresolved tension between the central government and the lower echelons of the state that have become enmeshed in market processes. The fact that lower-level officials are deeply implicated in these processes means that the central state has struggled to control and limit market dynamics.[10] As such, marketisation according to Smith proved resilient in the face of repression from 'military rule from above'.[11]

In this chapter, we build upon these insights but argue that the North Korean state became even more central to processes of marketisation than has typically been recognised. Indeed, the state played a leading role in the creation of market institutions in the country. While there was certainly a spontaneous element to marketisation in the 1990s when the ability of the state to provide for the basic needs of the population was drastically curtailed, government policies since the early 2000s and into the Kim Jong Un era served to formalise a wide range of hitherto illegal and semi-legal private economic activities, thereby playing a key role in establishing the market mechanism.[12] The reason for the state's proactive role was that marketisation was a process that served to facilitate both the reproduction of the state–bureaucratic class as a whole and thereby enabled the state to pursue its strategic goals. Faced with a severe fiscal crisis, the central state established a variety of mechanisms to stimulate market activity and absorb the resulting profits into state coffers. From the perspective of North Korea's emergent entrepreneurial class, the lack of clearly defined property rights meant that market activities required the cover of an affiliation with a state entity in order to engage in profit-oriented private economic activities. The relevant state entity, on the other hand, entered into a partnership with *de facto* private capital as a means of securing needed resources. Thus, the result was not a zero-sum relationship between the state and market actors but rather a mutually dependent one that was, to a certain extent, based on shared interests.

As such, while some scholars have sought to apply the concept of the 'shadow' or 'second economy' to the case of North Korean marketisation,[13] theses notions have become increasingly unable to capture the sheer scope and depth of marketisation in the country. Marketisation was no longer a

---

[10] Ibid., pp. 218–20.   [11] Ibid., p. 234.

[12] Yang Moon-Soo, "'Economic Management System in Our Style' Observed through the Revised Laws in the Kim Jong Un Era [Kimjŏngŭn chipkwŏn ihu kaejŏng pŏmnyŏngŭl t'onghae pon 'urisik kyŏngjegwallibangbŏp']", *Unification Policy Studies*, 26.2 (2017), pp. 100–105.

[13] Hyung-min Joo, 'Visualizing the Invisible Hands.'; Hong-Tack Chun, 'The Second Economy in North Korea', *Seoul Journal of Economics*, 12.2 (1999), pp. 173–94; Dukalskis, 'North Korea's Shadow Economy'. On the Soviet case, see Gregory Grossman, 'The "Second Economy" of the USSR', *Problems of Communism*, 16.5 (1977), pp. 25–40.

phenomenon that existed within the interstices of a statist economy but came to be a strategic goal pursued by the state. The state has been central to establishing the key underpinnings of market activity, including for example, not just the physical infrastructure of the marketplaces but the establishment of a mobile telecommunications sector and a range of legal reforms that provide at least partial recognition of the role of private capital in the economic life of the country. As we also argue, however, marketisation was somewhat uneven. It progressed most in the production of basic necessities as well as in the light industry, retail and service sectors, and amongst small-scale regional enterprises. It was much more limited in the military and defence sectors, and in energy production, railways and heavy industries.[14] As such, the unevenness of marketisation was not so much to be found on a vertical axis between the central state and lower-level officialdom but rather was a process that displayed marked sectoral variations.

5.1   The Rise of the Market in North Korea

The dominant view of marketisation in North Korea is that the process emerged as a result of the economic collapse of the 1990s and the public's resort to grassroots market activities as a means of survival. In this view, marketisation could be '. . . traced in part to the coping strategies of local party, government, and military units together with individual enterprises and households'.[15] As the PDS ground to a halt, the public had little choice but to acquire their own sources of food and basic necessities. In the countryside, farmers were to some extent able to rely on their own kitchen gardens (*tŏtbat*), while urban areas saw the emergence of workplace plots (*puŏpbat*). Mountainous regions that were unsuitable for conventional farming also saw the expansion of illegal reclaimed plots (*ttwaegibat*) following the crisis. Surplus produce was sold in local farmers' markets (*changmadang*), which rapidly became a key source of food for the majority of the population.

The existence of these markets was not a new phenomenon. On 5 March 1950, the state established farmers' markets in major cities to facilitate the sale of agriculture produce and livestock to urban residents.[16] While the completion of the collectivisation of agriculture and the nationalisation of commerce in

---

[14] Lim Kang-Taeg, *Analysis of the Condition of North Korea's Informal Sector: Focus on Corporate Activity [Pukhan kyŏngjeŭi pigongsikbumun silt'ae punsŏk: Kiŏphwaldongŭl chungsimŭro]* (Seoul: Korea Institute for National Unification, 2013).

[15] Haggard and Noland, *Famine in North Korea*, pp. 15–16.

[16] *Rodong Sinmun,* 3 March 1950, 'Remarks by Minister of Commerce Chang Si-U: the establishment of farmers' markets will strength the economic connections between cities and villages [Changsiu sangŏpsangŭi damhwa – Nongminsijangŭi kaesŏlŭn tosiwa nong'ch'on'ganŭi kyŏngjejŏk yŏn'gyerŭl tŏuk konggohi handa]'.

1958 saw the abolishment of conventional market trade in consumer goods and processed foodstuffs, the farmers' markets remained open.[17] Farmers were allowed to sell output from their own kitchen gardens at these local markets, thereby contributing to their own incomes and to the living standards of urban residents.[18] However, the authorities regarded this arrangement as belonging to the transitional phase of socialism and were concerned that even limited market trade could lead to the pursuit of self-enrichment rather than collective goals. As such, tradable items were restricted to non-grain produce, such as vegetables and tobacco. In addition, markets were limited to just one or two per city or county and allowed to open just once every ten days. In the 1980s, however, as the supply of food and basic necessities became more erratic, the scale of the farmers' markets grew, albeit with continued restrictions on the types of goods sold.[19]

Though official restrictions remained in place, the 1990s crisis led to the markets opening every day and to a wider range of agricultural goods being sold. In addition, the collapse of industry and the state's deepening financial difficulties meant that ordinary North Koreans could not afford the market prices with their official wages. Many were forced to engage in sideline economic activities such as petty trading or household production. This included the selling of homemade food along with shoes, clothes, cigarettes, medicine and household appliances. At the height of the crisis, workers also engaged in widespread pilfering of equipment and materials from state-owned factories and sold them at the markets, which in turn exacerbated the collapse in industrial production.[20] Markets also saw an influx of Chinese imports, such as food, clothes and other basic necessities, and indeed, growing trade relations with China became a key pillar of North Korea's transition towards a market economy. These goods were imported by trading companies but also smuggled by individuals. Along with North Korean citizens who lived at the border regions near China, ethnic Chinese (*hwagyo*) with greater freedoms to travel took a leading role in this cross-border trade and in marketisation more broadly.

Given the severity of the crisis, the authorities had little choice but to tolerate this expansion of the markets. It is estimated that by the year 2000,

---

[17] Choi and Koo, 'Formation of North Korean Cities' "Farmers' Markets"', pp. 144–49.

[18] *Minju Choson*, 13 January 1966, 'Farmers' markets are well managed in accordance with rural district – At the Hongwon County People's Committee [Nongch'on chigubyŏllo nongminsijangŭl chal unyŏng – Hongwŏn'gun inminwuiwŏnhoeesŏ]'.

[19] Kim Young-Hui, 'The Change and Future Prospects of North Korea's Farmers' Markets [Pukhan nongminsijangŭi pyŏnhwawa hyanghu chŏnmang]', *KDB Global Economic Issues*, April (2009), pp. 151–52.

[20] Park Young-Ja, Hong Je-Hwan, Hyun In-Ae, and Kim Bo-Geun, *Enterprise Operational Reality and Corporate Governance in North Korea [Pukhan kiŏpŭi unyŏngsilt'ae mit chibaegujo]* (Seoul: Korea Institute for National Unification, 2016), p. 109.

there were between three to four hundred markets across the country.[21] Informal marketplaces also emerged in the vicinity of official farmers' markets as well as in densely populated areas near train stations and residential neighbourhoods. As a result, the number of North Koreans who survived through market activities increased sharply. According to Hyun-Sun Park's 1999 survey of North Korean defectors, around 75 per cent had engaged in small-scale trading activities in the marketplaces or in other commercial activities.[22]

Although many North Koreans left their workplaces to find food and earn extra incomes, the authorities subsequently sought to ensure that workers remained at their assigned workplaces, even in cases where factories were unable to operate due to lack of inputs. This reflected the role of the workplace as a key locus of social control. Official wages remained low, however, and were further undermined by soaring levels of inflation. Monthly wages were not even enough to buy 1–2 kilogrammes of rice at market prices. As such, incomes from market activities came to vastly exceed official wages, with earnings from the informal economy amounting to roughly 80 times that of the official economy.[23] Workers and their families thereby came to lead an 'economic double life' as they found it necessary to supplement their income through market activities.[24] Marketisation was also a highly gendered process, whereby female members of the household typically participated in market activities while male workers remained in their poorly paid official posts. As one female defector from Rason city explained:

'The people who do business in the market are women. Maybe men are there to help a little, but almost 95 percent are women ... If men don't go to work, they are sent to the correctional centre and also have to receive labour training (nodongdallyŏn). Men in North Korea should not become unemployed. So women engage in buying and selling to make a living for their family and husbands just go to the workplace. In fact, even when they go to the workplace, they don't have a proper income and they just socially have the status of being not unemployed ... Men adhere to socialism just by going to work'.[25]

In addition to this gendered division of labour, a further key social transformation accompanying marketisation was the appearance of an entrepreneurial

[21] Yang Moon-Soo, *The Marketisation of the North Korean Economy: Nature – Character – Mechanism – Significance [Pukhan'gyŏngjeŭi sijanghwa: Yangt'ae – sŏnggyŏk – mek'anijŭm – hamŭi]* (Seoul: Hanul Books, 2010), p. 23.

[22] Park Hyun-Sun, *Contemporary North Korean Society and Family [Hyŏndae Pukhansahoewa kajok]* (Seoul: Hanul Books, 2003), p. 202.

[23] Byung-Yeon Kim, *Unveiling the North Korean Economy*, p. 103.

[24] Daniel Tudor and James Pearson, *North Korea Confidential: Private Markets, Fashion Trends, Prison Camps, Dissenters and Defectors* (Tokyo: Tuttle, 2015), p. 24.

[25] Interview with defector who left North Korea in 2012, 19 May 2018.

class known as the '*donju*' (literally, 'money masters'). The *donju* can be seen as both a product and driver of marketisation. In its early stages, many of their activities were deemed unequivocally illegal. For example, a large portion of the China-sourced goods that appeared in North Korean markets in the 1990s were acquired through smuggling, with such activities running the risk of severe punishment. However, these activities were also highly profitable. Subsequent reform measures expanded the legal space for private economic activities, and as will be argued below, the *donju* increasingly entered into the manufacturing, mining, fisheries and seafood, transport as well as real estate sectors. As their wealth grew, they also engaged in lending at high-interest rates, though this remained strictly illegal.[26] The rise of the *donju* was at the same time part of a broader process of societal polarisation, with the weakest in society unable to adapt to the changed economic environment and placed in increasing poverty. Indeed, estimates of the North Korean Gini coefficient suggest that the gap between rich and poor reached 'extremely high' levels by international standards, at above 0.6.[27] Thus, despite the fact that marketisation played an important role in improving the livelihood of the population, many still suffered from food shortages and deprivation.

5.2   Marketisation and Economic Reforms in the Early 2000s

As a result of the crisis, economic reform arguably became the most pressing issue facing North Korean policymakers. However, with the death of Kim Il Sung in 1994, the regime entered a period of official mourning and largely failed to adopt any significant measures to deal with the rapidly worsening situation, with the partial exception of the attempted restructuring of the agricultural work teams in the mid-1990s. However, in 1998 the constitution was revised to upgrade the Foreign Trade Committee of the State Administrative Council to the Ministry of Foreign Trade within the Cabinet. This revision also included amended provisions that expanded the legal scope for private economic activities, albeit with significant restrictions remaining. The late 1990s and early 2000s saw the enactment or revision of dozens of regulations related to foreign economic activities, including the introduction of the Foreign Trade Law.[28] These changes were accompanied by the emergence of new ideas and concepts that indicated policymakers' increased concern with the improvement of economic management, such as an emphasis on

---

[26] Lim Eul-Chul, 'The Formation and Development of Private Financing in North Korea: Patterns, Implications and Tasks [Pukhan sagŭmyungŭi hyŏngsŏnggwa paljŏn: Yangt'ae, hamŭi mit kwaje]', *The Korean Journal of Unification Affairs*, 27.1 (2015), p. 210.

[27] Byung-Yeon Kim, *Unveiling the North Korean Economy*, p. 110.

[28] Jong-Woon Lee, *North Korea's Economic Reform under An International Framework* (Seoul: Korea Institute for International Economic Policy, 2004), p. 13.

'practicalism' (*sillijuŭi*), as well as concepts such as the 'new thinking' (*shinsago*) and the 'great leap' (*tanbŏndoyak*). Following Kim Jong Il's four-day visit to Shanghai in January 2001, where he witnessed first-hand the results of China's policy of reform and opening, the emphasis was also placed on the need to establish economic competitiveness. Though there was no explicit approval of the Chinese experience, there was a nonetheless greater rhetorical emphasis on North Korea's own process of economic reform.[29]

Subsequently, on 1 July 2002, the government promulgated what came to be known as the 'July 1st Economic Management Improvement Measures'.[30] On the one hand, these measures were reactive and reflected the fact that the Kim Jong Il regime had little choice but to accept and legitimise the expanded role of the market. Yet, the reforms also represented a proactive shift away from the remnants of a rigid centrally planned economy towards one in which market dynamics played an increasingly important role.[31] The reforms took place in the context of an improvement in North Korea's international environment, including the warming of inter-Korea relations following the North–South summit held in Pyongyang in June 2000, improved relations with Washington during the latter years of the Clinton administration and the expansion of diplomatic relations with European countries. These developments also led to an increase in foreign trade and economic assistance in the early 2000s, creating a favourable context for reform. On 6 August 2002, *Rodong Sinmun* published an editorial that clearly expressed North Korean thinking behind the measures:

'The continuous improvement and completion of economic management is in accordance with the legitimate demand of socialist economic construction. . . . It is important to resolve all problems in the realm of economic management in accordance with the principle of securing the largest practical results . . . Production and enterprise management in the most rational and economic manner, either at the national level or in individual sectors or units, is an important method of securing practical results in the realm of economic management'.[32]

In terms of their substantive content, a key element of the July 1st measures was an increase in the state-designated prices of basic goods, thereby reducing

---

[29] Yonhap News Agency, *North Korea Handbook* (New York: East Gate, 2003), p. 238.

[30] Whilst the term 'reform' (*kaehyŏk*) is commonly used by South Korean and international observers, the North Korean state itself prefers more moderate terms, such as 'improvement measures' (*kaesŏn choch'i*). In this book, the North Korean and South Korean/international terms are used interchangeably.

[31] Phillip H. Park, 'Introduction: Economic Reform and Institutional Change in the DPRK', in *The Dynamics of Change in North Korea: An Institutionalist Perspective*, ed. by Phillip H. Park (Seoul: IFES Kyungnam University, 2009), pp. 30–31.

[32] *Rodong Sinmun*, 6 August 2002 'Socialist Economic Management and the Securing of Practical Results [Sahoejuŭi kyŏngjegwalliwa sillibojang]'.

their large disparity with market prices. Previously, the prices of food and basic necessities were set well below their actual value. With deepening shortages, however, market prices had reached many hundreds of times that of official prices. The price increases under the July 1st measures were therefore applied to food and basic necessities as well as public services such as transport, electricity, water and fuel. The aim was to reduce the burden on state finances by making official prices reflect more closely the cost of production. In addition, the official exchange rate was set at a level closer to the market exchange rate.

The July 1st measures also increased workers' wages to reflect these price increases, with average basic wages for manufacturing workers increasing 18-fold. The precise level of the increase was dependent on occupation, with increases for technicians, highly skilled workers and scientists higher than those for white-collar and service sector workers. The measures also curtailed the scope of what remained of the PDS, although specific social security schemes were maintained, such as free medical care, free compulsory education and the retired soldier support system.[33] Furthermore, material incentives were strengthened to improve workers' productivity, such as paying workers according to the quantity and quality of their work as well as the performance of their work units. This represented a departure from the well-established principle of 'equalism' (p'yŏnggyunjuŭi) that had hitherto characterised North Korean wage policy. As Professor Ri Ki Ban argued in a 2003 edition of the North Korean journal Economic Research (Kyŏngje Yŏn'gu):

'In the realm of distribution, equalism has a negative effect both on those who are good at their work and those who are lazy, and it reduces the effort and enthusiasm of the labour collective as a whole and encourages the lack of a serious attitude and preference for easy work, thereby creating an atmosphere of laziness (kŏndalp'ung). Thus, the elimination of equalism ... is an important requirement for improving economic management to increase workers' enthusiasm ... In a socialist society, failing to do one's own work and simply expecting free handouts is the old way of thinking, and leads to a decline in workers' enthusiasm. Therefore, the elimination of free handouts is an important issue in bringing the thought of workers into line with the demands of socialist economic management and maximising their loyal enthusiasm and creativity'.[34]

---

[33] KIEP, 2003/04 North Korean Economy Report [2003/04 Pukhan'gyŏngjebaeksŏ], (Seoul: Korea Institute for International Economic Policy, 2004), pp. 266–69.

[34] Ri Ki Ban, 'The Accurate Implementation of the Principle of Socialist Distribution Is an Important Requirement of the Completion of the Improvement of Economic Man agement [Sahoejuŭi punbaewŏnch'ikŭl chŏnghwakhi kuhyŏnhanŭn kŏsŭn kyŏngjegwalligaesŏn wansŏngŭi chungyohan yogu]', Economic Research [Kyŏngje Yŏn'gu], 2 (2003), p. 21.

The results of the reforms were mixed, however. With continued shortages of basic goods in state outlets, the reforms led to high levels of inflation. For example, between 2003 and 2008, the market price of rice saw an average annual increase of 62.4 per cent.[35] Furthermore, the effects of the increased material incentives were offset by the fact that wage levels in the state sector remained so low that workers were still unable to purchase goods at market prices. Nonetheless, the measures did suggest that the authorities recognised the problems caused by the unrealistic pricing and wage system along with the need for greater utilisation of market dynamics.

The July 1st measures also sought to increase productivity in the manufacturing sector by conferring more decision-making rights on SOEs and allowing for an increased share of profits to be retained by management. Enterprises were given responsibility in drawing up their plans and were henceforth to be assessed according to their 'earned income' (*pŏnsuib*). If enterprises surpassed their production goals, the resulting surplus could be sold and the profits either reinvested or paid as employee bonuses. The earned income system thus created a legal means for engaging with the market outside of the state plan.[36] As a result, enterprises showed greater interest in increasing production, trading with foreign enterprises and attracting new investment. For example, in a 2003 interview with *Choson Sinbo*, the director of Pyongyang's 3.26 Electric Wire Factory stated that 'In the past, investment in facilities for expanded reproduction was the responsibility of the state ... Each unit waited for the state to solve the problems of the supply of equipment. But from last year, with the improvement of the socialist economic management system, the 'earned income' is spent at the discretion of the factories and enterprises for the purposes of widened reproduction'.[37]

In March 2003, the authorities also transformed the existing farmers' markets into so-called 'general markets' (*chonghap sijang*). Through Cabinet Directive 24 (General Market Establishment Directive), the government provided detailed guidelines on how general markets were to be established and managed. The general markets were registered as regional-level SOEs, and were permitted to open every day and to trade in a broader range of industrial goods than the farmers' markets were able to. In addition to the expansion of existing facilities, markets on the outskirts of cities were moved closer to city centres and provided with permanent structures including walled perimeters and roofs. The fact that the markets were regulated by the state meant they took

---

[35] Sung Min Mun and Sung Ho Jung, 'Dollarization in North Korea: Evidence from a Survey of North Korean Refugees', *East Asian Economic Review*, 21.1 (2017), p. 82.

[36] Yang and Shepard, 'Changes in North Korea's Corporate Governance', p. 151.

[37] *Choson Sinbo*, 3 December 2003, 'The Complete Renewal of the Production Process after the Passing of about Forty Years – Leading Investment for the Future [40 yŏnyŏn mane iruŏjin saengsan'gongjŏng chŏnmyŏn'gaengsin – miraerŭl wihan sŏnhaengt'uja]'.

a similar form across the country in terms of opening hours, arrangement of stalls and permitted tradable goods. Following the payment of a market stall registration fee, traders were provided with a licence to operate a stall and were required to pay a 'market usage tax' on a daily basis.[38] A market management office took responsibility for the collection of fees and taxes.

Some markets were of considerable size. When Tongil Street Market in Pyongyang's Rangnang District first opened in August 2003, it was 6,000 square metres in size, had around 100,000–150,000 visitors a day and contained around 1,400 market stalls.[39] Furthermore, general markets became widespread throughout North Korea. Based on Google Earth satellite images and interviews with defectors, a 2016 report by the Korea Institute for National Unification put the number of formal general markets at 404.[40] The North Korean Development Research Institute, a research organisation of North Korean defectors in Seoul, put the figure somewhat higher at 461.[41] In any case, the markets continued to grow, even during periods of attempted crackdown such as in the late 2000s. Cities where markets saw the fastest growth include Sinuiju on the Chinese border as well as port cities such as Nampo and Haeju, suggesting that good transport links with the outside world were a key factor in their growth.[42]

General markets thus played a central role in North Korea's broader marketisation. Some of the larger markets came to serve as wholesale markets for the rest of the country.[43] These were initially established in cities close to the border with China, thereby acting as a conduit for the supply of imported Chinese products to other regions in North Korea. As marketisation

---

[38] Joung Eun-Lee, 'An Analysis of the External Changes and Development of the Public Market in North Korea [Pukhan kongsŏlsijangŭi woehyŏngjŏk paldale kwanhan yŏn'gu]', *Journal of Northeast Asian Economic Studies*, 23.1 (2011), p. 236.

[39] *Choson Sinbo*, 10 September 2004, 'Research and explorations from the employees of the Tongil Street Market – Facilitating the convenience of people's lives through the operation of a wholesale unit [T'ongilgŏrisijang chongŏbwŏndŭrŭi t'amguwa mosaek – tomaeban unyŏngŭro inminsaenghwarŭi p'yŏnŭidomo]'.

[40] Hong Min, Cha Moon-Suk, Joung Eun-Lee, and Kim Huk, *Information on North Korean Markets: Focusing on the Current Status of Official Markets [Pukhan chŏn'guk sijang chŏngbo: Kongsiksijang hyŏnhwangŭl chungsimŭro]* (Seoul: Korea Institute for National Unification, 2016).

[41] North Korea Development Institute, 'The Present Status and Outlook of North Korean Marketisation: A Focus on Market Change [Pukhanŭi sijanghwa hyŏnhwanggwa chŏnmang: Sijangbyŏnhwarŭl chungsimŭro]'. (Unpublished Paper, 2016).

[42] Benjamin Katzeff Silberstein, 'Growth and Geography of Markets in North Korea New Evidence from Satellite Imagery', (Washington, DC: US-Korea Institute at SAIS, 2015), p. 8.

[43] Hong Min et al., *Information on North Korean Markets*, p. 12. General markets that act as wholesale markets include Pyongyang's Tongil Street market, Rason City's Ch'ongpyong market, Pyongson City's Doksan market (South Pyongan Province), Sinuiju City's Ch'eha market (North Pyongan Province), Hyesan City's Hyesin market (Ryanggang Province), Hamhung City's Sapo market (South Hamkyoung Province), Ch'ongjin City's Sunam market (North Hamgyong Province), Wonsan City's Kalma market (Kangwon Province).

progressed, general markets in interior cities also developed into wholesale markets. An example of this was Doksan market, which had around 12,000 stalls in the market itself and a further 6,000 informal stalls in the surrounding streets and alleys. Located in the city of Pyongsong, close to Pyongyang, Doksan became the country's largest wholesale market and the centre of a national domestic trade network, selling both China-sourced consumer goods as well as domestic goods.[44] The market's importance also reflected Pyongsong's role as a rail and road transport hub, along with its proximity to Pyongyang but a more lax system of entry permits.

In addition to their role in the daily economic life of North Korean citizens, the government's motivations for the establishment of the general markets also lay in the significant financial benefits it gained through the collection of the fees and taxes. These vary in accordance with the location of the markets, the size of the stall and the types of goods being sold. According to research carried out in 2016 by the North Korean Development Institute, in Hyesan city's Hyesin market, clothing and textile stalls were the most expensive, with the cost of registration set at about 5,000 Chinese yuan (about US$ 750). Market stalls selling shoes, bags, electrical goods and cosmetics traded on average for 2,000 yuan (US$ 300), whereas food stalls cost around 300–500 yuan. Moreover, one day's taxes for a single stall at Hyesin market was typically between 1,000 and 3,000 won. With around 7,000 traders, the management office of Hyesin market could collect around seven million won (roughly US$ 800) in taxes per day. Annually, this amounted to 2.52 billion won (roughly US$ 290,000).[45] If estimates of 404 general markets and roughly 1,093,000 market stalls nationwide are accurate, one day's taxes nationally could reach between 1.45 and 1.85 billion won a day (US$ 174,525–222,604).[46]

The reforms of the early 2000s also allowed SOEs to sell their output in the general markets. On the one hand, this reflected the fact that SOEs had already undergone a significant degree of marketisation as a result of the crisis. When the material supply system collapsed, managers had little choice but to procure inputs and sell outputs outside of the central planning system. This often involved selling finished goods at market prices rather than at the much lower state prices. Prices, therefore, began to follow supply and demand rather than state-mandated prices.[47] As SOEs were permitted to sell directly in the general markets, their presence increased significantly. It was reported in the early 2000s, for example, that around 5 per cent of stalls in general markets were

[44] North Korea Development Institute, 'The Present Status and Outlook', pp. 94–99.
[45] Ibid., pp. 79–83.   [46] Hong Min et al., *Information on North Korean Markets*, p. 54.
[47] Yang and Shepard, 'Changes in North Korea's Corporate Governance', pp. 145–46.

assigned to SOEs.[48] The profits could then be used by the enterprise to procure needed inputs or as general operating funds.

5.3   The Marketisation of Agriculture

The rise of marketisation also impacted the agricultural sector. In 1996, the authorities introduced the New Sub-Work Team Management System, which sought to reduce the size of the agricultural sub-work teams (*bunjo*). Previously, each cooperative farm typically had around five to ten work teams, with each work team consisting of three to four sub-work teams of around fifteen to twenty-five members each.[49] The new system aimed to reduce the size of the sub-work team further to between seven and ten people, and in certain cases, to between five and eight people. Farmers were also to be given increased rights of disposal. In the past, all of the annual harvests were procured by the state, with the exception of a fixed portion of food, seeds and animal feed that could be retained by the farmers. Under the new system, farmers were to be allowed to retain any harvest in excess of a government-designated target.[50] However, the context of the crisis meant that despite the reforms the state continued to confiscate surpluses due to the shortages in the cities and the military. In any case, the reforms were never implemented nationwide and appeared to have been applied only on an experimental basis in certain regions such as Kangwon Province.[51]

Many of the underlying principles of these aborted reforms were, however, taken up once again in the early 2000s. Through the July 1st measures, the North Korean authorities introduced the 'actual results system' (*siljŏkje*) for cooperative farms, whereby farmers were granted expanded decision-making rights with regards to production. As with the abandoned reforms of the mid-1990s, the sub-work team was reduced from fifteen to twenty-five people to seven to twelve people.[52] The sub-work team thereby became the basic unit of agricultural production, evaluation and distribution, and was given rights to retain output in excess of government targets.[53] Members of the sub-work team could either consume the surplus or sell it to the state. However, the

---

[48] *Choson Sinbo,* 24 December 2003, 'Probing the Vitality of Improvement Measures [Kŏmjŭngtoenŭn kaesŏnjoch'iŭi saenghwallyŏk]'.
[49] KIEP, *2002 North Korean Economy Report,* pp. 138–40.
[50] Lim Soo-Ho, *Co-Existence of Plan and Market,* pp. 64–66.
[51] Sung-wook Nam, 'Chronic Food Shortages and the Collective Farm System in North Korea', *Journal of East Asian Studies,* 7.1 (2007), p. 109.
[52] Jeong Eunmee, 'Dual Track of Agricultural Policy in North Korea: Focusing on Interaction between Collective Agriculture and Farmers' Private Economy [Pukhan nongŏbjŏngch'aekŭi ijunggwaedo: Jibdannongŏpgwa nongminsagyŏngjeŭi sanghosŏngŭl chungsimŭro]', *The Korean Journal of Unification Affairs,* 19.1 (2007), p. 267.
[53] KIEP, *2003/04 North Korean Economy Report,* p. 91.

continued precariousness of the food supply suggested the limitations of the reforms. The broad contours of socialist agricultural management and the handing down of excessive crop targets remained in place and the system of government procurement of staple foods was maintained. Furthermore, the State Food Procurement Agency's purchasing price was much lower than the going market price, thereby adversely affecting farmers' incomes.

In reality, the increase in farmers' incentives in the 2000s was not due to attempted reform of cooperative farm management but to the ongoing spread of marketisation, the establishment of the general markets and the rising influence of the *donju*. Marketisation and the rising consumption of urban residents increased demand for a broad variety of foodstuffs. Farmers sold their surpluses unofficially to the markets, while some expanded private farming in their kitchen gardens as well as illegal plots. Indeed, Joung Eun-Lee's research on farming in Musan county in North Hamgyong Province provides evidence of private reclaimed plots of over 2,000 *pyŏng* (0.66 hectares).[54] This trend coincided with a growing shift towards more valuable cash crops such as chillies, garlic, tomatoes and tobacco. As private farming grew, the produce came to be distributed not just in regional markets but throughout the entire country via intermediary traders. As such, the private farming of land by individuals shifted from being largely for direct consumption towards profit-oriented farming.[55] Indeed, the *donju* also lent money to work teams or to individual farmers in cooperative farms to produce grain and cash crops, with the profits shared following the sale of harvest in the marketplace.[56] This trend contributed to the increased availability of food. For example, stalls selling staple foods, vegetables, fruits and livestock products came to account for between 10 and 20 per cent of all general market stalls.[57]

The government's efforts to absorb market-generated income also led to the legalisation of hitherto illegal plots. A new tax known as the Land Usage Fee was introduced in July 2002 and was applied to the land of the cooperative farm and farming households' kitchen gardens of over 30 *pyŏng* as well as

---

[54] Joung Eun-Lee, 'A Study on the Food Procuring Mechanism of City Workers in North Korea – Land Farming Cases of Musan Region in Hamgyeongbuk-Do [Pukhan tosinodongjaŭi singnyangjodal mek'ŏnijŭme kwanhan yŏn'gu: Hamgyŏngbukdo musanjiyŏgŭi sot'oji kyŏngjaksaryerŭl chungsimŭro]', *Journal of Northeast Asian Economic Studies*, 26.1 (2014), pp. 261–302.

[55] Lim Eul-Chul, *North Korea's Economy in the Kim Jong Un Era: Private Financing and Masters of Money [Kimjŏngŭn sidaeŭi Pukhan'gyŏngje: Sagŭmyunggwa tonju]* (Seoul: Hanul, 2016), p. 108.

[56] Yoon In Joo, 'A Study of Privatisation in North Korea: Current Status and Its Implications [Pukhanŭi sayuhwa hyŏnsang yŏn'gu: Silt'aewa hamŭirŭl chungsimŭro]', *North Korean Studies Review*, 18.1 (2014), p. 68.

[57] Kwon Tae-Jin, *The Current Situation and Outlook of Marketisation in North Korea's Agricultural Sector [Pukhanŭi nongŏppumun sijanghwa silt'aewa chŏnmang]* (Seoul: GS & J Institute, 2018), p. 11.

reclaimed plots.[58] The authorities expanded the scope of the tax through the enactment of the Real Estate Usage Fee (*pudongsan sayongnyo*) in 2006. According to North Korean sources, the Real Estate Usage Fee refers to '... the money that socialist institutions, enterprises, organisations and residents pay to the state in exchange for the use of the real estate that forms part of the country's wealth'.[59] State regulations also made explicit reference to the use of land by individuals, representing at least the partial legalisation of private farming activities, and by extension, of the market-based distribution of agricultural produce. This levying of fees on hitherto illegal private plots thereby constituted a significant shift from the principle laid out in North Korea's 1977 Land Law, which stated that: 'In the DPRK, land is the property of the state and of cooperative organisations. The country's entire land is a collective possession of the people so that nobody can sell and buy land or make it their private possession'.[60] As such, agriculture saw the rise of marketisation, although the strategic importance of food production meant that agricultural management nonetheless, for the most part, remained based on collectivist principles and subject to high levels of state intervention and control via collective farm management.

5.4   The Uneven Marketisation of State-Owned Enterprises

The process of marketisation in North Korea was an uneven one. While much of the central planning system had collapsed, factories in sectors regarded as 'strategic' continued to rely on funds and materials from the state. The defence, energy and railroad sectors along with large enterprises in heavy industry were all considered crucial for system maintenance and thus remained highly regulated as part of what remained of the planned economy. On the other hand, smaller-scale regional enterprises lacked state support and thus were more likely to receive private investment and rely heavily on the market.[61] During the Kim Jong Il era, state investment in light industry and regional

---

[58] Cho Han-Bum, Lim Kang-Taeg, Yang Moon-Soo and Lee Seog-Ki, *The Effects of Private Economic Activities on Public Economic Sectors in North Korea [Pukhanesŏ sajŏggyŏngjehwaldongi kongsiggyŏngjebumune mich'inŭn yŏnghyang punsŏk]* (Seoul: Korea Institute for National Unification, 2016), pp. 165–66.

[59] Ho Chol Hwan, 'Principles and Methods of Real Estate Pricing [Pudongsan kagyŏk chejŏngŭi wŏlliwa pangbŏp]', *Journal of Kim Il Sung University Philosophy, Economics*, 61.4 (2015), p. 115.

[60] Article 9 of the DPRK Land Law (Adopted by the Supreme People's Assembly on 29 April 1977, revised by the Supreme People's Assembly Presidium on 16 June 1999).

[61] For details on North Korean SOEs' divergent levels of reliance on the state and market, see Lee Seog-Ki, Kim Suk-Jin, Kim Kye Hwan and Yang Moon-Soo, *North Korean Industries and Firms in the 2000s: Recovery and Operation Mechanism [2000 nyŏndae Pukhanŭi sanŏpgwa kiŏp: Hoebok silt'aewa chakdong pangsik]* (Seoul: Korea Institute for Industrial Economics and Trade, 2010); Lim Kang-Taeg, *Analysis on the Condition*.

small and medium-sized factories was almost non-existent. The subsequent Kim Jong Un regime did place rhetorical emphasis on the development of the light industrial sector, and in his speech at the National Light Industry Convention in March 2013, Kim argued that: 'It is a primary task to normalise production at factories and enterprises and increase production of the basic necessities desperately needed for people's livelihood. In particular, there needs to be a decisive increase in the production of basic foods and primary consumer goods'.[62] However, there is little evidence of actual material support from the state. The majority of light industrial enterprises, small and medium-sized regional factories, as well as non-strategic enterprises in the heavy-industrial sector, had little choice but to engage in market activities to secure their profits.

As such, the July 1st measures were not so much a replacement of the state sector with the market but rather a recognition of the reality of marketisation alongside an attempted strengthening of what remained of the state sector through greater utilisation of market forces. As Yang Moon-Soo has argued, the authorities adopted a strategy of utilising an emergent dualistic economic structure in which the formal and informal sectors co-existed and mutually influenced each other. On the one hand, the state sought to expand the supply capacity of the formal sector through policy improvements within the existing planned economic system, and on the other hand, to partially expand the market mechanism in the broader economy.[63] This dualism also meant that marketisation exhibited specific spatial dimensions. For example, in Jagang Province, where many defence-related factories, hydropower stations and machinery tools factories were located, the majority of workers continued to receive food rations and monthly wages from the state. As such, Jagang Province underwent less marketisation than other regions.[64] However, while a broadly dualistic industrial structure came into being, there were also a variety of forms of enterprise management in between the two extremes, with varying levels of state control and market dependence across the various economic sectors.[65]

Outside of the strategic sector, the July 1st measures saw a shift away from targets represented in terms of the number of units to be produced (*hyŏnmul*

[62] *Rodong Sinmun*, 9 March 2013, 'Respected Comrade Kim Jong Un's speech given at the National Light Industry Convention [Kyŏngaehanŭn Kimjŏngŭn tongjikkesŏ chŏn'gukkyŏng-gongŏptaehoeesŏ hasin yŏnsŏl]'.
[63] Yang Moon-Soo, *Marketisation of the North Korean Economy*, pp. 46–53.
[64] North Korea Development Institute, 'Present Status and Outlook of North Korean Marketisation', p. 6.
[65] Yang Moon-Soo, 'North Korea's Marketisation: Trends and Structural Change [Pukhanŭi sijanghwa: Ch'usewa kujo pyŏnhwa]', *KDI Review of the North Korean Economy*, 15.6 (2013), pp. 54–55.

gyehoek) towards targets based on monetary value (*aeksang gyehoek*).[66] In a December 2004 interview with *Choson Sinbo*, vice trade minister Kim Yong Sul stated that the State Planning Commission was now imposing unit-based production targets only for strategically important materials, while targets for enterprises producing non-strategic goods were now expressed mainly in monetary values. Furthermore, in contrast to past practice whereby the government strictly regulated how enterprise profits were to be spent, enterprises were now able to spend their profits according to their own plans, once requisite payments were made to the state.[67] In addition, the reforms allowed materials to be sold at an agreed price between enterprises, thereby increasing the production of goods for sale on the market.[68] This led to cases whereby enterprises sold products at both state and market prices. Kumsong Tractor Factory based in Nampo city, for example, continued to engage in the production of tractors and farming equipment but also organised separate work teams to produce machinery for which there was high market demand, such as injection and shoemaking equipment.[69]

This shift of SOEs into profitable sidelines was also underpinned by the legal and institutional basis established by the August 3rd People's Consumer Goods Production Movement. As noted in the previous chapter, the August 3rd movement was originally launched in the mid-1980s by Kim Jong Il, and at the time, was largely unsuccessful in increasing the domestic production of consumer goods. However, the importance of this movement was re-emphasised by the authorities in the 2000s. A February 2007 editorial of *Minju Choson*, the official newspaper of the Presidium of the Supreme People's Assembly and the Cabinet, stated that:

'Through mobilising to the fullest extent all internal resources, we must positively increase the production of all kinds of people's consumer goods within workplace units producing basic necessities as well as within work teams organised in factories and enterprises. Through making great efforts to continue the August 3rd People's Consumer Goods Production Movement, we need to produce a greater variety of consumer products. Regional People's Committees must actively utilise household work teams and side-line production teams (*puŏbban*) that possess idle labour, and positively mobilise industrial by-products, agricultural products, natural resources,

---

[66] Park Young-Ja et al., *Enterprise Operational Reality*, pp. 31–32.
[67] *Choson Sinbo*, 13 December 2004, 'Strengthening of unified guidance, increase in powers below – An interview with Department of Trade Vice Minister Kim Yong Sul [T'ongiljŏgin chidoganghwa, araee manŭn kwŏnhan – Chosŏnmuyŏgsŏng Kimyongsul int'ŏbyu]'.
[68] Lim Kang-Taeg, *Analysis of the Condition*, pp. 81–84.
[69] Lee Seog-Ki, Yang Moon-Soo and Joung Eun-Lee, *Analysis on the Markets of North Korea [Pukhan sijangsilt'ae punsŏk]* (Sejong: Korea Institute for Industrial Economics and Trade, 2014). pp. 113–14.

farming materials in order to produce good quality people's consumer items such as daily necessities'.[70]

As marketisation progressed, the definition of 'August 3rd production' saw something of a shift, however, and came to refer more broadly to production that took place outside of the state plan with the resulting output sold at market prices. Part of the income gained from selling August 3rd goods could thus be used to meet the monetary targets handed down by the state or as part of the enterprise's operating funds. The term 'August 3rd' also came to be applied to workers who did not turn up to work but retained their jobs by paying a fee to their workplace managers so that they could participate in their own market-oriented activities.[71] Such practices were in the interests of both workers and enterprise directors. Though still technically illegal, they became established in many non-strategic regional enterprises as state control was relaxed. The authorities' position of benign neglect reflected the fact that this was a key means by which enterprises were able to maintain operations. However, the sideline activities of SOEs and the so-called August 3rd payments from workers have been a source of bribery and corruption amongst government officials and enterprise managers since the money handling involved were easily hidden and evaded from the state's oversight.[72]

5.5   The Donju and 'Wearing the Red Cap'

A key feature of North Korean marketisation was the emerging partnership between SOEs and the *donju*. Enterprises attracted investment from the *donju* in the form of either capital or the supply of materials, which were then used to manufacture goods for sale on the market. In return, the *donju* received either a portion of the sales income or products in kind which they could then sell directly on the market. Yoon In Joo's 2012 survey of 153 North Korean defectors found that 73 per cent knew of cases in which enterprises had received loans or investment from private individuals. A further 50 per cent stated that they were aware of cases in which individuals had asked enterprises to make goods on the basis of consignment-based processing arrangements. There were also increasing instances of private investors who effectively conducted their own business under the auspices of an SOE.[73] In the latter

[70] *Minju Choson,* 21 February 2007. 'Strongly light the flame of the light industrial revolution and bring about a decisive transformation in the production of people's consumer goods [Kyŏnggongŏb hyŏngmyŏngŭi pulgilŭl sech'age ilŭk'yŏ inminsobip'um saengsangesŏ kyŏl-jŏngjŏk chŏnhwanŭl ilukhaja]'.

[71] Park Young-Ja et al., *Enterprise Operational Reality,* pp. 136–37.

[72] Interviews with defectors, including a former SOE worker, trading firm manager and school-teacher, November 2017.

[73] Yoon In Joo, 'Study of Privatisation in North Korea', pp. 68–69.

case, the *donju* would pay a fee to the enterprise and in return use their own capital and equipment and hire their own employees. This allowed the *donju* to register their activities in the name of a patron organisation and would often result in them being appointed to some nominal position such as manager, deputy manager or general director. In the context of a lack of clearly defined property rights and legal proscription of the private ownership of the means of production, this enabled the *donju* to receive a degree of protection for their investments.[74] As such, marketisation moved well beyond the stage of private entrepreneurs engaged in simple buying and selling or household production. Private investment in SOEs became widespread in restaurants and shops, and thereafter, spread to trading companies, factories, cooperative farms, fisheries, mining and construction enterprises.

This process represents the emergence of a distinctive form of property rights in North Korea. Property can be defined as a 'bundle of rights' that can be disaggregated into rights of control, income and transfer. These rights might be enforced through several mechanisms ranging from formal law to social custom.[75] For countries undergoing transitions from a centrally planned economy towards a market system, these forms of property rights are likely to take particular hybrid forms.[76] In North Korea, state or collective public ownership had traditionally been the principal property form. As noted, however, the *donju* came to own various means of production as *de facto* private property through the establishment of contracts with state entities. This sometimes took the form of written contracts that explicitly specified profit-sharing arrangements, though such contracts remained informal rather than legally recognised. Nonetheless, through these contracts, the *donju* effectively obtained rights of the use and control of the assets they possessed, though disputes could occur upon the termination of the contract period.[77] Furthermore, the emergence of these hybrid property rights could not have taken place without the permissive stance of the state. This reflected a mutual interest in terms of the need on the part of the *donju* for the protection of their investments and the inability of the state to support SOEs in the non-strategic sectors and the resulting need for enterprises to attract private capital. As such, a large proportion of private economic activities take place under the protection of SOEs or other state

---

[74] Sung Chull Kim, *North Korea Under Kim Jong Il*, pp. 157–60.
[75] Harold Demsetz, 'Toward a Theory of Property Rights', *The American Economic Review*, 57.2 (1967), pp. 347–59.
[76] Andrew G. Walder and Jean C Oi, 'Property Rights in the Chinese Economy: Contours of the Process of Change', in *Property Rights and Economic Reform in China*, ed. by Jean C. Oi and Andrew G. Walder (Stanford, CA: Stanford University Press, 1999), pp. 6–10.
[77] Sung Chull Kim, *North Korea Under Kim Jong Il*, pp. 160–63.

entities.[78] For the authorities, a portion of the profits generated can be absorbed into the state's finances.

For the *donju,* this practice resembled that of 'wearing the red cap', as seen in China during the early Deng Xiaoping reform era. What precise forms did this 'wearing the red cap' take? One example could be found in the lease of state retail outlets by private investors. In the early 2000s, trading companies and factories were granted the right to independently manage state retail outlets. While the *donju* themselves were not allowed to directly rent state retail outlets, they could effectively borrow the name of an SOE or trading company, procure their own goods and thereby manage an outlet.[79] Under this arrangement, a certain portion of the profits made from sales is handed over to the enterprise or government agency. By doing so, private investors could pursue their profit-oriented activities with a relative degree of security. Similar arrangements existed with regards to a variety of other service-oriented businesses, such as beauty salons, snooker halls, public baths and karaoke rooms.

Restaurants also came to be managed as private enterprises. Smaller restaurants, for example, were formally owned by regional administrative organs but the necessary equipment and ingredients were purchased by individual investors with the food sold at market prices. Larger restaurants that were part of the state's food distribution network similarly received investment from the *donju.* In such situations, however, restaurants might typically sell food at both state and market prices, with profits shared between the enterprise and the *donju.* One example of this was Amnokgag Restaurant in Pyongyang's Tongdaewon District, a large state-operated restaurant that leased part of its space to a private investor. In this case, a three-year contract stipulated that a portion of the investor's profits was paid to the restaurant. The *donju* took care of remodelling the premises, the purchase of equipment and materials, the drawing up of the menus, sales and payment of wages to the workers. Food ingredients were also purchased from the markets and the food sold at prices well above state prices.[80] This higher price reflected the fact that the food was far superior in quantity and quality to that sold at state prices.

The *donju* also invested in manufacturing, reflecting the increasing market demand for consumer goods and the speed at which profits could be made on such investments.[81] In addition to the legal restrictions on private ownership and the need for political protection, partnering with an SOE in the

---

[78] Lee Seog-Ki et al., *Analysis of the Markets of North Korea,* pp. 287–99.

[79] Yang Moon-Soo, *Marketisation of the North Korean Economy,* pp. 233–37.

[80] Choi Seo-yoon, 'North Korean Restaurant Industry: Ryanggang Province-Style Restaurant Amnokgag [Pukhanŭi ŭmsigŏp, Yanggangdo t'ŭksanmul sikdang Amnoggag]', *KDB North Korean Development,* Autumn (2016), pp. 177–78.

[81] Cho Han-Bum et al., *Effects of Private Economic Activities,* p. 142.

manufacturing sector had the advantage that the daily supply of electricity to state-owned factories lasted roughly twice as long as that to residential buildings, thus giving the state-owned facilities a considerable advantage over household production.[82] Interviews with North Korean defectors provide anecdotal evidence of cases in which private entrepreneurs rented small regional factories, held full operating rights and engaged in the production and sales of consumer goods. One former manager of a trading company discussed such emergent forms of partnership between *donju* and SOEs:

'If an individual is capable, they can invest in and manage a factory or mine ... But in North Korea, private ownership is not legally allowed, right? Everyone in North Korea belongs to an organisation, and if you are of working age, you are a member of some workplace or other ... You do not have the legal right to manage a company under your own name. Because there's no private property, you have to piggyback on a state organ, that is to say, a large factory. The company is given the name of the state organ. Since the investor borrowed the name and is recognised as an employee, they have to pay a certain amount of the profit each month. This is all agreed upon. The name is that of a state organ, but that organ is not involved in the management. In reality, it belongs to the *donju*'.[83]

The transport sector also saw increased private investment, reflecting the chronic lack of investment from the state as well as continued energy shortages. Under the planned economy, the state-run rail network was the most important means of transport, but following the crisis, saw a much-reduced capacity. Given the difficulties and expense of modernising the rail network, the government made efforts to renovate the roads around Pyongyang and other major cities, which helped to promote the development of the marketised transport sector. Private individuals purchased Chinese-made second-hand goods trucks or vans, known in North Korea as servi-cars (*sŏbich'a*), and used them to transport people and goods. Servi-cars were used, for example, to transport imported goods from China to North Korea's interior as well as between the country's major cities. These vehicles were registered with an SOE such as Pyongyang Transportation Trading Company but were in reality used for private profit-making activities.[84] The definition of 'servi-car' subsequently came to include buses, which again were typically imported from China. North Korea thereby saw the emergence of a privately operated national bus network.[85] The need to register with an SOE again reflected the fact that

---

[82] Yoon In Joo, 'Study of Privatisation in North Korea', p. 72.
[83] Interview with a defector from Sinuiju, 16 June 2018.
[84] Lim Eul-Chul, *North Korea's Economy*, pp. 171–72.
[85] Yang Moon-Soo, '2015 Trends and Outlook in North Korea's Marketisation [2015 nyŏn Pukhan sijanghwa tonghyanggwa hyanghu chŏnmang]', *KDI Review of the North Korean Economy*, 18.1 (2016), p. 23.

private ownership of vehicles remained prohibited in North Korea. The authorities tolerated the operation of servi-cars not only because of the direct fees received but also because of the positive role that private transport played in stimulating the economy.

As can be seen, the partnership between the state and *donju* was apparent in a variety of sectors. While this relationship was in certain respects mutually dependent, the political power of the *donju* remained weak. Speculation that the emergent entrepreneurial class might represent a nascent form of civil society in North Korea would be premature, to say the least. As noted, the rise in the economic status of the *donju* took place in a context whereby they had little choice but to rely on the state in their pursuit of profit-oriented activities, and as such, the *donju* were only able to operate within the limits of political authority.[86] While serving as a key agent of marketisation, the *donju* remained in a politically precarious situation. In this respect, processes of marketisation were based upon the unity of interests between a variety of strata of bureaucrats and *donju*, central and regional state organs, as well as productive units.[87]

In certain instances, however, the state took the lead in establishing entirely new market sectors. A key example is the mobile communications sector. As with other aspects of marketisation, a key motivation for the state was the absorption of private capital into state finances via mobile phone fees and the sale of handsets. While the spread of mobile phones represents a potential challenge to authoritarian rule, it was primarily this economic motivation that underpinned the state's proactive role in promoting the use of mobile phones. In 2008, the Ministry of Communications established Koryolink, a joint venture with the Egyptian telecommunications company Orascom Telecom. This joint venture provided a communications service based on 3G technology that included both voice phone calls and a messaging service. North Korea subsequently established its own state-owned mobile communications company, Kangsong Net in 2012, thereby creating a more competitive market. The number of mobile phone subscribers thereupon increased significantly. Starting from around 20,000 subscribers in early 2009, the number of subscribers reached 1 million in 2012 and 3.6 million by 2016.[88] This amounted to more than a threefold increase within five years, with around one in seven North Koreans owning a mobile phone by 2016.

[86] Lim Eul-Chul, *North Korea's Economy*, pp. 211–12.
[87] Hong Min et al., *Information on North Korean Markets*, p. 12.
[88] *KOTRA Overseas Market News*, 4 January 2018, 'Current situation of the development of North Korea's mobile phone industry [Pukhan hyudaep'on sanŏp palchŏn hyŏnhwang]'.

The government thus adopted the role of the creator as well as a monopolistic provider of the mobile communications market.[89] While communications had been the most backward sector of North Korea's infrastructure, this increase in mobile phone usage represented its modernisation as well as an impetus for further marketisation. By facilitating the exchange of market information such as regional variations in price and demand as well as shifts in foreign exchange rates, mobile phones became indispensable for market traders. They accelerated the distribution of goods across the country, making it possible for traders in different regions as well as producers and distributors, wholesalers and retailers to determine more accurately the quantity and price of the goods to be traded.[90] Traders were also able to exchange information regarding periodic crackdowns on overtly illegal market activity. The government was also closely involved in the sale of mobile phone handsets via state retail outlets. In 2017, a low-end North Korean designed and manufactured handset was sold for around US$ 250 and a high-end smartphone model for around US$ 690.[91] While mobile subscription charges and handset prices were extremely high compared to official wages, the rising purchasing power of the public as a result of market activities contributed to the rapid increase in their usage.

5.6   Attempted Reversals of the Late 2000s

Despite the role that marketisation played in economic daily life following the crisis, the late 2000s saw attempts by the Kim Jong Il regime to reverse its existing market-friendly policy and instead repress market activities. In October 2005, the authorities attempted to reopen the PDS. Furthermore, in December 2007, the authorities banned women aged 49 and under from trading in the marketplace, while men under the age of 60 were expected to remain at their official workplaces and were prohibited from resigning from their jobs unless they were unable to work. In November of the following year, the Ministry of Commerce announced the reduced operation of the general markets and the transition back towards the former farmers' markets.[92] These measures thereby reflected an effort to re-establish the planned economy and return to collectivist principles. As a *Rodong Sinmun* editorial argued in February 2008:

---

[89] Yang Moon-Soo, '2015 Trends and Outlook in North Korea's Marketisation', p. 32.
[90] Lim Eul-Chul, *North Korea's Economy*, pp. 180–81.
[91] *KOTRA Overseas Market News*, 4 January 2018, 'Current situation of the development of North Korea's mobile phone industry [Pukhan hyudaep'on sanŏp palchŏn hyŏnhwang]'.
[92] Kim Young-Hui, 'Change and Future Prospects', p. 155.

'This year's joint editorial highlighted the Party's economic thought, ideology and policy as a firm guide to the construction of an economically powerful nation, and emphasised the importance of close adherence to the principles of socialism and collectivism in the realm of economic management. . . . What is also important in this task is the planned management and operation of the economy under the unified leadership of the state. The socialist economy is a planned economy'.[93]

This shift towards what Rudiger Frank has termed as 'socialist neoconservatism'[94] could also be seen in the renewed emphasis on mass mobilisation as a means of achieving economic goals, such as in the 150-day Battle initiated in April 2009 and the 100-day Battle the following September. This mass mobilisation was given added urgency due to the leadership's longstanding claims that the country would achieve the status of a 'great, powerful and prosperous nation' (kangsŏng daeguk) by April 2012, the 100th anniversary of Kim Il Sung's birth. Finally, on 30 November 2009, the North Korean authorities announced a currency reform. Without advance warning, this took the form of a redenomination measure whereby the old currency was replaced with the new currency at a rate 1:100 in the space of just one week. However, exchange was limited to just 100,000 won of the old currency per household. As many citizens held cash savings far in excess of that level, the measure caused considerable public anger. In response, the authorities allowed a further 50,000 won of the old currency to be exchanged per person. Nonetheless, the reform served to wipe out the cash savings of a large number of North Koreans. As one female market trader recalled:

'In previous currency reforms, if the exchange limit was set at 10 million won, you would first exchange 10 million won officially but then you would unofficially go back to the bank and exchange a further 20 or 30 million won. People didn't expect the money to become worthless. After all, it had the portrait of Kim Il Sung and Kim Jong Suk [Kim Jong Il's mother] on it . . . This time, the money exchange lasted for 3-4 days, but afterwards, the government wouldn't exchange any more. Would that not raise people's blood pressure? . . . In Hyesan, some people protested in front of the bank, and there was a man who threw the money into the Yalu River, and there were also people who burned the money'.[95]

It appears then that the authorities sought to use the currency reform to dispossess the *donju* and weaken marketising processes.[96] As Lee Seok has argued, the authorities also wished to gain the advantages of seigniorage by exploiting the differential between the costs of printing the new currency and

---

[93] *Rodong Sinmun*, 18 February 2008, 'The thorough implementation of socialist principles in economic management [Kyŏngjegwalliesŏ sahoejuŭi wŏnch'igŭi ch'ŏlchŏhan kuhyŏn]'.
[94] Rüdiger Frank, 'Socialist Neoconservatism'.
[95] Interview with defector previously engaged in market trade, 27 July 2018.
[96] Lee Seog-Ki et al., *North Korean Industries and Firms*, p. 203.

the value of what could be bought with that money. As such, redenomination was a means of addressing the state's chronic lack of finances and regaining control over the marketised economy.[97] The currency reform and the broader policy of market repression was a resounding failure, however. Without first ensuring the proper distribution of food and basic necessities through the PDS, the measures led to sharp increases in the prices of agricultural and consumer goods. Given the loss of confidence in the state's economic policy and the national currency, ordinary North Koreans sought to stockpile goods, which in turn exacerbated the price increases and caused a sharp drop in the market value of the new currency. Furthermore, in December 2009, the government banned citizens from holding and using foreign currencies, resulting in a further sharp rise in the exchange rate. Given the unstable economic situation at the time, the inflow of Chinese foodstuffs and consumer goods into North Korea's markets were sharply curtailed, creating further public hardship.[98]

Contrary to the government's expectations, the state-owned sector was also negatively impacted. The reason for this was related to the mutual dependence between the *donju* and the SOEs discussed above. Given that the *donju* suffered heavy losses as a result of the currency reform, the SOEs' dependence on those *donju* for capital and inputs meant that they too were badly affected.[99] However, those traders who stockpiled goods and the *donju* who held onto their savings in foreign currencies managed to avoid significant losses. Indeed, interviews with defectors suggest that some officials and traders made significant speculative profits, typically on the basis of leaked information prior to the official announcement of the reform.[100] However, as noted, public opinion in general turned negative in the wake of the confiscatory currency reform, the hyperinflation and the economic disorder. As Andrei Lankov has argued, '[f]or a brief while in January and February 2010, a major outbreak of public discontent seemed to be within the realms of possibility'.[101]

As a result, the regime was forced to abandon its policy of market repression. To alleviate public anger, the government paid the wages of SOEs' workers in the new currency at the same nominal amount as before the currency exchange, thereby resulting in what was in real terms a one-

---

[97] Lee Seok, 'Overview: Evaluation and Hypotheses Relating to Trends in the 2016 North Korean Economy [Ch'onggwal: 2016 nyŏn Pukhan kyŏngje tonghyangpyŏnggawa sŏlmyonggasŏl]', *KDI Review of the North Korean Economy*, 19.1 (2017), p. 13.

[98] Interviews with several former market traders and employees of SOEs who defected from North Korea, June and July 2018.

[99] Lee Seog-Ki et al., *North Korean Industries and Firms*, p. 203.

[100] Interviews in June and July 2018.

[101] Andrei N. Lankov, *The Real North Korea: Life and Politics in the Failed Stalinist Utopia* (Oxford: Oxford University Press, 2015), p. 131.

hundred-fold increase in wages. Moreover, Pak Nam Ki, Director of the KWP's Planning and Finance Department was held responsible for the debacle and was executed in the Spring of 2010. From May of that year, the general markets were reopened, and the government reverted to its former policy of utilising the market to support the state sector. As we will see in the next chapter, the Kim Jong Un regime maintained this broadly market-friendly policy. As such, the failed reversal of marketisation in the late 2000s turned out to be the exception that proved the rule in that it demonstrated not the opposition between the state and market but rather its mutual and irreversible interdependence. The state's ill-fated attempt to roll back the tide of marketisation was not without long-term impacts, however. As a result of the failed currency reform, there was a sharp increase in the price of goods and a more than 100-fold increase in the won–dollar market exchange rate between 2010 and 2012. Although the inflation rate began to stabilise in 2013, the experience of the currency reform served to accelerate the pace of dollarisation as ordinary citizens lost confidence in the North Korean won.[102]

5.7   Marketisation in the Kim Jong Un Era

With the onset of the Kim Jong Un regime in 2011, the process of marketisation continued unabated. Two particular aspects are worth mentioning here: the development of the real estate market and the continued marketisation of the transport sector. Reflecting the emergence of a vibrant informal real estate market, one of the most noticeable changes in the North Korean economy in the early to mid-2010s was the construction boom taking place in the country's major cities.[103] Under North Korea's socialist legal code, the state remained responsible for the provision of housing and thus formally adhered to the principle of state and collective ownership. As such, the buying, selling, exchange and renting of housing was technically illegal as there was no legal basis for the trade-in property.[104] Nonetheless, as in other areas of the

---

[102] Seung-Ho Jung, Ohik Kwon and Sung Min Mun, 'Dollarization, Seigniorage, and Prices: The Case of North Korea', *Emerging Markets Finance and Trade*, 53.11 (2017), p. 2463.

[103] Joung Eun-Lee, 'An Analysis of the Appearance and Significance of the North Korean Real Estate Development Sector: A Comparison with the the Development of the Chinese Real Estate Development Sector [Pukhan pudongsan kaebalŏpjaŭi tŭngjanggwa hamŭie taehan punsŏk: Chungguk pudongsan kaebalŏpjawaŭi pigyoyŏn'gurŭl chungsimŭro]', *KDI Review of the North Korean Economy*, 18.9 (2016), pp. 51–89; Henri Feron, 'Pyongyang's Construction Boom: Is North Korea Beating Sanctions?', *38 North*, 2017 www.38north.org/2017/07/hferon071817/ [accessed 24 April 2018].

[104] The North Korean government enacted the DPRK Housing Law on 21 January 2009. Article 3 of the law outlines the state's responsibility for the provision of housing, stating that 'It is the essential demand of the socialist system of our country that the state is responsible for amicably resolving the problem of people's housing'. The law also states that the construction and allocation of residence is limited to the local People's Committee and its agencies, enterprises

economy, hybrid forms of informal property rights emerged to allow for the trade-in housing. The market exchange of state housing between individuals involved the buying and selling of a government-issued Housing Usage Permit Certificate (*sallimjib riyonghŏgajŭng*). This thereby amounted to trade not in the ownership of real estate *per se* but rather in its usage. However, the emergence of this phenomenon and its expansion nonetheless suggests that a *de facto* real estate market took root in North Korea.

As the housing market grew, the cost of property in Pyongyang and other large cities rose sharply. As in any housing market, location played a key role in determining the price. In Pyongyang, the most expensive apartments were located in the Central District, where a five-room apartment in a high-rise building could typically sell for US\$ 200,000. In Pyongchon District, an apartment might cost between US\$ 120,000–130,000, in Potonggang District around US\$ 100,000, and in Moranbong District around US\$ 70,000.[105] State-led construction projects in Pyongyang contributed to the growth in the real estate market. In 2008, for example, the authorities launched the Pyongyang 100,000 House Construction Project as part of the goal of 'Building a Strong and Prosperous Nation'. Pyongyang thereafter saw the building of new apartment complexes in such areas as Changjon Street, Mirae Scientists Street and Ryomyong Street. Regional cities too saw the construction of new housing units. As private individuals were still not allowed to directly own the means of production, the *donju* typically approached state entities and enterprises in the construction sector and supplied their own capital and materials.[106] As in other sectors, SOEs provided the *donju* with a measure of protection for these highly profitable investments.

In addition, the marketisation of the retail sector continued, with a structure of competition emerging between stores operated by 'red cap' private investors and those directly operated by SOEs. Pyongyang, for example, saw an increasing number of state-owned food stores, butchers and fishmongers selling at market prices. An example of this was the emergence in December 2014 of the Hwanggumbol stores. Operated by Hwanggumbol Trading Company, these stores opened from 6 am to midnight, selling groceries and basic necessities which were bought in bulk from producers and sold at low prices. As the director of Hwanggumbol Trading Company stated: 'We started our business on the basis that people would like it if we sold all the goods necessary for their daily life, extended our opening times, set our prices more reasonably than

and organisations. Residents are required to obtain a Housing Usage Permit Certificate from an administrative agency before they can reside.

[105] *Yonhap News*, 2 April 2017, 'North Pyongyang luxury apartment price surge ... Up to 200 million won [Pukp'yŏngyang kogŭp ap'at'ŭ kagyŏk kŭptŭng ... ch'oego 2 ŏgwŏndae]'.
[106] Joung Eun-Lee, 'Appearance and Significance of the North Korean Real Estate', pp. 71–74.

other stores, and guaranteed the quality of goods'.[107] Furthermore, several large state-owned supermarkets and department stores opened, selling both domestically produced items and imported goods. These include the six-floor Changgwang Store on Mirae Scientists Street, Taesong Department Store in Taedonggang District and the Mirae Store in the Potonggang District. As such, SOEs became key market players in the retail sector, competing with private traders and general markets in terms of the quality of goods, price and customer service.

One further prominent manifestation of marketisation in North Korea's major cities was the rapid rise in the number of taxis. Prior to the late 2000s, a few dozen taxis operated in Pyongyang catering mainly for foreigners. As marketisation progressed, they were subsequently used as a means of transporting domestic passengers and goods. Indeed, it has been estimated that the number of taxis operating in Pyongyang alone grew from approximately 1,500 in early 2016 to as many as 6,000 in 2019, with several state-owned taxi companies participating in the sector.[108] While some of these SOEs were well established in the sector, such as Taedonggang Passenger Transport, others such as Air Koryo previously had no presence in the taxi business but were attracted by the potential profits. This was reflective of a broader trend whereby well-placed SOEs expanded into various sectors, and in that respect, came to resemble the conglomerate structure found in North Korea's capitalist neighbours.

5.8   Conclusion

As we have argued, the collapse of North Korea's centrally planned economy led to a process of marketisation. The majority of the country's citizens came to purchase their daily necessities from market traders, and in contrast to the poor-quality goods previously sold by the state retail outlets, goods in the marketplace were in strong demand. Furthermore, as marketisation progressed, there was growing competition over prices and consumer satisfaction. The money-earning activities of private individuals also became more diversified. Such processes occurred not just in the retail sector but in manufacturing, mining, seafood and fisheries, services and transport. However, this cannot be understood simply as a process of 'marketisation from below' that has gradually drawn in the lower-level officials and enterprises left to fend for

---

[107] *KBS News*, 28 March 2015, 'Twenty years of Marketplaces . . . how far to the changes in North Korean markets go? [Changmadang 20 nyŏn . . . Pukhan sijang pyŏnhwa ŏdikkaji?]'.

[108] *Hankyoreh*, 24 April 2019, 'Riding the wind of marketisation . . . the operation of Pyongyang Taxi's and Servi-cars [Sijanghwa param t'ago . . . P'yŏngyange t'aeksi ssŏbich'a tallinda]'.

themselves. As we have argued, the central state was a key actor in this process. Thus, instead of viewing the state and the market as being in a zero-sum relationship, it is more accurate to analyse contemporary socio-economic changes in North Korea as constituting the rise of a mutually dependent relationship between the state and the market.

In the first instance, much of the market activity that came to characterise contemporary daily economic life took place in the space created by government reforms. In particular, the July 1st measures in 2002 and the establishment of the general markets in 2003 acted as a spur to private economic activities and encouraged enterprises to engage with the market. The collapse of state planning in the 1990s led the market to replace the state planning system as the primary source of production materials for enterprises. The ability to retain profits also gave enterprises more scope to provide incentives to workers, thereby increasing overall operations.[109] As a result of their increased managerial autonomy and responsibility, SOEs became increasingly dependent on the *donju* through the latter's supply of capital and materials. These hybrid property forms emerged in the early 2000s in the retail and service sectors, but soon spread to the trading and manufacturing sectors.[110] As we have noted, reliance on the market varied according to the sector and geographic region. It was widespread in non-strategic regional-level enterprises that did not receive supplies of capital or raw materials from the state but more limited in strategic enterprises located in the heavy-industrial regions of the country's interior.

The state's proactive role in marketisation was a reflection of basic economic necessity. The chronic fiscal crisis meant that the authorities had to devise new ways in which to absorb income from market activities. As noted in the case of mobile communications, this also involved the creation of entirely new market sectors. While the currency reform of 2009 suggested the possibility of a conservative ideological backlash against marketising processes, its resounding failure and the return to a market-friendly policy under Kim Jong Un also pointed to both the mutual interdependence of state and market and to the irreversibility of marketisation. As such, the authorities continued to absorb profits from the market while the *donju* gained political protection, thereby promoting a variety of collusive relationships. This was not simply a 'domestic' process, however. The emergent post-crisis political economy can be considered in terms of how the country's developmental model was shaped by geopolitical contestation in Northeast Asia both during

---

[109] Cho Han-Bum et al., *Effects of Private Economic Activities*, p. 112.
[110] Yoon In Joo, 'Study of Privatisation in North Korea', pp. 76–77.

and after the Cold War. North Korea's marketisation was also dependent upon the geo-economic axis of the growing bilateral trade with China following the latter's own experience of reform and opening. This raises a further question: To what extent might North Korean marketising reforms repeat the successes of China's economic reform experience? In the following chapter, we examine this question with particular reference to economic reform during the Kim Jong Un era.

6   North Korean Economic Reform in the Shadow of China

Despite the crisis of the 1990s, the impulse to economic reform in North Korea by most accounts remained weak in comparison to other state socialist societies. The apparent failure to emulate China's state-guided transition to 'market socialism' is deemed as particularly surprising given its geographical proximity to North Korea, the longstanding economic and political linkages between the two countries and the correspondingly greater potential demonstrative effect of China's reforms. The literature has tended to view North Korea's limited reforms as resulting primarily from domestic politico–ideological factors, such as the obstinacy of the country's leadership and the threat that reform poses to the reigning ideologies of *Juche* or Military First Politics.[1] Observers have argued, for example, that North Korea's leadership fears that economic liberalisation would undermine its own authority and thereby loosen its hold over the populace. As a result, elites have taken no deliberate steps towards Chinese-style economic reform.[2]

However, such interpretations fail to adequately explain why, if the politico–ideological barriers to reform are so strong, North Korea has made any attempts at economic reform at all. As we saw in the previous chapter, the July 1st measures of 2002 sought to adjust the economic management system to ongoing processes of marketisation as well as increase management and worker incentives. Some observers did see in these measures an attempted emulation of the Chinese experience, suggesting that at the very least slogans such as *Juche* and Military First Politics were not as inflexible as to prevent what was in all but name an economic reform programme. However, the sincerity of these measures was widely doubted by others. For example, it has been argued that, rather than actively promote market reform, the primary aim of the July 1st measures was to overcome acute challenges such as the

---

[1] Tat Yan Kong, 'The Political Obstacles to Economic Reform in North Korea: The Ultra Cautious Strategy in Comparative Perspective', *The Pacific Review*, 27.1 (2014), p. 75; Eberstadt, *North Korean Economy*, p. xii–xiii; Andrei Lankov, 'Why North Korea Will Not Change', *Foreign Affairs*, 87.2 (2008), pp. 9–16.
[2] Oh and Hassig, 'North Korea between Collapse and Reform', p. 295.

paralysis of the PDS and were thereby designed to reinforce rather than relax centralised control over the economy and the expanding informal market sector.[3] Furthermore, it has been argued that the continued obsession with maintaining the self-reliant economy meant that the measures were unlikely to resolve ongoing problems of economic inefficiency.[4] They should therefore be seen as minor reforms *within* the system rather than a fundamental reform *of* the system, and thereby, as sharing more in common with the failed Soviet reforms of the 1960s than the Chinese experience.[5] As we have seen, by the late 2000s, such pessimism seemed to be vindicated as the government sought to reverse the reforms through cracking down on markets and dispossessing citizens of their new-found wealth. Reforms that may have offered a solution to the ongoing economic malaise thereby took second place to the imperative of regime maintenance, with the possible negative political consequences of genuine reform seen by the leadership as simply too dangerous.[6]

The Kim Jong Un regime, however, resumed the reform drive, announcing and to some degree implementing a new set of economic management policies. Under the slogan of 'Our-Style Economic Management Method' (*urisik kyŏngjekwalli pangbŏp*), the authorities sought to introduce measures aimed at improving economic efficiency and stimulating agricultural and industrial production. In many respects, they built upon the July 1st measures in reducing the scope of central planning and decentralising decision-making rights towards regions and individual production units. The formal introduction of the Socialist Enterprise Responsibility Management System (SERMS) in 2014, for example, expanded enterprise autonomy including greater responsibility for management performance as well as discretion over the utilisation of profits. In agriculture, the reforms similarly sought to increase farmers' incentives through the strengthening of cooperative farms' decision-making rights and discretion over the disposal of output. While the regime continued to emphasise socialist economic construction based on the principle of *Juche*, Our-Style Economic Management Method thereby sought to extend the reforms of the early 2000s. As with the July 1st measures, the reform measures under Kim Jong Un were to some extent reactive in that they represented an acceptance of the public's increased engagement in market activities.[7]

---

[3] Dae-Won Koh, 'Dynamics of Inter-Korean Conflict and North Korea's Recent Policy Changes: An Inter-Systemic View', *Asian Survey*, 44.3 (2004), p. 432.

[4] Un-Chul Yang, 'Reform without Transition: The Economic Situation in North Korea since the July 1, 2002, Measures', *North Korean Review*, 6.1 (2010), pp. 72–73.

[5] Bernhard Seliger, 'The July 2002 Reforms in North Korea: Liberman-Style Reforms or Road to Transformation?', *North Korean Review*, 1.1 (2005), pp. 22–37.

[6] Dongho Jo, 'Muddling along with Missiles', *EAI Issue Briefing*, 4 (2009), p. 5.

[7] Kwon Young-Kyong, 'Change and Outlook of North Korean Economic Policy in the Kim Jong Un Era [Kimjŏngŭn sidae Pukhan kyŏngjejŏngch'aekŭi pyŏnhwawa chŏnmang]', *Korean Eximbank North Korea Economic Review*, Spring (2014), pp. 17–19.

Certainly, the reality of marketisation was only mentioned obliquely through such terms as 'in line with the demands of actual development' or 'practical benefits'. While the language remained opaque, however, the measures adopted during the Kim Jong Un era established a favourable environment for continued marketisation. Although the success of the reforms was by no means assured, they did suggest that analyses emphasising the role of ideology or the imperatives of political survival as barriers to reform do not give a full account of the dynamics of economic reform in North Korea.

In this chapter, we provide an overview of the economic reforms pursued under Kim Jong Un and address the question of the extent to which North Korea followed in China's footsteps. We note that while North Korea's reform drive resembled the Chinese experience in many respects, the country faced particular challenges related to its distinctive model of political economy. These included the greater extent of economic decline in North Korea as a result of the crisis of the 1990s, bureaucratic resistance to reform due to the specificities of North Korea's economic structure and the dangers of inflation. Arguably the greatest challenge to the country's pursuit of Chinese-style 'reform and opening up' was its adverse external security environment. North Korea was by no means a passive actor within these broader regional tensions, but it remained the case that those tensions undermined the political standing of more pragmatic elements within the country and problematised efforts to attract foreign investment.

6.1   The Dynamics of Economic Reform under Kim Jong Un

There is little doubt that North Korea has historically adopted a cautious approach to economic reform. This caution stemmed both from the country's geopolitical environment and the structural features of its economy. Unlike China, where economic reform and opening took place after the improvement of its diplomatic relations with the United States, North Korea saw no such breakthrough and remained a hypermilitarised state and subject to stringent sanctions. Balazs Szalontai and Changyong Choi argue that successful instances of reform in China and Vietnam also required concessions to be made to the non-socialist powers. In Vietnam's case, this included the withdrawal of troops from Cambodia in 1989, though crucially this did not result in a significant weakening in Vietnam's bargaining position vis-à-vis the United States. For North Korea, however, the dismantling of its nuclear weapons programme would undermine the cornerstone of its deterrent.[8] As such, the

---

[8] Balazs Szalontai and Changyong Choi, 'The Prospects of Economic Reform in North Korea: Comparisons with China, Vietnam and Yugoslavia', *Europe-Asia Studies*, 64.2 (2012), p. 240.

international context for North Korean reform appears to be particularly inauspicious.

The structural features of the North Korean economy also raise questions as to the extent to which the country may follow Chinese-style reform and opening. Mainstream explanations of China's success versus the more problematic trajectory of the Soviet Bloc countries have typically cited the gradualist approach adopted by the former in contrast to the shock therapy approach of the latter.[9] Jeffrey Sachs and Wing Thye Woo argue that the cause of their divergent paths was not to be found not in the policies themselves but in their divergent prior structural conditions. China had embarked upon its reforms as a largely agricultural society with a large rural population, whereas the Soviet Bloc countries were mostly urban and (over)industrialised. Thus, at the outset of the reform era, 80 per cent of China's labour force was located outside of the conservative state sector, whereas in the Soviet Bloc, the state sector covered the majority of the population.[10] China's challenge was, therefore, one of 'normal' economic development, whereas the challenge for the Soviet Bloc countries was that of structural adjustment, namely cutting employment in inefficient and subsidised industries to allow for new jobs in more efficient industries and services. In this respect, China can be said to have enjoyed the advantages of backwardness.[11] The structural features of the North Korean economy, shaped as they were by post-war industrialisation and urbanisation, would suggest greater similarities with the more industrialised countries of the Soviet Bloc than with China.

Indeed, the challenge of reform can be seen as greater in (post) socialist countries with large heavy-industrial bases. As Michael Shafer has argued, in states in which the leading economic sectors are characterised by high levels of capital intensity and economies of scale, there are high sunk costs and thus high exit barriers. Any potential increase in competition resulting from restructuring can amount to disaster for enterprises in such sectors.[12] Such states also typically lack the institutions needed for the new sectors, while staff in the specialised agencies that monitor, regulate and service the old sectors fear for their own future in a new world where their specialised skills are of little use, and as such, they will resist the growth of new competing sectors. Restructuring can also threaten state revenues, thereby strengthening the

---

[9] John McMillan and Barry Naughton, 'How to Reform a Planned Economy: Lessons from China', *Oxford Review of Economic Policy*, 8.1 (1992), pp. 130–43.

[10] Jeffrey Sachs and Wing Thye Woo, 'Structural Factors in the Economic Reforms of China, Eastern Europe, and the Former Soviet Union', *Economic Policy*, 9.18 (1994), p. 112.

[11] Ibid., pp. 103–104.

[12] Michael D. Shafer, *Winners and Losers: How Sectors Shape the Developmental Prospects of States* (Ithaca, NY: Cornell University Press, 1994), p. 25.

tendency whereby leaders seek to preserve the status quo.[13] While Shafer's argument was originally applied to capitalist Third World countries, the implications of these sectoral interests can also be seen in state socialist countries.

The influence of such sectoral characteristics on the reform process can be seen in China's industrialised northeast. The strong legacies of the planned economy there led to bureaucratic resistance to reform amidst the relative absence of commercialism and entrepreneurism and the engrained custom of 'waiting, relying and asking' that emerged during the era of central planning.[14] Indeed, the politics of reform in China has been analysed in terms of this spatial distinction. Gilbert Rozman, for example, speaks of the struggle between the pro-reform forces concentrated in the Southeast of the country and the conservative forces who had their power bases inland and in the north. In this respect, Northeast China has been a 'bastion of conservatism'.[15] In the early reform era, North-eastern provincial authorities were slower to attract investment from neighbouring Japan and South Korea. Official economic cooperation between China's northeast and South Korea, for example, was restricted until the 1990s due to this general ambivalence, as conservative party officials sought to protect inefficient state-run industries from foreign competition. In addition, Japanese investments revived memories of colonial domination of the region.[16] Given the shared structural and historical characteristics between North Korea and northeast China, it is easier to grasp why Pyongyang has adopted a cautious and inconsistent approach towards economic reform.

Despite the fact that North Korea appears as a particularly inauspicious candidate for reform, the authorities have made efforts, albeit in a somewhat erratic manner. What then explains the stop-and-start pattern of economic reform in North Korea? One approach to understanding the dynamics of North Korean policymaking has been to examine the alleged contestation between economic reformists and the conservative Old Guard.[17] Patrick McEachern has argued, for example, that contestation over economic reform has been expressed through inter-institutional struggles between, on the one hand, the military and KWP, and on the other, the Cabinet. Whereas the military and KWP have tended to emphasise security concerns and ideological

---

[13] Ibid., pp. 37–38.

[14] Pingyu Zhang, 'Revitalizing Old Industrial Base of Northeast China: Process, Policy and Challenge', *Chinese Geographical Science*, 18.2 (2008), pp. 112–13.

[15] Gilbert Rozman, 'Northeast China: Waiting for Regionalism', *Problems of Post-Communism*, 45.4 (1998), p. 4.

[16] Outi Luova, 'Transnational Linkages and Development Initiatives in Ethnic Korean Yanbian, Northeast China: 'Sweet and Sour' Capital Transfers', *Pacific Affairs*, 82.3 (2009), p. 431.

[17] Selig Harrison, *Korean Endgame: A Strategy for Reunification and US Disengagement* (Princeton, NJ: Princeton University Press, 2002), p. 25.

correctness respectively, McEachern argues that the Cabinet has adopted a reformist position more favourable towards attracting foreign aid and investment as means of achieving economic rehabilitation.[18] This inter-institutional competition can also be seen in the rise and fall of particular individuals within the state bureaucracy. For example, Premier Pak Bong Ju had been responsible for several of the key reform measures of the early 2000s, a period that coincided with the ascendance of the Cabinet's political stature and its role in economic management. However, the decreasing influence of economic technocrats, Premier Pak's dismissal in April 2007 and the shift in authority over economic policymaking from the Cabinet back towards the KWP coincided with the attempted reversals of the late 2000s.[19]

Such views also see this backlash against economic reform as strongly influenced by the increasingly hostile external environment of the 2000s. This hostility dates back to the State of the Union 'axis of evil' address by George W. Bush in 2002 and the implied threat posed by the US-led coalition's 2003 invasion of Iraq. As Rüdiger Frank has argued, through adopting an aggressive stance of containment towards North Korea, the West '... failed to support the reformers. Indigenous reforms need domestic promoters. These take a great risk and must be able to show a few successes every once in a while to convince the leadership to stay the course. But we never gave pro-reform forces in North Korea a chance'.[20] Indeed, the hawkish international response to North Korea's first nuclear test in 2006 can be seen as having further undermined the standing of domestic reformers. Faced with sanctions, the KWP became vocal in emphasising planning over markets, arguing that commitment to socialist economics was in line with *Juche* ideology and thus must be adhered to. The KWP's call for retreat from the reform measures of the early 2000s thereby came to shape North Korea's economic policymaking.[21]

Some qualification is needed with regards to analyses of divisions between reformists and conservatives, however. In terms of inter-institutional competition, key North Korean political figures, in reality, hold concurrent positions in the KWP, government and military, thereby problematising the notion of clear-cut institutional positions. It is also important to be clear what is meant by the term 'reformist'. As yet, there is little clear evidence of calls for reform that explicitly question the legitimacy of the existing *Juche*

---

[18] Patrick McEachern, *Inside the Red Box: North Korea's Post-Totalitarian Politics* (New York: Columbia University Press, 2010), pp. 34–35.

[19] Jinwook Choi and Meredith Shaw, 'The Rise of Kim Jong Eun and the Return of the Party', *International Journal of Korean Unification Studies*, 19.2 (2010), p.183.

[20] Rüdiger Frank, 'Ideological Risk versus Economic Necessity: The Future of Reform in North Korea', *Japan Focus*, 7.30 (2009), p. 5.

[21] McEachern, *Inside the Red Box*, pp. 211–13.

self-reliant socialist economy. Indeed, calls for radical change would be politically dangerous and entail the loss of the existing privileged status of the bureaucratic class. As such, it is more accurate to speak of the increased influence of economic technocrats rather than 'reformists' per se. This influence reflects a broader generational shift within the economy-related ministries as key officials in their forties and fifties have replaced their retiring more-ideologically inclined elders. These emerging younger technocrats are more likely to propose pragmatic improvements to the existing system. Despite the more cautious discourse in North Korea, this resembles the manner in which Chinese reforms too were initially framed as 'reform within the system', with strong continuities in terms of the role of the authoritarian state.[22] As in China, therefore, the extent to which these more pragmatic policymakers are likely to gain influence in North Korea will strongly shape the future trajectory of reform.

Kim Jong Un's rise to power became the occasion of much media speculation over whether he might prove to be a reformer or whether his lack of revolutionary credentials might compel him to prove himself through provocative military acts and through associating himself with a hard-line version of his grandfather's *Juche* ideology.[23] In certain respects, both of these possibilities were realised. On the one hand, Kim Jong Un significantly accelerated the country's nuclear weapons programme, thereby heightening tensions with the United States and its allies in East Asia. At the same time, he resumed and deepened the country's economic reform programme. At the Plenary Meeting of the KWP Central Committee on 31 March 2013, this approach was given official standing as the dual '*Pyŏngjin*' line of the simultaneous development of the economy and nuclear weapons.[24] At the very least, this policy line suggested that the role of the external security environment in shaping economic policymaking should not be understood in any mechanistic sense. At a time when North Korea's relations with the United States had barely been worse, the fact that Pyongyang appeared to be adopting some of the most far-reaching economic reforms yet suggests that there was still considerable room for agency in terms of the leadership's policy initiatives. Indeed, as we discuss below, the tightening of sanctions in fact made the task of addressing the inefficient system of economic management all the more pressing. Whether the reforms could be

---

[22] You Ji, *China's Enterprise Reform: Changing State/Society Relations after Mao* (London: Routledge, 1998), p. 8.

[23] Victor D. Cha, 'Kim Jong Un Is No Reformer', *Foreign Policy [Online]*, 2012 http://foreignpolicy.com/2012/08/21/kim-jong-un-is-no-reformer/ [accessed 31 March 2020].

[24] *Rodong Sinmun*, 2 April 2013, 'The report given by Respected Comrade Kim Jong Un at the March 2013 Plenum of the KWP Central Committee [Kyŏngaehanŭn Kimjŏngŭn tongjikkesŏ Chosŏnnodongdang chungangwiwŏnhoe 2013 nyŏn 3 wŏl chŏnwŏnhoeŭiesŏ hasin pogo]'.

successful in the context of a hostile geopolitical environment is another question, however.

Despite deepening geopolitical tensions, there was under Kim Jong Un a clear shift in the top economic leadership back towards pragmatic technocrats. Early in his tenure, for example, Kim Jong Un dismissed his father's closest advisors, such as his aunt Kim Kyong Hui and her husband Jang Song Thaek (the latter of whom was executed in December 2013). Four key military figures who had accompanied Kim Jong Il's funeral hearse on 28 December 2011, including Chief of General Staff Vice-Marshal Ri Yong Ho, were also purged within two years. By the end of 2014, Kim Jong Un had replaced over half of the key figures in the Party, the government (including the Cabinet) and the military.[25] Kim Jong Un's rise to power also coincided with a shift in emphasis back towards the Cabinet. Key officials with economic expertise were assigned important ministry posts, and the role of the Cabinet as 'the nation's economic headquarters' was repeatedly emphasised in the official media. As a September 2015 article in *Minju Choson* argued:

'The Cabinet is the county's economic headquarters and the highest sovereign administrative executive organ for the Party's economic policies. If we wish to thoroughly establish Our-Style Economic Management Method and make it effective in carrying out economic work, we must decisively strengthen the Cabinet responsibility system and the Cabinet-centred system'.[26]

This shift in emphasis back towards pragmatic economic policymaking was also manifested in the reappointment of Pak Bong Ju in April 2013 to the position of Premier. Pak was charged with improving the system of economic management in agriculture and industry, and his position was further strengthened following his election to the Politburo Standing Committee at the KWP's 7th Party Congress in May 2016. This strengthening of the Cabinet's role in economic policy occurred alongside the weakening of the military's influence. Under Kim Jong Il's Military First Politics, the military had operated various trading companies, mines, farms and factories, and was, as a result, a significant earner of foreign currency. However, its role in the economy was significantly curtailed following Kim Jong Un's rise to power.

---

[25] The Institute for Far Eastern Studies, 'The Situation on the Korean Peninsula: An Evaluation of 2014 and the Outlook for 2015 [Hanbando Chŏngse: 2014 nyŏn p'yŏnggawa 2015 nyŏn chŏnmang]', *IFES Report*, 2014.

[26] *Minju Choson*, 17 September 2015, 'Let's strengthen the cabinet-responsibility system and the cabinet-centered system and make a transformation in the construction of an economically powerful nation [Naegakch'aegimje, naegakchungsimjerŭl kanghwahayŏ kyŏngjegangguk kŏnsŏresŏ chŏnhwanŭl irŭkhija]'.

6.2   Agricultural Reform

In terms of the actual reform measures put in place, they bore a strong resemblance to Deng Xiaoping's economic reforms. As such, it is worth first examining briefly China's own experience in order to shed light on the potential of as well as the barriers to applying similar reforms in the North Korean context. China's reforms involved, in the first instance, an increase in agricultural procurement prices as a means of tackling the low incentives inherent in the collective farming system. In 1979, prices paid by the state for agricultural produce saw an increase of 22.1 per cent on the previous year. This increase alone was successful in inducing an almost immediate rise in output, with a corresponding improvement in farmers' incomes and purchasing power. Between 1979 and 1981, farmers received an extra 46,290 million yuan as a result of these price adjustments.[27] An additional key reform was the reduction in the size of the collective production teams, thereby strengthening the link between individual effort and reward. Prior to the reforms, each production team had consisted of about twenty to thirty households, but due to difficulties in monitoring, rewards to individual farmers were not tied directly to their own efforts.[28] At the outset of the reform era, collective farms took the initiative in contracting pieces of collective land out to individual households. These experiments were eventually tolerated by provincial governments in Sichuan and Anhui.[29] They subsequently spread spontaneously throughout the country and full official acceptance of this Household Responsibility System (HRS) was finally given in late 1981. By the end of 1983, 98 per cent of all production teams had adopted the HRS.[30]

The manifest efficiency of the HRS served to undermine existing views amongst policymakers that larger farms were more appropriate to the application of modern farming technologies. Indeed, the HRS encouraged peasants to shift from the superficial application of fertilisers towards the practice of 'stratified insertion' into the soil for quickening nutrient absorption by plant roots.[31] Furthermore, while land contracts were originally set for just one or two years, in 1984, they were extended to 15 years to discourage over-exploitation of the soil and to promote investment and intensive farming while

---

[27] Robert F. Ash, 'The Evolution of Agricultural Policy', *The China Quarterly*, 116.December (1988), p. 540.

[28] Justin Yifu Lin, 'Rural Reforms and Agricultural Growth in China', *The American Economic Review*, 82.1 (1992), p. 37.

[29] Barry Naughton, *The Chinese Economy: Transitions and Growth* (Cambridge, MA: The MIT Press, 2007), p. 241.

[30] Lin, 'Rural Reforms and Agricultural Growth', p. 37.

[31] Yak-Yeow Kueh, 'China's New Agricultural-Policy Program: Major Economic Consequences, 1979-1983', *Journal of Comparative Economics*, 8.4 (1984), pp. 371.

conserving soil fertility.[32] Between 1978 and 1984, per capita grain output had seen an average yearly increase of 3.8 per cent, and between 1983 and 1984 alone, China's gross agricultural output increased by 14.5 per cent.[33] These successes encouraged policymakers to reduce the state's compulsory grain purchases. Thus, when farmers contracted their land, they agreed to turn over a certain amount of grain to the government, with the rest released to the market. The success of agricultural reform led to the same principles being applied to industry and commerce, extending the pattern whereby powers and resources from central planners were decentralised to local actors while core interests were protected through contracts.[34]

North Korean reform measures under Kim Jong Un, in several important respects, resemble those of the Chinese experience. In April 2012, Kim vowed in his first public speech that the North Korean people would 'not tighten their belts again' and would enjoy the wealth and prosperity of socialism.[35] A set of new agricultural and industrial reform measures was reportedly rolled out later that year, albeit seemingly on a pilot basis. Although there were no available official government documents that provided a definitive statement on the content of the reforms, at the plenary meeting of the KWP Central Committee on 31 March 2013, Kim Jong Un spoke of the need to 'study and complete Our-Style Economic Management Method', a term that would come to encapsulate the broad range of economic reforms pursued by the regime.[36] Further details of the reforms were given in Kim Jong Un's statement on 30 May 2014 titled 'On Establishing Our-Style Economic Management Method in Accordance with the Demands of Actual Development'. A *Rodong Sinmun* editorial in October 2014 emphasised the basic principle underpinning the reforms:

'The securing of practical benefits in economic work is a very important issue. If we are not concerned with practical benefits, there will be huge wastage, with a lot of human and material losses and economic disruption to all sectors, units, and even to the whole nation ... In order to obtain the utmost practical benefits in economic work, production

---

[32] Ash, 'Evolution of Agricultural Policy', p. 537.

[33] Carl Riskin, *China's Political Economy: The Quest for Development Since 1949* (Oxford: Oxford University Press, 1987), pp. 291–93.

[34] Naughton, *Chinese Economy*, p. 90.

[35] *Rodong Sinmun*, 16 April 2012, 'The Address given by the Supreme Leader of Our Party and People Comrade Kim Jong Un on the occasion of the military parade to commemorate the 100th Anniversary of The Great Leader Kim Il Sung's birthday [Widaehan suryŏng Kimilsŏng taewŏnsunim t'ansaeng 100 tol kyŏngch'uk yŏlbyŏngsigesŏ hasin uri tanggwa inminŭi ch'oegoryŏngdoja Kimjŏngŭndongjiŭi yŏnsŏl]'.

[36] *Rodong Sinmun*, 2 April 2013, 'The report given by Respected Comrade Kim Jong Un at the March 2013 Plenum of the KWP Central Committee [Kyŏngaehanŭn Kimjŏngŭn tongjikkesŏ chosŏnnodongdang chungangwiwŏnhoe 2013 nyŏn 3 wŏl chŏnwŏnhoeŭiesŏ hasin pogo]'.

and management must meet the demands of objective economic laws and modern science and technology'.[37]

In terms of their content, agricultural reforms were adopted to increase farmers' incentives by reducing the size of work teams. The reforms introduced a so-called 'Field Responsibility System' (*P'ojŏndamdangch'aegimje*), which bore strong parallels to the Chinese HRS. Under the North Korean version, each work team would consist of four to five farmers or less and would be assigned an individual plot of land. This measure was not entirely new. Mention had been made of the Field Responsibility System as part of the July 1st measures in the early 2000s. In a 2004 interview with *Choson Sinbo*, Vice Trade Minister Kim Yong Sul stated that 'Cooperative farms are currently introducing the Field Responsibility System on a pilot basis ... We also gave the authority to make the sub-work team smaller ... If it is possible to produce more crops on the same land with the same labour, then that is precisely 'practicalism' (*sillijuŭi*)'.[38] However, it appears that the reforms were not implemented nationally at that time.

In contrast, the Kim Jong Un government put the Field Responsibility System on a firm legal footing through revisions to the Agricultural Farm Law.[39] While the reforms were initially carried out on a pilot basis, the new system was, in 2014, expanded in scope and rolled out more extensively. In February that year, a convention of 8,000 sub-work unit leaders was held in Pyongyang, where they received a letter from Kim Jong Un containing details of the new system. This letter amounted to the most publicised statement of agricultural policy in decades and served to reaffirm the government's commitment to the reforms.[40] Furthermore, on 7 April 2015, a *Rodong Sinmun* article discussed the case of Sokhwa Cooperative Farm in Sonchon County of North Pyongan Province, whereby 'the format of the sub-work team, which is the basic production unit, has been reorganised to focus on members of a single family working together'.[41] Numerous *Rodong Sinmun* articles further demonstrated that the main goal of this measure was to improve farm

[37] *Rodong Sinmun*, 22 October 2014, 'Basic requirements for establishing Our-Style Economic Management Method [Urisik kyŏngjegwallibangbŏbŭi hwangnibesŏ nasŏnŭn kibonyogu]'.

[38] *Choson Sinbo*, 13 December 2004, 'Strengthening of unified guidance, increase in powers below – An interview with Department of Trade Vice Minister Kim Yong Sul [T'ongiljŏgin chidoganghwa, araee manŭn kwŏnhan – Chosŏnmuyŏgsŏng Kimyongsul int'ŏbyu]'.

[39] Legislation Press, *Legal Code of the Democratic People's Republic of Korea (Supplementary Edition) [Chosŏn Minjujuŭi Inmin'gonghwaguk pŏpchŏn (chŭngbop'an)]* (Pyongyang: Legislation Press, 2016), p. 295.

[40] Randall Ireson, 'DPRK Agricultural Policy: Chinese-Style Reform or Muddling Towards Autonomy?', *38 North*, 2015 http://38north.org/2015/01/rireson012715/ [accessed 31 March 2020].

[41] *Rodong Sinmun*, 7 April 2015, 'The secret of a year-long breakthrough – The efforts of workers in *Songch'ŏn* County's *Sŏkwa* collective farm that increased grain production by 1,000 tonnes

productivity and raise food production through increasing farmers' work incentives. Along with denunciation of 'equalism' in distribution, emphasis was given to differentiated compensation for individual farmers according to their performance.[42]

What the measures did not do was dismantle the collective farm units themselves, in contrast to China where the People's Communes were abolished in 1982. With the state's procurement system, restrictions on the direct sales of staple food in marketplaces remained in place. However, cooperative farms were given increased autonomy. While grain, meat, fruit and dried chillies were still covered by the central plan index and sold to the government at state prices, surpluses could be sold at a negotiated price to designated organisations such as enterprises. This represented a departure from past practice, whereby surpluses could only be sold to the state at a fixed low price. Other crops, however, were covered under the cooperative farms' own plan (*nongjangjip'yo*) and could be sold at higher market prices.[43] As Kwon Tae-Jin has argued, once the farm met its obligations under the central index, cooperative farms possessed rights in relation to the distribution and transfer of income, the setting of prices and sale of surplus produce and the use of profits for reinvestment. Farms were also given a degree of flexibility with regards to how they use central government funds as well as proceeds from market sales. They could also receive investments from private individuals, thereby strengthening the linkage between farms and the market.[44] As a result, farm management became increasingly monetised, and in line with this, the government imposed new taxes such as the land use fee, the irrigation fee and the electricity fee.[45]

To what extent were these agricultural reforms successful? In the early to mid-2010s, the evidence suggests that North Korea saw a moderate increase in its agricultural output. According to figures produced by South Korea's Rural Development Administration, overall crop production in 2014 was estimated

---

last year [Tan hanhae tongane piyakŭl irŭkhin pigyŏl – chinanhae algok 1,000 tŭl chŭngsuhan sŏnch'ŏn'gun sŏk'wahyŏptongnongjang ilgundŭrŭi saŏbesŏ]'.

[42] For example, *Rodong Sinmun*, 23 September 2015, 'For the Field Responsibility System to produce outcomes – the case of workers in Kangnyong County [P'ojŏndamdangch'aegimjega ŭni nage- kangnyŏnggun ilgundŭrŭi saŏbesŏ]'; *Rodong Sinmun*, 6 February 2016, 'The Field Responsibility System and the spirit of competition [P'ojŏndamdangch'aegimjewa kyŏngjaengsim']; *Rodong Sinmun*, 11 October 2017, 'Application of the Field Responsibility System to the actual situation – the case of workers in Pakchun County [P'ojŏndamdangch'aegimjerŭl silchŏnge matke chŏkyonghayŏ- pakch'ŏn'gun ilgundŭrŭi saŏbesŏ]'.

[43] Article 50 of the Agricultural Farm Law (revised 23 December 2014) outlines that farms can price their agricultural produce subject to the farm plan index to compensate for costs.

[44] Article 43 of the Agricultural Farm Law states that 'Farms may use the "idle money funds" (*yuhyu hwap'yejagŭm*) of the residents directly for the management activities according to procedures set by the relevant agency.'

[45] Kwon Tae-Jin, *Current Situation and Outlook*, pp. 6–9.

to have increased by 2.7 per cent compared over that of 2012, from 4.7 million tonnes to 4.8 million tonnes.[46] North Korean economist Chi Myong Su of the Academy of Agricultural Sciences argued that these trends could be taken as evidence of the effectiveness of the Field Responsibility System and its ability to increase farmers' 'patriotism' and productivity.[47] However, it should be noted that in 2015, crop production fell again to 4.5 million tonnes.[48] This decline was largely a result of poor rains and limited availability of water for irrigation.[49] After recovering somewhat, production in the year 2018 fell again to almost the same level seen in 2015 due to drought, high temperatures and floods.[50] As such, increased farmers' incentives were in themselves unable to offset the susceptibility of North Korean agriculture to adverse climatic events. In any case, it is difficult to draw macro-level correlations between the Field Responsibility System and overall harvest trends in North Korea due to lack of precise data as to exactly how extensively the agricultural reforms were rolled out across the country.

Furthermore, the reforms faced several challenges if they were to significantly improve food production. The first relates to the potential lack of clear direction from the central authorities as to the content and permanency of the reforms. Hyeong-Jung Park of the (South) Korea Institute for National Unification has suggested that inconsistency in their implementation led to a reluctance amongst farmers to take advantage of the new measures.[51] This is in marked contrast to the Chinese experience where, in light of the previous reversals of the Cultural Revolution, reformers explicitly sought to stress the continuity and durability of the new measures.[52] In addition, while the government intended a transition towards a family-based system, bureaucratic resistance at the local level meant that there were sharp variations in the degree to which the reforms were implemented across the country.[53] This resistance likely stemmed from the fact that an estimated one in ten collective farm members held positions in farm management, which were well paid and did not require any physical labour but received the same food allowance as

---

[46] Rural Development Administration. Data draw retrieved at www.kosis.kr [accessed 7 June 2020].

[47] *Tongil Sinbo*, 27 June 2015, 'Clear Evidence of the Effectiveness of the Field Responsibility System [Pojŏndamdangch'aegimje, kŭ saenghwalyŏk dduryŏsi siljŭng]'.

[48] Rural Development Administration. Data draw retrieved at www.kosis.kr [accessed 7 June 2020].

[49] FAO GIEWS Update, *The Democratic People's Republic of Korea Outlook for Food Supply and Demand in 2015/16.*

[50] FAO/WFP, *FAO/WFO Joint Rapid Food Security Assessment,* May 2019, p. 4.

[51] Hyeong-jung Park, 'North Korea's 'New Economic Management System': Main Features and Problems', *Korea Focus*, January (2014), p. 8

[52] Yasheng Huang, *Capitalism with Chinese Characteristics: Entrepreneurship and the State* (Cambridge: Cambridge University Press, 2008), p. 91.

[53] Hyeong-jung Park, 'North Korea's "New Economic Management System"', p 8.

labourers.[54] As such, this non-productive stratum would directly lose out if there was a shift away from the collective farm system, and thus had strong motivations to resist reform.[55]

Also, China's improvements in agricultural productivity were not only a result of greater incentives and more efficient use of labour, but also due to the import of new technologies and equipment. This led to a reduction in the production costs of key inputs such as fertilisers and pesticides. Indeed, from 1979 to 1980, prices for such inputs had declined by between 10 and 15 per cent, thereby enhancing incomes in rural China and improving incentives for further increased production.[56] Questions can be raised, however, as to how far increased incentives are likely to resolve North Korea's difficulties in food production. As Haggard and Noland have argued, there are competing datasets on North Korean grain production, including those from the Food and Agricultural Organization (FAO) that suggest a sudden and drastic drop between 1994 and 1995, and those from the US Department of Agriculture and South Korea's Ministry of Unification that suggest a more gradual secular decline from the mid-1980s.[57] In any case, it is clear that the collapse in food production during the 1990s was not a result of the sudden decline in farmers' motivations but part of a broader industrial collapse, and in particular, severe energy and fertiliser shortages. Given that the industrial sector had still seen only a partial recovery since the crisis, it was questionable whether North Korea's reforms could see the kinds of increase in output seen in China or even a return to former levels of production achieved in the 1980s. As such, the recovery of industry is essential for the full recovery of agriculture, thereby raising the question of reforms to industrial management.

6.3   State-Owned Enterprise Reform

The recovery of North Korea's industrial sector has indeed been lethargic. During the 2000s, the government increased investment in the so-called 'four leading sectors': the metal industry, electricity generation, railroads and the mining industry. Despite positive official media reports, these efforts were, in reality, met with mixed results. For example, the recovery of the metal industry was slow, with the output of crude steel estimated to have remained at around 1.2 million tonnes during the 2010s, thereby failing to reach the levels of the

---

[54] Sung-Wook Nam, 'Chronic Food Shortages', p. 106.
[55] Hyeong-jung Park, 'North Korea's "New Economic Management System"', p. 7.
[56] Michel Aglietta and Guo Bai, *China's Development: Capitalism and Empire* (London: Routledge, 2013), p. 89.
[57] Haggard and Noland, *Famine in North Korea*, pp. 34–38.

late 1980s.[58] The chemical industry was badly affected by the reduced supply of electricity and raw materials, leading to a sharp decline in the supply of inputs for light industry and agriculture. Although state media reported in the late 2000s increased investment in chemical plants and an increase in the production of fertiliser, the subsequent decline in the number of such reports suggests that further increases proved difficult due to continued energy and raw material shortages. Indeed, the ongoing energy shortage was a particularly strong barrier to economic rehabilitation. As such, the government engaged in the construction of several hydro-electric power plants, such as the Huichon Hydro Power Plant. As of the mid-2010s, North Korea reportedly had nine major thermal facilities. However, eight of them were coal-burning plants that suffered from an insufficient supply of good quality coal as well as delays in plant and equipment repairs.[59] The country's power generation facilities thus operated at far less than their combined potential output, and as a result, industrial recovery was modest at best, with production in most sectors failing to return to levels seen prior to the crisis.

However, as with agriculture, the authorities sought to facilitate industrial recovery through the decentralisation of decision-making rights and an increase in responsibility and incentives. In this respect, industrial management reforms again bore strong similarities to the Chinese experience, although it is important to keep in mind that Chinese SOE reforms were themselves far from an unmitigated success. In China, prices, as well as quantitative production targets in industry, had, as in North Korea, been set by the state. To increase the role of the market in determining price levels and guiding production-related decisions, a dual price system was introduced whereby SOEs were permitted to sell any output above the plan openly on the market. They were given greater freedoms to purchase inputs and make decisions over what to produce and at what quantity, with the right to introduce new product lines. SOEs were also given the right to retain a share of the profits, with the exact percentage subject to negotiation with the state. With these new rights, SOEs were also able to determine how they rewarded managers and where new investments were to be made.[60]

Chinese SOE reforms also included attempts to introduce a labour market, with greater flexibility for managers to adjust employment levels in accordance with market conditions, leading to an end to permanent employment. In 1985,

[58] Lee Seog-Ki, Byun Hak-moon and Na Hye-Seon, *North Korea's Industry and Industrial Policy in the Kim Jong Un Era [Kimjŏngŭn sidae Pukhanŭi sanŏp mit sanŏpchŏngch'aek]* (Sejong: Korea Institute for Industrial Economics and Trade, 2018), pp. 107–11.

[59] KDB, *North Korean Industry 2015 [Pukhanŭi sanŏp 2015]* (Seoul: Korean Development Bank, 2015), pp. 169–70.

[60] David Dollar, 'Economic Reform and Allocative Efficiency in China's State-Owned Industry', *Economic Development and Cultural Change*, 39.1 (1990), pp. 89–90.

contract workers accounted for just 4 per cent of total employment, but by 1995, this had increased to 29 per cent. Until the late 1990s, the dismissal of workers was still tightly regulated, however, with enterprises allowed to dismiss no more than 1 per cent of their workforce each year.[61] In general, SOE reform in China was slow. However, the share of SOEs in industrial production declined from 77.6 per cent in 1978 to 34 per cent in 1995.[62] Around half of these industrial SOEs were losing money.[63]

This decline resulted from the fact that most of the dynamism in urban reform in the 1980s came from the private sector. In contrast to the experience of the former Soviet Bloc, there was no widespread privatisation of SOEs in the early stages of reform. The Chinese government did, however, permit the establishment of private businesses, commonly referred to as *getihu,* or sole industrial and commercial proprietorships. These *getihu* were seen by the government as only supplementary to collective units and SOEs, with an initial cap of seven employees for each *getihu.* Nonetheless, the number of *getihu* expanded rapidly due to the fact that the dual-track price system had released a considerable amount of resources outside of the planning system, and that rising purchasing power boosted demand for lower-priced consumer goods.[64] In rural areas, a further source of private-sector dynamism came from the rapid rise of town and village enterprises (TVEs). These were an outcome of farmers' new-found freedom in the allocation of their own labour as a result of increased grain output and a reduction in the number of days spent in the field.[65] In 1980, there were 1.4 million TVEs with 30 million employees, though this grew to 23.4 million TVEs in 1996, with 135 million employees.[66]

In North Korea, the reform measures under Kim Jong Un resembled early Chinese attempts at reforming the SOE sector. These reforms took the form of the 'Socialist Enterprise Responsibility Management System' (SERMS, *sahoejuŭigiŏp ch'aegimgwallije*), the concrete details of which were formally announced through Kim Jong Un's statement on 30 May 2014. This new management system was underpinned by revisions to the Enterprise Law

---

[61] Fang Cai, Albert Park and Yaohui Zhao, 'The Chinese Labor Market in the Reform Era', in *China's Great Economic Transformation,* ed. by Loren Brandt and Thomas G. Rawski (Cambridge: Cambridge University Press, 2008), pp. 171–72.

[62] Loren Brandt, Thomas G. Rawski and John Sutton, 'China's Industrial Development', in *China's Great Economic Transformation,* ed. by Loren Brandt and Thomas G. Rawski (Cambridge: Cambridge University Press, 2008), p. 573.

[63] World Bank, 'China's Management of Enterprise Assets: The State as Shareholder', *World Bank Report,* 1997, p. 1.

[64] Ligang Song, 'Emerging Private Enterprise in China: Transitional Paths and Implications', in *China's Third Economic Transformation: The Rise of the Private Economy,* ed. by Ross Garnaut and Ligang Song (London: RoutledgeCurzon, 2004), pp. 31–32.

[65] Naughton, *Chinese Economy,* p. 90.

[66] Enrico C. Perotti, Laixiang Sun and Liang Zou, 'State-Owned versus Township and Village Enterprises in China', *UNU-Wider Working Paper,* 1998, p. 1.

(2014 and 2015), the People's Economy Planning Law (2015) and Public Finance Law (2015). Laws relating to trade, the supply of materials, local budgets, the central bank and commercial banks were also revised. As a result, the SERMS came to form the core of the economic reform programme during the late 2010s. Indeed, it was codified as the state's new economic management method in the revised constitution of April 2019. At the same time, the *Taean* Work System that had been Kim Il Sung's main institutional innovation in the 1960s was removed from the constitution.[67] The new management system was also frequently cited in North Korean literature:

'The SERMS is a management method that factories, enterprises, and cooperative organisations, on the basis of socialist ownership of the means of production, possess real management rights and conduct enterprise activities creatively, thereby carrying out their duty to the Party and the State and making workers, as the masters of production and management, to fulfil their responsibility and roles'.[68]

The legal revisions formalised the reduction in the central government's role in economic planning and increased decision-making rights of enterprises, factories and cooperative units. Although its function was in practice greatly reduced after the crisis of the 1990s, the State Planning Commission was formally still responsible for handing down production and supply plans to SOEs. Following the legal amendments, however, the State Planning Commission's responsibilities were limited to planning in the strategic sectors via the 'central index' (*chungang jip'yo*), while other targets were separated into the newly established 'regional index' (*chibang jip'yo*) and the 'enterprise index' (*kiŏpso jip'yo*).[69] Mandatory 'in-kind' planning indicators (*hyŏnmul kyehoekjip'yo*) for individual enterprises were also either reduced or completely removed from the plan. These changes thereby constituted an expanded role for the relevant ministries, regional organisations, and in particular, individual enterprises themselves in the formulation of economic planning indicators.[70] Indeed, in the Enterprise Law revision of 2014, a new clause was inserted: 'The enterprise has planning rights and can establish realistic plans in accordance with its own situation. ... The enterprise index is planned and executed by the enterprise itself in accordance with contracts reached with

---

[67] Article 33 of DPRK Constitution (revised 11 April 2019, 1st Meeting of the 14th Supreme People's Assembly).
[68] Ri Tong Su, 'Socialist Enterprise Responsibility Management System, Business Strategy and Enterprise Strategy [Sahoejuŭigiŏpch'aegimgwallijewa kyŏngyŏngjŏllyak, kiŏpchŏllyak]'. *Chollima*, 10 (2016), p. 73.
[69] DPRK People's Economy Planning Law (revised 25 June 2015), Article 13 – Division of People's Economy Planning Indexes.
[70] Yang Moon-Soo, 'Economic Management System in Our Style', pp. 99–100.

consumer institutions, enterprises and organisations'.[71] Thus, even though the term 'planning rights' was still used, the introduction of the SERMS gave SOEs significant authority over their own operations.

SOEs saw a formal expansion in their rights and autonomy but were also expected to be self-sufficient and responsible for their own performance.[72] North Korean economic publications emphasised SOEs' increased responsibilities and decision-making rights related to production, sales and finance management. They were also expected to support the livelihood of their employees as well as contribute to the national budget.[73] Managers were to make their own decisions regarding the sale of output and disposal of any remaining earned income after requisite payments were made to the state. The enterprise's expenses and sales prices were to be calculated at market prices, and its products sold openly on the market. It was also reported that 'direct supply centres' were to be established in each province, from which enterprises were able to purchase materials. Trade was permitted between enterprises in production equipment, materials and energy.[74] They were therefore required to secure their own funds, raw materials and equipment and expected to sell their output by means of agreements reached autonomously between suppliers and consumers.[75] The fact that the government officially granted enterprises the right to set prices autonomously and deal directly with consumers was thus a significant departure from the *Taean* Work System.

The authorities also expanded the rights of individual SOEs to engage directly in foreign trade and establish joint ventures with overseas partners. In the past, foreign trading rights had been granted only to trading companies or joint ventures. Provided they possessed a foreign trading licence (*wak'u*), such companies were officially allowed to engage in imports and exports.

---

[71] DPRK Enterprise Law (revised 5 November 2014), Article 31 – The Execution of People's Economic Plan.

[72] Lim Eul-Chul, *North Korea's Economy*, p. 82; Yang Moon-Soo, 'The Search for the Our-Style Economic Management Method after the Appearance of the Kim Jong Un System [Kimjŏngŭn ch'eje ch'ulbŏm ihu 'urisik kyŏngjegwallibangbŏp' ŭi mosaek: Hyŏnhwanggwa p'yŏngga]', *KDI Review of the North Korean Economy*, 16.3 (2014), pp. 14–15.

[73] Jo Hyok Myong, 'Economic Content of Business Expenditure Compensation under Socialist Enterprise Responsibility Management System [Sahoejuŭigiŏpch'aegimgwallije haesŏ kyŏngyŏngjich'ulbosangŭi kyŏngjejŏk naeryong]', *Economic Research [Kyŏngje Yŏn'gu]*, 4 (2017), pp. 18–19; Kang Chol Su, 'Financial Strategy for Obtaining Actual Results in the Contemporary Socialist Enterprise Responsibility Management System [Hyŏnsigi sahoejuŭigiŏpch'aegimgwallijega silchi ŭnŭl naedorok hagi wihan chaejŏngjŏk pangdo]', *Economic Research [Kyŏngje Yŏn'gu]*, 4 (2018), pp. 56–57.

[74] Choi Yong Nam, 'Important Problems in the Contemporary Era Related to the Improvement of the Supply of Materials [Hyŏnsigi chajaegonggŭpsaŏbŭl kaesŏnhanŭndesŏ nasŏnŭn chungyohan munje]', *Journal of Kim Il Sung University Philosophy, Economics*, 62.3 (2016), pp. 103–104.

[75] DPRK Enterprise Law (revised 5 November 2014), Article 39 – The Establishment of the Price and Sale of Products.

However, under Article 37 of the Enterprise Law, as amended in 2014, enterprises were permitted to establish independent contracts with foreign enterprises to procure capital, materials and equipment and to sell their output. Enterprises were also given the right to make direct payments to domestic and foreign banks, and to distribute profits in accordance with their own plans.[76] These increased rights served to promote the role of market prices in the operations of North Korean SOEs, thereby acting as a further spur to marketisation more broadly.

Under the new management system, not only were enterprises permitted to reinvest their own profits but were allowed to receive investment from private individuals. As with the revision of Agricultural Farm Law, Article 38 of the Enterprise Law stipulated that SOEs could directly mobilise and use 'idle money' held by residents.[77] Indeed, as discussed in the previous chapter, it had become established practice for SOEs to receive investments from the *donju*. While this was technically illegal, the authorities had adopted a position of benign neglect. In 2014, however, such practices were legalised. It is true that the reforms still did not fully recognise individual property rights, but there are again parallels here with the Chinese case. As noted, one of the key features of the Chinese experience was the proliferation of TVEs nominally owned by various local administrative organs but operating outside of the central planning system. While they were *de facto* private firms, they continued to wear the red cap in order to maintain access to supplies, credit and tax benefits. They were therefore an adaptive informal institution during the early stages of economic reform when private enterprises with more than eight employees were not legally permitted.[78] A parallel situation emerged in North Korea, whereby enterprises remained *de jure* public entities, but in reality, were invested in and operated by private individuals.

As also noted, however, the North Korean economy saw the emergence of a dualistic industrial structure following the crisis consisting of strategic and non-strategic sectors. In the Kim Jong Un era, North Korean academic publications were explicit about this dualism, arguing that in order to normalise production in strategic sectors, the state must concentrate its efforts on the supply of materials, machinery and other means of production required by

---

[76] Kim Hong Il, 'Important Issues Arising from the Multidimensional Development of Foreign Economic Relations [Taeoegyŏngjegwan'gyerŭl tagakchŏkŭro palchŏnsik'inŭndesŏ nasŏnŭn chungyo munje]', *Journal of Kim Il Sung University: Philosophy, Economics*, 61.4 (2015), pp. 72–73.

[77] Article 38 of DPRK Enterprise Law (revised 5 November 2014) states that 'Enterprises shall have the right to manage their financial resources and actively make management funds ... The enterprise may borrow funds from the bank or make use of residents' idle money to mobilise management activities that are lacking funds.'

[78] Kellee S. Tsai, *Capitalism without Democracy: The Private Sector in Contemporary China* (Ithaca, NY: Cornell University Press, 2007), p. 53.

SOEs in those sectors. While priority should be given to defence, the state should also guarantee the supply of cement and steel for the construction of hydroelectric power plants, coal for the operation of thermal power plants, steel and explosives for the coal mining industry, concentrate and electricity for the metal industry, synthetic resin and chemical fibres for light industry.[79] For these sectors, the central planning system still remained responsible for supplying materials to strategic enterprises according to the central plan index. As Jo Kil Hyon of Kim Il Sung University has argued, the exchange of equipment and materials amongst enterprises plays a key role in the effective utilisation of productive resources and the normalisation of production. However, for strategic enterprises: '... adhering to socialist principles in the exchange of materials between enterprises should be supplementary to the supply of goods according to the state plan'.[80] As such, the SERMS expanded enterprise autonomy, but in the strategic sector, the state still took responsibility for the supply of raw materials, with the latter remaining subject to state pricing.[81] SOEs in the infrastructure and the heavy-industrial sector thus remained far less likely to procure inputs and sell their output via the market.

Again, there is a lack of on-the-ground data as to exactly how far the SERMS has been implemented. The announcement of the Five-Year Strategy for National Economic Development 2016–2020 at the KWP's 7th Party Congress in May 2016 provided some clues, however. The Five-Year Strategy was the first national economic development plan since the failed Third Seven-Year Plan (1987–1993) of the Kim Il Sung era. The use of the term 'strategy' (chŏllyak) rather than 'plan' (kyehoek), however, reflected the fact that no quantitative production targets were made public. In the context of ongoing economic difficulties, the goal of the Five-Year Strategy was a more general one of 'laying the foundations for continued development of the nation's economy by revitalising the people's economy as a whole and ensuring a balance between the economic sectors'.[82] In terms of the sector-specific content, there was continued emphasis on resolving energy problems, normalising basic infrastructure and industries, and expanding the production of food and light industries. These were the same sectors that had been continually

[79] Choi Yong Nam, 'Important Problems', p. 103.
[80] Jo Kil Hyon, 'Important Problems Relating to the Rational Organisation of the Exchange of Materials between Enterprises [Kiŏpch'edŭl saiŭi mulchagyoryurŭl hamnijŏkŭro chojikhanŭndesŏ nasŏnŭn chungyohan munje]', Journal of Kim Il Sung University Philosophy, Economics, 64.3 (2018), p. 96.
[81] Tu Kwang Ik, 'Price Setting Methods in Enterprises [Kiŏpch'edŭresŏŭi kagyŏkchejŏngbangbŏp]', Journal of Kim Il Sung University Philosophy, Economics, 64.3 (2018), p. 138.
[82] Rodong Sinmun, 9 May 2016, 'Decisions of the 7th Congress of the KWP [Chosŏnnodongdang che 7 ch'a taehoe kyŏlchŏngsŏ]'.

emphasised since the Kim Jong Il era, suggesting limited progress in achieving these goals.

At the same Party Congress, Kim Jong Un argued that '... the SERMS should be implemented immediately. Factories, enterprises and cooperative organisations should establish management strategies in accordance with the requirements of the SERMS and should actively and creatively engage in enterprise activities, thereby, normalising, expanding and developing production. We must make sure that conditions are fully guaranteed so that management rights granted by the state can be fully utilised'.[83] This suggests that the new reforms had at that time still not been fully rolled out across the industrial sector. As with agriculture, however, it would appear that the problems in the industrial sector could not be addressed by increased managerial responsibilities and incentives alone, but that foreign investment would be a key prerequisite of industrial recovery.

6.4   Opening the Door?

As the Chinese experience suggests, the influx of foreign capital is a key means of revitalising the industrial sector. Emulating the experience of capitalist developmental states elsewhere in East Asia, China's experience with attracting foreign investment dates back to 1979 and the establishment of Special Economic Zones (SEZs) in Shenzhen, Zhuhai and Shantou in Guangdong Province as well as Xiamen in Fujian Province. On the one hand, these SEZs were deliberately located far from the centre of power in Beijing, thereby minimising potential political risks. However, the sites in Guangdong and Fujian were also chosen for their long history of contact with the outside world as a result of outward migration and proximity to Hong Kong, Macao and Taiwan.[84] In 1984, a total of fourteen further coastal cities were established, including Dalian, Qinhuangdao, Tianjin, Yantai, Qingdao, Lianyungang, Nantong, Shanghai, Ningbo, Wenzhou, Fuzhou, Guangzhou, Zhanjiang and Beihai. Hainan Island was also turned into an SEZ in 1988 and the Pudong region of Shanghai was established as an SEZ with regulations even more flexible than those found in other SEZs. Following Deng Xiaoping's 'Southern Tour' of 1992, a further two dozen major cities in inland China also adopted measures to attract foreign direct investment. As Shaun Breslin argues, it is no coincidence that the following year marked China's

---

[83] *Rodong Sinmun,* 8 May 2016, 'Party Central Committee report presented at the 7th KWP Congress – Kim Jong Un [Chosŏnnodongdang che 7 ch'a taehoeesŏhan tang chungangwiwŏn-hoe saŏpch'onghwabogo – Kimjŏngŭn]'.

[84] Yue-man Yeung, Joanna Lee and Gordon Kee, 'China's Special Economic Zones at 30', *Eurasian Geography and Economics,* 50.2 (2009), p. 223.

emergence as a major recipient of Foreign Direct Investment (FDI), with the figure for that year exceeding the entire preceding 14 years of reform put together.[85]

Despite the increasingly stringent sanctions of the 2010s, the North Korean authorities pursued the development of SEZs, thereby ostensibly creating the conditions for the opening of the economy along Chinese lines. In addition to Rason SEZ established in 1991, the Kim Jong Il regime had already established four further national-level SEZs, including the Sinuiju Special Administrative District, the Kaesong Industrial Complex, the Hwanggumpyong–Wihwa Economic Zone and the Mt. Kumgang Tourist Region. Under Kim Jong Un, however, the number of SEZs rose sharply. At the March 2013 Plenum of the KWP Central Committee, a new policy was adopted emphasising the establishment of 'Economic Development Zones' (*kyŏngjegaebalgu*) in accordance with the actual conditions of the local regions.[86] As a result, between November 2013 and December 2017, a further twenty-three SEZs were announced.[87] In contrast to Kim Jong Il's SEZ policy, the Kim Jong Un government divided SEZs into central and provincial-level zones. Four SEZs were added to those already under the direct management of the central government, including Kangnyong International Greening Demonstration Zone in South Hwanghae Province, Unjong High Technology Development Zone in Pyongyang and Jindo Exports Processing Zone in Nampo.[88]

The remainder of the new SEZs were managed by the provincial People's Committees. This reflected the stated principle that SEZs should be located in regions '... favourable to foreign economic cooperation and exchange and possess the conditions that will enable the zones to contribute to the economic and scientific development of the country'.[89] The purpose of the SEZs was, therefore, to improve local industry and infrastructure by attracting foreign

---

[85] Shaun Breslin, *China and the Global Political Economy* (Basingstoke: Palgrave Macmillan, 2013), p. 86.

[86] Ri Il Chol,'Concept and Main Types of Economic Development Zone [Kyŏngjegaebalguŭi kaenyŏmgwa chuyo yuhyŏng]', *Economics Journal*, 2 (2015), p. 42.

[87] With the designation of Kangnam Economic Development Zone in Pyongyang in December 2017, there were twenty-eight SEZs in North Korea. However, after North Korea's fourth nuclear test in January 2016, the operations of 124 South Korean enterprises in Kaesong Industrial Complex, the symbol of inter-Korean economic cooperation, were brought to an end. Following its closure, the Zone was removed from the official list of SEZs.

[88] Ri Il Chol, 'Concept and Main Types', p. 43; Korea Economic Development Association, *DPRK Special Economic Zones* (Pyongyang: Foreign Languages Publishing House, 2019), pp. 37–42.

[89] Ro Myong Song, 'Some Problems in Creating and Operating Economic Development Zones According to the Actual Conditions of Each Province [Kak todŭrŭi silchŏnge matke kyŏngjegaebalgudŭrŭl ch'angsŏl, unyŏnghanŭndesŏ nasŏnŭn myŏtkaji munje]', *Economic Research [Kyŏngje Yŏn'gu]*, 2 (2015), p. 41.

investment in line with the comparative advantage of each region. For example, the Hungnam Industrial Development Zone in South Hamgyong Province sought to take advantage of the fact that Hamhung City was since the early stages of industrialisation a key location for the chemical and machinery industries. As such, this SEZ was designated as an industrial district specialising in bonded processing as well as the production of chemicals, machinery and pharmaceuticals.[90] On the other hand, the two export processing zones of Jindo and Waudo in Nampo on the West coast were established to take advantage of the city's central role in North Korea's maritime trade.

In addition to Rason and Sinuiju zones, the Kim Jong Un government further designated SEZs on the Sino–North Korean border aimed at attracting Chinese investment, including Wiwon Industrial Development Zone (Jagang Province), Hyesan Economic Development Zone (Ryanggang Province), Kyongwon Economic Development Zone (North Hamgyong Province) and Manpo Economic Development Zone (Jagang Province). However, stringent sanctions meant that the goal of attracting Chinese investment into these new zones saw limited success, though there was also little in the way of government investment in the necessary infrastructure. The exception was the development of SEZs in the tourism sector, reflecting the fact that the latter was not subject to sanctions and remained a legitimate channel for earning foreign exchange. Key investments in this regard included an international tourism zone linking Wonsan and Mt. Kumgang in Kangwon Province. There was significant investment in the construction of recreational facilities and infrastructure in the Kalma Coastal Tourism district of Wonsan. In addition, Mubong Special Zone for International Tourism in the Mt. Baekdu region close to China's Jilin Province saw the construction of transport infrastructure and recreational facilities.

A key difference between the Kim Jong Un's SEZ policy and that of his father was that under the former, new SEZs were established in the vicinity of Pyongyang and its neighbouring cities, suggesting further evidence of a more positive attitude towards foreign investment. In particular, part of Unjong District on the northeast outskirts of Pyongyang was in July 2014 designated as the Unjong High Technology Development Zone. Unjong District had functioned as a hub of North Korean science and technology research due to the fact that the National Academy of Sciences, Pyongsong College of Natural Science and dozens of research institutions and enterprises were located there. The government's aim in establishing its first high-tech SEZ was to promote

---

[90] Ri Myong Jin, 'The Positive Promotion of the Development of Economic Development Zones Is an Important Task of Our Age [Kyŏngjegaebalgu kaebalsaŏbŭl chŏkkŭk milgonaganŭn kŏsŭn hyŏnsigi uri ap'e nasŏnŭn chungyohan kwaŏp]', *Journal of Kim Il Sung University: Philosophy, Economics*, 61.4 (2015), p. 76.

investment by foreign firms in IT, nanotechnology and biological engineering.[91] In addition, on 21 December 2017, the authorities designated part of Kangnam County in the southwestern part of Pyongyang as an economic development zone.

The Kim Jong Un government's SEZ policy thus demonstrated a desire to utilise foreign investment as a means of facilitating economic recovery. Indeed, the state's continued interest in the development of SEZs was apparent in Kim's official visits to SEZs in China in 2018 and 2019. During his first visit to China in March 2018, Kim visited the Chinese Academy of Sciences in Zhongguancun, the district in northwest Beijing known as China's 'Silicon Valley'. During his third 2018 trip to China in June, Kim visited the Chinese Academy of Agricultural Science's National Agricultural Science and Technology Innovation Park, and on his fourth trip in January, he visited the state-level Economic and Technological Development Zone in the Yizhuang area of Beijing. As such, these successive visits symbolised Kim Jong Un's interest in China's reform and opening as well as its scientific and technological development.

It goes without saying, however, that without a significant improvement in its foreign relations, Kim Jong Un's SEZ policy was unlikely to be a success. While the SEZ strategy suggested a potential means of addressing longstanding economic difficulties, the increasingly adverse external environment led the authorities to pursue a more familiar policy of 'nationalising production'. In his 2015 New Year's speech, Kim Jong Un emphasised that 'All factories and enterprises should wage a dynamic struggle to get rid of the proclivity to import and ensure the domestic production of raw and other materials and equipment'.[92] This campaign was further emphasised as the country was faced with the Trump administration's 'maximum pressure' campaign. In July 2017, through a *Rodong Sinmun* editorial titled 'Domestic production is an essential requirement of the construction of an economically powerful country', it was revealed that 'the economy is suffering from troubles and difficulties due to the barbaric high-intensity sanctions of the hostile forces. The nationalisation of production is a critical problem that cannot be delayed'.[93] As such, geopolitics played a critical role in whether North Korea would integrate itself more closely with the world economy or instead fall back on well-established tropes of 'autonomous development'.

---

[91] Korea Economic Development Association, *DPRK Special Economic Zones*, p. 41.

[92] *Rodong Sinmun*, 1 January 2015, 'New Year's Speech – Kim Jung Un'.

[93] *Rodong Sinmun*, 21 July 2017 'The nationalisation of production is an essential requirement of the construction of an economically powerful nation [Kuksanhwanŭn kyŏngjeganggukkŏnsŏrŭi p'ilsujŏk yogu]'.

6.5   Conclusion

As we have argued, conventional discussions of economic reform in North Korea present a picture of a domestic political culture that inhibits measures that might liberalise the existing system. However, such analyses do not adequately take into account the degree to which economic management and the daily life of the population have already diverged from the principles of the centrally planned economy. Although the regime was indeed unlikely to undertake radical reform measures that might lead to the weakening of political control, reform within the system was a task that the authorities could not avoid. In this respect, there are clear parallels between North Korea's reforms and the Chinese experience of the late 1970s and early 1980s. As Jin Jingyi has argued, a key characteristic of China's economic reforms was the decentralisation of power by passing down decision-making rights from the state to a multitude of economic subjects. In North Korea, reforms to agricultural and industrial management similarly amounted to an abandonment of 'equalism' and a transition towards a 'get rich first' ideology.[94] A key feature of Our-Style Economic Management Method was also that it put the nexus between the state and the market on firmer legal ground, thereby strengthening mutual dependence between the two.[95] In agriculture, it was reasonable to expect that if the Field Responsibility System was consistently implemented, farmers would have greater incentives to increase production. However, North Korean agriculture's heavy dependence on fertiliser and other industrial inputs meant that the revitalisation of industry remained a crucial task. The Chinese experience also suggests that the reform of the SOE sector was likely to face continued difficulties and would depend on the extent to which the country was able to attract foreign investment. In this respect, the greatest challenge for North Korea remained its adverse international environment.

While there had been a 'stop and go' cyclical rhythm to the reforms, the economic reform programme of the Kim Jong Un government was unlikely to see the kinds of reversals witnessed in the late 2000s. In his 2016 New Year's speech, for example, Kim Jong Un spoke of the need of '. . . [e]stablishing on a full scale Our-Style Economic Management Method which embodies the *Juche* idea thus giving full play to its advantages and vitality'.[96] Certainly, reform should not be understood as a linear process. In China too, economic policy was also characterised by a 'stop and go' rhythm, with each cycle

---

[94] Jin Jingyi, 'North Korea's Silent Change and North-South Relations [Pukhanŭi choyonghan pyŏnhwawa nambuggwangye]', *The Hankyoreh [Online]*, 21 September 2014, http://happyvil .hani.co.kr/arti/SERIES/58/656072.html [accessed 25 April 2020].

[95] Yang Moon-Soo, 'Economic Management System in Our Style', p. 112.

[96] *KCNA*, 1 January 2016, 'Kim Jong Un's New Year Address'.

characterised by an initial push forward with reform measures followed by the appearance of certain problems, including fears amongst policymakers of 'unhealthy' cultural and ideological currents, followed by attempts to pull in the reins to stabilise the situation.[97] North Korea's reversals have at times been severe. Yet despite their somewhat erratic nature, the underlying context of irreversible marketisation meant that continued attempts at economic reform were likely. As noted, however, the extent to which the reforms were likely to facilitate broader economic recovery depended much on regional and global context. Resolving the ongoing geopolitical standoff with the United States would require significant concessions on the nuclear programme, though this could only take place as part of a quid pro quo whereby the United States and allied powers made guarantees on North Korea's external security. The partial exception to North Korea's increasingly unfavourable external environment was China, and it is to this question of Sino–North Korean economic relations that our analysis now turns.

[97] Gordon White, *Riding the Tiger: The Politics of Economic Reform in Post-Mao China* (Basingstoke: Macmillan, 1993), pp. 58–59.

7   Dependency in Chinese–North Korean Relations?

It is little exaggeration to say that the most important geopolitical event in East Asia in the past few decades has been the rise of China. In the previous chapter, we examined the extent to which North Korea may be following the Chinese path towards market reform. Yet, the impact of China's rise can be examined from another perspective, namely that of the extent to which North Korea has been integrated into the emergent China-centred regional political economy. In the latter part of the twentieth century, North Korea remained largely isolated from the extraordinary regional growth centred on Japan and the so-called 'Asian tigers' of South Korea, Taiwan, Hong Kong and Singapore. However, the shift in the locus of regional dynamism towards mainland China in recent years coincided with the marketisation of the North Korean economy alongside a more porous Sino–North Korean border. There was, as a result, a marked deepening of bilateral trade and investment relations between China and North Korea. In 2003, North Korea's trade with China surpassed US\$ 1 billion for the first time. By 2013, however, trade had grown to US\$ 6.54 billion. The share occupied by China in North Korea's external trade increased from 39 per cent in 2006 to 57 per cent in 2010. By 2013, North Korea's total external trade was estimated at US\$ 8.48 billion, with China's share amounting to around 77 per cent of that trade.[1] According to Chinese official statistics, authorised investment by Chinese firms in North Korea increased from just US\$ 6.5 million in 2005 to US\$ 109.5 million in 2012. Despite a slight reduction the following year, the stock of Chinese investment in North Korea by 2013 amounted to US\$ 585.5 million.[2]

---

[1] These figures include inter-Korean trade and are drawn from statistics released by South Korea's Korea Trade-Investment Promotion Agency (KOTRA) and the Ministry of Unification. If inter-Korean trade is excluded, China's share in North Korea's foreign trade reached 89 per cent in 2013.
[2] PRC Ministry of Commerce, *2013 Statistical Bulletin of China's Outward Foreign Direct Investment* (Hong Kong: Purple Culture, 2014), p. 132. There are no concrete statistics on overall foreign investment in North Korea. However, one of the authors of this book attended the Northeast Asia Think Tank Forum in Changchun, September 2011, where Kim Cheol, head of the Economic Research Institute of the North Korean Academy of Social Sciences, stated that 78.7 per cent of foreign corporations investing in Rason were Chinese. After 2011, Chinese

As noted in the introductory chapter, opinions on the nature of China's rise and its implications for global development have been divided. Some see the country as potentially challenging global neoliberalism and as playing a leading role in providing Global South countries with alternatives to the trade, investment and development assistance of the Global North and the international financial institutions. Others, however, see China's emerging relations with Global South countries as representing the resurgence of neocolonialism. In this view, the country is regarded as being primarily concerned with securing the supply of resources to its growing economy, in providing profitable opportunities for its SOEs abroad, and more generally, in projecting its political and economic power in pursuit of its national interests. In light of this debate, the questions posed in this chapter are severalfold: What are the implications of China's increased economic engagement for North Korea's developmental prospects? Are we now witnessing the emergence of a neocolonial dependency between the two countries? Or has China's increased economic presence in North Korea provided a mutually beneficial form of engagement whereby North Korea has been able to utilise trade and investment flows to reverse its economic decline and pursue a path of recovery and renewed development?

This chapter proceeds by examining the substantive nature of the emerging trade and investment relations between China and North Korea. As we shall see, these relations were in the first instance underpinned by the shared strategic objectives of both countries, namely the maintenance of the stability of the North Korean regime and of the geopolitical status quo on the Korean peninsula. Chinese central and regional governments had a further objective in that engagement with North Korea came to play a key role in plans to revitalise China's struggling north-eastern regional economy. In the context of China's economic reforms and North Korean marketisation, however, the actual mode of economic engagement is in substance market-driven, taking the form of trade and investment by Chinese enterprises. This chapter will conclude by examining the potential risks inherent in China's engagement with North Korea in terms of the latter's longer-term developmental prospects.[3]

---

investment in Rason increased even further. Given that other countries reduced their investments due to the nuclear issue and international sanctions, it can be assumed that Chinese investment constitutes the vast majority of foreign investment.

[3] In this chapter, we primarily focus on Sino–North Korean relations from the early 2000s to 2017. The Trump administration's 'maximum pressure' campaign, the marked tightening of international sanctions and Beijing's more enthusiastic enforcement of those sanctions from late 2017 led to a curtailment of many of the forms of economic exchange detailed here. While we discuss these latter developments in detail in the following chapter, it is worth noting here that 2018 also saw an unprecedented level of diplomacy between Kim Jong Un and Xi Jinping, leading to signs that China's strict enforcement of sanctions was being partially relaxed. It is too early to say whether Sino–North Korean economic relations are likely to revert to their pre-2017

One caveat should be made before proceeding with the analysis. Much of Sino–North Korean trade and investment takes place on an informal basis and thus is not captured by official statistics.[4] Smuggling, for example, became widespread following the 1990s. Prior to China's tightening of sanctions in 2017, lax inspections at Chinese customs points meant that traders found it relatively easy to make false declarations and load undeclared and prohibited dual-use and luxury items onto container trucks together with permitted goods. This was not simply due to sanctions but often for the purpose of tax evasion and the avoidance of burdensome customs procedures. Trade settlement also typically made use of barter and cash, and often took the form of the spot trading of goods due to low levels of trust between traders as well as lack of reliable dispute resolution mechanisms.[5] North Korean banking institutions were also slow and tended to charge high fees. As such, informal methods of trade settlement were used even in transactions amounting to the value of hundreds of thousands of US dollars.[6] North Korean enterprises and government agencies purchased goods in Chinese border city markets in cash while Chinese investors tended to use cash to avoid the use of official financial channels. Large amounts of cash were thus physically carried across the border, often by the staff of North Korean trading companies or government agencies. Thus, while Chinese official statistics are the most accurate means to quantitatively gauge the scope of Sino–North Korean economic relations, the prominence of informal and often illicit methods of settling trade and investment-related transactions means that the true scale of economic exchange between the two countries was likely to be far greater than statistics suggest.

7.1   From Politics to Economics in Sino–North Korean Relations

Although China and North Korea are typically considered to be close allies, we have already seen how in the context of the Sino–Soviet split, bilateral relations underwent numerous twists and turns. Trade relations tended to follow closely the vicissitudes of political relations between the two countries. In the

---

pattern. Nonetheless, the economic engagement outlined in this chapter sheds light on North Korea's future economic potential should sanctions be lifted or China's enforcement of those sanctions be significantly relaxed.

[4] For a more in-depth discussion of the Sino–North Korean informal border economy, see Jong-Woon Lee and Kevin Gray, 'Cause for Optimism? Financial Sanctions and the Rise of the Sino-North Korean Border Economy', *Review of International Political Economy*, 24.3 (2017), pp. 424–53.

[5] Stephan Haggard, Jennifer Lee and Marcus Noland, 'Integration in the Absence of Institutions: China–North Korea Cross-Border Exchange', *Journal of Asian Economics*, 23.2 (2012), p. 132.

[6] Interviews with Chinese merchants engaging in trading business with North Korea, June 2009, April 2011 and November 2012.

1950s, when Chinese troops were still stationed in North Korea, bilateral trade was relatively strong. Trade declined during the Cultural Revolution though rose again following the US–China détente of the 1970s. Following the launch of China's reforms in the late 1970s, trade declined again as North Korea lent more heavily towards Moscow. Trade recovered somewhat following the collapse of the Soviet Union but declined again after 1993 as a result of China's removal of 'friendship prices' and its demands for payments in hard currency. This cooling of Sino–North Korean relations reflected the fact that, as a result of its deepening reform process, Beijing had reoriented its diplomatic strategy away from the support of anti-imperialist revolutionary movements and regimes in the Third World towards the goal of establishing friendly relations with China's anti-communist neighbours. Indeed, it was this 'good neighbour policy' that led China to join the Asia-Pacific Economic Cooperation in 1991 and the ASEAN Regional Forum in 1994, as well as to establish diplomatic ties with Indonesia, Vietnam, Singapore and, to Pyongyang's particular displeasure, South Korea in 1992.[7] Sino–North Korean trade relations thus remained cool throughout the 1990s, with China supplying only limited amounts of strategic goods such as crude oil and food. Despite being North Korea's largest trade partner since the demise of the Soviet Union, China's share in North Korea's total trade did not exceed 30 per cent throughout that decade. Following Kim Jong Il's official visit to Beijing in 2000, however, improving relations helped to boost trade by 31.8 per cent to US\$ 488 million. As noted, by 2013, this bilateral trade had grown to US\$ 6.54 billion (see Figure 7.1), an increase that took place in the context of continued stagnation of North Korean trade with other countries.

China's exports to North Korea ranged from basic necessities and foodstuffs to industrial equipment and crude oil. Although North Korean imports of Chinese grain saw a decline as a result of the partial recovery of the former's agricultural sector, imports of machinery parts, electrical equipment, vehicles, plastic products and chemical goods from China saw an increase. From the late 2000s, North Korea also increased its imports of building materials as a result of the construction boom taking place in North Korea's cities. Furthermore, Chinese firms invested in the export-oriented mining and apparel sectors as well as in manufacturing and the retail sector. North Korean exports were largely centred around coal and textile manufactures, and to a lesser extent, iron ore and seafood (see Figure 7.2).

What then explains this rapid increase in economic relations between the two countries? From China's perspective, this can in the broadest sense be said to stem from broader strategic concerns. In the context of North Korea's

---

[7] Chien-peng Chung, 'The "Good Neighbour Policy" in the Context of China's Foreign Relations', *China: An International Journal*, 7.1 (2014), p. 110.

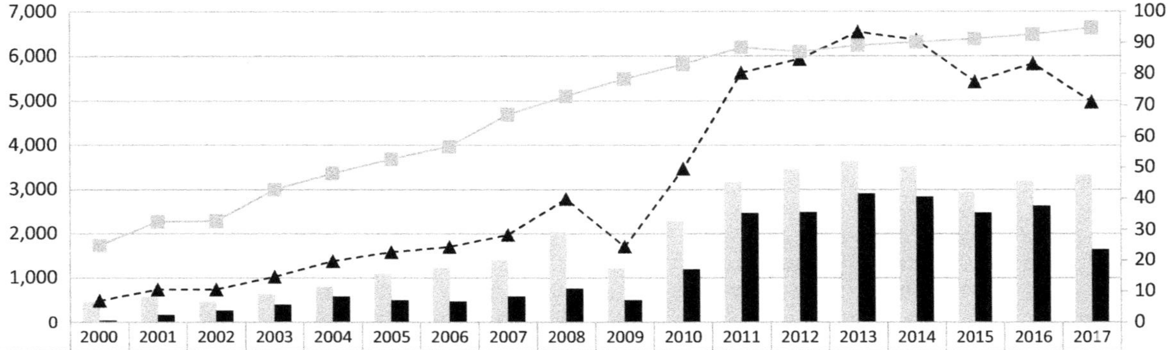

	2000	2001	2002	2003	2004	2005	2006	2007	2008	2009	2010	2011	2012	2013	2014	2015	2016	2017
Import	451	571	467	628	795	1,085	1,232	1,392	2,033	1,210	2,278	3,165	3,446	3,633	3,523	2,946	3,192	3,328
Export	37	167	271	396	582	497	468	582	754	501	1,188	2,464	2,485	2,912	2,841	2,484	2,634	1,650
Total Trade	488	738	738	1,024	1,377	1,582	1,700	1,974	2,787	1,711	3,466	5,629	5,931	6,545	6,364	5,430	5,826	4,978
China's Share	24.8	32.5	32.7	42.8	48.1	52.7	56.7	67.1	73.0	78.5	83.1	88.5	87.1	89.1	90.2	91.3	92.7	94.8

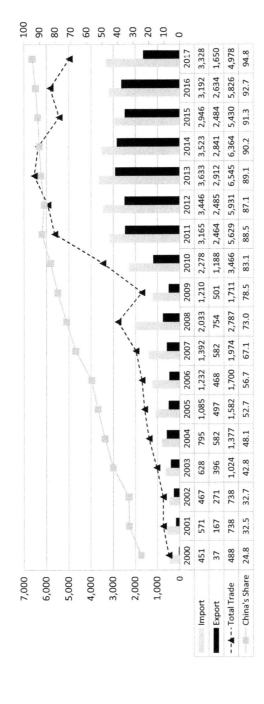

Figure 7.1: Trends in North Korea's trade with China (2000–17).
(Units: Million US$, %).

Source: China Customs data. China's share of North Korean trade is based on estimates made by the Korea Trade-Investment Promotion Agency.
Note: China Customs appears to have omitted North Korean trade data between August and November 2009. Chinese exports of crude oil have also been omitted from official customs data since 2014.

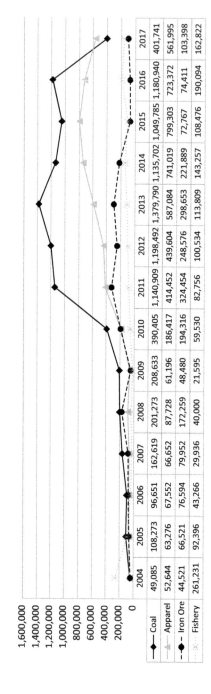

	2004	2005	2006	2007	2008	2009	2010	2011	2012	2013	2014	2015	2016	2017
Coal	49,085	108,273	96,651	162,619	201,273	208,633	390,405	1,140,909	1,198,492	1,379,790	1,135,702	1,049,785	1,180,940	401,741
Apparel	52,644	63,276	67,552	66,652	87,728	61,196	186,417	414,452	439,604	587,084	741,019	799,303	723,372	561,995
Iron Ore	44,521	66,521	76,594	79,952	172,259	48,480	194,316	324,454	248,576	298,653	221,889	72,767	74,411	103,398
Fishery	261,231	92,396	43,266	29,936	40,000	21,595	59,530	82,756	100,534	113,809	143,257	108,476	190,094	162,822

Figure 7.2: Trends in North Korea's major exports to China.
(Unit: US$ 1,000).
Source: China Customs data

increasing diplomatic isolation, the task of maintaining the geopolitical status quo on the Korea peninsula became a key concern for Beijing, reflecting the fear that a North Korean collapse might have catastrophic humanitarian as well as more traditional security implications for China and the Northeast Asia region. Indeed, China would lose a valuable buffer state and face the prospect of US-aligned unified Korea on its doorstep. There is little evidence to suggest, however, that China's approach to North Korea was driven by an ideological affinity with the country, given China's more extensive economic relations with South Korea and the fact that Sino–North Korean relations throughout most of the 1990s had remained relatively cool.

As we discuss in more detail in the following chapter, this rapid growth of economic relations coincided with the intensification of the multilateral sanctions regime against Pyongyang following the country's first nuclear test in 2006. On the one hand, as a permanent member of the United Nations Security Council, these sanctions could not be imposed without China's support, although the fact that Beijing largely failed to enforce those sanctions prior to 2017 was a key factor in their ineffectiveness. On the other hand, much of the growth in North Korean exports to China consisted of what were at the time non-sanctioned items. However, Sino–North Korean trade also included items explicitly proscribed by the sanctions regime, such as those belonging to the vaguely defined category of luxury goods as well as that of dual-use goods.[8]

While geopolitical considerations shaped the broad parameters of China's renewed engagement with North Korea, bilateral relations should also be seen as an integral part of China's more specific objective of developing its north-eastern provinces of Liaoning, Jilin and Heilongjiang, specifically in terms of addressing their needs for resources, cheap labour and profitable investment opportunities. In the midst of China's deepening regional disparities, the northeast remained distinctive in that it constituted the country's primary rust belt but also included relatively undeveloped border regions. Much as in northern Korea, Japanese colonialism in Manchuria had led to the development of heavy industries, most notably in steel, chemicals, hydroelectric power generation and automobile production.[9] Following 1949, the new Chinese state made further large-scale investments in heavy and chemical industries in the region, to the extent that the northeast became known as the 'cradle of

---

[8] The reports released by the UN Panel of Experts provide a comprehensive overview of sanctions evasion. See: www.un.org/sc/suborg/en/sanctions/1718/panel_experts/reports [accessed 22 May 2020].

[9] Cumings, 'The Origins and Development of the Northeast Asian Political Economy', pp. 12–13.

Chinese industry'.[10] Indeed, many of China's largest SOEs were located there. As noted in the previous chapter, the region fared badly, however, in the context of the growing interprovincial inequality that characterised the country's experience of reform. This was due to the fact that the reforms saw a shift in the locus of China's economic dynamism towards the labour-intensive export-oriented industries located in the coastal regions, and from SOEs to private and foreign-invested enterprises.

This resultant 'Northeast Phenomenon' (*dongbei xianzhuang*) of stalled growth was not simply a result of the region's ageing heavy-industrial structure, however. Relative geographical isolation and the fact that both Jilin and Heilongjiang provinces are both landlocked meant that the northeast was ill-placed to take advantage of the investment by overseas Chinese capital that formed a key impetus of China's post-1978 growth. Due to this combination of factors, the northeast economy's dependency on foreign trade in 2001 was just 20.37 per cent, less than half the national average of 43.57 per cent. Foreign direct investment to the region was recorded at US$ 3.19 billion in the same year, accounting for just 6.89 per cent of the national total.[11] With its outdated industrial base and limited new investment, the northeast's share in China's overall industrial production saw a sharp decline from 17 per cent in the late 1970s to just 8.6 in 2002.[12]

This decline became of increasing concern to the Chinese authorities. As a result, local government in the northeast from the 1990s sought to revitalise the region through cooperation with neighbouring countries, including North Korea. For example, the Tumen River Area Development Programme (TRADP) was aimed at promoting regional economic cooperation centred on China, North Korea, South Korea, Russia and Mongolia, with Japan adopting the position of an observer. Sponsored by the United Nations Development Programme, TRADP sought to achieve these goals through several mechanisms including plans to establish a duty-free shipping and processing zone inclusive of the North Korean cities of Rason and Chongjin, the Chinese cities of Hunchun and Yanji, and the Russian city of Vladivostok. However, TRADP's progress was erratic due to ongoing security tensions surrounding the Korean peninsula and limited interest on the part of firms in neighbouring

---

[10] Jae Ho Chung, Hongyi Lai and Jang-Hwan Joo, 'Assessing the 'Revive the Northeast'(Zhenxing Dongbei) Programme: Origins, Policies and Implementation', *The China Quarterly*, 197 (2009), p. 110.

[11] Kim Su-Hwan, *An Analysis of Sino–North Korean Cross-Border Cooperation and Its Implication for Incheon Metropolian City [Pukchung chŏpkyŏnghyŏmnyŏk punsŏgwa Inch'ŏnsiŭi taeŭngbanghyang]* (Incheon: Incheon Development Institute, 2012), p. 45.

[12] Kang Sung-Ho, 'The Revitalisation Plan for Northeasten China: Focusing on the Interrelations between South Korea and China [Chunggugŭi tongbukjinhŭngjŏllyak: Hanjung hyŏmnyŏggwaŭi kwallyŏnsŏngŭl chungsimŭro]', *Korea and World Politics*, 21.1 (2005), p. 194.

countries in investing in the Tumen River border region.[13] Furthermore, there were tensions between central and local governments in these member countries with regards to the extent to which cross-border regional cooperation should occur.[14] Beijing was also seemingly wary of North Korean initiatives to promote border region developmental projects on China's doorstep. In addition to providing little initial support to North Korea's Rajin–Sonbong Free Economic and Trade Zone, Beijing also appeared to adopt a negative stance towards Pyongyang's efforts to establish the Sinuiju Special Administration District in 2002.

From the mid-2000s, however, Beijing began to place more emphasis on economic cooperation with North Korea as a means of facilitating the northeast's economic recovery. In line with the policy of 'going out' (*zouchuqu*), the State Council in June 2005 adopted a proactive strategy of encouraging Chinese enterprises in the northeast to gain access to natural resources, transport infrastructure and markets in neighbouring countries. This included the adoption of a proposal made by Jilin provincial government for a 'Road Port Zone Integration Project' (*lugangqu yitihua*).[15] This cross-border infrastructural project would facilitate Jilin Province's strategy of 'borrowing the harbour to access the sea' (*jiegang chuhai*), whereby the landlocked province would overcome its isolation by acquiring rights to use the warm water ports such as Rajin on North Korea's north-eastern coast.

Similar principles underpinned China's more targeted regional development plans announced in the late 2000s. In July 2009, for example, the State Council ratified the Liaoning Coastal Economic Belt Development Plan aimed at revitalising the province's industrial base. The plan was first proposed by the Liaoning provincial government in 2005 and sought to connect the six coastal cities of Dalian, Dandong, Jinzhou, Yingkou, Panjin and Huludao into a single

---

[13] In 2005, the TRADP was rebranded as the Greater Tumen Initiative (GTI) following the transfer of full ownership from the UNDP to the member states. However, North Korea withdrew from the GTI in 2009 as a result of tensions surrounding its nuclear programme as well as the disappointing results of the TRADP/GTI and the failure of significant FDI to materialise. Given North Korea's geographical centrality to the broader multilateral Tumen River cooperation, this withdrawal was a major blow to multilateral efforts to develop the region. As such, the results of the TRADP/GTI can be seen as having fallen well short of its aims.

[14] Christopher W. Hughes, 'Tumen River Area Development Programme (TRADP): Frustrated Microregionalism as a Microcosm of Political Rivalries', in *Microregionalism and World Order*, ed. by Shaun Breslin and Glenn D. Hook (London: Palgrave Macmillan, 2002), pp. 115–43.

[15] Won Dong Wook, 'The Bright and Dark Sides of Economic Cooperation between North Korea and China: Changjitu and Sino-NK Economic Cooperation [Pukchunggyŏnghyŏbŭi pitgwa kŭlimja: 'Ch'angjit'u kaebalgyehoeg' kwa Pukchunggan ch'oguggyŏng yŏn'gyegaebalŭl chungsimŭro]', *Contemporary China Studies*, 13.1 (2011), p. 47.

regional industrial hub.[16] However, the State Council's plan also included the development of Dandong New City, which with downtown Dandong, Dandong Harbour and the neighbouring North Korean Hwanggumpyong–Wuihwa SEZ, would form a more focused regional industrial zone. A further key component of the plan was the building of the 3 km four-lane New Yalu River Bridge connecting Dandong New City with the outskirts of Sinuiju. An agreement on this project was announced on the occasion of Chinese Premier Wen Jiabao's visit to Pyongyang in October 2009 and construction of the bridge began in December 2010, with China as the sole investor.

In August 2009, the State Council also approved the Changchun–Jilin–Tumen (abbreviated to 'Changjitu') Pilot Area, covering the cities of Changchun and Jilin as well as Hunchun in Jilin Province's Yanbian Korean Autonomous Prefecture, along with Rason SEZ and Chongjin city on North Korea's north-eastern coast. Again, Wen Jiabao's visit in October unveiled China's acquisition of utilisation rights for North Korean ports. It was reported, for example, that the Chuangli Group was granted with a long-term lease for the use of Rajin harbour's pier No. 1. This was accompanied by a joint venture contract with North Korea's Kangsung Trading Company and was accompanied in early 2009 by a Chinese investment of 26 million yuan for the pier's modernisation.[17] Securing access to Rajin harbour meant that raw materials could be shipped from Jilin Province to China's own southern provinces more quickly and cheaply than by road or rail transport. Shipping times from China's northeast to its key markets of South Korea and Japan would also be significantly reduced.[18] Indeed, to facilitate cross-border cooperation, Jilin Province's Changjitu plan involved investment in border infrastructure, such as the building of the New Tumen River Bridge between Quanhe customs district in Hunchun and the North Korean border town of Wonjong, as well as the building of a new 53 km road from the border to Rason. The renewed interest of China in the North Korean border region from the mid-2000s was enhanced as Beijing and Pyongyang in November 2010 agreed a

---

[16] State Council Information Office of the PRC, 6 February 2010, 'Plan for the Development of Liaoning Coastal Economic Belt Development Plan – Full Document [Liaoningyanhai jingjidai fazhanguihua quanwen]' www.scio.gov.cn/ztk/xwfb/04/4/Document/542279/542279.htm [accessed 17th April 2019].

[17] Bae Jong-Ryeol and Yoon Seung-Hyun, *An Analysis of Jilin Province's Economic Cooperation with North Korea: Focus on Investment [Kilimsŏngŭi taebuggyŏngjehyŏmnyok silt'ae punsŏk: Taebukt'ujarŭl chungsimŭro]* (Seoul: Korea Institute for National Unification, 2015), pp. 55–58.

[18] Russia also invested in Rajin Port. It secured the right to use Pier No. 3 and completed the modernisation of the pier terminal in 2014. The groundbreaking ceremony for the modernisation of the 54 km railroad linking the Russian border town of Khasan and Rajin Port began in October 2008, and the railroad opened in September 2013.

plan of 'joint development and management' for Rason SEZ as well as Sinuiju's two islands of Hwanggumpyong and Wihwa on the Yalu River.

Following Xi Jinping's rise to power in 2013, however, Beijing became increasingly reluctant to pursue large-scale cooperation projects with North Korea. This reflected in part increased tensions over the latter's nuclear programme, but also the fact that many of the existing high-profile projects simply failed to progress as planned. For example, the New Yalu River Bridge remained unopened despite having been completed in October 2014. Indeed, there appeared to have been no effort on the North Korean side to connect the bridge to the existing road network, and thus, the bridge remained unused. It thereby stood for some observers as a testament to the futility of economic engagement with North Korea. Regional governments in the northeast, however, continued to make efforts to pursue smaller scale cooperation with North Korea. For example, in October 2015, the Liaoning provincial government opened the China–Korea Border Trade Zone in Dandong's New City, which allowed tax-free purchase of goods by border residents up to a value of 8,000 yuan (US$ 1,260) per day.[19] Though the failure to open the nearby New Yalu River Bridge negatively affected the zone's prospects, more successful border cooperation zones were established in Jilin Province's Yanbian region.

The fact that efforts continued at the regional level can be understood in the context of the northeast's continued economic difficulties. In 2015, for example, Liaoning's economic growth rate reached just 3 per cent, the lowest amongst China's thirty-one administrative provinces, and fell further to −2.5 per cent in 2016. Jilin and Heilongjiang Provinces fared somewhat better, but the north-eastern provinces were still the lowest-performing in the country. At the same time, exchange with North Korea increased in importance to the region. In Jilin Province, for example, North Korea accounted for 12.1 per cent of the province's total exports (US$ 6.25 billion) in 2014, making North Korea Jilin Province's biggest export destination for the first time, exceeding Japan, Russia and South Korea.[20] Thus, while high-profile engagement projects promoted by the central government appeared to grind to a halt, regional and local governments continued to encourage the expansion of economic exchange with North Korea. The freedom of regional governments to engage with North Korea should not be exaggerated, however. Following the onset of Trump's 'maximum pressure' campaign in 2017, the Chinese central government pressured regional governments to curtail their economic cooperation with North Korea. Nonetheless, the point here is that the different emphases between central and regional governments suggest that China's North Korea

[19] *Voice of America*, 30 June 2016, 'Dandong China–North Korea Border Trade Customs Pilot in Operation [Dandong Pukchung hosimuyŏggu segwan sihŏm unyŏng]'.
[20] Bae and Yoon, *Analysis of Jilin Province's Economic Cooperation,* p. 14.

policy cannot simply be reduced to the desire to maintain a buffer state on the Korean peninsula but instead represents a more complex amalgam of geopolitical and geoeconomic objectives pursued at multiple scales and by a variety of actors.

The expansion of Sino–North Korean economic engagement in the 2000s also coincided with a shift in the kinds of entities involved. Until the late 1990s, border trading rights for local Chinese firms and residents had been tightly controlled by the provincial authorities, with the trade itself largely monopolised by SOEs. However, with the Chinese government's easing of restrictions on cross-border trade in the early 2000s, the number of private firms engaging with North Korea rose sharply. In the case of the Dandong region, for example, there were by the early 2010s around 6,700 registered trading companies, with more than a third of these estimated to be involved in economic exchange with North Korea.[21] Several of these were companies that had grown from being small private traders to become major enterprises dealing with the large-scale import and export of coal, metals, fertiliser, foodstuff, machinery, vehicles and building materials.[22] There were also many small-scale Chinese traders and merchants based in Liaoning and Jilin Provinces, some of whom acted as trade agents for North Korean firms and Chinese enterprises in other provinces. Thus, although the Chinese government encouraged the development of this cross-border economy, the majority of the entities involved were profit-seeking private businesses.

The dominance of private enterprises in Sino–North Korean relations underlines the latter's profit-oriented nature. Indeed, in talks with Kim Jong Il in Changchun on 27 August 2010, Chinese President Hu Jintao emphasised that ties between the two countries were to be based upon the principles of being 'government-led, enterprise-based, market-operated, and for mutual benefit'. These remarks indicated that economic cooperation between the two countries would operate on market principles, albeit with the two governments establishing the underpinning framework. Furthermore, in contrast to Pyongyang's past preference for 'no strings attached' aid, this approach was accepted and indeed actively pursued by Pyongyang. This was perhaps out of necessity rather than choice, due to North Korea's increased diplomatic isolation resulting from its nuclear programme alongside the regime's ambitious stated goal of turning the country into a 'strong and prosperous nation' (kangsŏngdaeguk). Indeed, the dynastic succession from Kim Jong Il to his son Kim Jong Un in late 2011 meant that the task of economic revival

---

[21] Interview with a local government official, Dandong, November 2012.
[22] Interview with the managing staff of Hongxiang Industrial Development Company, a major trading company in Dandong, November 2012.

had become all the more important to legitimation and maintaining political stability.

7.2   Shifting Forms of Trade and Investment

Reflecting the demands of the booming Chinese economy, the vast majority of trade and investment between China and North Korea was centred on the mineral resources sector. The growth in North Korean exports of anthracite to China is particularly noteworthy, reaching a level of US$ 1.38 billion in 2013 (see Figure 7.2). This increase in mineral exports to China underlines how Japanese and South Korean unilateral sanctions alongside the booming Chinese economy led to a restructuring of North Korea's external economic relations in a manner that resembles the dependence on mineral exports found in other developing countries. However, the ensuing slowdown of the Chinese economy, the end of the global commodity boom and the tightening of environmental regulations in China led to a subsequent sharp decline in anthracite prices from about 100 dollars per tonne in 2011 to 50 dollars per tonne in early 2016.[23] North Korea initially responded to this decline by increasing the physical quantity of its coal exports, and as such, in 2015, North Korea replaced Russia as China's third-largest source of coal (see Table 7.1). However, the continuing fall in prices meant that the total value of exported anthracite fell to US$ 1.05 billion that year. In a similar fashion, China Customs data show that iron ore exports to China grew from a value of US $529,000 in 2000 to $324 million in 2011, but thereafter sharply declined to a value of $72.8 million by 2015. These fluctuations further suggest that the importers of North Korean mineral resources are largely Chinese enterprises making decisions on the basis of profit rather than political factors.

In the mid-2000s, larger Chinese enterprises also began to invest in other mineral resources, such as iron ore, gold, coal and copper. According to one report, in the latter half of the 2000s, Chinese enterprises invested in a total of twenty major mines, including Musan Mine in North Hamgyong Province, Sangnong Gold Mine in South Hamgyong Province, Hyesan Youth Copper Mine in Ryanggang Province, Tokhyon Mine in North Pyongan Province, 2.8 Jikdong Youth Coal Mine in South Pyongan Province, and Unpa Zinc Mine in North Hwanghae Province.[24] Given the dilapidated state of North Korea's mining sector, such investments typically required significant prior

---

[23] Interviews with managers of Chinese trading companies importing anthracite from North Korea, July 2016.

[24] North Korean Resources Research Institute, *Analysis of North Korean Mineral Resources Development [Pukhan chawŏn'gaebalsaŏp silt'aebunsŏk]* (Seoul: North Korean Resources Research Institute and Korea Resources Corporation, 2010), pp. 9–10.

Table 7.1 *China's major anthracite import sources, 2014–16*
(Value unit: Million US$, %)

	2014			2015			2016		
	Country	Value	%	Country	Value	%	Country	Value	%
1	Australia	8,912	47.2	Australia	5,295	52.3	Australia	5,530	48.3
2	Indonesia	3,316	17.6	Indonesia	1,552	15.3	Indonesia	2,046	17.9
3	Russia	2,183	11.6	North Korea	1,050	10.4	North Korea	1,181	10.3
4	North Korea	1,136	6.0	Russia	1,043	10.3	Russia	1,126	9.8
5	Canada	980	5.2	Canada	554	5.5	Mongolia	992	8.7
6	Mongolia	945	5.0	Mongolia	536	5.3	Canada	491	4.3
7	South Africa	451	2.4	Vietnam	43	0.4	New Zealand	45	0.4
8	Vietnam	440	2.3	New Zealand	24	0.2	Vietnam	25	0.2

Source: China Customs data

modernisation of the mines and the improvement of their transport links. The overall result was that minerals continued to grow sharply as a percentage of North Korea's overall exports to China, from 17 per cent in 2000 to 52 per cent in 2015.

Most Chinese investors chose not to demand management control but preferred to invest through joint ventures with local partners as a means of lowering the risks associated with investments in North Korea.[25] However, joint ventures with North Korean partners were not without frictions over the method of investment, contract conditions and distribution of profits. Perhaps the most well-known example of such frictions is the case of the Xiyang Group, who in 2012 publicly accused the North Korean government of sabotaging its US$ 40 million investment. The complaints made by Xiyang were numerous, the most serious being that once the North Korean partners had learned the process of commercially separating valuable minerals from their ores, they then reneged on the contract and forced the Chinese company to leave. The North Korean side responded, however, that much of the US$ 40 million stipulated in the contract was never actually delivered. Similar allegations against North Korean partners were made by an affiliated company of the Wanxiang Group in relation to its investments in Hyesan Youth Copper Mine.[26] These widely publicised experiences did not, however, appear to temper flows of trade and investment between the two countries.

[25] Byung-kwang Park, 'China-North Korea Economic Relations during the Hu Jintao Era', *International Journal of Korean Unification Studies*, 19.2 (2010), p. 142.
[26] *New York Times*, 20 October 2012, 'China–Korea Tensions Rise after Failed Venture'.

In line with North Korea's marketisation, Chinese enterprises also increased their investments in the country's retail sector. Although the size of these investments was smaller in comparison to those in the mineral sector, they held the potential for a more direct impact on the livelihood of North Korean citizens. A key example of this was the establishment of the Potonggang Trade Market in June 2005 and the Kwangbok Area Commerce Centre in 2012. Potonggang Trade Market sold imported goods from China for wholesale or retail, including construction materials, steel products, machine parts as well as rubber products and agricultural machinery. The market was a joint venture with the Ministry of Foreign Trade's Central Import–Export Trade Company, the Liaoning Taixing International Trading Company and three private Chinese enterprises.[27] The Kwangbok Area Commerce Centre, situated in Pyongyang's Mangyongdae district, was opened in January 2012 following the major renovation of the twenty-year-old Kwangbok Department Store. This supermarket was Pyongyang's first large-scale shopping outlet, based on a joint venture between the Chinese Feihaimengxin International Trade Company and the Korea Daesong Trading Company.[28] China-sourced goods accounting for around 60 per cent of all goods sold, although the proportion of domestically produced goods sold in retail outlets subsequently increased over time.[29]

In the context of declining revenues from mineral exports, investment in labour-intensive manufacturing became a key growth area for North Korea in the 2010s. Some of this investment was for the purposes of targeting growing North Korean domestic demand for consumer goods, electrical appliances, food manufacturing equipment, construction materials, etc. More important in terms of the country's foreign currency earnings, however, was the expansion of export-oriented manufacturing, which served to integrate the country into China-centred regional and global production networks despite the increasingly stringent sanctions. Investment in North Korean manufacturing for export typically took the form of consignment-based processing (CBP), whereby Chinese enterprises supplied the funds, production equipment and materials while North Korean companies provided the workers. The finished products were then re-exported back to China. Under CBP, when Chinese enterprises received orders beyond their capacity to fulfil, orders were placed with North Korean SOEs located

---

[27] Bae Jong-Ryeol, 'An Evaluation of Foreign Investment in North Korea: Focusing on EU and Chinese Enterprises [Pukhanŭi woegugint'uja silt'aewa p'yŏngga: EUwa chungguk kiŏbŭi taebukjinch'ulŭl chungsimŭro]', *EXIM North Korean Economic Review*, Fall (2008), p. 61.

[28] *KCNA*, 5 January 2012, 'Kwangbok Area Supermarket Opens.'

[29] *Choson Sinbo*, 22 January 2018, 'A commercial area favoured by the people – competition between department stores for higher-level service [Inmindŭri chŭlgyŏch'annŭn sangŏp kongganŭro - poda sujunnop'ŭn pongsarŭl wihan paekhwajŏmdŭrŭi kyŏngjaeng]'.

mostly in Pyongan Province, such as the Unha, Daesong, and Bonghwa trading companies. Raw materials such as cotton and related equipment were supplied by the Chinese enterprises, thereby avoiding issues relating to the unreliability of supply chains within North Korea itself. Wage-related payments were then made to the North Korean authorities or to the trading company directly. On the basis of these arrangements, exports to China of CBP-based clothing and related items (HS 61, 62) saw particularly rapid growth, from US$ 186.4 million in 2010 to US$ 799.3 million in 2015 (see Figure 7.3), amounting to an increase from 16 per cent of total exports to 33 per cent (see Figure 7.4).

China thereby largely replaced South Korea as the main destination of CBP clothing exports from North Korea. Indeed, Chinese enterprises that had previously acted as intermediaries between North and South Korean companies began to engage in North Korean CBP directly.[30] This was much to the displeasure of South Korean SMEs who were prohibited from maintaining their operations in North Korea as a result of the 'May 24th' sanctions put in place by Seoul in 2010 following the sinking of the *Ch'ŏnan* corvette. By 2013, clothing accounted for about 20 per cent of North Korea's total exports to China, thereby reducing North Korea's heavy dependence on mineral resources. This growth in CBP textile manufacturing also contributed to rising North Korean employment levels. The 2008 national census had already recorded almost 400,000 workers as working in the clothing industry, amounting to 13.84 per cent of the entire manufacturing sector employment.[31] This figure is therefore likely to have increased with the growth in CBP-based production. Should the tensions surrounding North Korea's nuclear programme be resolved, there is therefore potential for North Korea's cost advantages to be generalised so that the country can enter the global clothing market from a position whereby it can compete not only with Chinese labour costs but also with that of low-wage producers in Southeast Asia.

North Korea's integration into regional and global production networks occurred in the context of rising labour costs within China. The latter took place as a result of increases in the minimum wage, labour unrest and demands for wage increases, as well as a tightening labour market due to demographic shifts associated with the impacts of the one-child policy. For clothing manufacturers in China's more prosperous coastal provinces, the challenge of rising wages led to the relocation of production either to China's inland/western

---

[30] Interviews with Chinese firm owners engaged in trade business and CBP, November 2012 and March 2013 in Dandong and Shenyang.

[31] DPRK Central Bureau of Statistics, *DPRK 2008 Population Census National Report* (Pyongyang: DPRK Central Bureau of Statistics, 2009), p. 193.

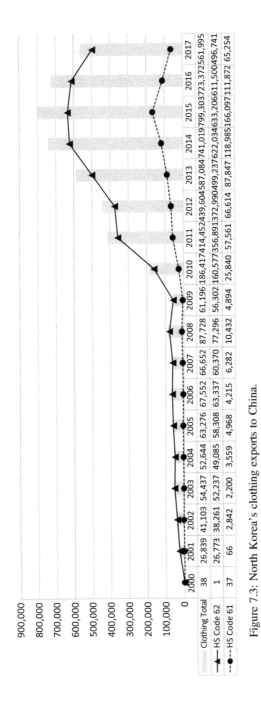

Figure 7.3: North Korea's clothing exports to China.

(Unit: US$ 1,000).

Notes: HS Code 61 refers to knitted or crocheted articles of apparel and clothing accessories; HS Code 62 refers to articles of apparel and clothing accessories that are not knitted or crocheted. Source: China Customs data.

	2000	2001	2002	2003	2004	2005	2006	2007	2008	2009	2010	2011	2012	2013	2014	2015	2016	2017
Clothing Total	38	26,839	41,103	54,437	52,644	63,276	67,552	66,652	87,728	61,196	186,417	414,452	439,604	587,084	741,019	799,303	723,372	561,995
HS Code 62	1	26,773	38,261	52,237	49,085	58,308	63,337	60,370	77,296	56,302	160,577	356,891	372,990	499,237	622,034	633,206	611,500	496,741
HS Code 61	37	66	2,842	2,200	3,559	4,968	4,215	6,282	10,432	4,894	25,840	57,561	66,614	87,847	118,985	166,097	111,872	65,254

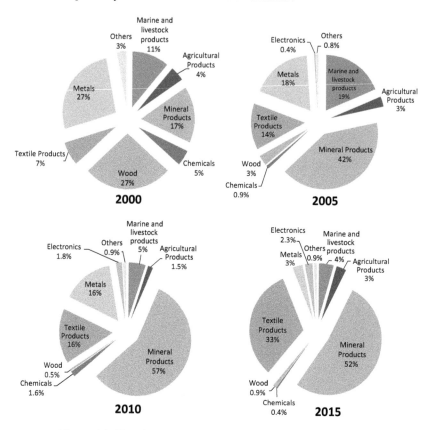

Figure 7.4: Changing structure of North Korea's exports to China.
Source: China Customs data

regions or overseas.[32] However, the latter strategy of 'going out' was also adopted by clothing manufacturers in the northeast, particularly in border regions adjacent to North Korea. Indeed, China's northeast was by no means spared from wage increases. Labour-intensive factories in the clothing and footwear sectors, for example, experienced greater difficulties in recruiting workers, with some of them operating at less than half their capacity. Dandong experienced one of the most serious labour shortages in Liaoning Province,

---

[32] Shengjun Zhu and John Pickles, 'Bring In, Go Up, Go West, Go Out: Upgrading, Regionalisation and Delocalisation in China's Apparel Production Networks', *Journal of Contemporary Asia*, 44.1 (2014), pp. 36–63.

and in the early 2010s, the number of apparel companies in the city declined from 120 to 70.[33]

As such, North Korea came to perform the role of what David Harvey terms a 'spatial fix' for China's north-eastern clothing manufacturers by providing new sources of low-cost labour.[34] CBP-based production enabled Chinese manufacturers to avoid exposure to the risks of direct investment in the country. This was a strategy supported by regional governments. For example, several major clothing manufacturers in Hunchun and Dandong cities were granted official permits by the customs authorities so that local companies would only have to pay 20 per cent of customs duties when re-importing finished clothing items back into China from North Korea.[35] Furthermore, the Jilin provincial authorities regarded clothing manufactured in North Korea under CBP arrangements as produced in China, thereby giving preference in terms of quality and safety inspections.[36]

In addition to CBP-based production, the early 2010s saw a marked rise in the dispatch of North Korean workers to China's northeast, and in particular, to border cities such as Dandong. While CBP-based production was less risky than direct investment for Chinese firms, the use of dispatched North Korean labour represented a further reduction of risk. As noted, there were widespread reports of difficulties faced by Chinese enterprises operating in North Korea. Chinese enterprises feared the appropriation of their assets and had significant concerns about the poor infrastructure as well as arbitrary changes in rules and practices.[37] The strict quarantine procedures put in place during the winter of 2015–16 in response to the Ebola crisis further demonstrated how seemingly arbitrary actions taken by the North Korean authorities could greatly inconvenience Chinese investors.[38] The dispatch of North Korean labour to production sites in China thereby helped to mitigate such risks.

Local governments in China's northeast played a key role in facilitating this process. In 2012, for example, the Tumen municipal authorities signed an agreement with the DPRK Joint Venture and Investment Committee to

---

[33] Choi Jangho, Kim Junyoung, Im So Jeong and Choi Yoojeong, *Economic Cooperation between North Korea and China, and Implications for Inter-Korean Economic Cooperation [Pukchung punŏpch'egye punsŏggwa taebuk kyŏngjehyŏmnyŏge taehan sisajŏm]* (Sejong: Korea Institute for International Economic Policy, 2015), p. 109.

[34] David Harvey, 'Globalization and the "Spatial Fix"', *Geographische Revue*, 2 (2001), pp. 23–30 .

[35] *People's Daily*, 5 February 2013, 'Opening Cross-border CBP trade with North Korea [Taejosŏn wit'akkagongmuyŏk pitchang yŏnda]'.

[36] Bae and Yoon, *Analysis of Jilin Province's Economic Cooperation*, pp. 167–68; Choi Jangho et al, *Economic Cooperation between North Korea and China*, pp. 108–109.

[37] Haggard and Noland, *Hard Target*, p. 153..

[38] Andray Abrahamian, 'North Korea's Very Bad Year and China's Role in It', *Reuters [Online]*, 2015 http://blogs.reuters.com/great-debate/2015/07/22/north-koreas-very-bad-year-and-chinas-role-in-it/ [accessed 2 April 2020].

dispatch 20,000 North Korean workers to the city's newly established Choson Industrial Park.[39] The actual number of North Korean workers employed there grew rapidly from around 600 at the end of 2013 to 4,000 in August 2016.[40] As Chinese enterprises pressured local governments to permit further employment of North Korean workers, those governments also competed with each other. Following the approval by the Tumen authorities for Choson Industrial Park to employ North Korean labour, Hunchun, a neighbouring city, signed a separate contract with North Korean labour supplier Choson Rungnado Company to dispatch more North Korean workers.[41] The employment of North Korean workers was therefore largely a local level initiative. The central Chinese government did not formally express a position on such practices, though as with local efforts to promote exchange with North Korea more generally, it appears that it turned a blind eye to this practice given the continued economic slowdown in the northeast.

Large numbers of North Korean workers were reportedly dispatched to Chinese firms in the clothing, food and service sectors. This represented a significant cost advantage for those firms since the cost of employing a North Korean skilled worker in Dandong and Hunchun amounted to around 1,500–1,600 yuan per month, compared to 2,700–3,000 yuan for Chinese workers.[42] For the workers themselves, wages compared favourably to an average North Korean family income, thus making overseas work an attractive proposition despite reported restrictions on personal freedom while in China.[43] Thus, CBP within North Korea and the dispatch of North Korean workers to the Chinese border regions served to create a pattern of Chinese engagement that extended beyond that of the enclave format that allegedly characterises Chinese investments in Africa, reflecting, of course, North Korea's significant wage advantages.[44] The scope of Sino–North Korean engagement more

[39] *JiLinXinWen*, 27 December 2013, 'Tumen is fully promoting the development of China (Tumen) Korea Industrial Complex [Domun Chungguk (Domun) Chosŏn gongŏpdanjibaljŏn chollyŏk ch'ujin]'.

[40] Choi Yong-Jin, 'Economic Technology Development Zone, Micro-Regional Cooperation, and One Belt-One Road in the Northeast Asian Borderlands [Dongbuga chŏpgyŏngjiyŏgŭi kyŏng-jegisulgaebalgu, sojiyŏnghyŏmnyŏk kŭrigo ildaeillo]', *The Korean Journal of Area Studies*, 34.3 (2016), p. 104.

[41] Kim Sung-Jae, 'Firms' Fighting of Tumen vs Hunchun?: Struggles of Local Governments to Have North Korean Labours [Tumen vs Hunch'un kiŏp morichae chabgo momssaum wae? Chungguk chibangjŏngbuggiri Pukhan illyŏk dalla]', *Weekly Donga*, 13 January 2014, pp. 40–42.

[42] KITA, 'The Status of North Korean Workers in China and Related Implications', *KITA Beijing Office Brief*, 2014, p. 4.

[43] Andrei Lankov, 'North Korean Workers Abroad Aren't Slaves', *NK News*, 2014 www.nknews .org/2014/11/north-korean-workers-abroad-arent-slaves/ [accessed 2nd April 2020].

[44] It is questionable, however, to what extent such characterisations are accurate in the case of China–Africa relations, see Brautigam, *The Dragon's Gift*; Giles Mohan, 'Beyond the Enclave:

broadly came to make increasing use of North Korean labour, thereby integrating North Korea into China-centred production networks beyond the export of mineral resources.

Initially, small groups of North Koreans worked primarily in the service sector, and particularly in restaurants. This then expanded to textiles, timber processing, machinery assembly, fisheries processing, construction and IT sectors. In the Dandong region alone, in 2016, there were estimated to be around as many as 30,000 workers, largely in unskilled jobs in clothing, seafood, wood product and construction material factories.[45] A further 9,000 North Korean workers were employed in Jilin's Yanbian Korean Autonomous Prefecture.[46] Some of these operations were reported to be quite large in scale. In 2015, for example, a major Chinese manufacturer of men's clothes, the Youngor Group, established a factory in Hunchun's industrial zone in 2015 with the support of the city government.[47] In 2016, the employment of 1,500 North Korean workers made up around 75 per cent of the total workforce, and there were plans to increase this to 5,000 North Korean workers.[48] In addition to low-wage unskilled labour, North Korea also dispatched relatively highly skilled IT workers in line with the country's comparative strengths in software development and animation. Dandong Dongfang Measurement and Control Technology, for example, employed forty to fifty doctoral researchers from the (North) Korean Academy of Sciences.[49] Media reports suggested that there were more than 2,400 North Korean IT workers in the Chinese northeast, including about 1,000 workers in Yanji, Jilin Province and 500–600 workers in Shenyang, Liaoning Province.[50]

7.3   Win-Win Cooperation or an Emerging Neocolonial Relationship?

The pattern of Sino–North Korean relations described in this chapter provides support for China's rhetoric of the 'win-win' nature of its cooperation with the developing Global South. For China, this deepening mode of engagement provided both geopolitical stability on its frontiers and played a crucial role in efforts to overcome internal regional disparities within China through facilitating the revitalisation of the north-eastern region. From Pyongyang's

Towards a Critical Political Economy of China and Africa', *Development and Change*, 44.6 (2013), pp. 1255–72.

[45] Choi Yong-Jin, 'Economic Technology Development Zone', p. 104.

[46] Interview with Hunchun municipal government official, July 2016.

[47] Bae and Yoon, *Analysis of Jilin Province's Economic Cooperation*, p. 170.

[48] Interviews with factory managers, Hunchun industrial zone, July 2016.

[49] Interviews with IT staff, Dandong, November 2012.

[50] *Yonhap News*, 22 February 2016, 'Thousands of North Korean IT workers earn foreign currency in China's Northeast in the midst of international sanctions [Taebukchejae kungmyŏnsŏ Pukhan ITillyŏk such'ŏnmyŏng, chungguksŏ oehwabŏri]'.

perspective, economic cooperation with China compensated for the loss of foreign exchange earnings resulting from the freezing of its relations with South Korea along with its general diplomatic isolation and associated 'aid fatigue' on the part of international donors. As such, China's engagement served to maintain North Korea's connections with the world economy in what would otherwise be a situation of almost total isolation. It is true that the dominance of mineral resources in Sino–North Korean trade and investment relations suggested broad parallels with critical analyses of China's impact on developmental prospects in other parts of the developing world and posed a significant vulnerability for North Korea. Yet, China's economic engagement also increased the supply of basic necessities for the country's citizens, thereby addressing the chronic lack of supply of such goods. Furthermore, as argued above, China-sourced CBP provided both employment as well as the possibility for North Korea to achieve greater integration into global production networks.

It should also be noted that the relatively positive dimension to this relationship owed much to the fact that North Korea's developmental trajectory differed somewhat to other parts of the developing world. By way of comparison, it is useful here to consider briefly the case of Southeast Asia. It has been noted, for example, that China's economic rise led to increased fears in Southeast Asia of export losses.[51] For the ten years between 1995 and 2004, the share of ASEAN manufactures in US and Japanese imports for most sectors saw a decline at the expense of Chinese manufactures. In addition, there was a decline in the absolute value of ASEAN exports to the United States and Japan.[52] Southeast Asia thereafter became a key source of intermediate components, the bulk of which were shipped to China for final assembly and then exported to the West. Indeed, during the 1990s, there was a fourfold increase in the value of ASEAN exports to China. While a significant proportion of this trade was driven by the boom in China's demand for Southeast Asia's raw materials, there was also an increasing share of component manufactures within this trade.[53] With rising costs in Southeast Asia and resulting changes in the investment strategies of transnational corporations, component production thereafter began to shift to China itself.[54]

---

[51] Sanjaya Lall and Manuel Albaladejo, 'China's Competitive Performance: A Threat to East Asian Manufactured Exports?', *World Development*, 32.9 (2004), p. 1441.

[52] John Ravenhill, 'Is China an Economic Threat to Southeast Asia?', *Asian Survey*, 46.5 (2006), pp. 668–69.

[53] Ibid., pp. 670–72; see also John Humphrey and Hubert Schmitz, 'China: Its Impact on the Developing Asian Economies', *IDS Working Paper*, 296, (2007).

[54] Jeffrey Henderson, 'China and Global Development: Towards a Global-Asian Era?', *Contemporary Politics*, 14.4 (2008), p. 384.

In contrast to Southeast Asia, however, the narrowing of North Korea's industrial base occurred largely prior to the resurgence of economic relations with China. Given the poor state of North Korea's industrial sector, the prospects for reconstructing the country's model of self-reliant industrialisation appeared remote. Indeed, it can be questioned whether this would be a viable option for developing countries more generally given the increasingly restrictive international environment for autonomous developmental strategies.[55] It is further problematised by the rapidly changing nature of technology and the increased obsolescence of reverse engineering and licensing as strategies for development. Such changes in the international environment have led to a shift from classic Gerschenkronian late-development strategies towards greater engagement with the world economy through global value chains as the primary mode of development. In line with these trends, North Korea experienced increased economic enmeshment into China-centred production networks, and thereby, into a new model of industrial economic and spatial organisation, experiencing deindustrialisation alongside tentative industrialisation through integration at the same time. Indeed, in the North Korean context, this appeared to be the country's only viable strategy for economic recovery, and as such, the mode of China's engagement can be viewed as relatively positive for North Korea's development prospects.

Should the nuclear issue be resolved, what might the longer-term impact of China's engagement be on North Korean economic recovery and growth? Much has been written on so-called 'growth triangles', such as those found in Singapore–Johor (Malaysia)–Riau (Indonesia), Hong Kong–Shenzhen and a variety of cross-border cooperation patterns in the European Union. Such arrangements have proven conducive towards attracting foreign capital as well as encouraging the collective utilisation of resources through cross-border industrial cooperation. Through increasing complementarities between border cities and regions such as Sinuiju and Dandong, and Rason and Yanbian, China could potentially play a key role in the upgrading of North Korean infrastructure through the supply of capital and technical skills. The promotion of economic cooperation in the border regions might also have the potential to encourage the influx of South Korean and foreign capital into North Korea, particularly if planned projects of the Trans-Korean Railway connecting the Korean peninsula with China and Russia or North Korea's establishment of SEZs are advanced. The dangers inherent in the emerging economic relationship with China are clear, however. Mineral exports, the dispatch of labour and simple CBP operations could conversely encourage the North Korea leadership to adhere to a strategy of muddling through rather than continue with its

---

[55] Ha-Joon Chang, *Kicking Away the Ladder: Development Strategy in Historical Perspective* (London: Anthem, 2002).

programme of economic reforms. Much then depends on the developmental strategies adopted by Pyongyang.

Excessive dependence on China means that North Korea is greatly exposed to any potential external shock such as a change in prices in the raw materials market or in Beijing's broader policy towards North Korea. Indeed, in the next chapter, we will examine the extent to which this has been the case since 2018 when China's enforcement of sanctions was significantly tightened. Even before this, however, the slowdown of the Chinese economy and corresponding decline in commodity prices meant, for example, that prices per tonne of anthracite had declined from $102 per tonne in 2011 to $73.4 per tonne in 2014.[56] Furthermore, there are clear risks that North Korea might remain stuck at the level of simple supplier of low-wage labour and natural resources as demanded by the rapidly growing Chinese economy. Without a proactive approach on the part of Pyongyang aimed at facilitating upward mobility within global production networks, the expansion of economic relations with China is unlikely in itself to aid the reform of North Korea's existing industrial structure or strengthen international competitiveness beyond reliance on low wages.

Even the more developed Southeast Asian countries have faced significant challenges in taking advantage of such networks and facilitating industrial upgrading. Jeffrey Henderson and Richard Phillips have argued, for example, that following the emergence of the Malaysian electronics sector in the 1980s, there was little in the way of industrial upgrading in the country.[57] Southeast Asian countries with weaker industrial bases such as Cambodia, Laos and Myanmar were largely limited to the role of exporters of raw materials and resources, and as such, the benefits that they could receive through trade with China were even more limited.[58] Thus, when considering the pattern of North Korea's exports to China, it is this latter group of countries that arguably presents a more likely vision of North Korea's future than the miracle economies found elsewhere in Northeast Asia.

7.4   Conclusion

The rise of China can be seen as a key dimension of the development–geopolitics nexus, as it relates to North Korea. From China's perspective, the

---

[56] Jong-kyu Lee, 'Decline in the DPRK's Anthracite Export to China: Causes and Implications', *KDI Focus*, 57 (2015), p. 4.

[57] Jeffrey Henderson and Richard Phillips, 'Unintended Consequences: Social Policy, State Institutions and the "Stalling" of the Malaysian Industrialization Project', *Economy and Society*, 36.1 (2007), pp. 78–102.

[58] Barry Eichengreen, Yeongseop Rhee and Hui Tong, 'China and the Exports of Other Asian Countries', *Review of World Economics*, 143.2 (2007), pp. 201–26; Humphrey and Schmitz, 'China'.

deepening of Sino–North Korean relations was driven by strategic considerations, and specifically, by Beijing's efforts to maintain the geopolitical status quo on the Korean peninsula. Economic exchange with North Korea was also seen as central to China's attempts to revitalise its north-eastern region and particularly its border regions. For Pyongyang, economic relations with China provided a much-needed source of trade and investment in the context of otherwise increasing international isolation. The substantive content of these relations thereby reflected a complex combination of geopolitical and geoeconomic imperatives, albeit undergoing a transition from being primarily politically constituted to being constituted by market actors. As we shall see in the next chapter, the international sanctions regime and China's more enthusiastic enforcement of those sanctions have, however, significantly curtailed many of the forms of economic exchange detailed in this chapter. This included trade and investment in mineral resources, textiles and the seafood sectors, investment in the service sector, as well as the dispatch of North Korean labour to China. There was no doubt a significant degree of evasion of sanctions, however, and many of the forms of trade and investment detailed here likely continued at much-reduced levels.[59]

A further aim of this chapter has been to examine the past record of Sino–North Korean relations with a view to exploring North Korea's future developmental prospects. Indeed, the record of bilateral engagement between the two countries has mixed implications for the North Korean political economy. Faced with significant challenges in revitalising its existing heavy-industrial basis, North Korea came to occupy the role of supplier of natural resources and low-cost labour to China's economy. Consignment-based processing was also an important mode of integration into global production networks for North Korea, though it remained to be seen to what extent this could provide an opportunity for the country to further share in the benefits of Northeast Asia's vibrant economic development. Nonetheless, given that China's engagement largely came *after* the collapse of North Korean industry, it is questionable as to whether the relationship between the two countries could properly be referred to as 'neocolonial'. Pyongyang's international isolation meant that China came to provide much needed foreign exchange and to some degree facilitated the upgrading of infrastructure while providing employment opportunities for North Korean workers.

One question that we have not been able to address adequately in this chapter is that of the substantive social and environmental impact of China's increased engagement with North Korea. The difficulties of conducting fieldwork in the country, the lack of civil society and the resultant scarcity of

---

[59] Interviews with Chinese traders engaging in business with North Korea, August 2018 (Yanbian region) and November 2019 (Dandong).

reliable qualitative information prevent full consideration of the substantive impact of China's impact on the everyday livelihood of North Korean citizens. Given that exchange was centred around mineral resources, the dispatch of labour and low-wage manufacturing, there is little ground for optimism that China's presence was accompanied by stringent environmental and labour standards. This is particularly so since such standards have hardly been a defining feature of China's own recent developmental experience. There also appears to be little likelihood that the North Korean government had either the volition or the capacity to seriously tackle the negative social impacts of increased engagement with China. The broader issues of human rights and of whether engagement or further isolation are likely to be more conducive to political change in North Korea are also beyond the scope of this chapter. It is important to note, however, the parallels between North Korea's current situation and that of China in the late 1970s at the outset of its reform programme. The success of the Chinese reform programme was based, to a large degree, on the influx of foreign capital, though this led to the emergence of new collective subjectivities that resisted capitalist exploitation, not least in the export-oriented manufacturing sector.[60] As such, North Korea's increased engagement with the outside world and resulting socio-economic transformations is unlikely to leave the country's system of authoritarian rule unaffected, and indeed, it is for this reason that the North Korean leadership has sought to maintain a firm grip on the process.

In the short to medium term, however, there are significant challenges and risks in North Korea's emerging relationship with China. As discussed, these include in the first instance the challenge of industrial upgrading and moving into higher-value-added activities within cross-border production networks. Indeed, prospects for a successful upgrading strategy on the part of the North Korean state seem less than promising. There are also inherent dangers of excessive reliance on China, or indeed, on any single country. North Korea urgently needs to diversify its external relations, particularly with regards to its sources of trade and investment. China's more stringent enforcement of sanctions since 2018 also underlines the challenges faced by Kim Jong Un's *Pyŏngjin* dual line of the development of nuclear weapons and the economy. It is to the issue of international sanctions that our final chapter now turns.

---

[60] Kevin Gray and Youngseok Jang, 'Labour Unrest in the Global Political Economy: The Case of China's 2010 Strike Wave', *New Poltiical Economy*, 20.4 (2015), pp. 594–613.

8 International Sanctions and North Korean Development

International sanctions form a key axis through which the development–geopolitics nexus has shaped the North Korean political economy. Indeed, the country has been subject to sanctions for most of its existence. Unilateral sanctions were imposed by the United States at the time of the Korean War. Pyongyang was, however, able to offset the impacts of these sanctions through expanding its economic relations with the Socialist Bloc countries in the early post-war era, and from the 1970s, with Western Europe and Japan. The democratic transition in South Korea also led to rapid growth in inter-Korean trade from the late 1990s. However, North Korea's nuclear and missile programme led the United Nations Security Council (UNSC) to impose multilateral sanctions from the mid-2000s. Despite the increasing stringency of the sanctions regime, the measures largely failed to dissuade Pyongyang from pursuing nuclear weapons or from engaging in other illicit activities. As the broader literature on sanctions suggests, this should not be surprising. The mainstream debate on sanctions has largely revolved around the question of whether sanctions are 'effective' or not, usually understood in terms of the extent to which they are successful in altering the behaviour of the target state, or more ambitiously, in facilitating regime change. However, even in the most optimistic accounts, sanctions are more likely to fail than meet their stated objectives, often as a result of evasive practices but also due to the political resilience of the targeted regime to outside pressure.

In this chapter, we seek to examine the range of economic and political impact of sanctions on North Korean development. Though sanctions shaped the geographies of North Korea's external economic relations, they did not for most of the history of their implementation appear to exert any discernible macroeconomic shock on the country. Indeed, the imposition of multilateral sanctions from 2006 coincided with continued marketisation and gradual economic recovery, largely as a result of the deepening trade and investment relations with China. The tightening of financial sanctions against North Korea and international banks with dealings with the country also intensified informal and often illicit forms of trade, including smuggling, barter trade and the use of cash in trade-related transactions. The evidence suggests, however, that as sanctions were strengthened after 2017, the drastic reduction in the country's trade and investment did have certain sectoral impacts. Sanctions also shaped North Korean economic policymaking, most notably through Pyongyang's renewed emphasis on import-substitution policies. Yet the country's leadership also appeared to be no closer to making concessions on the key issue of its nuclear weapons programme, thereby raising questions not only with regards to the effectiveness of sanctions but the degree to which they provoke counter-responses which actively undermine the explicit objectives of sanctions.

8.1   A Brief History of Sanctions against North Korea

Unilateral US sanctions against North Korea date back to the time of the Korean War. North Korean assets in the United States were frozen and restrictions placed on trade and investment with the country. Most-favoured-nation status was also denied to North Korea, thereby further restricting the country's ability to export to the United States. Restrictions were later placed on non-humanitarian aid under the Foreign Assistance Act of 1961. Following the bombing of the Korean Air Lines Flight 858 by North Korean agents in November 1987, the country was added to the State Sponsors of Terrorism list, which brought enhanced sanctions on trade, travel and financial transactions.[1] However, as a result of the 1990s humanitarian crisis, the 1994 Agreed Framework and the 1999 moratorium on missile testing, US sanctions were partially relaxed. This was also followed by a visit of North Korean Vice Marshal Jo Myong Rok to Washington and Secretary of State Madeleine Albright to Pyongyang in October 2000. However, renewed tensions over Pyongyang's resumption of its nuclear programme in the early 2000s led to further sanctions. These included financial sanctions that targeted North Korea's integration into the international financial system. In September 2005, the US Department of the Treasury accused Macao-based bank Banco Delta Asia of facilitating North Korean money laundering as well as trafficking in counterfeit currency. This accusation alone led the Macao banking authorities to freeze fifty-two North Korean accounts worth US$ 25 million and made foreign banks and businesses wary of having even legitimate dealings with North Korea for fear of being designated complicit in money laundering.[2]

---

[1] Semoon Chang 'A Chronology of U.S. Sanctions Against North Korea', in *Economic Sanctions Against a Nuclear North Korea: An Analysis of United States and United Nations Actions Since 1950*, ed. by Suk Hi Kim and Semoon Chang (Jefferson: McFarland, 2003), pp. 34–54.
[2] Bruce Klingner, 'Banco Delta Asia Ruling Complicates North Korean Nuclear Deal', *The Heritage Foundation WebMemo*, 1398. March (2007).

Following an agreement reached at the Six-Party Talks on 13 February 2007, the United States removed North Korea from its State Sponsors of Terrorism list in October 2008. However, as relations worsened again from 2009, a new set of 'smart sanctions' targeted individuals and organisations suspected of involvement in North Korea's nuclear weapons programme along with various illicit trade and financial activities. Furthermore, in November 2017, the Trump administration put North Korea back on the State Sponsors of Terrorism list and imposed a ban on US citizens travelling to the country without prior approval. The Office of Foreign Assets Control under the US Treasury rapidly expanded the list of sanctioned North Korean entities including government organs, enterprises and banks. In addition, secondary sanctions were imposed on third-country corporations, financial institutions and businesspeople with dealings with North Korea. Dozens of foreign companies and individuals, including mainly Chinese nationals involved in economic exchange with North Korea, were placed on US Treasury sanction lists. Due to risks associated with being labelled a 'sanctions evader', this caused large numbers of foreign companies to halt their dealings with North Korea.

While the United States has never been a significant economic partner of North Korea, Japanese and South Korean bilateral sanctions had a more measurable impact on the country's external economic relations. Following the collapse of the Soviet Union, Japan had become North Korea's second-largest trade partner after China. Annual bilateral trade reached approximately US$ 400–500 million in the 1990s, or around 25 per cent of North Korea's total foreign trade. Remittances from the pro-North Korean residents in Japan became a significant source of revenue for Pyongyang. However, Pyongyang's admission in September 2002 that it had kidnapped thirteen Japanese citizens in the 1970s and 1980s led to a significant souring of relations between the two countries and to Tokyo halting its humanitarian assistance to North Korea. The first nuclear test in October 2006 led to a strengthening of Japanese sanctions, including a ban on North Korean imports, the freezing of North Korean financial assets in Japan, the suspension of cash remittances, the imposition of stringent export controls and a ban on Japanese visits and charter flights and vessels to North Korea. As a result, bilateral trade saw a 98 per cent drop between 2000 and 2007, from US$ 464 million to just US$ 9 million. Tokyo subsequently imposed a complete embargo on Japanese exports to North Korea in June 2009 following Pyongyang's second nuclear test.

Inter-Korean trade and investment had become a key axis of North Korea's external economic relations from the late 1990s. The 'Sunshine Policy' of engagement pursued by the Kim Dae-Jung government saw a sharp increase in inter-Korean trade from US$ 333 million in 1999 to US$ 1.82 billion in 2008. The Kaesong Industrial Complex (KIC) played a key role in this growth after South Korean enterprises began operating there in December 2004. Following the sinking of the *Ch'ŏnan* corvette on 26 March 2010, however, the so-called 'May 24th measures' banned North Korean vessels from entering South Korean territorial waters and ports and suspended all inter-Korean trade outside of the KIC. There was also a ban on investment in new and ongoing cooperation projects in North Korea, meaning that no new investments in the KIC were permitted. Henceforth, all inter-Korean trade was to consist solely of the export of raw materials to the KIC and the import of manufactured goods. Following Pyongyang's fourth nuclear test in January 2016, however, Seoul shut down the KIC completely, putting an end to the era of economic cooperation between the two Koreas.

In addition to bilateral sanctions, North Korea from the mid-2000s became subject to UNSC multilateral sanctions as a result of the country's nuclear and missile programme (see Table 8.1). Between 2006 and 2016, UN resolutions (1695, 1718, 1874, 2087, 2094) largely took the form of so-called 'smart sanctions'.[3] The latter is seen as mitigating the negative humanitarian consequences of comprehensive trade sanctions of the kind imposed on Iraq in the 1990s.[4] As such, UN sanctions against North Korea sought to forestall the further development of North Korea's nuclear programme but also avoid collateral damage to society more broadly. Specifically, the measures included a ban on the transfer of missiles and missile-related materials and technology to North Korea; a ban on the sale to North Korea of conventional arms and on North Korean arms exports; a ban on the export of dual-use and luxury goods to North Korea; a ban on new grants, financial assistance or concessional loans to North Korea, except for 'humanitarian and developmental purposes'. In terms of 'smart' measures aimed at North Korea's elite, they also included travel bans on figures and state entities connected to the nuclear programme as well as sanctions on North Korean financial institutions.

However, in 2016, as North Korea markedly increased the pace of its nuclear and missile programme, there was a shift from smart sanctions towards more comprehensive trade sanctions. Resolution 2270, passed on 2 March 2016 in response to North Korea's fourth nuclear test, included a ban on North Korean exports of coal, iron, iron ore and several other minerals. However, the resolution included a somewhat vague exemption clause for trade in minerals conducted for 'livelihood purposes', effectively giving China no reason to enforce the sanctions. This clause was partially removed under UNSC Resolution 2321 on 30 November 2016. Resolution 2321 banned the export of copper, nickel, silver and zinc, placed a quantitative cap on North Korean

[3] David Cortright and George A. Lopez, *Smart Sanctions: Targeting Economic Statecraft* (Lanham, MD: Rowman and Littlefield, 2002).

[4] Denis J. Halliday, 'The Impact of the UN Sanctions on the People of Iraq', *Journal of Palestinian Studies*, 28.2 (1999), pp. 29–73.

Table 8.1 *UNSC resolutions related with North Korea*

UNSCR 1695 (15 July 2006)	• Ban on exports to North Korea of missiles and missile-related items.
UNSCR 1718 (14 October 2006)	• Ban on sale to North Korea of conventional military arms (excluding small arms) and related services or assistance.
	• Ban on export of luxury goods to North Korea.
	• Ban on export of materials related to nuclear programme as well as freezing of related financial funds.
	• Permission for states to inspect cargo to and from North Korea to enforce the sanctions.
	• Travel ban on figures connected to nuclear programme.
UNSCR 1874 (12 June 2009)	• Tightening of sanctions relating to North Korea's imports and exports of arms and related materials (excluding small arms) as well as related services; calls for increased vigilance over such activities.
	• Prior notification to Security Council in advance of selling small arms or light weapons to North Korea.
	• Member states authorised to inspect North Korean cargo within their territory if suspected of being related to nuclear programme.
	• Measures such as freezing of assets to prevent financial assistance to North Korea that could contribute to weapons of mass destruction (WMD)-related programmes.
	• No new commitments for financial assistance to North Korea except if related to humanitarian/development programmes or potential nuclear agreement.
	• Setting up of expert panel to assist enforcement and implementation of resolution.
UNSCR 2087 (22 January 2013)	• Strengthening of Resolutions 1718 and 1874 through clarifying the right of states to seize and destroy materials suspected of heading to and from North Korea for the purposes of weapons development and research.
UNSCR 2094 (7 March 2013)	• Targeting of illicit activities of diplomatic personnel, including travel bans and asset freezes on key figures.
	• Ban on financial services that might be used to evade sanctions including prohibition of new branches of North Korean banks in member states territories.
	• States authorised to inspect all cargo originating from North Korea.
	• Denial of permission to any aircraft to take off from, land in or overfly their territory if suspected of containing prohibited items.
UNSCR 2270 (2 March 2016)	• All states to inspect cargo within or transiting through their territory (airports, seaports, free trade zones) destined to or originating in North Korea.
	• Prohibition of North Korean nationals and those in their own territories from leasing or chartering their flagged vessels or aircraft to North Korea or providing it with crew services.

Table 8.1 *(cont.)*

	• Ban on use of states' vessels for North Korean purposes, that is, restriction against 'flagship of convenience'. • Ban on North Korea exports of coal, iron, iron ore, gold, titanium ore, vanadium ore and rare earth materials (though with exemption for 'livelihood purposes'). • Ban on sales of aviation fuel to North Korea. • States to expel diplomats involved in sanctions evasion, and a ban on education of North Korean nationals in fields that might assist nuclear/weapons programme.
UNSCR 2321 (30 November 2016)	• North Korean iron and iron ore exports permitted only if for livelihood purposes. • Export bans also placed on copper, nickel, silver and zinc, helicopters, vessels and statues. • Limits on number of bank accounts held by diplomatic missions and consular posts, and on number of diplomats. • Members states to close existing representative offices, subsidiaries, bank accounts in North Korea (humanitarian exception). • Suspension of scientific and technical cooperation (except medical). • More individuals added to travel bans/asset freezes.
UNSCR 2371 (5 August 2017)	• Complete ban on coal, iron, iron ore, lead and lead ore exports and seafood. • Prohibition of new joint ventures with North Korean entities, or the expansion of existing investments. • Individuals and entities added to the travel bans/ asset freezes. • Ban on the hiring of additional North Korean dispatch workers.
UNSCR 2375 (11 September 2017)	• Cap on sales of refined petroleum, crude oil and natural gas liquids to North Korea. • Ban on North Korean textile exports. • Ban on new work permits for overseas North Korean workers. • Ban on existing joint ventures with North Korean entities.
UNSCR 2397 (22 December 2017)	• Limit on North Korean imports of petroleum to 500,000 barrels per year. • Crude oil capped at current levels. • Repatriation of all North Korean workers earning income abroad within 24 months.

Sources: UN Security Council Documents on North Korea www.securitycouncilreport.org/un-documents/dprk-north-korea/ [accessed 24 May 2020].

exports of coal (which were not to exceed either a monetary value of US$ 400.9 million or the volume of 7.5 million tonnes), though it maintained a livelihood exemption for iron and iron ore exports.

UNSC Resolution 2371, passed on 5 August 2017, removed this exemption entirely. Coal, iron and iron ore, lead ore as well as seafood were all banned, and there was a prohibition on new joint ventures with North Korean entities and expansion of existing investments. This removal of the livelihood exemption thus potentially sat at odds with the claim made in Article 26 of Resolution that the measures '. . . are not intended to have adverse humanitarian consequences for the civilian population of the DPRK'. Furthermore, under Resolution 2375, passed on 11 September 2017, quantitative caps were placed on the sales of crude oil, refined petroleum and natural gas liquids to North Korea. Significantly, a ban was also placed on North Korean textile exports and new permits for overseas North Korean workers. Finally, Resolution 2397, passed on 22 December 2017, limited North Korean imports of petroleum to 500,000 barrels per year, capped crude oil at current levels, and called for the repatriation of all North Korean nationals earning income abroad within 24 months. As such, by 2017, UN sanctions had come to target nearly all sectors underpinning Sino–North Korean economic cooperation.

8.2   The Economic Impacts of Sanctions on North Korea

To what extent then have the broad array of unilateral and multilateral sanctions outlined earlier been successful in exerting economic pressure on North Korea? To answer this question, it is first worth considering the broader academic literature on the efficacy of sanctions.[5] Commonly regarded as representative of the optimistic camp in terms of the effectiveness of sanctions, Gary Hufbauer and others conducted a study of 115 cases of largely trade-based sanctions between 1914 and 1990, finding that sanctions were at least partially successful in just 34 per cent of all the cases. As such, the study concluded that sanctions are of limited utility in compelling a target country to take actions it resists, though they noted that the success rate varied in accordance with the type of policy or governmental change sought.[6] Others have argued that even this analysis overstates the success rate of sanctions. Robert Pape, for example, re-examined Haufbauer and others' database and

[5] Gary Clyde Hufbauer, Jeffrey J. Schott and Kimberly Ann Elliott, *Economic Sanctions Reconsidered: History and Current Policy* (Washington, DC: Institute for International Economics, 1990); Robert A. Pape, 'Why Economic Sanctions Do Not Work', *International Security*, 22.2 (1997), pp. 90–136; Robert A. Pape 'Why Economic Sanctions Still Do Not Work', *International Security*, 23.1 (1998), pp. 66–77; Kimberly A. Elliott, 'The Sanctions Glass: Half Full or Completely Empty?', *International Security*, 23.1 (1998), pp. 50–65.

[6] Hufbauer et al., *Economic Sanctions Reconsidered*, pp. 158–59.

argued that almost none of the claimed forty cases of effective economic sanctions can realistically be interpreted as 'successful'.[7]

There are several reasons for the low efficacy of sanctions. For example, the degree to which the sender state is able to ensure that other states, particularly allies, support the sanctions is often seen as crucial to their success.[8] It is rare for a sender state, however, to be able to achieve a complete blockade of a targeted country, since alternative sources of supply and shipment of goods typically undermine the intended effects of sanctions.[9] Powerful or wealthy allies might assume the role of a so-called 'black knight'.[10] Even if sanctions are successfully applied on a multilateral basis, target states often find it relatively easy to evade sanctions. In Johan Galtung's study of Rhodesia in the 1960s, for example, the country's extensive land borders and opportunities for smuggling played a key role in undermining the impact of multilateral sanctions.[11] Evasion strategies often mean that sanctions have unintended outcomes such as the expansion of illicit and criminal economies. In the case of the Federal Republic of Yugoslavia in the 1990s, trade-based sanctions contributed to the criminalisation of the state, economy and civil society of both the targeted country and its immediate neighbours, thereby fostering a symbiosis between political leaders, organised crime and transnational smuggling networks.[12]

Given that they have been in place in some form since the time of the Korean War, the economic impact of US sanctions on the North Korean economy is particularly difficult to measure.[13] The economic exchange between the two countries has historically been minimal, making it difficult to gauge with any level of accuracy the cost of sanctions in relation to 'normal' US–North Korean trade relations. Sanctions imposed in the 2000s by North Korea's erstwhile key trading partners of Japan and South Korea have had a more measurable impact (see Figure 8.1). However, China came to play the role of the 'black knight' vis-à-vis North Korea, with the burgeoning economic relations between the two countries more than compensating for the loss of

---

[7] Pape, 'Why Economic Sanctions Do Not Work', p. 93.

[8] James Mayall, 'The Sanctions Problem in International Economic Relations: Reflections in the Light of Recent Experience', *International Affairs*, 60.4 (1984), p. 639; but see Daniel W. Drezner, 'Bargaining, Enforcement, and Multilateral Sanctions: When Is Cooperation Counterproductive?', *International Organization*, 54.1 (2000), pp. 73–102.

[9] Thomas D. Willett and Mehrdad Jalalighajar, 'U.S. Trade Policy and National Security', *Cato Journal*, 3.3 (1983), p. 723.

[10] Hufbauer, Schott, and Elliott, *Economic Sanctions Reconsidered*, p. 8.

[11] Johan Galtung, 'On the Effects of International Economic Sanctions, With Examples from the Case of Rhodesia', *World Politics*, 19.3 (1967), p. 398.

[12] Peter Andreas, 'Criminalizing Consequences of Sanctions: Embargo Busting and Its Legacy', *International Studies Quarterly*, 49.2 (2005), pp. 335–60.

[13] For an example of one such attempt, see Hafbauer et al., *Economic Sanctions Reconsidered*, p. 116.

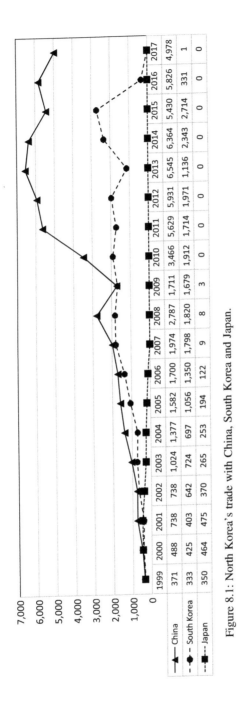

	1999	2000	2001	2002	2003	2004	2005	2006	2007	2008	2009	2010	2011	2012	2013	2014	2015	2016	2017
China	371	488	738	738	1,024	1,377	1,582	1,700	1,974	2,787	1,711	3,466	5,629	5,931	6,545	6,364	5,430	5,826	4,978
South Korea	333	425	403	642	724	697	1,056	1,350	1,798	1,820	1,679	1,912	1,714	1,971	1,136	2,343	2,714	331	1
Japan	350	464	475	370	265	253	194	122	9	8	3	0	0	0	0	0	0	0	0

Figure 8.1: North Korea's trade with China, South Korea and Japan.
(Unit: Million US$).
Sources: Drawn from Chinese Customs data and from the South Korean Ministry of Unification and Korea Trade-Investment Promotion Agency.

227

trade with Japan and South Korea. Until early 2017, North Korea's economic relations with China meant that the country was largely able to escape the negative impact of other trading country's bilateral sanctions.

What then have been the economic impacts of the increasingly stringent UNSC resolutions imposed on North Korea since 2006? On the surface at least, it appears that one of the paradoxes of multilateral sanctions is that they coincided with North Korea's gradual economic recovery and with the expansion of the country's foreign trade. As noted in the previous chapter, between 2006 and 2016, North Korea's trade with China increased from US$ 1.7 billion to US$ 5.8 billion. Available data on the market prices of goods and the exchange rate also suggests a degree of macro-economic stability. To be sure, the high level of inflation following the crisis of the 1990s was a driving force behind dollarisation in the country. Indeed, the economy was adversely affected by the failed currency reforms of 2009, which caused the price of grain and consumer goods to rise sharply and the market value of the won to decline vis-à-vis the dollar. After 2013, however, the market exchange rate remained remarkably stable (see Figure 8.2). The Chinese renminbi also traded in North Korea at around 1,200 won per yuan during the late 2010s.

Food prices also appeared to stabilise, with the price of rice in local markets tending to average out at around 5,000 won per kg (see Figure 8.3). Some seasonal fluctuation existed particularly during the so-called 'lean season' before the harvest, but the tightening of sanctions did not impact the cost of food.[14] Indeed, it can be argued that North Korean food markets actually increased their resilience in the face of strengthened sanctions. While imported foodstuffs from China such as grains, fruits, wheat flour and pork accounted for a significant proportion of the food sold in North Korean markets, domestic produce also saw an increase in quantity and quality. One indicator of the greater availability of food was that, in contrast to the early 2000s, trade in food became one of the least profitable marketplace activities, and instead, trade in clothing, cosmetics and consumer electronics stalls were much more profitable, though these had higher overhead costs such as stall fees.[15] At the same time, there was a steady improvement in socio-economic health indicators in the country. For example, between 2009 and 2017, the prevalence of chronic malnutrition in children under age five, as measured by stunting, fell from 32.4 per cent to 19.1 per cent. Acute malnutrition, as measured by

---

[14] Data on exchange rates and grain prices are provided by Daily NK, and are based on observations in Pyongyang, Sinuiju and Hyesan.

[15] Interviews with North Korean defectors who had previously been market traders in cities such as Hyesan (Ryanggang Province) and Sariwon (North Hwanghae Province), July 2018.

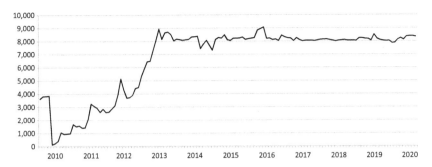

Figure 8.2: Market exchange rate of North Korean won to US dollar.
(Unit: Won/US$).
Source: Daily NK

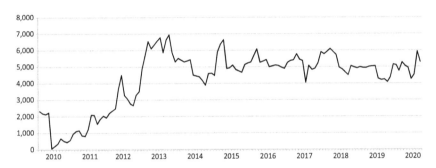

Figure 8.3: Trends in price of high-quality rice.
(Unit: Won/kg).
Source: Daily NK.

wasting, fell from 5.2 per cent to 2.5 per cent.[16] North Korea also saw significant improvements in child mortality, with a decline from 72.8 deaths per 1,000 under five-year-olds in 1998 to 18.2 in 2018.[17]

Until 2017, much of the officially recorded trade consisted of goods that were not yet covered by sanctions, though the growth of North Korea's external trade relations was also facilitated by China's lax enforcement of

[16] Central Bureau of Statistics, *DPRK Multiple Cluster Survey 2009* (Pyongyang: Central Bureau of Statistics, 2010); Central Bureau of Statistics, *DPRK Multiple Cluster Survey 2017* (Pyongyang: Central Bureau of Statistics, 2017).
[17] World Bank, 'World Development Indicators' https://databank.worldbank.org/home.aspx [accessed 24 May 2020].

sanctions. But as UNSC 1718 Sanctions Committee Panel of Experts reports suggest, North Korea also engaged in widespread smuggling. This included, for example, North Korean arms exports to raise foreign currency as well as the import of components and materials related to its nuclear programme. The country also continued to engage in the import of luxury goods. This illicit trade typically involved deceptive practices including false description and mislabelling of shipments alongside the use of intermediaries and shell companies. Evasive techniques were also deployed to disguise financial transactions through use of overseas entities, shell companies, informal transfer mechanisms, cash couriers and barter arrangements. Prohibited activities were often conducted through otherwise legitimate commercial networks using aliases, agents, offices and complicit companies. Designated entities and banks continued to operate through the use of non-DPRK national agents with experience in moving money, people and goods. Such activities were also facilitated by North Korean diplomats, officials and trade representatives based overseas. Indeed, diplomatic missions have provided logistical support for arms transfers, military technicians and intelligence operations, acting as fronts for designated entities and individuals and engaging in commercial activities.[18]

Much of this trade was in goods and services that might otherwise be regarded as legitimate for countries not under sanctions. However, accusations have long been made that North Korea engaged in the smuggling of strictly illegal goods such as narcotics, counterfeit goods as well as fake banknotes.[19] As Rudiger Frank has argued, these activities reflect in part the denial of legal channels for North Korea to acquire much needed hard currency. Given the regime's strong normative emphasis on ideology and moral superiority, the trade involves a clear reputational loss and reflects the fact that North Korea views itself as having no other choice.[20] Haggard and Noland note, however, that due to the greater scrutiny of North Korea's external activities as well as the expansion of legitimate Sino–North Korean trade, this trade in overtly illegal goods likely saw a decline after 2006.[21] With the imposition of sectoral sanctions from 2017, however, it remained to be seen to what the impact of the closing off of legitimate trade channels had on this trade.

---

[18] See Panel of Expert Reports: S/2010/571, S/2012/422, S/2013/337, S/2014/147, S/2015/131, S/2016/157, S2017/150.

[19] Justin V. Hastings, *A Most Enterprising Country: North Korea in the Global Economy* (Ithaca: Cornell University Press, 2016). For a critical engagement with such accusations, see Smith, *North Korea,* pp. 36–39.

[20] Ruediger Frank, 'The Political Economy of Sanctions Against North Korea', *Asian Perspective,* 30.3 (2006), pp. 30–31.

[21] Stephan Haggard and Marcus Noland, *Hard Target: Sanctions, Inducements, and the Case of North Korea* (Stanford, CA: Stanford University Press, 2017), pp. 85–86.

In recent years, financial sanctions have been promoted as capable of inflicting considerable costs on the economies of target states.[22] These sanctions work by pressuring banks rather than governments to act as agents of international isolation. Typically, banks are expected to observe the US Treasury watchlists and block suspicious assets and transactions, thereby cutting individuals and organisations off from the global financial system. As seen in the case of Banco Delta Asia, reputational concerns regarding the danger of being labelled a 'money laundering concern' mean that US and non-US banks alike have strong motivations to adhere to the watchlists, even when they are not required to do so by domestic or international law.[23] Yet by closing off legitimate channels of trade settlement, North Korean firms and government agencies expanded their use of informal methods of cross-border trade and trade settlement. Indeed, the overall impact of these actions was that North Korea's ability to engage in financial dealings with the outside world was curtailed and that traders increased their reliance on secretive financial transactions as an evasive measure.[24] Even UN agencies and European NGOs conducting humanitarian work in North Korea have been affected, as many of these organisations had relied on Chinese or European banks to make transfers to North Korea's Foreign Trade Bank for payments related to their operations.[25]

8.3   The Political Impact of Sanctions

Even if sanctions succeed in exerting a significant economic impact on the target state, sanctions cannot be said to 'work' unless that impact translates into the desired political outcomes. The assumption that economic hardship will in itself force policy change or even lead to the overthrow of the government is overly simplistic. Sanctions can indeed elicit unintended responses from targeted populations. Again, as Galtung argued in his study of Rhodesia, sanctions may induce a 'rally round the flag' effect within the target country and thereby strengthen rather than weaken political unity.[26] Furthermore, if sanctions succeed in bringing hardship to the population but fail to induce regime change, the sender country or the international community as a whole

---

[22] Akbar E. Torbat, 'Impacts of the US Trade and Financial Sanctions on Iran', *The World Economy*, 28.3 (2005), pp. 407–34.

[23] Rachel L. Loeffler, 'Bank Shots: How the Financial System Can Isolate Rogues', *Foreign Affairs*, 88.2 (2009), pp. 101–10.

[24] See Lee and Gray, 'Cause for Optimism?'

[25] Daniel Wertz, 'The Evolution of Financial Sanctions on North Korea', *North Korean Review*, 9.2 (2013), pp. 76–77.

[26] Galtung, 'Effects of International Economic Sanctions', p. 389; see also David M. Rowe, *Manipulating the Market: Understanding Economic Sanctions, Institutional Change, and the Political Unity of White Rhodesia* (Ann Arbor: University of Michigan Press, 2001).

might be explicitly regarded by that population as engaging in imperialistic behaviour. As Adeno Addis argues, target regimes may successfully shift the blame for their economic mismanagement onto the international community. Indeed, sanctions do in reality often fail to make a distinction between the state and its people, treating both as outlaws.[27] Target states can in the face of sanctions also adopt strategies of restructuring the domestic economy, for example, through focusing on domestic production rather than on external trade. If such efforts fail, sanctions provide a convenient scapegoat, but if they succeed, these efforts can be presented as proof of local ingenuity.[28] Sanctions may also induce more of the aggressive or repressive behaviour that they are often designed to deter through impacting upon the domestic balance of forces within the target state. Even the most authoritarian governments are typically influenced by a diverse range of inner views, meaning that sanctions are as likely to strengthen the hand of hawks as they are the hand of doves, and as such, they may serve to increase the possibility of further aggressive behaviour.[29]

In the North Korean case, stringent sanctions appeared to contribute to a renewed commitment to self-reliance, despite simultaneous commitment to economic reform measures. In his 2015 New Year's speech, for example, Kim Jong Un spoke of the need to counter what he saw as the 'import disease' (*suibbyŏng*). The context of international sanctions notwithstanding, this domestic production campaign was in many respects an extension of the strategy pursued by Kim Il Sung in the 1960s. Much was made in the official media of successes in the production of 'Juche steel', the domestic production of nitrogen fertiliser and the spread of Computer Numerical Control (CNC) in the machinery industry.[30] However, considering that these aims had been continuously promoted since the Kim Jong Il era and that North Korea continued to lack the funds necessary for the recovery of its capital-intensive infrastructure, such claims of success are dubious.

Indeed, in sectors dependent on capital and advanced technology, product quality remained poor and foreign imports still dominated the market. This led to increased emphasis by the authorities on technological upgrading on the basis of domestic resources. In his 2018 New Year's address, Kim Jong Un stated that '... [t]he scientific research sector should prioritise the resolution of

[27] Adeno Addis, 'Economic Sanctions and the Problem of Evil', *Human Rights Quarterly*, 25.3 (2003), pp. 611–612.
[28] Galtung 'Effects of International Economic Sanctions', pp. 393–96.
[29] Willett and Jalalighajar, 'U.S. Trade Policy and National Security', p. 725.
[30] *Rodong Sinmun*, 12 April 2018, 'The Cabinet's work in Juche Year 106 (2017) and tasks for Juche Year 107 (2018) for the implementation of the Five-Year Strategy of National Economic Development [Kukkagyŏngjebalchŏn 5 kaenyŏn chŏllyaksuhaengŭl wihan naegagŭi chuch'e 106 (2017 nyŏn) saŏpchŏnghyŏnggwa chuch'e 107(2018nyŏn) kwaŏbe taehayŏ]'.

the scientific and technological problems arising in the establishment of *Juche*-oriented production in our own style, ensuring the domestic production of raw and other materials and equipment, and perfecting the structure of the self-supporting economy'.[31] As such, government policy was to direct production units as well as universities and research institutes towards the goal of import substitution, with a strong emphasis on 'the unification of science and technology with production'.[32] In addition, the revised Enterprise Law of 2014 explicitly stated the aim of actively promoting new technologies and products through the granting of greater product development rights to enterprises. The Law also emphasised enterprises' technological innovation and provided incentives for employees' technical training and the development of their creativity.[33]

Successes in import substitution were more apparent in the light industrial sector, though this can arguably be explained with reference to ongoing processes of marketisation and enterprise reform rather than the state's facilitative role *per se*. Anecdotal evidence suggests, for example, that domestic products gradually replaced Chinese imports at marketplaces and retail outlets. *Choson Sinbo* reported that in Pyongyang's Kwangbok Area Commerce Centre, around 60 per cent of the merchandise in 2012 was sourced from China, whereas in January 2018, around 70 per cent of goods were domestically produced.[34] Furthermore, the quality of domestically manufactured goods reportedly improved, with foodstuffs and clothing proving popular with North Korean consumers.

As such, the authorities actively sought to mitigate the impact of sanctions. What then was the potential for sanctions to achieve their goals? As noted, for sanctions to be regarded as successful, they not only need to exert a negative economic impact on the target country but also need to lead to the desired policy change. One potential mechanism whereby sanctions might be expected to 'work' is by exploiting divisions amongst elites and strengthening the hand of those who favour the desired policy change. Some scholars have indeed

---

[31] *Rodong Sinmun*, 1 January 2018, 'New Year's Speech – Kim Jung Un'.

[32] Joung Chun Shim, 'An Important Issue in Realising the Nationalization of Production of Facilities and Raw Materials in All Sectors of the People's Economy [Inmin'gyŏngje modŭn pumunesŏ sŏlbi, wŏllyo chajaeŭi kuksanhwarŭl sirhyŏnhanŭndesŏ nasŏnŭn chungyomunje]', *Journal of Kim Il Sung University Philosophy, Economics*, 62.2 (2016), pp. 68–71.

[33] DPRK Enterprise Law (Revised 5 November 2014) contained several specific clauses related with the science and technology, including Article 6 (the *Juche*-isation of management activities, modernisation, the principle of science and technology), Article 34 (the development of production), Article 36 (the nurturing of talent), Article 41 (the development projects of science and technology) and Article 42 (technological innovation).

[34] *Choson Sinbo*, 22 January 2018, 'A commercial area favoured by the people – competition between department stores for higher level service [Inmindŭri chŭlgyŏch'annŭn sangŏpkongganŭro – poda sujunnop'ŭn pongsarŭl wihan paekhwajŏmdŭrŭi kyŏngjaeng]'.

identified divisions within policymaking elites that might potentially form the basis of such splits.[35] However, such analyses have largely been applied to the Kim Jong Il era, with little evidence to suggest that such divisions exist under the incumbent Kim Jong Un regime.[36] Furthermore, to the extent that such divisions have been identified, they relate not to the specific issue of the development of nuclear weapons but rather more generally to the priority given to security versus economic reform.

A more modest goal of sanctions is that they will deprive the North Korean regime of the funds needed to support its nuclear programme. However, North Korea is already the lowest spending nuclear state in the world today.[37] The regime claims with some justification that the development of nuclear weapons is a cheaper option than the modernisation of its conventional forces. As Kim Jong Un argued in 2013, 'the *Pyŏngjin* line will strengthen the nation's defence capability at low cost without the increase of defence expenditure, while turning great energy towards economic construction and the improvement of the people's livelihood'.[38] Indeed, despite the marked acceleration of its nuclear weapons programme in 2017, there did not appear to have been a major shift in the portion of the national budget devoted to defence. The state budget recorded defence spending at 15.8 per cent in 2017 and 15.9 per cent in 2018, thereby at a level broadly similar to that of the early 2010s.[39] As such, the level of economic stress that would likely be required to starve the country's nuclear weapons programme of funds is likely to be unattainable, at least without significant humanitarian costs. A further widespread assumption regarding the impact of sanctions is that such economic stress on the population may cause the North Korean public to rebel against the state and potentially facilitate regime change from within. However, the fact that civil society in North Korea has been eliminated to an arguably unparalleled degree does not bode well for such a scenario.[40] Given that the country experienced

---

[35] McEachern, *Inside the Red Box*; Robert L. Carlin and Joel S. Wit, 'Debate and Policy Formation', *The Adelphi Papers*, 46.382 (2006), pp. 15–19.

[36] Patrick McEachern, 'Centralizing North Korean Policymaking under Kim Jong Un', *Asian Perspective*, 43.1 (2019), pp. 35–67.

[37] The International Campaign to Abolish Nuclear Weapons (ICAN) www.icanw.org/the-facts/catastrophic-harm/a-diversion-of-public-resources/ [accessed 24 May 2020].

[38] *Rodong Sinmun*, 2 April 2013, 'The report given by Respected Comrade Kim Jong Un at the March 2013 Plenum of the KWP Central Committee [Kyŏngaehanŭn Kimjŏngŭn tongjikkesŏ chosŏnnodongdang chungangwiwŏnhoe 2013 nyŏn 3 wŏl chŏnwŏnhoeŭiesŏ hasin pogo]'.

[39] *Rodong Sinmun*, 12 April 2018 'On the results of the execution of DPRK's Juche Year 106 (2017) budget and the state budget for Juche Year 107 (2018) [Chosŏnminjujuŭi Inmin'gonghwaguk chuch'e 106 (2017) nyŏn kukkayesanjip'aengŭi kyŏlsan'gwa chuch'e 107 (2018) nyŏn kukkayesane taehayŏ]'.

[40] Antonio Fiori and Sunhyuk Kim, 'Jasmine Does Not Bloom in Pyongyang: The Persistent Non-Transition in North Korea', *Pacific Focus*, 29.1 (2014), 44–67.

widespread starvation in the 1990s with only sporadic overt resistance suggests that this is not a likely scenario.

Indeed, the relative improvement of the economy since the 2010s might in any case undermine the potential for resistance against the state. According to a 2017 report by Daily NK, an outlet by no means sympathetic to North Korea, the broader economic improvements in the country meant that '... [a]s rates of absolute poverty and malnourishment have declined, so too have overall living standards risen, and dissatisfaction with the government dropped'.[41] There is certainly evidence to suggest that as marketisation progressed, market traders increasingly engaged in small isolated incidents of unrest. These tended, however, to be related to defending trading rights and protecting income rather than constituting any substantive challenge to the regime itself.[42] As we discuss below, the Trump administration's 'maximum pressure' campaign from 2017 had more noticeable economic impacts on North Korea. Yet the question remains how economic pressure translates into political outcomes. As noted above, sanctions can, in fact, strengthen the regime's narrative of a hostile external environment, potentially producing a 'rally round the flag' effect whereby foreign powers can credibly be blamed for domestic economic hardship. The North Korean regime clearly propagated this message domestically, but in the absence of public opinion polling, it can only be speculated as to the extent to which the North Korean public supported the regime and to which they believed that their economic difficulties were a result of sanctions.

8.4   Sanctions under 'Maximum Pressure'

The onset of the Trump administration in 2017 coincided with a marked tightening of the international sanctions against North Korea. In terms of multilateral UN sanctions, this involved a shift from smart sanctions back towards more comprehensive trade sanctions. On paper at least, the broad measures outlined in UNSC Resolutions 2321, 2371, 2375 and 2397 had the potential to have an adverse effect on people's livelihood through targeting North Korean mineral, seafood and textile exports, restricting energy sales to North Korea, as well as banning the dispatch on North Korean workers overseas. Certainly, the sanctions were aimed at placing significant economic pressure on the country, mainly through the drastic reduction in North Korea's foreign currency earnings and subsequent decline in its imports. Any attempt to restrict energy imports, for example, could not but have an impact on the North Korean people themselves. While the military was likely to have access

---

[41] In Ho Park, 'The Creation of the North Korean Market System', (Seoul: Daily NK, 2017), p. 12.
[42] Andrew Jackson, 'Why Has There Been No People's Power Rebellion in North Korea?', *European Journal of Korean Studies*, 18.1 (2018), pp. 14–15.

to considerable stockpiles of oil, ordinary citizens would not.[43] Textile manufacturing was a significant employer of North Korean women, with the most recent census showing that nearly 400,000 workers were employed in the apparel manufacturing sector, with 87 per cent of those female workers.[44] Though the confiscation of passports and restriction of movement of North Korean workers abroad have led to accusations of 'slave labour' in the mainstream media, there was nonetheless strong competition for these jobs. Again, the majority of dispatched workers working in restaurants and labour-intensive clothing factories were women. North Koreans had a strong preference for overseas work due to the higher levels of pay, and they often paid bribes to the managers of the trading companies in order to be selected for such work.[45] Returning workers typically invested their earnings and brought back goods for sale in North Korea's general markets, thereby contributing to marketisation and the rise of an entrepreneurial class.[46]

The key question, however, is the extent to which these new sanctions were enforced. As noted, China's lax enforcement of multilateral sanctions had frequently been cited as a key factor in sanctions' ineffectiveness. This led the Trump administration to promote the so-called 'China responsibility theory' in dealing with the North Korean nuclear programme. This approach was supported by the threat of secondary US sanctions against Chinese entities that have dealings with North Korea, which may have played a key role in China's more proactive enforcement of UN sanctions from 2017. Yet, China's increased willingness to enforce sanctions against North Korea was also a response to the fact that Pyongyang's continued development of nuclear weapons appeared to be drawing counter-responses from the United States and its allies that were opposed to China's interests. Beijing, for example, reacted vociferously to the deployment of the Terminal High Altitude Area Defence (THAAD) missile system in South Korea in 2017. Though ostensibly a defensive system, China's main objections to THAAD were that the United States would be able to use its radar system to look deep into Chinese territory and that its deployment would form part of a broader regional missile system aiming at encircling China. In this respect, Beijing's objections were reminiscent of the Soviet Union's objection to the US deployment of anti-ballistic

---

[43] Peter Hayes and David Von Hippel, 'Sanctions on North Korean Oil Imports: Impacts and Efficacy', *Nautilus Peace and Security Special Report*, 2017. https://nautilus.org/napsnet/napsnet-special-reports/sanctions-on-north-korean-oil-imports-impacts-and-efficacy/ [accessed 25 May 2020].

[44] DPRK Central Bureau of Statistics, *DPRK 2008 Population Census National Report*, p. 193.

[45] Interviews with North Korean defectors previously engaged in foreign trade and labour dispatch, May and June 2018.

[46] Andrei Lankov, 'North Korean Workers Abroad Aren't Slaves'.

missiles (ABM) that led to the 1972 ABM Treaty.[47] Increased tensions between Beijing and Washington over trade also arguably diminished the former's willingness to resist the latter's pressures over North Korea. In sum, North Korea's development of nuclear weapons came to be seen as having particularly negative implications for China's regional security, thereby undermining North Korea's traditional role as a buffer state.

Thus, on 18 February 2017, Beijing announced that, on the basis of the UNSC Resolution 2321, the quota for coal imports from North Korea that year had already been reached, and that further imports would be banned for the rest of the year. As a result, Chinese Customs statistics show a sharp drop in monthly imports of coal to zero in 2017. Although North Korea's 2017 imports recorded a slight increase in value, the collapse in mineral exports to China led to a sharp decline in overall trade from late 2017 onwards. The Chinese authorities also took measures against its own enterprises with dealings with North Korea. In September 2016, for example, Beijing took the unusual step of launching an investigation into a Chinese company, the Dandong Hongxiang Industrial Development Corporation, one of the largest trading companies dealing with North Korea and one suspected by the United States of flouting sanctions.[48]

In 2018, China's official imports from North Korea for the year dropped to just US$ 195 million, a decline of 88.2 per cent on the previous year. Chinese exports to North Korea also fell by about 33.4 per cent, with the annual volume of total Sino–North Korean trade in 2018 declining by more than half to just US$ 2.4 billion.[49] This decline in trade coincided with Beijing's restrictions on investment by Chinese firms in North Korea and on local government involvement in cross-border economic cooperation projects. Chinese tourism to North Korea also saw periodic crackdowns, despite the fact that tourism remained outside the scope of UN sanctions. There is little doubt, however, that widespread smuggling and illicit trade continued to take place. As the Panel of Experts reported, this included continued coal exports, typically involving transhipment via the Russian Far East. Multiple evasion techniques, routes and deceptive shipping tactics were deployed, including manipulation of Automatic Identification Systems, loitering, voyage deviations and fraudulent documentation. Ship-to-ship transfers of petroleum also took place.[50] Other

---

[47] Mark Tokola, 'Why Is China so Upset about THAAD?', *Korea Economic Institute of America Website*, 2017 http://keia.org/why-china-so-upset-about-thaad [accessed 19 October 2018].

[48] *New York Times*, 20 September 2016, 'China Announces Inquiry Into Company Trading with North Korea'.

[49] China Customs data drawn from the Korea International Trade Association database.

[50] Report of the Panel of Experts established pursuant to resolution 1874 (2009), 5 March 2018. www.un.org/ga/search/view_doc.asp?symbol=S/2018/171 [accessed 24 May 2020].

measures, such as the ban on joint ventures with North Korean entities, proved difficult to implement, as the Chinese government was simply unable to keep track of the activities of small-scale traders and businesspeople in the border regions. On the ground reports at the August 2018 Rason International Trade Fair, for example, suggest that there was no shortage of interest from Chinese investors, many of whom appeared to be unaware of the details of the most recent sanctions and the restrictions on investment.[51]

One potential source of evidence on the overall impact of the sanctions on the North Korean economy is the annual GDP estimates made by South Korea's central bank, the Bank of Korea. The sudden drop from an estimated growth rate of 3.9 per cent in 2016 to −3.5 per cent in 2017 and −4.1 per cent in 2018 was widely interpreted as an outcome of the sanctions. This decline was underpinned by a sharp contraction in particular of the mining sector and heavy and chemical industries as well as construction sector[52] Though questions have long been raised about the reliability of the Bank of Korea's estimates, it seems logical that the marked strengthening of sanctions negatively affected the growth of North Korea's major economic sectors. This impact also appeared to cause problems for the Five-Year Strategy for National Economic Development from 2016. As Premier Pak Bong Ju remarked at the 6th Meeting of the 13th Supreme People's Assembly in April 2018, 'there were serious deficiencies in the Cabinet's work last year'.[53]

Despite the dramatic decline in North Korean exports and the growing trade deficit, the market exchange rate remained remarkably stable. How Pyongyang managed to maintain the stability of the exchange rate amidst such a drastic contraction of trade is indeed something of a puzzle. One argument has been that Pyongyang's monetary authorities, mindful of the social unrest caused by the 2009 currency reform, were keeping a close eye on the informal exchange rate and may have intervened by spending its reserves of dollars and renminbi.[54] There is little concrete evidence for such speculation, however, and the longer the currency remains stable, the less convincing such an explanation appears. Prices of a range of market goods also remained stable and fluctuations in food prices continued to be seasonal rather than related to sanctions.

---

[51] Andray Abrahamian, 'The Sanctions Effect in North Korea: Observations from Rason', *38 North*, 2018 www.38north.org/2018/10/aabrahamian101918/ [accessed 20 October 2018].

[52] Bank of Korea, Economic Statistics System http://ecos.bok.or.kr/ [accessed 24 May 2020].

[53] *Rodong Sinmun,* 12 April 2018, 'The Cabinet's work in Juche Year 106 (2017) and tasks for Juche Year 107 (2018) for the implementation of the Five-Year Strategy of National Economic Development [Kukkagyŏngjebalchŏn 5 kaenyŏn chŏllyaksuhaengǔl wihan naegagǔi chuch'e 106 (2017 nyŏn) saŏpchŏnghyŏnggwa chuch'e 107(2018nyŏn) kwaŏbe taehayŏ]'.

[54] William B. Brown, *North Korea's Shackled Economy, 2018* (Washington, DC: National Committee on North Korea, 2018), p. 16.

Reporting by outlets such as Daily NK alongside our interviews with North Korean defectors and Chinese traders provides further anecdotal evidence as to the impacts of sanctions. While it is important to avoid overgeneralising from individual reports, they suggest that sanctions did have an impact although this was not uniform and varied according to economic sector, region and social class. On the one hand, the number of taxis and private servi-cars increased despite fluctuations in fuel prices, while competition continued to grow in the retail and service sectors.[55] However, the ban on mineral exports unsurprisingly had a negative impact on mining regions, and in particular, on miners and their families in the sector. Restaurant managers, transport operators and sellers of consumer goods in coal-producing regions also saw a sharp drop in their profits. The embargo on iron ore in late 2017 reportedly led to an almost complete halt in production at Musan Mine. However, at the same time, it has been reported that sanctions led to more coal being supplied to North Korean power plants and thus to an improved electricity supply.[56] It should be noted, however, that minerals such as coal remained subject to state pricing and thus the scope for replacing foreign markets with the domestic market was limited. Even large-scale 'basic mines' (*kibont'an'gwang*) within the state sector exported a portion of their output to earn the foreign exchange needed to cover their running costs, and as such, they too were likely to be negatively impacted by the sanctions.[57] Textiles and seafood on the other hand are sold at market prices and thus there was in theory more scope for redirection towards the domestic market.

However, anecdotal reports by Daily NK suggest that the drastic reduction in North Korea's external trade had a negative impact on marketplace activities.[58] This is seemingly contradicted by their own market data that suggests continued stability of market prices. However, the fact that dollarisation means that market prices are largely denominated in foreign currency and that Chinese and North Korean markets for non-sanctioned essential items are well integrated, it is possible that supply quickly adapted to changes in demand resulting from the reduction in the public's purchasing power.[59] In this respect,

---

[55] Interviews with North Korean defectors in Seoul (June and July 2018).

[56] *Daily NK*, 19 September 2018, 'Sanctions on coal exports lead to improvements in electricity supply'.

[57] Lim Soo-Ho, 'Sanctions on North Korea in the Medium to Long Term: the Influence of Sanctions on Coal and Iron Ore Exports on the Domestic Economy of North Korea [Taebukchejaeŭi chungjanggi hyogwa: sŏkt'an ch'ŏlgwangsŏk such'ulchejaega Pukhan naesugyŏngjee mich'inŭn yŏnghyang]' in *KDI Review of the North Korean Economy*, 21.12 2019, pp. 18–19.

[58] *Daily NK*, 9 August 2019, 'Sanctions lead to continued stagnation of North Korea's markets'; *Daily NK*, 11 November 2018, 'Sanctions hit North Korea's South Pyongan Province hard'; *Daily NK*, 25 April 2019, 'Pyongyang's economy faces possible stagnation'.

[59] Lee Seok, 'Summary: the North Korean Economy in 2018, in Crisis or Holding Up? [Ch'onggwal: 2018 nyŏn Pukhan'gyŏngje, wigiin'ga pŏt'igiin'ga]' in *KDI Review of the North Korean Economy*, 21.2 2019, p. 22.

the slowdown of the construction sector may be a more reliable indicator of the state of the market economy in North Korea. High-quality apartments in Pyongyang's Central District that were reportedly selling for US$200,000– US$300,000 in June 2018 had declined by more than US$50,000 by August that year, with sanctions and a resulting shortage of capital amongst potential buyers cited as a key factor.[60] As such, the decline in the price of real estate might indicate a decline in the public's purchasing power, since the supply of housing cannot quickly adapt to reduced consumer demand.

There is also evidence to suggest that sanctions had a negative impact on agricultural production in the country. In May 2019, the World Food Programme (WFP) released a Joint Rapid Food Security Assessment, which noted that droughts followed by flooding in 2018 had led to a 12 per cent decline in the harvest compared to the previous year's near-average level, thereby the lowest level since the 2008/09 season. As a result, 10.1 million North Korean citizens were placed in the category of being 'food insecure'. Though this reflects long-term issues in North Korean agriculture and its vulnerability to climatic events, the WFP's report also highlighted the impact of sanctions on the agricultural sector's poor performance. As the report states, recent sanctions impeded the import of items essential for agricultural production, such as fuel, fertilisers, machinery and spare parts for equipment. Shortages of fuel, electricity and pumping equipment had a negative impact on irrigation, thereby reducing yields and making crops susceptible to extreme weather. The level of mechanisation was also undermined by ageing machinery and lack of spare parts and fuel, thereby increasing reliance on animal and human labour. The resulting delays in production reduced the possibilities for double cropping and increase post-harvest losses. Lack of energy, ageing machinery and the lack of spare parts also created problems in the processing of food, thereby negatively impacting storage life and the availability of food during the lean months.[61]

The strengthening of sanctions also coincided with a decline in humanitarian assistance to North Korea. As shown in Figure 8.4, after 2013 humanitarian aid to North Korea remained below US$ 50 million, thereby reaching only about 30 per cent of requested funds. Assistance was thereby limited to the most basic humanitarian projects targeting vulnerable groups. It should be noted that this decline was also a result of the lessening urgency of the food crisis, declining levels of goodwill towards the country due to its nuclear programme, as well as frustrations with the North Korean government over restrictions on

---

[60] *Daily NK*, 12 October 2018, 'Buyers disappear as apartment prices plummet in Sinuiju, North Korea'.
[61] FAO and WFP, 'Democratic People's Republic of Korea FAO/WFP Joint Rapid Food Security Assessment', (Bangkok: FAO and WFP, 2019).

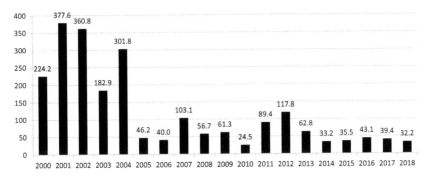

Figure 8.4: Trends in international humanitarian aid to North Korea.
(Unit: Million US$).
Sources: the data drawn from the United Nations Office for the Coordination of
Humanitarian Affairs, Financial Tracking Service http://fts.unocha.org [accessed
24 May 2020].

the distribution and monitoring of aid. Nonetheless, as a recent UN report
argues, sanctions were having adverse consequences for the civilian population. Humanitarian activities were often significantly delayed and disrupted,
notably due to risk perceptions relating to sanctions violation on the part of
banks, suppliers and officials. Aid agencies were unable to transfer funds into
the country and the reluctance of suppliers and transport companies to transport goods into North Korea led to breakdowns in supply chains. Sanctions
thereby added to reluctance amongst donors to provide funds to North
Korea.[62] Indeed, sanctions severely problematised the import of items needed
for humanitarian goods in North Korea. The UN mechanism for case-by-case
humanitarian exemptions was also inadequate. Requests for exemptions made
by humanitarian organisations typically involved delays of months and long
lead times, thereby significantly impeding the work of such organisations.
Furthermore, Pyongyang was held responsible for the needs of the population
yet was not itself able to apply for exemptions.[63] Unilateral measures by states
also impeded the work of humanitarian organisations. South Korea's May 24th
measures effectively placed an embargo on humanitarian aid, while the US
travel ban on American citizens to the country severely constrained the ability
of US-based NGOs to provide assistance.

---

[62] DPRK Humanitarian Country Team, '2018 DPR Korea Needs and Priorities', p. 8 https://
dprkorea.un.org/sites/default/files/2019-07/unct_kp_NP2018.pdf [Accessed 11 January 2021].
[63] Henri Feron, Ewa Eriksson, Kevin Gray, Suzy Kim, Marie O'Reilly, Kee Park and Joy Yoon.
'The Human Costs and Gendered Impact of Sanctions on North Korea'. Korea Peace Now!,
October 2019, pp. 10–11 https://dprkorea.un.org/sites/default/files/2019-07/unct_kp_NP2018
.pdf [accessed 11 January 2021].

Sanctions under maximum pressure, therefore, appeared to have a negative impact upon the North Korean economy, even if they were no closer to forcing the regime to relinquish its nuclear weapons programme. However, the year 2018 saw the North Korean leadership embark upon an unprecedented diplomatic overture to both South Korea and the United States, raising the possibility that sanctions were finally forcing Pyongyang's hand. Certainly, one of the key demands made by Pyongyang was that negotiations over denuclearisation should be accompanied by sanctions relief. Furthermore, there was some evidence that year of the shifting priorities of the North Korean state. In April, for example, there was a transition in rhetoric at least from the *Pyŏngjin* dual line of nuclear weapons and economic development towards a sole emphasis on economic goals.[64] At the same time, Pyongyang was strongly critical of sanctions. As a *Rodong Sinmun* editorial on 2 October 2018 stated, 'What the U.S. should clearly know is that sanctions and pressure cannot work on the DPRK. Sanctions and dialogue can never go together. It is a contradiction that the United States is talking about the dialogue with its partner while ratcheting up sanctions and pressure on it.'[65]

It was unclear, however, whether in fact sanctions really were forcing Pyongyang to reconsider its nuclear policy. Negotiations between North Korea and the United States quickly becoming bogged down in familiar issues of the sequencing of mutual concessions, an issue that has frequently derailed talks in the past.[66] The failure of the Hanoi Summit in February 2019 suggested at the very least that while sanctions may have played some role in bringing North Korea to the table, they failed to induce Pyongyang to abandon its nuclear weapons as a precondition for such relief. If Pyongyang continued to regard denuclearisation as a price too large to pay for sanctions relief, then it is difficult to speak of sanctions having 'worked' in any substantive sense.

Despite the deadlock of the US–North Korea negotiations, 2018 did appear to see some relaxation of Chinese pressure on North Korea. Media reports suggested that following Kim Jong Un's summit with Xi Jinping in March, customs inspections in Dandong were already being reduced. Whereas customs officers had been checking each item with x-ray scans, they were now only searching around half of all vehicles.[67] Furthermore, the summits

---

[64] *Rodong Sinmun*, 21 April 2018, 'At the Third Plenum of the 7th KWP Central Committee, Kim Jong Un, Chairman of the KWP, proudly declares the great victory of the *Pŏngjin* Line and proposes a new strategic direction for the Party [Chosŏnnodongdang chungangwiwŏnhoe che 7 ki che 3 ch'a chŏnwŏnhoeŭi chinhaeng Chosŏnnodongdang wiwŏnjang Kimjŏngŭn tongjikkesŏ pyŏngjillosŏnŭi widaehan sŭngnirŭl kŭngjinop'i sŏnŏnhagigo tangŭi saeroun chŏllyakchŏk rosŏnŭl chesihasiyŏtta]'.

[65] *Rodong Sinmun*, 2 October 2018, 'Sanctions and Dialogue Can Never Go Together'.

[66] Haggard and Noland, *Hard Target*, p. 190.

[67] *Radio Free Asia*, 15 June 2018, 'China Relaxes Customs Inspections on Border with North Korea, Despite Sanctions Assurances'.

also created widespread expectations concerning potential economic engagement with North Korea. During his visits to China in 2018, Kim Jong Un visited sites symbolising the achievements of China's reform and opening, such as Beijing's special economic zones. This created expectations that North Korea would open up externally and that there would be a revitalisation of Sino–North Korean economic cooperation. Following the third inter-Korean summit, South Korea's Moon Jae-In government also moved towards launching a set of ambitious economic projects aimed at integrating both Koreas to the Asian mainland, though with the risk of causing frictions with the United States over whether this would violate existing sanctions. Even President Trump himself publicly commented on North Korea's prospects for economic development and the active support of the United States in that process. Whether these ambitious plans come to fruition depends greatly on diplomacy between North Korea and the United States, though it does seem though that the warming of relations with China at least creates the potential for the cross-border economy to return to its pre-2017 form.

8.5   Conclusion

International sanctions constituted a key mechanism whereby geopolitical contestation served to shape North Korea's developmental trajectory. Yet, their precise impacts were complex and often counter-intuitive. Indeed, there is little evidence to suggest that until 2017, sanctions exerted any measurable macroeconomic shock on North Korea. US, South Korean and Japanese bilateral sanctions mainly served to increase North Korea's economic reliance on China. Indeed, the strengthening of multilateral sanctions since 2006 alongside China's lax enforcement of those sanctions underpinned a tentative period of economic recovery. This was aided by ongoing marketisation and the government's reform of economic management. Sanctions did, however, serve to intensify informal and illicit trading practices. International sanctions also led the Kim Jong Un regime to place increased emphasis on the nationalisation of production, thereby potentially ameliorating the impact of sanctions to some degree. Overall, the North Korean case confirms the general scepticism in the literature on the efficacy of sanctions and their limited scope for inducing political change or a shift in the country's nuclear policy.

In this chapter, we have also examined the extent to which the tightening of sanctions under Trump's maximum pressure campaign impacted the North Korean economy. The evidence is mixed. Key indicators such as trade and GDP estimates suggest a significant impact, although price and exchange rate data appear relatively stable. There is also anecdotal evidence to suggest that certain regions, sectors and social strata were negatively impacted. However, there is continued widespread evasion of sanctions, and even where sanctions have caused economic stress, they did not force the authorities to abandon its nuclear programme. While North Korea's turn towards diplomacy in 2018 led to views in some quarters that sanctions were indeed working, Pyongyang's negotiations with Washington quickly became bogged down in familiar issues of the sequencing of any potential *quid pro quo* agreement. Furthermore, sanctions continued to be interpreted by the North Korean leadership as part of the 'hostile policy' facing the country and adopted strategies that sought to mitigate the effects of that hostility.

Conclusion

At its most fundamental level, development refers to a long-term historical project of the liberation of peoples and nations from the vestiges of colonialism, poverty, oppression and underdevelopment. For states emerging from periods of colonial rule, development has typically taken the form of nationalist projects involving the mobilisation of resources by means of a strong interventionist state for the purposes of 'catching up' with the advanced industrialised countries. In this sense, the late developmental project can be seen as a reflection of the fundamental inequalities of the international system and as a conscious attempt to achieve security and overcome those inequalities. There has, however, been great variation in terms of the extent to which such projects of national development have been successful. That variation cannot be explained solely with reference to the domestic internal attributes of the individual states concerned or as a result of generalised notions of dependency. Rather, the substantive character of projects of national development can be explained only with reference to their mutually constitutive relations with broader processes of geopolitical contestation. Indeed, key geopolitical moments such as colonialism and decolonisation, the Cold War, and the rise of China are central to explaining both the material and ideological underpinnings of late development projects in the Third World and their substantive successes and failures.

As we have argued in this book, the framework of the development–geopolitics nexus sheds light on the specificity of North Korea's developmental experience, including its initial successes in catch-up industrialisation, its subsequent secular decline followed by the collapse in the 1990s and its partial recovery since then. Understanding the continuities and changes of the North Korean political economy has necessarily involved a historically informed analysis of how catch-up industrialisation was shaped by the country's location on one of the key fault lines of regional and global geopolitics. North Korea is often examined from the perspective of state socialism, reflecting the fact that the early period of state-building was strongly influenced by the Soviet model. Yet, the North Korean polity has also been fundamentally postcolonial in its outlook, with its developmental trajectory profoundly shaped by the legacies of three and a half decades of imperial rule by Japan. On the one hand, the brutally repressive and exploitative nature of Japanese rule alongside a simultaneous albeit partial process of colonial modernisation laid the basis for the emergence of a Korean national identity that was anti-colonial in nature and underpinned by a strong developmental ethos. As elsewhere in the colonial world, nationalists envisaged a future in which Korea would join the ranks of modern independent nations and achieve security through a process of state-led national development. In the immediate post-liberation era at least, there was no contradiction between these aims and a close alliance with the Soviet Union, with that alliance seen as the most expedient means by which modernisation and catch-up industrialisation could be rapidly achieved.

The colonial experience was crucial to North Korea's future developmental path in other ways. The uneven impact of colonial development meant that much of the heavy industry established in Korea during the late 1930s and the early 1940s was located in the north of the country, close to Korea's natural resources and the frontline of the Sino–Japanese War. This establishment of an initial industrial base thereby created opportunities for North Korea that were unavailable to many other nations emerging from colonial rule. Indeed, a key objective of national economic planning after the Korean War was the reconstruction and continued development of this heavy-industrial base. With generous aid from the Socialist Bloc owing to North Korea's geostrategic importance, the country made the rapid industrial transition from war-torn and largely agrarian postcolonial society. However, Kim Il Sung's heavy industry–first strategy would ultimately have a negative impact on the country's subsequent developmental trajectory, particularly in terms of its adaptability to ongoing shifts in the world economy. Thus, while North Korea shared important commonalities with aspiring developing countries elsewhere in the postcolonial world, geopolitics in a sense overdetermined its pursuit of statist catch-up industrialisation.

A further feature of North Korea's distinctive experience of late development was the country's status as a divided country. National division meant that North Korea was continually engaged in an ongoing competition for legitimacy and military security with the South, a competition in which the North was from the 1970s increasingly on the losing side. Of course, North Korea was not the only divided nation during the post-war era, and national division cannot be used as an explanation for the nature of North Korea's political economy in any deterministic sense. In contrast to East Germany, for example, the Korean War and the unstable and shifting nature of North Korea's external alliances had a profound impact on the country's subsequent political development and the leadership's heightened sense of geopolitical vulnerability and threat. In the more immediate term, however, the generous assistance from the Socialist Bloc countries bolstered Kim Il Sung's ability to pursue a heavy industry–first strategy. At the same time, the Korean War led to the strengthening of the US alliance with South Korea and Japan, laying the basis for capitalist East Asia's 'miracle growth' and thereby presenting a further material and ideational challenge to the North Korean leadership in subsequent decades.

South Korea did not face any major shocks to its external alliances and the substance of the US–South Korean alliance has remained in place to the present day. For North Korea, however, the geopolitical environment took a marked turn for the worse in the 1960s. The Soviet Union's policy of peaceful coexistence with the United States, the deepening of the Sino–Soviet split and the emergence of a military regime in the South all posed challenges to the North Korean regime. This ongoing uncertainty served to deepen the leadership's commitment to the building of a strong defence sector based on heavy industry and also contributed towards the increasing militarisation of society. Towards these goals, the leadership explicitly justified the sacrifice of living standards in North Korea. The shifting nature of the country's external alliances also led Pyongyang to pursue an independent line in its foreign policy, through for example, utilising the Non-Aligned Movement to expand its relations with Third World countries.

The 1960s also saw the introduction of major institutional modifications that would come to characterise North Korea's distinctive approach to economic management, such as the *Ch'ŏngsan-ri* Method, the *Taean* Work System and unified and detailed planning. Nonetheless, North Korea faced problems typical of centrally planned economies, namely chronic economic inefficiency and the challenges of transitioning from extensive to intensive development. Nonetheless, there is little doubt that the rapidly rising defence-related expenditures in the 1960s significantly contributed towards this stalling of North Korea's developmental model. While the shifting of resources away from broad-based development towards militarisation was a common trend throughout the postcolonial Third World, the sheer scope of North Korea's defence burden is difficult to comprehend without considering the specificity of the country's position on the frontline of the Asian Cold War as a divided country.

The parallels between North Korea and elsewhere in the postcolonial Third World can also be seen in its failed attempts to tackle its developmental impasse through increased engagement with the global economy in the 1970s. In order to address slowing economic growth, North Korea established foreign trade relations with Western Europe and Japan for the purpose of purchasing new machinery and capital equipment. By doing so, however, North Korea became exposed to the increasing volatility of the world capitalist economy during that decade. As the global decline in raw material prices contributed to the country's growing balance of payments difficulties, North

Korea defaulted on its debt and was subsequently shut out of global capital markets. Subsequent efforts to attract foreign investment in the 1980s foundered, and North Korea experienced continued economic decline as its dependence on cheap energy inputs from its socialist allies increased. With the end of the Cold War in the early 1990s, the Soviet Union and China drastically curtailed their economic support for North Korea, thereby immediately exposing the dangerous extent to which North Korea had become reliant on the country's external alliances. With the benefit of hindsight, it could be seen that North Korea's avowed self-reliance was a chimaera.

The question of why North Korea at this juncture did not collapse is frequently posed. In contrast to the uprisings in the Soviet Bloc or even the failed 1989 uprising in China, North Korea did not appear to show signs of significant popular unrest despite increasing hardship and the onset of famine. Given the oft-spontaneous nature of popular uprisings, it is deceptively easy to make post-hoc justifications of why a particular revolt or revolution did or did not happen. No doubt, a part of the answer relates to the monolithic nature of North Korean political culture and the highly developed mechanisms of social and political control. Indeed, North Korea lacks any tradition of popular protest or even nascent civil society outside the realm of the all-powerful Leviathan state. In the early years of state formation, social forces that might have potentially opposed the new regime largely fled south. The elimination of factionalism in the 1950s also minimised the likelihood that elite manoeuvrings might have brought about a political aperture of some sort. Furthermore, with the firm establishment of the monolithic ideological system of *Juche* thought in the late 1960s, the hierarchical ruling structure of the *Suryŏng* significantly curtailed any independent space outside of the corporatist polity. Indeed, the hereditary successions of Kim Jong Il and later Kim Jong Un were able to take place with seemingly minimal overt resistance. It is clear, therefore, that at the point at which the North Korean system might have most been expected to collapse, the state was largely able to cope with the crisis, notwithstanding the widespread loss of life through famine. On the one hand, crisis management included political measures such as Military First Politics. With the collapse of the PDS, however, North Koreans at all levels of the social hierarchy had little choice but to turn to market activities as a form of survival.

Despite periodic crackdowns, marketisation was a process that was largely accepted by the state, particularly as the latter had absolved itself of responsibility for much of the former centrally planned economy. Non-strategic SOEs were left to fend for themselves and had to engage in market-based activities to survive. At the same time, marketisation led to a form of mutual interdependence between state organs and emergent forms of private capital. The state came to rely on income derived from grassroots market activities in the form of both official fees and bribes, while the absence of clear private property rights led the emergent entrepreneurial class to establish informal relations with state officials to protect their investments and gain access to state-owned means of production. Indeed, it was this mutual dependence that underpinned the fundamental irreversibility of marketisation. While the central government carried out periodic crackdowns on certain illicit market-based activities, it could not eliminate market dynamics given its inability to provide material support to lower-level bureaucratic organs and SOEs. The state also in certain instances played a key role in extending the realm of the market, through for example, the establishment of the telecommunications sector. For this reason, the North Korean political economy has been fundamentally transformed to the extent that, with the exception of the defence industry and the strategic industrial sector, there are few parts of economy and society that have been unaffected by marketisation.

Though it is inaccurate to refer to North Korea as a case of unreformed socialism, the relatively cautious nature of the reform process is indeed a paradox. Mainstream explanations emphasise the monolithic nature of the Kim dynasty and the inhibiting role of *Juche* ideology. In doing so, they focus almost entirely on the internal attributes of the North Korean system and argue that the regime's domestic characteristics largely determine its integration with the global economy. There is certainly little doubt that North Korean state ideology remains strongly shaped by norms of self-reliant autonomous development. Yet, this begs the question of why such ideas have maintained such a hold in North Korea compared to other state socialist societies. On the one hand, the structural characteristics of the North Korean economy problematise expectations that the country will pursue Chinese-style reform and opening up. North Korea's urbanisation and heavy industrialisation create considerably less scope for the kinds of rural-based experiments with market socialism seen in China, or in Vietnam for that matter. There is less in the way of a surplus rural population that can be easily transferred to export-oriented factories without undermining the collective agricultural system. More immediate geopolitical factors also play a role. Both China and Vietnam launched their economic reform programmes following a marked improvement of their relations with the United States. Though there is little available empirical evidence of a split between hardliners and reformers in North Korea, it stands to reason that the continued strong perception of a hostile external environment is likely to be less conducive to economic reform.

To regard the country as isolated, however, would be to neglect the profound impact that the China boom has had on the North Korean economy in recent years. Indeed, it was the influx of goods across the Sino–North Korean border that in many respects underpinned the country's tentative economic recovery and marketisation. The resulting availability of cheap consumer goods had a mostly positive impact on the livelihoods of North Korean citizens, and Chinese imports underpinned the expansion of light manufacturing, retail, construction, transport and the service sectors. While mineral resources constituted the bulk of North Korean exports to China, growing Chinese investment in North Korea's garment manufacturing sector also served to integrate the country into regional production networks. The dispatch of North Korean workers further utilised the country's comparative advantage in labour costs. On the one hand, this trade relationship resembled in its broad contours a situation of classic economic dependency. Yet, North Korea's economy collapsed prior to the deepening of economic relations between the two countries, though this relationship does make North Korea highly vulnerable to shifts in political relations between the two countries.

Although US unilateral sanctions have been in place since the time of the Korean War, the fact that North Korea's economy was, during the early post-liberation decades, oriented towards the Socialist Bloc meant that those sanctions had relatively limited impact. They also did little to impede North Korea's unprecedented expansion of trade relations with Western Europe and Japan in the 1970s. More consequential were the stringent sanctions imposed by North Korea's erstwhile trading partners of South Korea and Japan in the late 2000s, though this mainly served to reorient the country's economic relations towards China. Indeed, the booming Chinese economy led to the paradox in which tightening multilateral sanctions coincided with the gradual recovery of the North Korean economy. For the most part then, the history of sanctions against North Korea has been one of evasion alongside non-enforcement. Nonetheless, from 2017, China too became increasingly proactive in the enforcement of sanctions. While official trade figures show a precipitous decline in trade, much remains unclear regarding the precise impact of sanctions on the North Korean economy. Anecdotal evidence suggests that their impact is uneven. There is also a vast difference between sanctions having a negative economic impact and sanctions 'working' in the sense of bringing about the desired change in North Korean policy. While the US–North Korean summit in Hanoi in February 2019 saw Pyongyang make demands for sanctions relief, it appeared to be no closer to accepting the US demand of complete and verifiable denuclearisation as a precondition for that relief.

While it is no doubt a cliché to conclude with the 'crossroads' metaphor, it seems so apt in the case of North Korea at the present juncture as to be unavoidable. In early 2018, Donald Trump's campaign of 'maximum pressure' gave way to an unprecedented wave of diplomacy. By February 2019, Kim Jong Un had met with South Korean president Moon Jae-In on three occasions, with Chinese President Xi Jinping four times, and with US President Trump twice. One of the key inducements that the Trump administration offered Kim Jong Un in return for the country's nuclear disarmament was the possibility of large-scale investment in North Korea. Indeed, at the Singapore summit in June 2018, Trump reportedly showed Kim a promotional video depicting an imagined future for North Korea in which the '... doors of opportunity are ready to be open: investment from around the world, where you can have medical breakthroughs, an abundance of resources, innovative technology, and new discoveries'.[1] In South Korea, the prevailing discourse surrounding the renewed warming of inter-Korean relations also focussed more on the potential opportunities of economic cooperation rather than on any sense of ethnic brotherhood. In terms of nuclear negotiations, the aspiration in Washington and Seoul was that the prospect of transforming North Korea into the next China or Vietnam would be attractive enough to induce Kim Jong Un to relinquish his weapons and pursue a path of reform and greater integration into the global economy.

It appeared also that economic development has weighed more heavily upon the minds of policymakers in Pyongyang than at any time in recent decades. Much of this is to do with the legitimacy challenges faced by Kim Jong Un. Two generations removed from North Korea's founding leader, Kim Jong Un's rule increasingly rested on a social contract with the population that promised improved living standards in return for continued public support for the regime, albeit backed up by the still considerable repressive capacities of the state. In his first public speech as new leader, Kim stated that the people would 'not tighten their belts again' and would enjoy the wealth and prosperity of socialism. The 'improvement of people's livelihood' (*inminsaenghwal hyangsang*) thereupon became a key element of North Korea's developmental discourse. As in the Kim Jong Il era, primary blame for the country's economic hardship continued to be placed on external powers, and specifically, on the 'harsh economic blockade and sanctions' imposed by the United States. Nonetheless, Kim Jong Un presented himself as a pragmatic leader seeking to bring about economic development. Kim's on-the-spot guidance visits increasingly included factories, commercial facilities, construction sites, schools, farms and fisheries. He also sought to nurture the image of a benevolent leader through promising to eradicate 'authority, bureaucratism, and corruption' as an urgent national task.[2] However, this emphasis on economic development continued to be conveyed through the well-established tropes of charismatic leadership. The emphasis on public livelihood did not, for example, change the fact that on-the-spot guidance visits were themselves a

---

[1] 'United States - North Korea Singapore Summit Video' www.youtube.com/watch?time_con tinue=231&v=A838gS8nwas [accessed 17 April 2019].
[2] *Rodong Sinmun*, 8 May 2016, 'Party Central Committee report presented at the 7th KWP Congress – Kim Jong Un [Chosŏnnodongdang che 7 ch'a taehoeesŏhan tang chungangwiwŏn-hoe saŏpch'onghwabogo – Kimjŏngŭn]'.

practice very much associated with North Korea's traditionalist modes of economic management.

As we have noted, Kim Jong Un's ascendance to power was accompanied by the adoption in 2013 of the *Pyŏngjin* dual line of the simultaneous development of nuclear weapons and the economy. As Kim Jong Un argued at the KWP's 7th Party Congress in May 2016: 'The construction of an economic powerhouse is the basic front on which our party and nation should concentrate their efforts. Our country has risen to the position of a political and military powerhouse, but the economic sector has not yet reached a reasonable level'.[3] The '*Pyŏngjin* line' was a direct reference to Kim Il Sung's *Pyŏngjin* Dual Line of Economic and Defence Construction adopted in the early 1960s. The difference was that Kim Il Sung facilitated a shift in emphasis from a focus on economic reconstruction to that of militarisation as a result of the increasingly uncertain geopolitical environment of the 1960s. Kim Jong Un's *Pyŏngjin* line, on the other hand, was a shift in the other direction, from the Military First Politics that began under his father's reign towards greater emphasis on economic goals, though crucially without any improvements in North Korea's security. As a result, there was arguably a greater contradiction between the twin goals of Kim Jong Un's *Pyŏngjin* line.

At the 3rd Plenary of the 7th KWP Central Committee held on 20 April 2018, however, the regime announced the completion of the country's nuclear weapons programme and thus an end to nuclear and intercontinental missile testing. As such, the *Pyŏngjin* line was ostensibly replaced by a new line based on '... concentrating all efforts on socialist economic construction in accordance with the new high stage of revolutionary development'.[4] The task of economic construction was thereby formulated as national priority, and to achieve this, party and state were called upon to prioritise economic work through the mobilisation of the country's human, material and technical potential.[5] The fact that this shift in strategy occurred shortly before Kim's 27 April summit with Moon Jae-In meant that it was interpreted by many as a sign of North Korea's commitment to denuclearisation.[6] A more pessimistic assessment, however, was that North Korea had developed a sufficient nuclear deterrent to be able to negotiate from a position of strength and was thereby seeking acceptance as a nuclear power. It can only be speculated as to the extent to which North Korea was willing to make substantive concessions over

---

[3] Ibid.

[4] *Rodong Sinmun*, 5 May 2018, 'With high spirit of victory, let's push forward the troops of economic construction [P'ilsŭngŭi sinsim tŭnop'i kyŏngjegŏnsŏl taejin'gunŭl himitke tagŭch'yŏ nagaja]'.

[5] Ibid.

[6] *New York Times*, 21 April 2018, Will Kim Jong-un Trade His Nuclear Arsenal to Rebuild Economy?

denuclearisation. It remains clear, however, that North Korea had in no sense reduced its commitment to national security, and for the time being at least, the substantive content of the *Pyŏngjin* remained in play.

Certain aspects of North Korea's economic programme can presumably meet with some success without the removal of international sanctions. For example, the adoption of Our-Style Economic Management Method and continued efforts to utilise market dynamics to strengthen the state sector has some potential in terms of nurturing domestic dynamism of the kind seen in China in the early stages of reform. In recent years, the regime has also placed a great deal of emphasis on developing the country's science and technology capacities. The development of science and technology as a means of countering economic dependency has been a well-established trope of North Korean developmental discourse since the time of Kim Il Sung. Yet, what is also distinctive about Kim Jong Un's science and technology policy is that through the introduction of the Socialistic Enterprise Responsibility Management System, there is a greater emphasis on improving the business performance of individual enterprises and increasing the development of new technologies and products as a means of promoting production. While the institutional modifications are clear enough, it is difficult to know exactly how successful individual enterprises have been in achieving such goals. However, in line with the policy goal of nationalising production, improvements in enterprises' technological capacities can be seen in the increased sales of domestic light industrial products in North Korean markets and the improvements in their quality and competitiveness.

It seems clear, however, that the ongoing economic blockade of North Korea presents a clear challenge to the Kim Jong Un government's efforts to attract foreign investment. As we have noted, North Korea's geographical location and existing pattern of integration into China-centred regional and global production networks suggest considerable potential for the country to capitalise on its advantages in low-cost skilled labour. Improvements in inter-Korean economic exchange would also further the potential for the match between North Korean labour and South Korean capital and technology, as has indeed been witnessed in the Kaesong Industrial Complex. As such, the resolution of the nuclear standoff with the United States remains an essential prerequisite for access to the foreign investment needed for the fulfilment of North Korea's broader economic development plans.

Yet, even if the nuclear issue is resolved and North Korea is able to integrate itself more fully into the regional and global economy, the vision of a self-reliant autonomous economy that has shaped North Korean developmental strategy for the past seven decades is likely to come into sharp conflict with the reality of the contemporary global capitalism based on transnational production networks. In this respect, questions might be raised as to how far North

Korean policymakers are likely to go in order to create a favourable environment for foreign investors, for example. Without providing for such an environment, integration into the world economy is likely to take place at a very low level, involving the export of natural resources and labour and the import of more sophisticated manufactured goods. Though this may bring an increase in living standards for some, this shallow integration is a developmental path that has stalled in other parts of Asia.

This is not to suggest that past developmental discourses necessarily pose an insurmountable barrier. North Korea is hardly alone in facing this dissonance between its developmental aspirations and the realities of contemporary global capitalism. Numerous postcolonial states have eventually had to abandon their ideals of autonomous national development and integrate themselves within global circuits of capital and technology in order to pursue continued development. Yet for North Korea, this requires a thorough transformation in its external threat perception. As we have seen, China's initial experimentations with market socialism took place far from the centres of political power due to concerns regarding their potential destabilising impact. There is one crucial difference, however, in that external threat perceptions weigh much more heavily on the minds of North Korean policymakers. North Korea is part of a divided nation on what remains one of the world's most entrenched geopolitical fault lines. It is faced with a vastly more powerful southern neighbour that continues to compete for legitimacy as 'true' representative of the Korean nation. This creates an inauspicious environment for North Korea's full integration into the global economy. Investment from South Korea, in many respects the country's most obvious potential economic partner, poses a challenge in terms of both regime stability and legitimacy in North Korea. While South Korean state and capital naturally see the North as providing a wealth of economic opportunities, this is more than matched by deep North Korean anxieties concerning potential economic dependency vis-à-vis the South. However, this may further strengthen North Korea's desire to normalise its relations with the United States, a key prerequisite for developing economic relations with a broader range of potential trade and investment partners.

While the resolution of the nuclear issue may pave the way for North Korea's entry into a US-centred regional and global liberal order, wider geopolitical tensions are leading to increasing polarisation in the Northeast Asian region. The US–China trade war, the new Indo–Pacific Strategy of the United States, alongside numerous other security conflicts within the region all have potential implications for North Korea. As US–North Korea summitry appeared to run into difficulties due to a lack of mutual trust between the two countries, North Korea's relations with Russia and China saw an improvement, with Kim Jong Un meeting Russian President Vladimir Putin in Vladivostok in April 2019, and President Xi Jinping making his first visit to Pyongyang the following June. In the absence of progress in its relations with Washington, the revival of North Korea's alliances with its traditional allies became a distinct possibility, with the potential for encouraging a strategy of muddling through rather a genuine transformation of its external relations and readmission into the international community and world economy.

Even as the country's domestic economy continued to deteriorate, Pyongyang appeared to be no closer to making concessions on its nuclear programme. Furthermore, in 2020, North Korea was confronted with the fallout of the COVID-19 pandemic. The self-imposed closure of the country's borders from late January unsurprisingly led to a further sharp drop in trade with the outside world. By July, North Korean exports to China were recorded at just US\$37 million, a decline of 69 per cent compared to the same period the previous year. Imports also fell by around 67 per cent.[7] This compounded the impact of the 'maximum pressure' campaign and led to some of the most challenging economic conditions faced by the country in over two decades. Yet, even this did not appear to significantly alter North Korea's position on its nuclear programme. Furthermore, in June 2020, amidst growing dissatisfaction with South Korea following the failure of the Hanoi Summit, Pyongyang sought to increase pressure on Seoul through blowing up the building of the Inter-Korean Joint Liaison Office that had been established less than two years prior following the April 2018 Panmunjom Declaration.

While North Korea's nuclear policy appears relatively impervious to economic pressure caused by either sanctions or the COVID-19 pandemic, there seems little doubt that a transformation in North Korea's geopolitical environment is crucial for economic recovery and for any sustained process of reform and opening up. The fact that the Korean War remains effectively unresolved after seven decades exerts a profound impact on the path that North Korea is likely to take. Indeed, geopolitical insecurity has shaped the North Korean development model since the time of state formation. Encouraging North Korea along the path of economic reform and integration into the global economy thus requires coming to terms with that history and creating a more favourable environment for North Korea's economic recovery and development. Although the North Korean political economy has evolved in important ways since the collapse in the 1990s, the resolution of the nuclear standoff and the removal of sanctions is a necessary if not sufficient step for North Korea's integration with the world economy. However, further moves in this direction will require considerable political imagination from the interested powers and the international community.

---

[7] China Customs data drawn from the KITA database.

Bibliography

Abrahamian, Andray, 'The Sanctions Effect in North Korea: Observations from Rason', *38 North*, 2018 www.38north.org/2018/10/aabrahamian101918/ [accessed 20 October 2018].

Addis, Adeno, 'Economic Sanctions and the Problem of Evil', *Human Rights Quarterly*, 25.3 (2003), pp. 573–623.

Aglietta, Michel, and Guo Bai, *China's Development: Capitalism and Empire* (London: Routledge, 2013).

Agov, Avram Asenov, 'North Korea in the Socialist World: Integration and Divergence, 1945-1970. The Crossroads of Politics and Economics'. (PhD thesis: University of British Columbia, 2010).

Akamatsu, Kaname, 'A Historical Pattern of Economic Growth in Developing Countries', *The Developing Economies*, 1.S1 (1962), pp. 3–25.

Alam, M. Shahid, *Governments and Markets in Economic Development Strategies: Lessons from Korea, Taiwan, and Japan* (New York: Praeger Publishers, 1989).

Amsden, Alice H., *Asia's Next Giant: South Korea and Late Industrialization* (Oxford: Oxford University Press, 1989).

An, Kwang Jup, 'The Development of Finance in Korea [Urinara chaejŏngŭi palchŏn]', in *The Development of the People's Economy in Korea, 1948-1958 [Urinaraŭi inmin'gyŏngje palchŏn 1948-1958]*, ed. by Kim Il Sung University Department of Economics (Pyongyang: State Publishing Company, 1958), pp. 269–308.

Andreas, Peter, 'Criminalizing Consequences of Sanctions: Embargo Busting and Its Legacy', *International Studies Quarterly*, 49.2 (2005), pp. 335–60.

Anievas, Alexander, *Capital, the State, and War: Class Conflict and Geopolitics in the Thirty Years' Crisis, 1914-1945* (Ann Arbor: University of Michigan Press, 2014).

Armstrong, Charles K., *The North Korean Revolution 1945-1950* (Ithaca, NY: Cornell University Press, 2003).

'The Role and Influence of Ideology', in *North Korea in Transition: Politics, Economy, and Society*, ed. by Kyung-Ae Park and Scott Snyder (Plymouth: Rowman and Littlefield, 2013), pp. 3–18

Ash, Robert F., 'The Evolution of Agricultural Policy', *The China Quarterly*, 116. December (1988), pp. 529–55.

Bae, Jong-Ryeol, 'An Evaluation of Foreign Investment in North Korea: Focusing on EU and Chinese Enterprises [Pukhanŭi woegugint'uja silt'aewa p'yŏngga: EUwa Chungguk kiŏbŭi taebukjinch'ulŭl chungsimŭro]', *EXIM North Korean Economic Review*, Fall (2008), pp. 43–70.

Bae, Jong-Ryeol, and Yoon Seung-Hyun, *An Analysis of Jilin Province's Economic Cooperation with North Korea: Focus on Investment [Kilimsŏngŭi taebuggyŏngjehyŏmnyok silt'ae punsŏk: Taebukt'ujarŭl chungsimŭro]* (Seoul: Korea Institute for National Unification, 2015).

Baek, Jun-Kee, 'North Korea's Political Changes and Power Realignment in the 1950s Following the Korean War Armistice [Chŏngjŏn hu 1950 nyŏndae Pukhanŭi chŏngch'i pyŏndonggwa kwŏllyŏk chaep'yŏn]', *Review of North Korean Studies*, 2.2 (1999), pp. 9–71.

Balassa, Bela, 'Exports and Economic Growth', *Journal of Development Economics*, 5.2 (1978), pp. 181–89.

Bedeian, Arthur G, and Carl R. Phillips, 'Scientific Management and Stakhanovism in the Soviet Union: A Historical Perspective', *International Journal of Social Economics*, 17.10 (1990), pp. 28–35.

Berger, Mark, 'From Nation-Building to State-Building: The Geopolitics of Development, the Nation-State System and the Changing Global Order', *Third World Quarterly*, 27.1 (2006), pp. 5–25.

Bernard, Mitchell, and John Ravenhill, 'Beyond Product Cycles and Flying Geese: Regionalization, Hierarchy, and the Industrialization of East Asia', *World Politics*, 47.2 (1995), pp. 171–209.

Bleiker, Roland, *Divided Korea: Toward a Culture of Reconciliation* (Minneapolis: University of Minnesota Press, 2005).

Bodenheimer, S., 'Dependency and Imperialism: The Roots of Latin American Underdevelopment', *Politics & Society*, 1.November (1971), pp. 327–57.

Bond, Patrick, 'BRICS and the Tendency to Sub-Imperialism', *Pambazuka News [Online]*, 2014 www.pambazuka.net/en/category/features/91303 [accessed 29 April 2020].

Brandt, Loren, Thomas G. Rawski, and John Sutton, 'China's Industrial Development', in *China's Great Economic Transformation*, ed. by Loren Brandt and Thomas G. Rawski (Cambridge: Cambridge University Press, 2008), pp. 569–632.

Brautigam, Deborah, *The Dragon's Gift: The Real Story of China in Africa* (Oxford: Oxford University Press, 2009).

Breslin, Shaun, *China and the Global Political Economy* (Basingstoke: Palgrave Macmillan, 2013).

Brezinski, Horst, 'International Economic Relations between the KDPR and Western Europe', in *The Economy of the Korean Democratic People's Republic 1945-1977*, ed. by Youn-Soo Kim (Kiel: German Korea-Studies Group, 1979), pp. 202–31.

Brown, William B., *North Korea's Shackled Economy, 2018* (Washington, DC: National Committee on North Korea, 2018).

Bruff, Ian, 'Overcoming the State/Market Dichotomy', in *Critical International Political Economy: Dialogue, Debate and Dissensus*, ed. by Stuart Shields, Ian Bruff, and Huw Macartney (Basingstoke: Palgrave Macmillan, 2011), pp. 80–98

Brun, Ellen, and Jacques Hersh, *Socialist Korea: A Case Study in the Strategy of Economic Development* (New York: Monthly Review Press, 1976).

Bunce, Valerie, 'The Empire Strikes Back: The Evolution of the Eastern Bloc from a Soviet Asset to a Soviet Liability', *International Organization*, 39.1 (1985), pp. 1–46.

Buzo, Adrian, *The Guerilla Dynasty: Politics and Leadership in North Korea* (London: I B Tauris, 1999).

Byman, Daniel, and Jennifer Lind, 'Pyongyang's Survival Strategy: Tools of Authoritarian Control in North Korea', *International Security*, 35.1 (2010), pp. 44–74.

Cai, Fang, Albert Park, and Yaohui Zhao, 'The Chinese Labor Market in the Reform Era', in *China's Great Economic Transformation*, ed. by Loren Brandt and Thomas G. Rawski (Cambridge: Cambridge University Press, 2008), pp. 167–214.

Callinicos, Alex, 'Bourgeois Revolutions and Historical Materialism', *International Socialism*, 43 (1989), pp. 113–71.

Carlin, Robert L., and Joel S. Wit, 'Debate and Policy Formation', *The Adelphi Papers*, 46.382 (2006), pp. 15–19.

Carmody, Pádraig R., and Francis Y. Owusu, 'Competing Hegemons? Chinese versus American Geo-Economic Strategies in Africa', *Political Geography*, 26.5 (2007), pp. 504–24.

Central Bureau of Statistics, *DPRK Multiple Cluster Survey 2009* (Pyongyang: Central Bureau of Statistics, 2010).

DPRK Multiple Cluster Survey 2017 (Pyongyang: Central Bureau of Statistics, 2017).

Cha, Victor D., 'Kim Jong Un Is No Reformer', *Foreign Policy [Online]*, 2012 http://foreignpolicy.com/2012/08/21/kim-jong-un-is-no-reformer/ [accessed 31 March 2020].

Chang, Ha-Joon, *Kicking Away the Ladder: Development Strategy in Historical Perspective* (London: Anthem, 2002).

Chang, Semoon, 'A Chronology of U.S. Sanctions Against North Korea', in *Economic Sanctions Against a Nuclear North Korea: An Analysis of United States and United Nations Actions Since 1950*, ed. by Suk Hi Kim and Semoon Chang (Jefferson: McFarland, 2003), pp. 34–55.

Chase-Dunn, Christopher, *Socialist States in the World-System* (Beverly Hills: Sage, 1983).

Cheong, Seong-Chang, *Contemporary North Korean Politics: History, Ideology and Power System [Hyŏndae Pukhanŭi chŏngch'i: Yŏksa – inyŏm – kwŏllyŏgch'aegye]* (Seoul: Hanul Academy, 2011).

Chernilo, Daniel, 'Social Theory's Methodological Nationalism Myth and Reality', *European Journal of Social Theory*, 9.1 (2006), pp. 5–22.

Cho, Han-Bum, Lim Kang-Taeg, Yang Moon-Soo, and Lee Seog-Ki, *The Effects of Private Economic Activities on Public Economic Sectors in North Korea [Pukhanesŏ sajŏggyŏngjehwaldongi kongsiggyŏngjebumune mich'inŭn yŏnghyang punsŏk]* (Seoul: Korea Institute for National Unification, 2016).

Cho, Myung-chul, *Economic Relations between North Korea and Russia and Their Implications for Economic Cooperation between Two Koreas [Pukhan'gwa Rŏsia saiŭi kyŏngjehyŏmnyŏk hyŏnhwanggwa nambukkyŏnghyŏbe chunŭn sisajŏm]* (Seoul: Korea Institute for International Economic Policy, 2003).

Cho, Soon Sung, 'Korea: Election Year', *Asian Survey*, 8.1 (1968), pp. 29–42.

Choi, Bong-Dae, and Koo Kab-Woo, 'Implications of the Implementation of the Process of the Formation of North Korean Cities' "Farmers' Markets": Centred on the Cases of Sinuiju, Chongjin and Hyesan in North Korea during the 1950s-1980s [Pukhan tosi "nongminsijang" hyŏngsŏng kwajŏngŭi yihaengnonjŏk hamŭi: 1950-1980 nyŏndae Sinŭiju, Ch'ŏngjin, Hyesanŭi saryerŭl chungsimŭro]', *Review of North Korean Studies*, 6.2 (2003), pp. 133–87.

Choi, Jangho, Kim Junyoung, Im So Jeong, and Choi Yoojeong, *Economic Cooperation between North Korea and China, and Implications for Inter-Korean Economic Cooperation [Pukchung punŏpch'egye punsŏggwa taebuk kyŏngjehyŏmnyŏge taehan sisajŏm]* (Sejong: Korea Institute for International Economic Policy, 2015).

Choi, Jinwook, and Meredith Shaw, 'The Rise of Kim Jong Eun and the Return of the Party', *International Journal of Korean Unification Studies*, 19.2 (2010), pp. 175–202.

Choi, Seo-yoon, 'North Korean Restaurant Industry: Ryanggang Province-Style Restaurant Amnokgag River [Pukhanŭi ŭmsigŏp, Yanggangdo t'ŭksanmul sikdang Amnokgag]', *KDB North Korean Development*, Autumn (2016), pp. 166–83.

Choi, Yong-Jin, 'Economic Technology Development Zone, Micro-Regional Cooperation, and One Belt-One Road in the Northeast Asian Borderlands [Dongbuga chŏpgyŏngjiyŏgŭi kyŏngjegisulgaebalgu, sojiyŏnghyŏmnyŏk kŭrigo ildaeillo]', *The Korean Journal of Area Studies*, 34.3 (2016), pp. 97–124

Choi, Yong Nam, 'Important Problems in the Contemporary Era Related to the Improvement of the Supply of Materials [Hyŏnsigi chajaegonggŭpsaŏbŭl kaesŏnhanŭndesŏ nasŏnŭn chungyohan munje]', *Journal of Kim Il Sung University Philosophy, Economics*, 62.3 (2016), pp. 103–106.

Choi, Yong Sub, 'North Korea's Hegemonic Rule and Its Collapse', *The Pacific Review*, 30.5 (2017), pp. 783–800.

Chun, Hong-Tack, 'Economic Conditions in North Korea and Prospects for Reform', in *North Korea after Kim Il Sung*, ed. by Thomas H. Henriksen and Jongryn Mo (Stanford: Hoover Institution Press, 1997), pp. 32–49.

'The Second Economy in North Korea', *Seoul Journal of Economics*, 12.2 (1999), pp. 173–94

Chung, Chien-peng, 'The "Good Neighbour Policy" in the Context of China's Foreign Relations', *China: An International Journal*, 7.1 (2014), pp. 107–23.

Chung, Chin O., *Pyongyang between Peking and Moscow: North Korea's Involvement in the Sino-Soviet Dispute, 1958-1975* (University, Alabama: University of Alabama Press, 1978).

Chung, Jae Ho, Hongyi Lai, and Jang-Hwan Joo, 'Assessing the "Revive the Northeast"(Zhenxing Dongbei) Programme: Origins, Policies and Implementation', *The China Quarterly*, 197 (2009), pp. 108–25.

Chung, Joseph Sang-Hoon, 'Economic Planning in North Korea', in *North Korea Today: Strategic and Domestic Issues*, ed. by Robert A. Scalapino and Jun-yop Kim (Berkeley, CA: Institute of East Asian Studies, University of California, 1983), pp. 164–96

'Foreign Trade of North Korea: Performance, Policy and Prospects', in *North Korea in a Regional and Global Context*, ed. by Robert A. Scalapino and Hongkoo Lee

(Berkeley, CA: Institute of East Asian Studies, University of California Press, 1986), pp. 78–114.

'North Korea's Seven Year Plan (1961-70): Economic Performance and Reforms', *Asian Survey*, 12.6 (1972), pp. 527–525.

The North Korean Economy: Structure and Development (Stanford: Hoover Institution Press, 1974).

Chung, Young Chul, *Research on Kim Jong Il's Leadership [Kimjŏngil ridŏsip yŏn'gu]* (Seoul: Sunin, 2005).

'The Suryŏng System as the Institution of Collectivist Development', *Journal of Korean Studies*, 12.1 (2007), pp. 43–73.

Clark, Cal, and Donna Bahry, 'Dependent Development: A Socialist Variant', *International Studies Quarterly*, 27.3 (1983), pp. 271–93.

Cliff, Tony, *State Capitalism in Russia* (London: Pluto Press, 1974).

Clough, Ralph N., *Embattled Korea: The Rivalry for International Support* (Boulder, CO: Westview Press, 1987).

Cortright, David, and George A. Lopez, *Smart Sanctions: Targeting Economic Statecraft* (Lanham, MD: Rowman and Littlefield, 2002).

Cumings, Bruce, *The Origins of the Korean War: Volume I. Liberation and the Emergence of Separate Regimes 1945-1947* (Princeton, NJ: Princeton University Press, 1981).

'The Origins and Development of the Northeast Asian Political Economy: Industrial Sectors, Product Cycles, and Political Consequences', ed. by Frederic C. Deyo, *International Organization*, 38.1 (1984), pp. 1–40.

'The Legacy of Japanese Colonialism in Korea', in *The Japanese Colonial Empire, 1895-1945*, ed. by Ramon H. Myers and Mark R. Peattie (Princeton, NJ: Princeton University Press, 1984), pp. 478–96.

The Origins of the Korean War: Volume II. The Roaring of the Cataract 1947-1950 (Princeton, NJ: Princeton University Press, 1990).

Korea's Place in the Sun: A Modern History (New York: W.W. Norton and Company, 1997).

Parallax Visions: Making Sense of American-East Asian Relations (Durham, NC: Duke University Press, 1999).

Curtin, Peter, *The World and the West: The European Challenge and the Overseas Response in the Age of Empire* (Cambridge: Cambridge University Press, 2000).

David-West, Alzo, 'Stalinism, Post-Stalinism, and Neo-Capitalism: To Be or Not to Be?', *North Korean Review*, 4.2 (2008), pp. 58–67.

Demsetz, Harold, 'Toward a Theory of Property Rights', *The American Economic Review*, 57.2 (1967), pp. 347–59.

Department of State, *North Korea: A Case Study of a Soviet Satellite* (Washington, DC: US Government Printing Office, 1961).

Desai, Radhika, 'Introduction: Nationalisms and Their Understandings in Historical Perspective', *Third World Quarterly*, 29.3 (2008), pp. 397–428.

Dollar, David, 'Economic Reform and Allocative Efficiency in China's State-Owned Industry', *Economic Development and Cultural Change*, 39.1 (1990), pp. 89–105.

DPRK Academy of Sciences, *The Development of the People's Economy in Korea after Liberation [Haebanghu urinaraŭi inmin'gyŏngjebaljŏn]* (Pyongyang: Academy of Sciences Publishing House, 1960).

DPRK Central Bureau of Statistics, *Statistics on the Development of the DPRK's People's Economy 1946-1960 [1946-1960 Chosŏn Minjujuŭi Inmin'gonghwaguk inmin'gyŏngjebaljŏn t'onggyejib]* (Pyongyang: State Publishing House, 1961).

DPRK 2008 Population Census National Report (Pyongyang: DPRK Central Bureau of Statistics, 2009).

Drezner, Daniel W., 'Bargaining, Enforcement, and Multilateral Sanctions: When Is Cooperation Counterproductive?', *International Organization*, 54.1 (2000), pp. 73–102.

Dukalskis, Alexander, 'North Korea's Shadow Economy: A Force for Authoritarian Resilience or Corrosion?', *Europe - Asia Studies*, 68.3 (2016), pp. 487–507.

Ebel, Robert E., *Communist Trade in Oil and Gas: An Evaluation of the Future Export Capability of the Soviet Bloc* (New York: Praeger, 1970).

Eberstadt, Nicholas, 'Financial Transfers from Japan to North Korea: Estimating the Unreported Flows', *Asian Survey*, 36.5 (1996), pp. 523–42.

The North Korean Economy: Between Crisis and Catastrophe (New Brunswick, NJ: Transaction Publishers, 2007).

'What Is Wrong with the North Korean Economy', *American Enterprise Institute*, 2011 www.aei.org/publication/what-is-wrong-with-the-north-korean-economy/ [accessed 15 January 2020].

Eberstadt, Nicholas, and Alex Coblin, 'Dependencia, North Korea Style', *The Asan Institute for Policy Studies Issue Brief*, 32 (2014).

Eberstadt, Nicholas, Marc Rubin, and Albina Tretyakova, 'The Collapse of Soviet and Russian Trade with the DPRK, 1989-1993: Impact and Implications', *The Korean Journal of National Unification*, 4 (1995), pp. 87–104.

Eckert, Carter J., *Offspring of Empire: The Koch'ang Kims and the Colonial Origins of Korean Capitalism, 1876-1945* (Seattle: University of Washington Press, 1991).

'The South Korean Bourgeoisie: A Class in Search of Hegemony', *Journal of Korean Studies*, 7 (1990), pp. 115–48.

Eckert, Carter J., Ki-baik Lee, Young Ick Lew, Michael Robinson, and Edward W. Wagner, *Korea Old and New: A History* (Cambridge, MA: Harvard University Press, 1990).

Edwards, Lawrence, and Rhys Jenkins, 'The Impact of Chinese Import Penetration on the South African Manufacturing Sector', *The Journal of Development Studies*, 51.4 (2013), pp. 447–463.

Eichengreen, Barry, Yeongseop Rhee, and Hui Tong, 'China and the Exports of Other Asian Countries', *Review of World Economics*, 143.2 (2007), pp. 201–26.

Elliott, Kimberly A., 'The Sanctions Glass: Half Full or Completely Empty?', *International Security*, 23.1 (1998), pp. 50–65.

Emmanuel, Arghiri, *Unequal Exchange: A Study of the Imperialism of Trade* (New York: Monthly Review Press, 1972).

Ericson, Richard E., 'The Classical Soviet-Type Economy: Nature of the System and Implications for Reform', *The Journal of Economic Perspectives*, 5.4 (1991), pp. 11–27.

FAO, IFAD, UNICEF, WFP and WHO, *The State of Food Security and Nutrition in the World 2017: Building Resilience for Peace and Food Security*. (Rome: FAO, 2017).

FAO and WFP, 'Democratic People's Republic of Korea FAO/WFP Joint Rapid Food Security Assessment', (Bangkok: FAO and WFP, 2019).

Ferdinand, Peter, 'Westward Ho - The China Dream and "One Belt, One Road": Chinese Foreign Policy under Xi Jinping', *International Affairs*, 92.4 (2016), pp. 941–57.

Feron, Henri, 'Pyongyang's Construction Boom: Is North Korea Beating Sanctions?', *38 North*, 2017 www.38north.org/2017/07/hferon071817/ [accessed 24 April 2018].

Ferraro, Vincent, 'Dependency Theory: An Introduction', in *The Development Economics Reader*, ed. by Giorgio Secondi (London: Routledge, 2008), pp. 58–64.

Fiori, Antonio, and Sunhyuk Kim, 'Jasmine Does Not Bloom in Pyongyang: The Persistent Non-Transition in North Korea', *Pacific Focus*, 29.1 (2014), pp. 44–67.

Foster-Carter, Aidan, 'North Korea: Development and Self-Reliance. A Critical Appraisal', in *Korea North and South*, ed. by Gavan McCormack and Mark Selden (New York: Monthly Review, 1978), pp. 115–46.

Francis, Corinna-Barbara, 'Quasi-Public, Quasi-Private Trends in Emerging Market Economies: The Case of China', *Comparative Politics*, 33.3 (2001), pp. 275–94.

Frank, Andre Gunder, 'The Development of Underdevelopment', in *Imperialism and Underdevelopment: A Reader*, ed. by Robert I Rhodes (New York: Monthly Review Press, 1970), pp. 4–17.

Frank, Ruediger, 'Classical Socialism in North Korea and Its Transformation: The Role and the Future of Agriculture', *Harvard Asia Quarterly*, X.2 (2006), pp. 15–33.

'The Political Economy of Sanctions Against North Korea', *Asian Perspective*, 30.3 (2006), pp. 5–36.

Frank, Rudiger, 'North Korea's Autonomy 1965–2015', *Pacific Affairs,* 87.3 (2015), pp. 791–99.

Frank, Rüdiger, 'Lessons from the Past: The First Wave of Developmental Assistance to North Korea and the German Reconstruction of Hamhùng', *Pacific Focus*, 23.1 (2008), pp. 46–74.

'Ideological Risk versus Economic Necessity: The Future of Reform in North Korea', *Japan Focus*, 7.30 (2009), 1–8.

'Socialist Neoconservatism and North Korean Foreign Policy', in *New Challenges of North Korean Foreign Policy*, ed. by Kyung-Ae Park (Basingstoke: Palgrave MacMillan, 2010), pp. 3–42.

Frieden, Jeff, 'Third World Indebted Industrialization: International Finance and State Capitalism in Mexico, Brazil, Algeria, and South Korea', *International Organization*, 35.3 (1981), pp. 407–431.

Galtung, Johan, 'On the Effects of International Economic Sanctions, With Examples from the Case of Rhodesia', *World Politics*, 19.3 (1967), pp. 378–416.

Gerschenkron, Alexander, *Economic Backwardness in Historical Perspective* (Cambridge, MA: Harvard University Press, 1962).

Gills, Barry, 'North Korea and the Crisis of Socialism: The Historical Ironies of National Division', *Third World Quarterly*, 13.1 (1992), pp. 107–30.

Korea versus Korea: A Case of Contested Legitimacy (London: Routledge, 1996).

Gleason, Gregory, 'The Political Economy of Dependency under Socialism: The Asian Republics in the USSR', *Studies in Comparative Communism*, 24.4 (1991), pp. 335–53.

Gold, Thomas B., 'Colonial Origins of Taiwanese Capitalism', in *Contending Approaches to the Political Economy of Taiwan*, ed. by Edwin A. Winckler and Susan M. Greenhalgh (Armonk, NY: M. E. Sharpe, 1988), pp. 101–17.

Goodrich, Leland M., *Korea: A Study of US Policy in the United Nations* (New York: Council on Foreign Relations, 1956).

Gordenker, Leon, *The United Nations and the Peaceful Unification of Korea: The Politics of Field Operations, 1947-1950* (The Hague: Martinus Nijhoff, 1959).

Gore, Charles, 'Methodological Nationalism and the Misunderstanding of East Asian Industrialisation', *European Journal of Development Research*, 8.1 (1996), pp. 77–122.

Gourevitch, Peter, 'The Second Image Reversed: The International Sources of Domestic Politics', *International Organization*, 32.4 (1978), pp. 881–912.

Grajdanzev, Andrew J., *Modern Korea* (New York: The John Day Company, 1944).

Gramsci, Antonio, *Selections from the Prison Notebooks of Antonio Gramsci* (London: Lawrence and Wishart, 1971).

Gray, Kevin, and Youngseok Jang, 'Labour Unrest in the Global Political Economy: The Case of China's 2010 Strike Wave', *New Poltiical Economy*, 20.4 (2015), pp. 594–613.

Gray, Kevin, *Labour and Development in East Asia: Social Forces and Passive Revolution* (London: Routledge, 2015).

Grossman, Gregory, 'The "Second Economy" of the USSR', *Problems of Communism*, 16.5 (1977), pp. 25–40.

Habib, Benjamin, 'The Enforcement Problem in Resolution 2094 and the United Nations Security Council Sanctions Regime: Sanctioning North Korea', *Australian Journal of International Affairs*, 70.1 (2016), pp. 50–68.

Haggard, Stephan, and Marcus Noland, *Famine in North Korea: Markets, Aid, and Reform* (New York: Columbia University Press, 2007).

Haggard, Stephan, Jennifer Lee, and Marcus Noland, 'Integration in the Absence of Institutions: China–North Korea Cross-Border Exchange', *Journal of Asian Economics*, 23.2 (2012), pp. 130–45.

Haggard, Stephan, and Marcus Noland, 'Reform from Below: Behavioral and Institutional Change in North Korea', *Journal of Economic Behavior and Organization*, 73.2 (2010), pp. 133–52.

Hard Target: Sanctions, Inducements, and the Case of North Korea (Stanford, CA: Stanford University Press, 2017).

Halliday, Denis J., 'The Impact of the UN Sanctions on the People of Iraq', *Journal of Palestinian Studies*, 28.2 (1999), pp. 29–73.

Halliday, Jon, 'The North Korean Enigma', *New Left Review*, 127 (1981), pp. 18–52. 'The North Korean Model: Gaps and Questions', *World Development*, 9.9 (1981), pp. 889–905.

Han, Sung Joo, 'North Korea's Security Policy and Military Strategy', in *North Korea Today: Strategic and Domestic Issues*, ed. by Robert A. Scalapino and Jun-yop Kim (Berkeley, CA: Institute of East Asian Studies, University of California Press, 1983), pp. 144–63.

Harrison, Selig, *Korean Endgame: A Strategy for Reunification and US Disengagement* (Princeton, NJ: Princeton University Press, 2002).

Hart-Landsberg, Martin, *Korea: Division, Reunification, & U.S. Foreign Policy* (New York: Monthly Review Press, 1998).

Hart-Landsberg, Martin, and Paul Burkett, 'China and the Dynamics of Transnational Capital Accumulation', in *Marxist Perspectives on South Korea in the Global Economy*, ed. by Martin Hart-Landsberg, Seongjin Jeong, and Richard Westra (Aldershot: Ashgate, 2007), pp. 115–38.

Harvey, David, *A Brief History of Neoliberalism* (Oxford: Oxford University Press, 2005).

'Globalization and the "Spatial Fix"', *Geographische Revue*, 2 (2001), pp. 23–30.

Hastings, Justin V., *A Most Enterprising Country: North Korea in the Global Economy* (Ithaca, NY: Cornell University Press, 2016).

Hatch, Walter, and Kozo Yamamura, *Asia in Japan's Embrace: Building a Regional Production Alliance* (Cambridge: Cambridge University Press, 1996).

Hayes, Peter, and David Von Hippel, 'Sanctions on North Korean Oil Imports: Impacts and Efficacy', *Nautilus Peace and Security Special Report*, 2017. https://nautilus .org/napsnet/napsnet-special-reports/sanctions-on-north-korean-oil-imports-impacts-and-efficacy/ [accessed 25 May 2020].

Henderson, Jeffrey, 'China and Global Development: Towards a Global-Asian Era?', *Contemporary Politics*, 14.4 (2008), pp. 375–92.

Henderson, Jeffrey, and Richard Phillips, 'Unintended Consequences: Social Policy, State Institutions and the "Stalling" of the Malaysian Industrialization Project', *Economy and Society*, 36.1 (2007), pp. 78–102.

Higgins, Rosalyn, *United Nations Peacekeeping 1946-1967: Documents and Commentary. 2. Asia* (Oxford: Oxford University Press, 1970).

Ho, Chol Hwan, 'Principles and Methods of Real Estate Pricing [Pudongsan kagyŏk chejŏngŭi wŏlliwa pangbŏp]', *Journal of Kim Il Sung University Philosophy, Economics*, 61.4 (2015), pp.115–18.

Holzman, Franklyn D., and Robert Legvold, 'The Economics and Politics of East-West Relations', *International Organization*, 29.1 (1975), pp. 275–320.

Hong, Min, Cha Moon-Suk, Joung Eun-Lee, and Kim Huk, *Information of North Korean Markets: Focusing on the Current Status of Official Markets [Pukhan chŏn'guk sijang chŏngbo: Kongsiksijang hyŏnhwangŭl chungsimŭro]* (Seoul: Korea Institute for National Unification, 2016).

Howard, Keith, 'Juche and Culture: What's New?', in *North Korea in the New World Order*, ed. by Hazel Smith, Chris Rhodes, Diana Pritchard, and Kevin Magill (Basingstoke: Macmillan, 1996), pp. 169–95.

Huang, Yasheng, *Capitalism with Chinese Characteristics: Entrepreneurship and the State* (Cambridge: Cambridge University Press, 2008).

Hufbauer, Gary Clyde, Jeffrey J. Schott, and Kimberly Ann Elliott, *Economic Sanctions Reconsidered: History and Current Policy* (Washington, DC: Institute for International Economics, 1990).

Hughes, Christopher W., 'Tumen River Area Development Programme (TRADP): Frustrated Microregionalism as a Microcosm of Political Rivalries', in *Microregionalism and World Order*, ed. by Shaun Breslin and Glenn D. Hook (London: Palgrave Macmillan, 2002), pp. 115–43.

Humphrey, John, and Hubert Schmitz, 'China: Its Impact on the Developing Asian Economies', *IDS Working Papers*, 295 (2007).

Hwang, Eui-Gak, *The Korean Economies: A Comparison of North and South* (Oxford: Clarendon Press, 1993).

The Institute for Far Eastern Studies, 'The Situation on the Korean Peninsula: An Evaluation of 2014 and the Outlook for 2015 [Hanbando chŏngse: 2014 nyŏn p'yŏnggawa 2015 nyŏn chŏnmang]', *IFES Report*, 2014.

Ireson, Randall, 'DPRK Agricultural Policy: Chinese-Style Reform or Muddling Towards Autonomy?', *38 North*, 2015 http://38north.org/2015/01/rireson012715/ [accessed 31 March 2020].

Jackson, Andrew, 'Why Has There Been No People's Power Rebellion in North Korea?', *European Journal of Korean Studies*, 18.1 (2018), pp. 1–34.

James, C.L.R., *State Capitalism and World Revolution* (Oakland, CA: PM Press, 2013).

Jang, In Sook, 'North Korea's Development of the Crisis and Reorganization of Mass Movement Line in the 1970s [1970 nyŏndae Pukhanŭi palchŏnwigiwa taejungundongnosŏn chaejŏngnip]', *Journal of North Korean Studies*, 15.1 (2011), pp. 247–77.

Jeon, Hyun Soo, 'The Nationalisation of Major Industry and the Planning of the People's Economy [Sanŏbŭi kugyuhwawa inmin'gyŏngjeŭi kyehoekhwa: Kongŏbŭl chungsimŭro]', *Review of North Korean Studies [Hyŏndaepukhanyon'gu]*, 2.1 (1999), pp. 63–121.

Jeung, Young-Tai, *North Korea's Civil-Military-Party Relations and Regime Stability* (Seoul: Korea Institute for National Unification, 2007).

Ji, You, *China's Enterprise Reform: Changing State/Society Relations after Mao* (London: Routledge, 1998).

Jin, Jingyi, 'North Korea's Silent Change and North-South Relations [Pukhanŭi Choyonghan Pyŏnhwawa Nambuggwangye]', *The Hankyoreh [Online]*, 21 September 2014 http://happyvil.hani.co.kr/arti/SERIES/58/656072.html [accessed 25 April 2020].

Jo, Dongho, 'Muddling along with Missiles', *EAI Issue Briefing*, 4 (2009), pp. 1–8.

Jo, Hyok Myong, 'Economic Content of Business Expenditure Compensation under Socialist Enterprise Responsibility Management System [Sahoejuŭigiŏpch'aegimgwallije haesŏ kyŏngyŏngjich'ulbosangŭi kyŏngjejŏk naeryong]', *Economic Research [Kyŏngje Yŏn'gu]*, 4 (2017), pp. 18–19.

Jo, Kil Hyon, 'Important Problems Relating to the Rational Organisation of the Exchange of Materials between Enterprises [Kiŏpch'edŭl saiŭi mulchagyoryurŭl hamnijŏkŭro chojikhanŭndesŏ nasŏnŭn chungyohan munje]', *Journal of Kim Il Sung University Philosophy, Economics*, 64.3 (2018), pp. 95–100.

Johnson, Chalmers, *MITI and the Japanese Miracle: The Growth of Industrial Policy, 1925-1975* (Stanford, CA: Stanford University Press, 1982).

Joung, Chun Shim, 'An Important Issue in Realising the Nationalization of Production of Facilities and Raw Materials in All Sectors of the People's Economy [Inmin'gyŏngje modŭn pumunesŏ sŏlbi, wŏllyo chajaeŭi kuksanhwarŭl sirhyŏnhanŭndesŏ nasŏnŭn chungyomunje]', *Journal of Kim Il Sung University Philosophy, Economics*, 62.2 (2016), pp. 68–71.

Joo, Hyung-min, 'Visualizing the Invisible Hands: The Shadow Economy in North Korea', *Economy and Society*, 39.1 (2010), pp. 110–45.

Joo, Seung-Ho, 'Soviet Policy toward the Two Koreas, 1985-1991: The New Political Thinking and Power', *Journal of Northeast Asian Studies*, 14.2 (1995), pp. 23–46.

Joung, Eun-Lee, 'An Analysis of the External Changes and Development of the Public Market in North Korea [Pukhan kongsŏlsijangŭi woehyŏngjŏk paldale kwanhan yŏn'gu]', *Journal of Northeast Asian Economic Studies*, 23.1 (2011), pp. 215–51.

'A Study on the Food Procuring Mechanism of City Workers in North Korea – Land Farming Cases of Musan Region in Hamgyeongbuk-Do [Pukhan tosinodongjaŭi singnyangjodal mek'ŏnijŭme kwanhan yŏn'gu: Hamgyŏngbukdo musanjiyŏgŭi sot'oji kyŏngjaksaryerŭl chungsimŭro]', *Journal of Northeast Asian Economic Studies*, 26.1 (2014), pp. 261–302.

'An Analysis of the Appearance and Significance of the North Korean Real Estate Development Sector: A Comparison with the the Development of the Chinese Real Estate Development Sector [Pukhan pudongsan kaebalŏpjaŭi tŭngjanggwa hamŭie taehan punsŏk: Chungguk pudongsan kaebalŏpjawaŭi pigyoyŏn'gurŭl chungsimŭro]', *KDI Review of the North Korean Economy*, 18.9 (2016), pp. 51–89.

Jeong, Eunmee, 'Dual Track of Agricultural Policy in North Korea: Focusing on Interaction between Collective Agriculture and Farmers' Private Economy [Pukhan nongŏbjŏngch'aekŭi ijunggwaedo: Jibdannongŏpgwa nongminsagyŏngjeŭi sanghosŏngŭl chungsimŭro]', *The Korean Journal of Unification Affairs*, 19.1 (2007), pp. 247–75.

Jung, Seung-Ho, Ohik Kwon, and Sung Min Mun, 'Dollarization, Seigniorage, and Prices: The Case of North Korea', *Emerging Markets Finance and Trade*, 53.11 (2017), pp. 2463–75.

Kang, Chol Su, 'Financial Strategy for Obtaining Actual Results in the Contemporary Socialist Enterprise Responsibility Management System [Hyŏnsigi sahoejuŭigiŏpch'aegimgwallijega silchi ŭnŭl naedorok hagi wihan chaejŏngjŏk pangdo]', *Economic Research [Kyŏngje Yŏn'gu]*, 4 (2018), pp. 56–57.

Kang, Chul Won, 'An Analysis of Japanese Policy and Economic Change in Korea', in *Korea Under Japanese Colonial Rule: Studies of the Policy and Techniques of Japanese Colonialism*, ed. by Andrew C. Nahm (Kalamazoo, MI: Center for Korean Studies, Western Michigan University, 1973), pp. 77–88.

Kang, Myoung-Kyu, and Keun Lee, 'Industrial Systems and Reform in North Korea: A Comparison with China', *World Development*, 20.7 (1992), pp. 947–58.

Kang, Myung-Kyu, 'Industrial Management and Reforms in North Korea', in *Economic Reforms in the Socialist World*, ed. by Stanislaw Gomulka, Yong-Chool Ha, and Cae-One Kim (Armont, NY: M. E. Sharpe, 1989), pp. 200–211.

Kang, Sung-Ho, 'The Revitalisation Plan for Northeasten China: Focusing on the Interrelations between South Korea and China [Chunggugŭi tongbukjinhŭngjŏllyak: Hanjung hyŏmnyŏggwaŭi kwallyŏnsŏngŭl chungsimŭro]', *Korea and World Politics*, 21.1 (2005), pp. 191–220.

Kay, Cristóbal, 'Why East Asia Overtook Latin America: Agrarian Reform, Industrialisation and Development', *Third World Quarterly*, 23.6 (2002), pp. 1073–1102.

KCNA, *Korean Central Almanac, 1954-1955 [1954-1955 nyŏnp'an Chosŏnjungangnyŏn'gam]* (Pyongyang: KCNA, 1955).

Korean Central Almanac 1958 [Chosŏnjungangyŏn'gam 1958] (Pyongyang: KCNA, 1958).

Korean Central Almanac 1959 [Chosŏnjungangyŏn'gam 1959] (Pyongyang: KCNA, 1959).

Korean Central Almanac 1961 [Chosŏnjungangnyŏn'gam 1961] (Pyongyang: KCNA, 1961).

Korean Central Almanac 1962 [Chosŏnjungangnyŏn'gam 1962] (Pyongyang: KCNA, 1962).

Korean Central Almanac 1965 [Chosŏnjungangnyŏn'gam 1965] (Pyongyang: KCNA, 1965).

KDB, *North Korean Industry 2015 [Pukhanŭi sanŏp 2015]* (Seoul: Korean Development Bank, 2015).

KDI, *The Economic Indicators of North Korea [Pukhan'gyŏngjejip'yojip]* (Seoul: Korea Development Institute, 1996).

KIEP, *2002 North Korean Economy Report [2002 Pukhan'gyŏngjebaeksŏ]* (Seoul: Korea Institute for International Economic Policy, 2003).

2003/04 North Korean Economy Report [2003/04 Pukhan'gyŏngjebaeksŏ] (Seoul: Korea Institute for International Economic Policy, 2004) .

Kim, Byong Sik, *Modern Korea: The Socialist North, Revolution Perspectives in the South, and Unification* (New York: International Publishers, 1970).

Kim, Byung-Yeon, *Unveiling the North Korean Economy: Collapse and Transition* (Cambridge: Cambridge University Press, 2017).

Kim, Gwang-Oon, *The History of North Korean Politics I: The Establishment of Party, State and Military [Pukhan chŏngch'isa yŏn'gu 1: Kŏndang, kŏn'guk, kŏn'gunŭi yŏgsa]* (Seoul: Sunin, 2003).

Kim, Hak-joon, *Korean Partition and the Soviet Military Rule of North Korea under International Politics among Major Powers (1863-January 1946) [Kangdaeguk kwŏllyŏgjŏngch'i araesŏŭi hanbando punhalgwa Soryŏnŭi Pukhan'gunjŏnggaesi (1863 nyŏn 1946 nyŏn 1 wŏl)]* (Seoul: Seoul National University Press, 2008).

Kim, Han-Kyo, 'The Japanese Colonial Administration in Korea: An Overview', in *Korea Under Japanese Colonial Rule: Studies of the Policy and Techniques of Japanese Colonialism*, ed. by Andrew C. Nahm (Kalamazoo, MI: Center for Korean Studies, Western Michigan University, 1973), pp. 41–53.

Kim, Hong Il, 'Important Issues Arising from the Multidimensional Development of Foreign Economic Relations [Taeoegyŏngjegwan'gyerŭl tagakchŏkŭro palchŏnsik'inŭndesŏ nasŏnŭn chungyo munje]', *Journal of Kim Il Sung University: Philosophy, Economics*, 61.4 (2015), pp. 71–77.

Kim, Il Sung, 'The Report of the Work of the DPRK Government Delegations Visiting the Soviet Union, the People's Republic of China and People's Democratic Countries [Ssoryŏn Chunghwainmin'gonghwaguk mit inminminjujuŭi chegukkadŭrŭl pangmunhan Chosŏn Minjujuŭi Inmin'gonghwaguk chŏngbudaep'yodanŭi saŏp kyŏnggwa pogo].' Reprinted by the Korean Central News Agency *Korean Central Almanac, 1954-1955 [1954-1955 nyŏnp'an Chosŏnjungangnyŏn'gam]* (Pyongyang: KCNA, 1955), pp. 19–29.

On the Summary of the Work of the Government Delegation Visiting Fraternal States and Some of the Challenges Facing Our Party [Hyŏngjejŏk che kukkarŭl pangmunhan chŏngbu taep'yodanŭi saŏp ch'onghwawa uri tangŭi tangmyŏnhan myŏtkaji kwaŏptŭre kwanhayŏ] (Pyongyang: Korean Workers Party, 1956).

On the Recovery and Development of the Post-War People's Economy [Chŏnhu inmin'gyŏngje pokkubalchŏnŭl wihayŏ] (Pyongyang: Korean Workers' Party Publishing House, 1956).

The Current Situation and Tasks of Our Party [Hyŏnjŏngsewa uri tangŭi kwaŏp] (Pyongyang: Korean Workers' Party Publishing House, 1966).

On Juche Ideology [Chuch'esasange taehayŏ] (Pyongyang: Korean Workers' Party Publishing House, 1977).

Kim, Jong Il, 'The Development of Industry in Korea [Urinara Kongŏbŭi Palchŏn]', in *The Development of the People's Economy in Korea, 1948-1958 [Urinaraŭi inmin'gyŏngje palchŏn 1948-1958]*, ed. by Kim Il Sung University Department of Economics (Pyongyang: State Publishing Company, 1958), pp. 101–41.

Kim, Joungwon Alexander, 'The "Peak of Socialism" in North Korea: The Five and Seven Year Plans', *Asian Survey*, 5.5 (1965), pp. 255–69.

Kim, Kook-Chin, 'South Korea's Policy toward Russia: A Korean View', *Journal of Northeast Asian Studies*, 13.3 (1994), pp. 3–12.

Kim, Kook-Hoo, *Pyongyang's Soviet Korean Elites [P'yŏngyangŭi k'areisŭk'i Ellit'ŭrŭl]* (Seoul: Hanul Books, 2013).

Kim, Myung-Ki, *The Korean War and International Law* (Claremont, CA: Paragon House, 1991).

Kim, Se Jin, 'South Korea's Involvement in Vietnam and Its Economic and Political Impact', *Asian Survey*, 10.6 (1970), pp. 519–32.

Kim, Su-Hwan, *An Analysis of Sino-North Korean Cross-Border Cooperation and Its Implication for Incheon Metropolian City [Pukchung chŏpkyŏnghyŏmnyŏk punsŏggwa Inch'ŏnsiŭi taeŭngbanghyang]* (Incheon: Incheon Development Institute, 2012).

Kim, Sung-bo, *North Korean History 1: The Experience of State Building and People's Democracy 1945-1960 [Pukhanŭi yŏgsa 1: Kŏn'guggwa inminminjujuŭi kyŏnghŏm 1945-1960]* (Seoul: Critical Review of History, 2011).

Kim, Sung-Jae, 'Firms' Fighting of Tumen vs Hunchun?: Struggles of Local Governments to Have North Korean Labours [Tumen vs Hunch'un kiŏp morichae chabgo momssaum wae? Ch'ungguk chibangjŏngbuggiri Pukhan illyŏk dalla]', *Weekly Donga*, 13 January 2014, pp. 40–42.

Kim, Sung Chull, *North Korea Under Kim Jong Il: From Consolidation to Systemic Dissonance* (New York: SUNY Press, 2012).

Kim, Sung Jun, 'The Development of Agricultural Management in Korea [Urinara Nongch'on'gyŏngniŭi Palchŏn]', in *The Development of the People's Economy in Korea 1948-1958 [Urinaraŭi inmin'gyŏngje palchŏn 1948-1958]*, ed. by Kim Il Sung University Department of Economics (Pyongyang: State Publishing Company, 1958), pp. 143–93.

Kim, Suzy, *Everyday Life in the North Korean Revolution, 1945-1950* (Ithaca, NY: Cornell University Press, 2013).

Kim, Yong Hyun, 'A Study on the Militarizing State of North Korea: The 1950s-1960s [Pukhanŭi kunsagukkahwae kwanhan yŏn'gu: 1950-1960 nyŏndaerŭl chungsimŭro]' (PhD thesis: Dongguk University, 2001).

Kim, Youn-Soo, 'The Economy of the KDPR - Its Development, Organization and Functioning', in *The Economy of the Korean Democratic People's Republic 1945-1977*, ed. by Youn-Soo Kim (Kiel: German Korea-Studies Group, 1979), pp. 13–105.

Kim, Youn Suk, 'Current North Korean Economy: Overview and Prospects for Change', *North Korean Review*, 4.2 (2008), pp. 16–30.

Kim, Young-Hui, 'The Change and Future Prospects of North Korea's Farmers' Markets [Pukhan nongminsijangŭi pyŏnhwawa hyanghu chŏnmang]', KDB *Global Economic Issues*, April (2009), pp. 149–57.

King, Betty L., 'Japanese Colonialism and Korean Economic Development, 1910-1945', *Asian Studies - Journal of Critical Prespectives on Asia*, 13.3 (1975), pp. 1–21.

KITA, 'The Status of North Korean Workers in China and Related Implications', *KITA Beijing Office Brief* (2014).

Klingner, Bruce, 'Banco Delta Asia Ruling Complicates North Korean Nuclear Deal', *The Heritage Foundation WebMemo*, 1398.March (2007).

Koh, B. C., 'North Korea and Its Quest for Autonomy', *Pacific Affairs*, 87.4 (2014), pp. 765–78

Koh, Byung Chul, *The Foreign Policy of North Korea* (New York: Praeger, 1969).

Koh, Dae-Won, 'Dynamics of Inter-Korean Conflict and North Korea's Recent Policy Changes: An Inter-Systemic View', *Asian Survey*, 44.3 (2004), pp. 422–41.

Kohli, Atul, 'Where Do High Growth Political Economies Come From? The Japanese Lineage of Korea's "Developmental State"', *World Development*, 22.9 (1994), pp. 1269–93.

Kong, Tat Yan, 'The Political Obstacles to Economic Reform in North Korea: The Ultra Cautious Strategy in Comparative Perspective', *The Pacific Review*, 27.1 (2014), pp. 73–96.

Kontorovich, Vladimir, 'Lesons of the 1965 Soviet Economy Reform', *Soviet Studies*, 40.2 (1988), pp. 308–16.

Korea Economic Development Association, *DPRK Special Economic Zones* (Pyongyang: Foreign Languages Publishing House, 2019).

Kornai, János, *The Socialist System: The Political Economy of Communism* (Princeton, NJ: Princeton University Press, 1992).

Köves, András, 'Socialist Economy and the World-Economy', *Review (Fernand Braudel Center)*, 5.1 (1981), pp. 113–133.

Krueger, Anne O., 'The Political Economy of the Rent Seeking Society', *The American Economic Review*, 64.3 (1974), pp. 291–303.

Kuark, Yoon T., 'North Korea's Industrial Development during the Post-War Period', *The China Quarterly*, 14.June (1963), pp. 51–64.

Kueh, Yak-Yeow, 'China's New Agricultural-Policy Program: Major Economic Consequences, 1979-1983', *Journal of Comparative Economics*, 8.4 (1984), pp. 353–75.

Kuznets, Paul W., *Economic Growth and Structure in the Republic of Korea* (New Haven, CT: Yale University Press, 1977).

Kwon, Tae-Jin, *The Current Situation and Outlook of Marketisation in North Korea's Agricultural Sector [Pukhanŭi nongŏppumun sijanghwa silt'aewa chŏnmang]* (Seoul: GS & J Institute, 2018).

Kwon, Tai-Hwan, 'International Migration of Koreans and the Korean Community in China', *Korea Journal of Population and Development*, 26.1 (1997), pp. 1–18.

Kwon, Young-Kyong, 'Change and Outlook of North Korean Economic Policy in the Kim Jong Un Era [Kimjŏngŭn sidae Pukhan kyŏngjejŏngch'aekŭi pyŏnhwawa chŏnmang]', *Korean Eximbank North Korea Economic Review*, Spring (2014), pp. 1–30.

KWP, *Reports and Decisions on the DPRK People's Economy First Five Year Plan (1957-1961) [Chosŏn Minjujuŭi Inmin'gonghwaguk inmin'gyŏngjebalchŏn che 1 ch'a 5 kaenyŏn (1957-1961) kyehoege kwanhan pogo mit kyŏlchŏngsŏ]* (Pyongyang: Korean Workers' Party Publishing House, 1958).

Lal, Deepak, *The Poverty of 'Development Economics'* (Cambridge, MA: Harvard University Press, 1983).

Lall, Sanjaya, and Manuel Albaladejo, 'China's Competitive Performance: A Threat to East Asian Manufactured Exports?', *World Development*, 32.9 (2004), pp. 1441–66.

Lane, David, *The Rise and Fall of State Socialism* (London: Polity Press, 1996).

Lankov, Andrei N., 'Kim Takes Control: The "Great Purge" in North Korea, 1956-1960', *Korean Studies*, 26.1 (2002), pp. 87–119.

'Why North Korea Will Not Change', *Foreign Affairs*, 87.2 (2008), pp. 9–16.

'North Korean Workers Abroad Aren't Slaves', *NK News*, 2014 www.nknews.org/2014/11/north-korean-workers-abroad-arent-slaves/ [accessed 2 April 2020].

The Real North Korea: Life and Politics in the Failed Stalinist Utopia (Oxford: Oxford University Press, 2015).

Lee, Hy-Sang, 'North Korea's Closed Economy: The Hidden Opening', *Asian Survey*, 28.12 (1988), pp. 1264–79.

'Supply and Demand for Grains in North Korea: A Historical Movement Model for 1966-1993', *Korea and World Affairs*, 18.3 (1994), pp. 509–52.

Lee, Jong-kyu, 'Decline in the DPRK's Anthracite Export to China: Causes and Implications', *KDI Focus*, 57 (2015), pp. 1–9.

Lee, Jong-Seok, *Research on the Korean Workers' Party: Focus on Changes in Leadership Thought and Structural Change [Chosŏnnodongdang yŏn'gu: Chidosasanggwa kujo pyŏnhwarŭl chungsimŭro]* (Seoul: Critical Review of History, 1995).

A New Approach to Understanding Contemporary North Korea [Saero ssŭn hyŏndae Pukhanŭi ihae] (Seoul: Critical Review of History, 2000).

Research on North Korean-Chinese Relations at the Time of the Cultural Revolution [Munhwadaehyŏngmyŏng sigi Pukhan-Chungguk kwan'gye yŏn'gu] (Seongnam: Sejong Institute, 2015).

Lee, Jong-Woon, *North Korea's Economic Reform under An International Framework* (Seoul: Korea Institute for International Economic Policy, 2004).

Lee, Jong-Woon, and Kevin Gray, 'Cause for Optimism? Financial Sanctions and the Rise of the Sino-North Korean Border Economy', *Review of International Political Economy*, 24.3 (2017), pp. 424–53.

Lee, Seog-Ki, Byun Hak-moon, and Na Hye-Seon, *North Korea's Industry and Industrial Policy in the Kim Jong Un Era [Kimjŏngŭn sidae Pukhanŭi sanŏp mit sanŏpchŏngch'aek]* (Sejong: Korea Institute for Industrial Economics and Trade, 2018).

Lee, Seog-Ki, Kim Suk-Jin, Kim Kye Hwan, and Yang Moon-Soo, *North Korean Industries and Firms in the 2000s: Recovery and Operation Mechanism [2000 nyŏndae Pukhanŭi sanŏpgwa kiŏp: Hoebok silt'aewa chakdong pangsik]* (Seoul: Korea Institute for Industrial Economics and Trade, 2010).

Lee, Seog-Ki, Yang Moon-Soo, and Joung Eun-Lee, *Analysis on the Markets of North Korea [Pukhan sijangsilt'ae punsŏk]* (Sejong: Korea Institute for Industrial Economics and Trade, 2014).

Lee, Seok, 'Overview: Evaluation and Hypotheses Relating to Trends in the 2016 North Korean Economy [Ch'onggwal: 2016 nyŏn Pukhan kyŏngje tonghyangpyŏnggawa sŏlmyonggasŏl]', *KDI Review of the North Korean Economy*, 19.1 (2017), pp. 3–26.

'Summary: the North Korean Economy in 2018, in Crisis or Holding up? [Ch'onggwal: 2018 nyŏn Pukhan'gyŏngje, wigiin'ga pot'igiin'ga]', *KDI Review of the North Korean Economy*, 21.2 2019, pp. 3–28.

Lee, Tae-Sup, *North Korea's Economic Crisis and System Change [Pukhanŭi Kyŏngje Wigiwa Ch'eje Pyŏnhwa]* (Seoul: Sunin, 2009).

Legislation Press, *Legal Code of the Democratic People's Republic of Korea (Supplementary Edition) [Chosŏn Minjujuŭi Inmin'gonghwaguk pŏpchŏn (chŭngbop'an)]* (Pyongyang: Legislation Press, 2016).

Lerner, Mitchell, '"Mostly Propaganda in Nature": Kim Il Sung, the Juche Ideology, and the Second Korean War', *Wilson Center Working Paper*, 2010.

Liberman, Peter, *Does Conquest Pay? The Exploitation of Occupied Industrial Societies* (Princeton, NJ: Princeton University Press, 1996).

Lim, Eul-Chul, *North Korea's Economy in the Kim Jong Un Era: Private Financing and Masters of Money [Kimjŏngŭn sidaeŭi Pukhan'gyŏngje: Sagŭmyunggwa tonju]* (Seoul: Hanul, 2016).

'The Formation and Development of Private Financing in North Korea: Patterns, Implications and Tasks [Pukhan sagŭmyungŭi hyŏngsŏnggwa paljŏn: Yangt'ae, hamŭi mit kwaje]', *The Korean Journal of Unification Affairs*, 27.1 (2015), pp. 205–42.

Lim, Hyun-Chun, and Byung-Kook Kim, 'Rethinking North Korean Self-Reliance: Reality and Facade', in *Dynamic Transformation: Korea, NICs and Beyond*, ed. by Gill-Chin Lim and Wook Chang (Urbana: Consortium on Development Studies, 1990), pp. 53–79.

Lim, Jae-Cheon, *Kim Jong Il's Leadership of North Korea* (Londong: Routledge, 2009).

Lim, Kang-Taeg, 'North Korea's Foreign Trade, 1962-1992' (PhD thesis: University at Albany, State University of New York, 1995).

Analysis of the Condition of North Korea's Informal Sector: Focus on Corporate Activity [Pukhan kyŏngjeŭi pigongsikbumun silt'ae punsŏk: kiŏphwaldongŭl chungsimŭro] (Seoul: Korea Institute for National Unification, 2013).

Lim, Phillip Wonhyuk, 'North Korea's Food Crisis', *Korea and World Affairs*, 21.4 (1997), pp. 568–85.

Lim, Soo-Ho, *The Co-Existence of Plan and Market: The Outlook for North Korea's Economic Reform and Systemic Change [Kyehoeggwa sijangŭi kongjon: Pukhanŭi kyŏngjegaehyŏggwa ch'ejebyŏnhwa chŏnmang]* (Seoul: Samsung Economic Research Institute, 2008).

'Sanctions on North Korea in the Medium to Long Term: the Influence of Sanctions on Coal and Iron Exports on the Domestic Economy of North Korea [Taebukchejaeŭi chungjanggi hyogwa: sŏkt'an ch'ŏlgwangsŏk such'ulchejaega

Pukhan naesugyŏngjee mich'inŭn yŏnghyang]', *KDI Review of the North Korean Economy,* 21.12 (2019), pp. 15–28.

Lin, Justin Yifu, 'Rural Reforms and Agricultural Growth in China', *The American Economic Review,* 82.1 (1992), pp. 34–51.

Loeffler, Rachel L., 'Bank Shots: How the Financial System Can Isolate Rogues', *Foreign Affairs,* 88.2 (2009), pp. 101–10.

Luova, Outi, 'Transnational Linkages and Development Initiatives in Ethnic Korean Yanbian, Northeast China: "Sweet and Sour" Capital Transfers', *Pacific Affairs,* 82.3 (2009), pp. 427–46.

Mao, Tse-Tung, *Selected Works of Mao Tse-Tung: Volume II* (Peking: Foreign Languages Press, 1965).

Selected Works of Mao Tse-Tung: Volume III (Peking: Foreign Languages Press, 1965).

Marer, Paul, 'Soviet Economic Policy in Eastern Europe', in *Reorientation and Commercial Relations of the Economies of Eastern Europe,* ed. by Joint Economic Commitee US Congress (Washington, DC: US Government Printing Office, 1974).

Marx, Karl, and Fredrich Engels, *The Communist Manifesto* (Harmondsworth, Middlesex: Penguin Books, 1967).

Mayall, James, 'The Sanctions Problem in International Economic Relations: Reflections in the Light of Recent Experience', *International Affairs,* 60.4 (1984), pp. 631–42.

Mazarr, Michael J., 'Orphans of Glasnost: Cuba, North Korea and US Policy', *Korea and World Affairs,* 15.1 (1991), pp. 58–84.

McEachern, Patrick, *Inside the Red Box: North Korea's Post-Totalitarian Politics* (New York: Columbia University Press, 2010).

'Centralizing North Korean Policymaking under Kim Jong Un', *Asian Perspective,* 43.1 (2019), pp. 35–67.

McMillan, John, and Barry Naughton, 'How to Reform a Planned Economy: Lessons from China', *Oxford Review of Economic Policy,* 8.1 (1992), pp. 130–43.

Millar, James R., 'A Note on Primitive Accumulation in Marx and Preobrazhensky', *Soviet Studies,* 30.3 (1978), pp. 384–93.

Mohan, Giles, 'Beyond the Enclave: Towards a Critical Political Economy of China and Africa', *Development and Change,* 44.6 (2013), pp. 1255–72.

Moody, Peter Graham, 'Chollima, the Thousand Li Flying Horse: Neo-Traditionalism at Work in North Korea', *Sungkyun Journal of East Asian Studies,* 13.2 (2013), pp. 211–33.

Moon, Chung-in, and Sangkeun Lee, 'Military Spending and the Arms Race on the Korean Peninsula', *Asian Perspective,* 33.4 (2009), pp. 69–99.

Moore, Aaron Stephen, 'The Yalu River Era of Developing Asia: Japanese Expertise, Colonial Power, and the Construction of Sup'ung Dam', *Journal of Asian Studies,* 72.1 (2013), pp. 115–39.

MOU, *North Korean Economic Statistics [Pukhan Kyŏngje t'onggyejip]* (Seoul: Ministry of Unification, 1996).

Understanding North Korea (Seoul: Ministry of Unification, 2014).

Mun, Sung Min, and Sung Ho Jung, 'Dollarization in North Korea: Evidence from a Survey of North Korean Refugees', *East Asian Economic Review,* 21.1 (2017), pp. 81–100.

Murray, Martin J., *The Development of Capitalism in Colonial Indochina (1870-1940)* (Berkeley, CA: University of California Press, 1980).

Myers, B. R., *North Korea's Juche Myth* (Busan: Sthele Press, 2015).

Nairn, Tom, 'The Modern Janus', *New Left Review*, 94 (1975), pp. 3–30.

Nam, Sung-wook, 'Chronic Food Shortages and the Collective Farm System in North Korea', *Journal of East Asian Studies*, 7.1 (2007), pp. 93–123.

Namkoong, Young, 'An Analysis of North Korea's Policy to Attract Foreign Capital: Management and Achievement', *Korea and World Affairs*, 19.3 (1995), pp. 459–81.

Naughton, Barry, *The Chinese Economy: Transitions and Growth* (Cambridge, MA: The MIT Press, 2007).

Nayyar, Deepak, *Catch Up: Developing Countries in the World Economy* (Oxford: Oxford University Press, 2013).

Nehru, Jawaharlal, 'Changing India', *Foreign Affairs*, 41.3 (1963), pp. 453–65.

Noland, Marcus, 'Why North Korea Will Muddle Through', *Foreign Affairs*, 76.4 (1997), pp. 105–18.

'Prospects for the North Korean Economy', in *North Korea after Kim Il Sung*, ed. by Dae-Sook Suh and Chae-Jin Lee (London: Lynne Rienner, 1998), pp. 33–58

North Korea Development Institute, 'The Present Status and Outlook of North Korean Marketisation: A Focus on Market Change [Pukhanŭi sijanghwa hyŏnhwanggwa chŏnmang: Sijangbyŏnhwarŭl chungsimŭro]' (Unpublished Paper, 2016).

North Korean Resources Research Institute, *Analysis of North Korean Mineral Resources Development [Pukhan chawŏn'gaebalsaŏp silt'aebunsŏk]* (Seoul: North Korean Resources Research Institute and Korea Resources Corporation, 2010).

Oh, Kongdan, and Ralph C. Hassig, 'North Korea between Collapse and Reform', *Asian Survey*, 39.2 (1999), pp. 287–309.

North Korea through the Looking Glass (Washington, DC: Brookings Institution, 2000)

Oh, Youngjin, *The Soviet Army's North Korea: One Testament [Sogunŭi Pukhan: Hanaŭi chŭngŏn]* (Seoul: Central Culture Publishing, 1983).

Okonogi, Masao, 'North Korean Communism: In Search of Its Prototype', in *Korean Studies: New Pacific Currents*, ed. by Dae-Sook Suh (Honolulu: University of Hawai'i, 1994), pp. 177–206.

Paige, Glenn D., '1966: Korea Creates the Future', *Asian Survey*, 7.1 (1967), pp. 21–30.

'North Korea and the Emulation of Russian and Chinese Behavior', in *Communist Strategies in Asia: A Comparative Analysis of Governments and Parties*, ed. by Arthur Doak Barnett (New York: Praeger, 1963), pp. 228–61.

Paige, Glenn D., and Dong Jun Lee, 'The Post-War Politics of Communist Korea', *The China Quarterly*, 14, June (1963), pp. 17–29.

Paik, Haksoon, *The History of Power in North Korea: Ideas, Identities, and Structures [Pukhan kwŏllyŏgŭi yŏgsa: Sasang, chŏngch'esŏng, kujo]* (Seoul: Hanul Books, 2010).

Pape, Robert A., 'Why Economic Sanctions Do Not Work', *International Security*, 22.2 (1997), pp. 90–136.

'Why Economic Sanctions Still Do Not Work', *International Security*, 23.1 (1998), pp. 66–77.

Park, Byung-kwang, 'China-North Korea Economic Relations during the Hu Jintao Era', *International Journal of Korean Unification Studies*, 19.2 (2010), pp. 125–50.

Park, Hyeong-jung, 'Introduction of Party-Centered Industrial Management System in the First Half of the 1960's in North Korea [1960 nyŏndae chŏnban'gi Pukhanesŏ chibangdang chungsimŭi kongŏpkwallich'egye surip kwajŏnggwa naeyong]', *Review of North Korean Studies*, 6.2 (2003), pp. 89–132.

'North Korea's "New Economic Management System": Main Features and Problems', *Korea Focus*, January (2014), pp. 1-12.

Park, Hyun-Sun, *Contemporary North Korean Society and Family [Hyŏndae Pukhansahoewa Kajok]* (Seoul: Hanul Books, 2003).

Park, In Ho, *The Creation of the North Korean Market System* (Seoul: Daily NK, 2017).

Park, Phillip H., *Rebuilding North Korea's Economy: Politics and Policy* (Seoul: IFES Kyungnam University, 2016).

The Development Strategy of Self-Reliance (Juche) and Rural Development in the Democratic People's Republic of Korea (London: Routledge, 2002).

'Introduction: Economic Reform and Institutional Change in the DPRK', in *The Dynamics of Change in North Korea: An Institutionalist Perspective*, ed. by Phillip H. Park (Seoul: IFES Kyungnam University, 2009), pp. 3–41.

Park, Seong-yong, 'North Korea's Military Policy under the Kim Jong-Un Regime', *Journal of Asian Public Policy*, 9.1 (2016), pp. 57–74.

Park, Tae-gyun, 'Beyond the Myth: Reassessing the Security Crisis on the Korean Peninsula during the Mid-1960s', *Pacific Affairs*, 82.1 (2009), pp. 93–110.

Park, Yong-Soo, 'The Political Economy of Economic Reform in North Korea', *Australian Journal of International Affairs*, 63.4 (2009), pp. 529–49.

Park, Young-Ja, Hong Je-Hwan, Hyun In-Ae, and Kim Bo-Geun, *Enterprise Operational Reality and Corporate Governance in North Korea [Pukhan kiŏpŭi unyŏngsilt'ae mit chibaegujo]* (Seoul: Korea Institute for National Unification, 2016).

Pempel, T. J., 'The Developmental Regime in a Changing World Economy', in *The Developmental State*, ed. by Meredith Woo-Cumings (Ithaca, NY: Cornell University Press, 1999), pp. 137–81.

Perotti, Enrico C., Laixiang Sun, and Liang Zou, 'State-Owned versus Township and Village Enterprises in China', *UNU-Wider Working Paper*, 1998 www.wider.unu.edu/publications/working-papers/previous/en_GB/wp-150/ [accessed 25 April 2020].

Perry, John Curtis, 'Dateline North Korea: A Communist Holdout', *Foreign Policy*, 80. Autumn (1990), pp. 172–91.

Person, James F., 'North Korea's Chuch'e Philosophy', in *Routledge Handbook of Modern Korean History*, ed. by Michael J. Seth (London: Routledge, 2016), pp. 211–20.

'North Korea in 1956: Reconsidering the August Plenum and the Sino-Soviet Joint Intervention', *Cold War History*, 19.2 (2019), pp. 253–74.

van der Pijl, Kees, 'State Socialism and Passive Revolution', in *Gramsci, Historical Materialism and International Relations*, ed. by Stephen Gill (Cambridge: Cambridge University Press, 1993), pp. 237–58.

Polanyi, Karl, *The Great Transformation* (Boston: Beacon Press, 1944).

Prashad, Vijay, *The Darker Nations: A People's History of the Third World* (New York: New Press, 2007).

PRC Ministry of Commerce, *2013 Statistical Bulletin of China's Outward Foreign Direct Investment* (Hong Kong: Purple Culture, 2014).

Rau, Zbigniew, *The Reemergence of Civil Society in Eastern Europe and the Soviet Union* (Boulder: Westview Press, 1991).

Ravenhill, John, 'Is China an Economic Threat to Southeast Asia?', *Asian Survey*, 46.5 (2006), pp. 653–74.

Ray, David, 'The Dependency Model of Latin American Underdevelopment: Three Basic Fallacies', *Journal of Interamerican Studies and World Affairs*, 15.1 (1973), pp. 4–20.

van Ree, Erik, *Socialism in One Zone: Stalin's Policy in Korea, 1945-1947* (Oxford: Berg, 1989).

'The Limits of Juche: North Korea's Dependence on Soviet Industrial Aid, 1953-1976', *Journal of Communist Studies*, 5.1 (1989), pp. 50–73.

Research Institute of Juche Economics - Academy of Social Sciences, *Dictionary of the Economy [Kyŏngjesajŏn]* (Pyongyang: Social Science Publishing House, 1985).

Rhee, Myong Seo, 'Our Party's Economic Policy on Heavy Industry-First Growth and the Simultaneous Development of Light Industry and Agriculture [Chunggongŏbŭi usŏnjŏk changsŏnggwa kyŏnggongŏp mit nongŏbŭi tongsijŏk palchŏne taehan uri tangŭi kyŏngjejŏngch'aek]', in *The Constructions of Socialist Economy in Our Country [Urinaraesŏŭi sahoejuŭi kyŏngje kŏnsŏl]*, ed. by DPRK Academy of Sciences, Economics and Legal Research Institute (Pyongyang: Academy of Sciences Publishing House, 1958), pp. 90–136.

Ri, Il Chol, 'Concept and Main Types of Economic Development Zone [Kyŏngjegaebalguŭi kaenyŏmgwa chuyo yuhyŏng]', *Economic Research [Kyŏngje Yŏn'gu]*, 2 (2015), pp. 42–43.

Ri, Ki Ban, 'The Accurate Implementation of the Principle of Socialist Distribution Is an Important Requirement of the Completion of the Improvement of Economic Management [Sahoejuŭi punbaewŏnch'ikŭl chŏnghwak'i kuhyŏnhanŭn kŏsŭn kyŏngjegwalligaesŏn wansŏngŭi chungyohan yogu]', *Economic Research [Kyŏngje Yŏn'gu]*, 2 (2003), pp. 19–21.

Ri, Myong Jin, 'The Positive Promotion of the Development of Economic Development Zones Is an Important Task of Our Age [Kyŏngjegaebalgu kaebalsaŏbŭl chŏkkŭk milgonaganŭn kŏsŭn hyŏnsigi uri ap'e nasŏnŭn chungyohan kwaŏp]', *Journal of Kim Il Sung University: Philosophy, Economics*, 61.4 (2015), pp. 75–77.

Ri, Tong Su, 'Socialist Enterprise Responsibility Management System, Business Strategy and Enterprise Strategy [Sahoejuŭigiŏpch'aegimgwallijewa kyŏngyŏngjŏllyak, kiŏpchŏllyak]' *Chollima*, 10 (2016), pp. 73–74.

Riskin, Carl, *China's Political Economy: The Quest for Development Since 1949* (Oxford: Oxford University Press, 1987).

Ro, Myong Song, 'Some Problems in Creating and Operating Economic Development Zones According to the Actual Conditions of Each Province [Kak todŭrŭi silchŏnge matke kyŏngjegaebalgudŭrŭl ch'angsŏl, unyŏnghanŭndesŏ nasŏnŭn myŏtkaji munje]', *Economic Research [Kyŏngje Yŏn'gu]*, 2 (2015), pp. 39–41.

Robinson, Joan, 'Korean Miracle', *Monthly Review*, 16.9 (1965), pp. 541–49.

Robinson, Michael, *Korea's Twentieth Century Odyssey: A Short History* (Honolulu: Hawaii University Press, 2007).

Rolf, Steven, 'Locating the State: Uneven and Combined Development, the States System and the Political', in *Theoretical Engagements in Geopolitical Economy*, ed. by Radhika Desai (Bingley: Emerald Group, 2015), pp. 113–53.

Rosenberg, Justin, 'The "Philosophical Premises" of Uneven and Combined Development', *Review of International Studies*, 39.3 (2013), pp. 569–97.

Rowe, David M., *Manipulating the Market: Understanding Economic Sanctions, Institutional Change, and the Political Unity of White Rhodesia* (Ann Arbor: University of Michigan Press, 2001).

Rozman, Gilbert, 'Northeast China: Waiting for Regionalism', *Problems of Post-Communism*, 45.4 (1998), pp. 3–13.

Sachs, Jeffrey, and Wing Thye Woo, 'Structural Factors in the Economic Reforms of China, Eastern Europe, and the Former Soviet Union', *Economic Policy*, 9.18 (1994), pp. 101–45.

Dos Santos, Theotonio, 'The Structure of Dependence', *The American Economic Review*, 60.1 (1970), pp. 231–36.

Saxonberg, Steven, *Transitions and Non Transitions from Communism: Regime Survival in China, Cuba, North Korea and Vietnam* (Cambridge: Cambridge University Press, 2013).

Scalapino, Robert A., 'Korea: The Politics of Change', *Asian Survey*, 3.1 (1963), pp. 31–40.

Scalapino, Robert A., and Chong-Sik Lee, *Communism in Korea: Part 1. The Movement* (Berkeley, CA: University of California Press, 1972).

Schurmann, Franz, *Ideology and Organisation in Communist China* (Berkeley, CA: University of California Press, 1966).

Seliger, Bernhard, 'The July 2002 Reforms in North Korea: Liberman-Style Reforms or Road to Transformation?', *North Korean Review*, 1.1 (2005), pp. 22–37.

Selverstone, Mark J., *Constructing the Monolith: The United States, Great Britain, and International Communism, 1945–1950* (Cambridge, MA: Harvard University Press, 2009).

Shafer, D. Michael, *Winners and Losers: How Sectors Shape the Developmental Prospects of States* (Ithaca, NY: Cornell University Press, 1994).

Shapiro, Jane P., 'Soviet Policy Towards North Korea and Korean Unification', *Pacific Affairs*, 48.3 (1975), pp. 336–52.

Silberstein, Benjamin Katzeff, *Growth and Geography of Markets in North Korea New Evidence from Satellite Imagery* (Washington, DC: US-Korea Institute at SAIS, 2015).

Simon, Sheldon W., 'Regional Security Structures in Asia: The Question of Relevance', in *East Asian Security in the Post-Cold War Era*, ed. by Sheldon W. Simon (Armonk, NY: M. E. Sharpe, 1993), pp. 11–27.

Singh, Nitya, and Wootae Lee, 'Survival from Economic Sanctions: A Comparative Case Study of India and North Korea', *Journal of Asian Public Policy*, 4.2 (2011), pp. 171–86.

Smith, Hazel, 'Overcoming Humanitarian Dilemmas in the DPRK (North Korea)', *United States Institute of Peace Special Report* (2002).

Hungry for Peace: International Security, Humanitarian Assistance, and Social Change in North Korea (Washington, DC: United States Institute of Peace, 2005).

North Korea: Markets and Military Rule (Cambridge: Cambridge University Press, 2015).

Snyder, Scott, *China's Rise and the Two Koreas: Politics, Economics, Security* (Boulder, CO: Lynne Rienner, 2009).

Social Science Publishing Company, *DPRK History of Foreign Relations 2 [Chosŏn Minjujuŭi Inmin'gonghwaguk taeoegwan'gyesa 2]* (Pyongyang: Social Science Publishing Company, 1987).

Son, Jon Hu, *The Experience of Land Reform [T'ojigaehyŏk kyŏnghŏm]* (Pyongyang: Social Science Publishing Company, 1983).

The History of Land Reform in North Korea [Urinara t'ojigaehyŏksa] (Pyongyang: Science and Encyclopedia Publishing Company, 1983).

Song, Ligang, 'Emerging Private Enterprise in China: Transitional Paths and Implications', in *China's Third Economic Transformation: The Rise of the Private Economy*, ed. by Ross Garnaut and Ligang Song (London: RoutledgeCurzon, 2004), pp. 29–47.

Steinfeld, Edward S., 'China's Shallow Integration: Networked Production and the New Challenges for Late Industrialization', *World Development*, 32.11 (2004), pp. 1971–87.

Strange, Gerard, 'China's Post-Listian Rise: Beyond Radical Globalisation Theory and the Political Economy of Neoliberal Hegemony', *New Political Economy*, 15.5 (2011), pp. 539–59.

Suh, Dae-Sook, 'A Preconceived Formula for Sovietization: The Communist Takeover of North Korea', *Journal of East and West Studies*, 1.1 (1973), pp. 101–14.

Kim Il Sung: The North Korean Leader (New York: Columbia University Press, 1988).

Suh, Dong-Man, 'North Korea's Political Struggles and Ideology Situation in the 1950s [1950 nyŏndae Pukhanŭi chŏngch'igaldŭnggwa idaeollogi sanghwan]', in *North and South Korea's Choice and Refraction in the 1950s [1950 nyŏndae nambukhanŭi sŏnt'aeggwa kuljŏl]*, ed. by The Institute of Korean Historical Studies (Seoul: Critical Review of History, 1998), pp. 307–50.

The History of Socialist System Formation in North Chosun 1945-1961 [Pukchosŏn sahoejuŭi ch'eje sŏngnipsa 1945-1961] (Seoul: Sunin, 2005).

Suh, Sang-Chul, 'North Korean Industrial Policy and Trade', in *North Korea Today: Strategic and Domestic Issues*, ed. by Robert A. Scalapino and Jun-yop Kim (Berkeley, CA: Institute of East Asian Studies, University of California, 1983), pp. 197–213.

Suny, Ronald Grigor, *The Revenge of the Past: Nationalism, Revolution and the Collapse of the Soviet Union* (Stanford, CA: Stanford University Press, 1993).

Szalontai, Balázs, *Kim Il Sung in the Khrushchev Era: Soviet–DPRK Relations and the Roots of North Korean Despotism, 1953–1964* (Washington, DC: Woodrow Wilson Center Press, 2005).

Szalontai, Balazs, and Changyong Choi, 'The Prospects of Economic Reform in North Korea: Comparisons with China, Vietnam and Yugoslavia', *Europe-Asia Studies*, 64.2 (2012), pp. 227–46.

Tan-Mullins, May, Giles Mohan, and Marcus Power, 'Redefining "Aid" in the China–Africa Context', *Development and Change*, 41.5 (2010), pp. 857–81.

Timmer, Charles Peter, 'Agriculture and Economic Development Revisited', *Agricultural Systems*, 40.1–3 (1992), pp. 21–58.

Tokola, Mark, 'Why Is China so Upset about THAAD?', *Korea Economic Institute of America Website*, 2017 http://keia.org/why-china-so-upset-about-thaad [accessed 19 October 2018].

Torbat, Akbar E., 'Impacts of the US Trade and Financial Sanctions on Iran', *The World Economy*, 28.3 (2005), pp. 407–34.

Tsai, Kellee S., *Capitalism without Democracy: The Private Sector in Contemporary China* (Ithaca, NY: Cornell University Press, 2007).

Tu, Kwang Ik, 'Price Setting Methods in Enterprises [Kiŏpch'edŭresŏŭi kagyŏkchejŏngbangbŏp]', *Journal of Kim Il Sung University Philosophy, Economics*, 64.3 (2018), pp. 137–41.

Tudor, Daniel, and James Pearson, *North Korea Confidential: Private Markets, Fashion Trends, Prison Camps, Dissenters and Defectors* (Tokyo: Tuttle, 2015).

Uchida, Jun, '"A Scramble for Freight": The Politics of Collaboration along and across the Railway Tracks of Korea under Japanese Rule', *Comparative Studies in Society and History*, 51.1 (2009), pp. 117–50.

Vanous, Jan, 'East European Economic Slowdown', *Problems of Communism*, 31.July-August (1982), pp. 1–19.

Wade, Robert, *Governing the Market: Economic Theory and the Role of Government in East Asian Industrialization* (Princeton, NJ: Princeton University Press, 1990).

Walder, Andrew G., and Jean C. Oi, 'Property Rights in the Chinese Economy: Contours of the Process of Change', in *Property Rights and Economic Reform in China*, ed. by Jean C. Oi and Andrew G. Walder (Stanford, CA: Stanford University Press, 1999), pp. 1–24.

Ward, Peter, Andrei Lankov, and Jiyoung Kim, 'Capitalism from Below with North Korean Characteristics: The State, Capitalist Class Formation, and Foreign Investment in Comparative Perspective', *Asian Perspective*, 43.3 (2019), pp. 533–55.

Weigle, Marcia A., and Jim Butterfield, 'Civil Society in Reforming Communist Regimes: The Logic of Emergence', *Comparative Politics*, 25.1 (1992), pp. 1–23.

Wertz, Daniel, 'The Evolution of Financial Sanctions on North Korea', *North Korean Review*, 9.2 (2013), pp. 69–82.

White, D. Gordon, 'The Democratic People's Republic of Korea through the Eyes of a Visiting Sinologist', *The China Quarterly*, 63.September (1975), pp. 515–22.

White, Gordon, 'North Korean Chuch'e: The Political Economy of Independence', *Bulletin of Concerned Asian Scholars*, 7.2 (1975), pp. 44–54.

Riding the Tiger: The Politics of Economic Reform in Post-Mao China (Basingstoke: Macmillan, 1993).

Whittaker, D. Hugh, Tianbiao Zhu, Timothy Sturgeon, Mon Han Tsai, and Toshie Okita, 'Compressed Development', *Studies in Comparative International Development*, 45.4 (2010), pp. 439–67.

Wiegersma, Nancy, *Vietnam - Peasant Land, Peasant Revolution: Patriarchy and Collectivity in the Rural Economy* (Basingstoke: Macmillan, 1988).

Wilczynski, Jozef, *The Economics of Socialism: Principles Governing the Operation of the Centrally Planned Economies in the USSR and Eastern Europe under the New System* (London: Allen and Unwin, 1972).

Willett, Thomas D., and Mehrdad Jalalighajar, 'U.S. Trade Policy and National Security', *Cato Journal*, 3.3 (1983), pp. 717–41.

Won, Dong Wook, 'The Bright and Dark Sides of Economic Cooperation between North Korea and China: Changjitu and Sino-NK Economic Cooperation [Pukchunggyŏnghyŏbŭi pitgwa kŭlimja: "ch'angjit'u kaebalgyehoeg" kwa Pukchunggan ch'oguggyŏng yŏn'gyegaebalŭl chungsimŭro]', *Contemporary China Studies*, 13.1 (2011), pp. 41–73.

Woo, Jongseok, 'Kim Jong-Il's Military-First Politics and beyond: Military Control Mechanisms and the Problem of Power Succession', *Communist and Post-Communist Studies*, 47.2 (2014), pp. 117–25.

World Bank, 'China's Management of Enterprise Assets: The State as Shareholder', *World Bank Report*, 1997 http://documents.worldbank.org/curated/en/1997/06/694720/chinas-management-enterprise-assets-state-shareholder [accessed 25 April 2020].

Yakubovsky, Vladimir B., 'Economic Relations between Russia and the DPRK: Problems and Perspectives', *Korea and World Affairs*, 20.3 (1996), pp. 451–76.

Yang, Moon-Soo, *The Structure of the North Korean Economy: The Mechanism of North Korean Development and Slowdown [Pukhan'gyŏngjeŭi kujo: Kyŏngjegaebalgwa ch'imch'aeŭi mek'aŏnijŭm]* (Seoul: Seoul National University Press, 2001).

The Marketisation of the North Korean Economy: Nature – Character – Mechanism – Signifiance [Pukhan'gyŏngjeŭi sijanghwa: Yangt'ae – sŏnggyŏk – mek'anijŭm – Hamŭi] (Seoul: Hanul Books, 2010).

'North Korea's External Loans: Trends and Characteristics [Pukhanŭi taeoech'aemu munje:Ch'usewa t'ŭkching]', *KDI Review of the North Korean Economy*, 14.3 (2012), pp. 18–37.

'North Korea's Marketisation: Trends and Structural Change [Pukhanŭi sijanghwa: Ch'usewa kujo pyŏnhwa]', *KDI Review of the North Korean Economy*, 15.6 (2013), pp. 45–70.

'The Search for the Our-Style Economic Management Method after the Appearance of the Kim Jong Un System [Kimjŏngŭn ch'eje ch'ulbŏm ihu "Urisik kyŏngjegwallibangbŏp" ŭi mosaek: Hyŏnhwanggwa p'yŏngga]', *KDI Review of the North Korean Economy*, 16.3 (2014), pp. 3–24.

'2015 Trends and Outlook in North Korea's Marketisation [2015 nyŏn Pukhan sijanghwa tonghyanggwa hyanghu chŏnmang]', *KDI Review of the North Korean Economy*, 18.1 (2016), pp. 13–34.

'Economic Management System in Our Style Observed through the Revised Laws in the Kim Jong Un Era [Kimjŏngŭn chipkwŏn ihu kaejŏng pŏmnyŏngŭl t'onghae pon 'Urisikkyŏngjegwallibangbŏp']', *Unification Policy Studies*, 26.2 (2017), pp. 81–115.

Yang, Moon Soo, and Kevin Shepard, 'Changes in North Korea's Corporate Governance', in *The Dynamics of Change in North Korea: An Institutionalist Perspective*, ed. by Phillip H. Park (Seoul: IFES Kyungnam University, 2009), pp. 135–80.

Yang, Un-Chul, 'Reform without Transition: The Economic Situation in North Korea since the July 1, 2002, Measures', *North Korean Review*, 6.1 (2010), 71–87.

Yeung, Yue-man, Joanna Lee, and Gordon Kee, 'China's Special Economic Zones at 30', *Eurasian Geography and Economics*, 50.2 (2009), pp. 222–40.

Yoon, Dae-kyu, 'The Constitution of North Korea: Its Changes and Implications', *Fordham International Law Journal*, 27.4 (2003), pp. 1289–305.

Yoon, In Joo, 'A Study of Privatisation in North Korea: Current Status and Its Implications [Pukhanŭi sayuhwa hyŏnsang yŏn'gu: Silt'aewa hamŭirŭl chungsimŭro]', *North Korean Studies Review*, 18.1 (2014), pp. 55–85.

Yonhap News Agency, *North Korea Handbook* (New York: East Gate, 2003).

Young, Benjamin 'The Struggle For Legitimacy- North Korea's Relations With Africa, 1965–1992', *BAKS Papers*, 16 (2015), pp. 97–116.

Yu, Chong-Ae, 'The Rise and Demise of Industrial Agriculture in North Korea', *Journal of Korean Studies*, 12.1 (2007), pp. 75–109.

Yu, Hong, 'Motivation behind China's "One Belt, One Road" Initiatives and Establishment of the Asian Infrastructure Investment Bank', *Journal of Contemporary China*, 26.105 (2017), pp. 353–68.

Zagoria, Donald S., 'North Korea: Between Moscow and Beijing', in *North Korea Today: Strategic and Domestic Issues1*, ed. by Robert Scalapino and Jun-Yop Kim (Berkeley, CA: Institute of East Asian Studies, University of California Press, 1983), pp. 351–71.

Zhang, Pingyu, 'Revitalizing Old Industrial Base of Northeast China: Process, Policy and Challenge', *Chinese Geographical Science*, 18.2 (2008), pp. 109–18.

Zhang, Zhihong, 'Rural Industrialization in China: From Backyard Furnaces to Township and Village Enterprise', *East Asia: An International Quarterly*, 17.3 (1999), pp. 61–87.

Zhebin, Alexander, 'Russia and North Korea: An Emerging, Uneasy Partnership', *Asian Survey*, 35.8 (1995), pp. 726–39.

Zhu, Shengjun, and John Pickles, 'Bring In, Go Up, Go West, Go Out: Upgrading, Regionalisation and Delocalisation in China's Apparel Production Networks', *Journal of Contemporary Asia*, 44.1 (2014), pp. 36–63.

Zimmerman, William, 'Dependency Theory and the Soviet-East European Hierarchical Regional System: Initial Tests', *Slavic Review*, 37.4 (1978), pp. 604–23.

Index